The
Freelance
Photographer's
Market
Handbook
1998

The Freelance Photographer's Market Handbook
1998

Edited by John Tracy & Stewart Gibson
Listings Coordinator: James Clancy

BFP BOOKS London

A catalogue record for this book is available from the British Library

ISBN 0-907297-45-5

Fourteenth Edition

Published for the Bureau of Freelance Photographers by BFP Books, Focus House, 497 Green Lanes, London N13 4BP. Typesetting and page layout by BFP Books. Text set in New Century Schoolbook. Printed in Great Britain by Selwood Printing.

CONTENTS

PREFACE.. 7
ABOUT THE BFP.. 9
HOW TO USE THIS BOOK.. 11
APPROACHING THE MARKET.. 14
MAGAZINES: Introduction.. 17
     New Listings, Changes and Deletions............................ 19
     Subject Index.. 21
MAGAZINE MARKETS: Angling.. 27
     Animals & Wildlife.. 29
     Arts & Entertainment... 34
     Aviation... 37
     Boating & Watersport... 40
     Building & Engineering.. 46
     Business.. 50
     Camping & Caravanning... 54
     Children's & Teenage... 56
     County & Country... 57
     Cycling & Motorcycling.. 63
     Electronics & Computing... 68
     Equestrian... 70
     Farming... 72
     Food & Drink... 74
     Gardening.. 76
     General Interest.. 79
     Health & Medical.. 83
     Hobbies & Crafts.. 85
     Home Interest... 91
     Industry... 94
     Local Government & Services... 99
     Male Interest... 103
     Motoring.. 107
     Music... 113

Parenting.. 119
Photography & Video.. 121
Politics & Current Affairs............................... 126
Railways.. 128
Religion... 130
Science & Technology...................................... 132
Sport.. 134
Trade... 148
Transport.. 154
Travel.. 155
Women's Interest... 158
NEWSPAPERS.. 166
BOOKS: Introduction... 172
        Subject Index.. 175
        Listings... 179
CARDS & CALENDARS.. 192
AGENCIES: Introduction.. 197
                Subject Index.. 200
                Listings... 203
SERVICES: Accessories & Specialised Equipment................ 224
              Art Services.. 225
              Computer Software.. 226
              Equipment Hire.. 227
              Equipment Repair.. 227
              Framing & Finishing.. 229
              Insurance.. 230
              Material Suppliers.. 231
              Model Agencies.. 232
              Postcard Printers... 232
              Processing & Printing.. 233
              Storage & Presentation....................................... 238
              Studio & Darkroom Hire..................................... 240
              Studio Services.. 240
USEFUL ADDRESSES.. 242
INDEX.. 244

PREFACE

The past twelve months have seen steady growth in most sectors of the publishing world.

Magazine launches have continued apace, but with a perhaps more measured approach which is allowing titles to establish themselves gradually and with less risk of failure. An equally positive sign is that there have been fewer notable closures than for many years, confirming that greater overall stability has returned to the market.

We can expect to see a good deal more activity over the next 12 months. Most major publishers have a variety of ideas under development and are promising a wide range of launches in the near future.

The newspaper scene continues to contract as far as circulations and manning levels are concerned. But as in each of the past few years the increasing emphasis on pictures coupled with the shedding of staff photographers is only opening up greater opportunities for freelances.

Book publishing has generally held steady, with few dramatic developments. Here, the area many once considered ripe for most rapid growth – multimedia CD-ROM – seems to have foundered somewhat as sales failed to take off. It seems that the general market is not yet ready for this sort of product – at least not at current pricing levels. Some companies have withdrawn from the field altogether, while others have reduced their range until such time as the market is considered more mature.

A different kind of CD-ROM product of interest of photographers has been alarming many in the picture agency world. This is the field of "royalty free" photography on CD, a development that is causing agencies to fear an erosion of their business as clients opt for the low-cost, readily-available image. Others argue that these products are in the main used by different types of markets than those seeking the individual, high-quality image provided by agencies, and that they are growing the market for photography by encouraging a more widespread use of images.

Whatever the arguments, these companies do offer a limited outlet for the freelance photographer, though currently most are sourced and produced in North America. But as yet only a handful operate a fee structure that would seem to make supplying them worthwhile in the long term. We continue to recommend that freelances looking for sales beyond their own direct marketing activities place their work with a good agency for maximum returns.

For the freelance photographer in 1998, the overall view is of a marketplace becoming both more exciting and more reliable than for some years.

ABOUT THE BFP

Founded in 1965, the Bureau of Freelance Photographers is today the major body for the freelance photographer. It has a worldwide membership, comprising not only full-time freelances, but also serious amateur and semi-professional photographers. Being primarily a service organisation, membership of the Bureau is open to anyone with an interest in freelance photography.

The most important service offered to members is the *Market Newsletter,* a confidential monthly report on the state of the freelance market. A well-researched and highly authoritative publication, the *Newsletter* keeps freelances in touch with the market for freelance work, mainly by giving information on the type of photography currently being sought by a wide range of publications and other outlets. It gives full details of new magazines and their editorial requirements, and generally reports on what is happening in the publishing world and how this is likely to affect the freelance photographer.

Redesigned and expanded in 1996, the *Newsletter* now also includes in-depth interviews with editors, profiles of successful freelances, examples of successful pictures, and other general features to help freelances in understanding and approaching the marketplace.

The *Newsletter* is considered essential reading for the freelance and aspiring freelance photographer, and because it pinpoints launches and changes in the marketplace as they occur, it also acts as a useful supplement to the *Handbook.* The *Handbook* itself is an integral part of BFP membership services; members paying the full annual fee automatically receive a copy every year as it is published.

Other services provided to members for the modest annual subscription include:

● Advisory Service. Individual advice on all aspects of freelancing is available to members.

● Mediation Service. The Bureau tries to protect its members' interests in every way it can. In particular, it is often able to assist individual members in recovering unpaid fees and in settling copyright or other disputes.

● Exclusive items and special offers. The Bureau regularly offers books and other items to members, usually at discount prices. It originated Editorial Submission Forms for use by members, and is also able to supply Model Release Forms.

● In the Services section of this *Handbook* can be found a number of companies providing special discounts to BFP members on production of a current membership card. Members can also obtain comprehensive photographic insurance cover at highly competitive rates through a scheme arranged by the BFP with a leading specialist company.

For further details and an application form, write to Bureau of Freelance Photographers, Focus House, 497 Green Lanes, London N13 4BP, telephone 0181-882 3315, or send a fax message on 0181-886 5174. Or if you wish to join right away, you'll find an application form at the back of this book.

HOW TO USE THIS BOOK

Anyone with the ability to use a camera correctly has the potential to make money from their pictures. Taking saleable photographs isn't difficult; the difficulty lies in finding the market. It isn't enough for you, the photographer in search of a sale, to find what you think *might* be a suitable market; rather you must find *exactly* the right magazine, publisher, agency or whatever for your particular type of work. Many a sale is lost when work which is, in itself, technically perfect fails to fulfil the total requirements of the buyer.

The Freelance Photographer's Market Handbook has been designed to help resolve these difficulties. It puts you in touch with major markets for your work, telling you exactly what each is looking for, together with hints and tips on how to sell to them and, wherever possible, an idea of the rates they pay.

The *Handbook* covers five big markets for your pictures: magazines (by far the largest), newspapers, book publishers, picture agencies, and card and calendar companies. There are three ways of using the book, depending on the way you need or wish to work:

1. If you are out to sell to magazines and you can offer coverage on a theme particularly applicable to a certain type of publication (i.e. gardening, angling, sport) turn to the magazine section and look for the subject. The magazines are listed under 36 categories, each of which has a broad heading covering specific magazines. The categories are in alphabetical order, as are the magazines within those categories. You need only read through them to discover which is best for your type of work.

2. If you have a set of pictures that fall into a specific photographic category (i.e. landscapes, children, glamour, etc.), turn to the subject index on page 21. Look up your chosen subject and there you will find a list of all the

magazines with a strong interest in that particular type of picture. You then have only to look up each one mentioned in the appropriate section for precise details of their requirements. (If in doubt as to where to find a particular magazine consult the general index at the back of the book.) There are separate subject indexes for book publishers and agencies on pages 175 and 200 respectively.

3. If you are looking for the requirements of a specific magazine, book publisher, agency, card or calendar publisher, whose name is already known to you, simply refer to the general index at the back of the book.

Some points to remember

With this wealth of information open to you, and with those three options for finding the right market, there is no reason why you shouldn't immediately start earning good cash from your camera. But before you rush off to put your pictures in the post, here are some points worth bearing in mind and which will help you to more successful sales:

1. The golden rule of freelancing: don't send people pictures they don't want. Read the requirements listed in the various parts of this directory and obey them. When, for instance, a Scottish magazine says they want pictures of all things Scottish with the exception of kilts and haggis, you can be sure they are over-stocked with these subjects. They are not going to make an exception just for you, however good you think your pictures might be.

2. If you are working in colour, and unless the listing states otherwise, always supply transparencies rather than prints. Unless otherwise stated, it can be assumed that any size of transparency, from 35mm up, can be accepted.

3. When submitting pictures, make sure they are accompanied by detailed captions. And don't forget to put your own name and address on each photograph.

4. If you have an idea for a picture or feature for a particular publication, don't be afraid to telephone first to discuss what you have in mind. Nearly every editor or picture buyer approached when the *Handbook* was being compiled said they would be delighted to hear from potential freelances in advance, rather than have inappropriate pictures or words landing on their desks.

5. If seeking commissions, always begin by making an appointment with the appropriate person in order to show your portfolio and/or cuttings. Do not turn up at a busy editor's office unannounced and expect to be met with open arms.

6. Never send anything to a market on spec without a stamped addressed envelope for its return.

APPROACHING THE MARKET

You've chosen your market, taken the pictures and written the captions. Full of hope and expectation, you put your work in the post. A week later, it comes back with a formal rejection slip. Why? Where did you go wrong?

You have only to look through the pages of this book to see that there are a lot of markets open to the freelance photographer, yet the sad fact remains that a great many of those who try their hand at editorial freelancing fail the first few times, and many never succeed at all. That isn't meant to be as discouraging as it might sound. On the contrary, because so many freelances fail, *you*, with the inside knowledge gleaned from these pages, stand a better chance of success than most. What's more you can gain from the experience of others.

So let's take a look at some of the areas where the inexperienced freelance goes wrong. Knowing the common mistakes, you can avoid them and consequently stand the best chance of success with your own work.

The first big mistake made by the novice is in the actual format of pictures supplied. The easiest type of photograph to take and produce today is the colour print. Unfortunately, colour prints are difficult to sell. Enprints, such as those produced by commercial processing houses, never sell – except in the most exceptional of circumstances. Most buyers in today's market require colour slides and/or black and white prints.

Look at your intended market to see just how much colour they use as opposed to black and white. Many magazines are all-colour, but a lot still use black and white. If the colour pages are in a minority compared with the mono pages, then do your best to restrict your submission to black and white prints. If your market uses mostly colour, then send transparencies.

The quality of your work must be first class. Colour slides should be pin-sharp and perfectly exposed to give strong, saturated colours. Slight under-exposure of around one-third to half a stop may be acceptable, but over-exposure never. Many publishers and agencies prefer to receive originals, but in most cases really good "reproduction-quality" dupes should be just as acceptable.

Mono prints should have a sharp bite of contrast, coupled with a good range of tones all the way from white through to black. The surface of the paper on which your prints are presented matters too. It is difficult for printers to make good reproductions from prints on matt or lustre surfaces, so stick to glossy.

Never send flat, grey mono prints or over-exposed, washed-out colour slides.

For some markets, the size of your transparencies is important. Most today accept 35mm, but some – such as calendars and greetings cards, or certain specialist picture libraries – continue to prefer larger formats: 6x6cm as a minimum and even 5x4in. If your chosen market stipulates a medium or larger format, don't send 35mm.

So much for picture format, but what of the actual subject of your pictures? Here again, a lot of fundamental mistakes are made. The oldest rule in the freelancing book is this: don't take pictures, then look for markets; find a market first and then shoot your pictures specifically with that market in mind.

Every would-be freelance knows that rule; yet the many who ignore it is frankly staggering. Remember that rule and act accordingly. First find your market, analyse it to see the sort of pictures it uses, then go all out to take *exactly* the right type of picture.

Editors see a lot of pictures every day, and the vast majority are totally unsuited to their market. Of those that are suited, many are still rejected because, despite being the right *type* of pictures, the subjects are still uninspiring. They are subjects the editor has seen over and over again; and the type that the magazine will already have on file. So once again, the work gets rejected.

Remember this and learn from it. Most of the pictures that fall on an editor's desk are pretty ordinary. If you want to make yours sell, you have to show them something different. It might be a fairly straightforward view of an unusual subject, or it might be a more common subject, seen and photographed from a new angle. Either way, it will be different.

So when you set out to take your pictures, really look at your subject and, even before you press the shutter, ask yourself, why am I taking this picture? Why will an editor want to buy it? What's so different or unusual about it? How can I make a few changes here and now to give it a better chance of success?

Good, traditional picture composition also plays a part in a picture's chances. Many would-be freelances submit pictures of people in which the principal subject is far too small and surrounded by a wealth of unwanted, distracting detail. So make a point, whenever you shoot, of moving in close and really filling the viewfinder with your subject.

Many potentially saleable landscapes are ruined by a flat perspective. So watch out for, and try to include, foreground interest in such pictures.

People at work on a craft or a hobby can be good sellers, but a good many pictures depicting such subjects are shot candidly without the necessary thought needed to really show the subject to its best. Always pose pictures like these before you take them.

Finally, a word about presentation. It's true that a good picture can often find a sale, no matter how badly it is presented; but it is equally true that bad presentation can just as easily influence an editor or picture buyer and so ruin your chances of success. So why make things difficult for yourself?

When you send prints, make sure they are stiffly packed between thick cardboard or in special cardboard envelopes. Present slides in plastic filing wallets and make them easy to view with the minimum of fuss. If you are sending words – either captions to pictures or a full-blown articles – always type them, rather than writing them by hand. Type on one side of the paper only and leave a double space between lines with good margins on each side. Send your submission with a brief letter, not with pages of explanations about the work. The sale will stand or fall by your pictures and/or words, never by the excuses you offer as to why certain pictures might not be too good. If they're not good enough, they won't sell.

Give your editor what he or she wants. Give them originality and sparkle, and present the whole package in the best way you can. Learn the rules and you'll be on your way to a good many picture sales.

But don't think that anyone is going to break those rules just for you. If your pictures don't measure up to what is required, there will always be another envelope right behind full of pictures that do. And there are no prizes for guessing which submission is going to make the sale.

MAGAZINES

The British magazine market is vast. Anyone who doubts that has only to look at the racks of periodicals in any major newsagent. And this is only the tip of the iceberg, the largest section of the consumer press. Beneath the surface there is the trade press, controlled circulation magazines and many smaller publications that are never seen on general sale. At the last count more than 8,000 magazines were being published on a regular basis in Britain.

In this section you will find detailed listings of magazines which are looking for freelances. Some pay a lot, others are less generous, but all have one thing in common – they are here because they need freelance contributions on a regular basis and they are willing to pay for them.

When you come to start looking at these listings in detail, you might be surprised by the number of magazines of which you have never heard. Don't let that put you off. What the newcomer to freelancing often fails to realise is that there are as many, if not more, trade magazines as there are consumer publications, and very few of these are ever seen on general sale.

Trade magazines, as the term implies, are aimed at people whose business is making money from the particular subject concerned. As such, their requirements are usually totally different to their consumer counterparts.

As an example, consider boating. A consumer magazine on that subject will be aimed at the boat owner or enthusiast and could contain features on boats and the way they are handled. A trade magazine on the same subject is likely to be more interested in articles about the profits being made by the boating industry and pictures of shop displays of boating accessories.

Trade magazines do not necessarily have a separate section to themselves. If the subject is a common one, such as the example above in which there are both trade and consumer publications, they have been listed for your convenience under a common heading. Despite that, however, there *is* a section specifically for trade. This contains trade magazines that have no consumer counterparts, as well as magazines whose subject is actually trade itself and trading in general.

As you go through these listings, therefore, it is important for you to realise that there is a very real difference between the two sides of the subject, but it is a difference which is explained under each publication's requirements. So don't ignore trade magazines of whose existence you were not previously aware. Very often such a magazine will have just as big a market for your pictures and the fees will be just as much, and in some cases more, than those offered by the consumer press.

It is often a good idea for the freelance to aim at some of the more obscure publications listed here. Simply because they are a little obscure, they may not have been noticed by other freelances and, as such, your sales potential will be higher.

Another factor that will become apparent as you look through this section of the *Handbook* is the degree to which black and white illustrations are still needed as well as colour. It's wise, then, to remember this when you are shooting pictures for publication. If possible, shoot both colour and mono for those markets that require both.

When you are looking through the entries, don't stop at the section on illustrations. Read what the magazine needs in the way of text too. A publication that might appear to have a very small market for individual pictures often has a larger potential for illustrated articles, and all you need to do to make a sale is add a few words.

You will also find that many publications talk about needing mainly commissioned work. Don't be misled by this. The commissions are given to freelances and, although this means they won't consider your work on spec, they could well be interested in giving you a commission if you can prove you are worth it. That's where previous experience comes in. When trying for commissions, you should always have examples of previously published work to show an editor.

Many of the larger magazines employ a specific editor to deal with picture submissions and with photographers. They may go under various titles – picture editor, art editor, art director – but this is the person directly responsible for picture selection and for commissioning photographers for specific jobs. This, therefore, is the person you should approach when sending pictures or seeking photographic assignments. When sending written material though, illustrated or not, your approach is best made direct to the editor.

The magazine market is one of the largest available to the freelance. You might not receive as large a fee per picture as you would from, say, the calendar market, or for certain sales that might be made on your behalf by an agency, but what this field does offer is a *steady* income.

There are so many magazines, covering so many different subjects, that freelances who have their wits about them would be hard put *not* to find one to which their own style and interests can be adapted. Make yourself known to a few chosen magazine editors, let them see that you can turn out good quality work on the right subject, at the right time, and there is no reason why this market shouldn't make you a good, regular income, either part time or full time.

New Listings, Changes & Deletions

The following is designed to alert readers to possible new markets as well as to important changes that have taken place since the last edition of the *Handbook*.

'New Listings' includes magazines that have been launched since the last edition appeared as well as established titles that appear in the *Handbook* for the first time. 'Title Changes' lists publications that have changed their names (previous titles in brackets). 'Deletions' lists publications that appeared in the previous edition but are omitted from this one. Publications under this heading have not necessarily ceased publication – they may have been deleted because they no longer offer a worthwhile market for the contributor.

To find the page number for any particular magazine, refer to the main index at the back of the book.

New Listings

The Art of Bonsai
Bizarre
Buckinghamshire Countryside
Cat World
Classic CD
Collect it!
Condé Nast Traveller
The English Garden
The European
FHM
Fun For Kids
Furniture & Cabinetmaking
Gallop!
Hockey Sport
Horse Magazine
Inside Rugby
Junior Education
Minx
Now
On the Ball
Paddles
Peter Purves' Mad About Dogs
Real Business
Sailing Today
Teddy Bear Scene
Touring Car World
Toymaking
Traction
Triumph World
Water Craft
What Digital Camera
Xtreme

Title Changes

Active Magazine (Get Active)
Babycare & Pregnancy (First Steps)
Caravan Life (Caravan Plus)
Classics (Retro)
Cricket World Monthly (Cricket Monthly)
Cycling & Mountain Biking Today
    (Cycling Today)

Desire Direct (Desire)
Fishing Monthly (Scottish Fishing Monthly)
J17 (Just Seventeen)
London 2000 (Arrival)
Planning (Planning Week)
Ski & Snowboard (Ski Survey)
Sports Boat & Waterski International (Sports
   Boat International)
Trace (True)

Deletions

Action Replay
Air Power International
Air World International
The Boatman
Coaching Journal & Bus Review
Complete Car
Computer Life

Countrylover's Magazine
1st in Line
Fishkeeping Answers
Here!
Ki Motorsport
Lakescene
Let's Go With Going Places
90 Minutes
Parrot Magazine
Practical Gardening
Rugby Magazine
Rush
Sky Sports
Sport First
Suffolk Countryside
Titbits Magazine
Today's Horse
Travel Agency
Vital

Subject Index

Only magazines are included in this index, but it should be noted that many of these subjects are also required by agencies, book publishers and card and calendar publishers.

Separate subject indexes for book publishers and picture agencies appear in the appropriate sections, on pages 175 and 200 respectively.

To find the page number for any magazine, refer to the main index at the back of the book.

Agricultural Scenes

Crops
Dairy Farmer
Farmers Weekly
Highbury House Communications
The Landworker
Pig Farming
Poultry World

Aircraft

Aeroplane Monthly
Air International
Airforces Monthly
Aviation News
Commuter World
Defence Helicopter
Flight International
Flyer
Helicopter World
Jane's Defence Weekly
Pilot
Popular Flying

Architecture & Buildings

Architecture Today
Build It
Building Today
Country Homes and Interiors
FX
Glass Age & Window Construction
House Builder
House & Garden
Local Government News
New Civil Engineer
Period Living & Traditional Homes
Perspectives on Architecture
Prestige Interiors
RIBA Journal
World of Interiors

Arts and Crafts

Best of British
Country Origins
Crafts Beautiful
Furniture & Cabinetmaking
Good Woodworking
Inspirations
The Lady
Popular Crafts
Practical Craft
This England
Toymaking
Woodcarving
Woodturning
Woodworker

Birds

Bird Keeper
Bird Life
Bird Watching
Birds
Birdwatch
Cage and Aviary Birds
Just Parrots
Racing Pigeon Pictorial
Wildfowl & Wetlands
The Wildlife Photographer

Boats & Watercraft

Boat Angler
Boat International
Canal & Riverboat
Classic Boat
International Boat Industry
Jet Skier & Personal Watercraft
Motor Boat and Yachting
Motor Boats Monthly
Paddles
RYA News
Regatta

Sailing Today
Sports Boat International
Water Craft
Waterways World
Yachting Monthly
Yachting World
Yachts and Yachting

Business Scenes

Accountancy Age
Business Life
Business Opportunity World
CA Magazine
Commerce Magazine
Computer Weekly
The Director
The Economist
Entrepreneur
Export Times
The Journal
MEED
Management Accounting
Marketing
People Management
Real Business

Celebrities

Bella
Big!
Chat
Eva
Hello!
Mizz
More!
Now
19
OK! Weekly
Options
Radio Times
Saga
The Stage
Sugar
TV Times
Theatre
Woman
Woman & Home

Children

Babycare & Pregnancy
Brownie
Fun for Kids

Guiding
Highbury House Communications
Junior Education
Mother & Baby
Nursery World
Our Baby
Parents
Parentwise
Right Start
Safety Education
Scouting
She
You and Your Baby

Domestic and Farm Animals

All About Cats
All About Dogs
Animal Action
Animal Life
Cat World
Cats
Dairy Farmer
Dogs Today
Gallop!
Horse Magazine
Horse and Pony
Horse and Rider
Kennel Gazette
Peter Purves' Mad About Dogs
Pig Farming
Pony
Riding
Your Cat
Your Dog

Fashion

Arena
Attitude
Bella
Best
Chat
Company
Cosmopolitan
Drapers Record
Elle
Esquire
Essentials
FHM
FW
Fashion Extras
France
GQ

Good Housekeeping
Harpers & Queen
Hello!
J17
The Lady
Loaded
Looks
Marie Claire
Maxim
Men's Wear
Mizz
Minx
More!
Ms London Weekly
19
Options
Prima
She
Sky Magazine
Trace
Woman
Woman's Journal
Woman's Own
Woman's Realm
Woman's Weekly

Flowers and Plants

Amateur Gardening
The Art of Bonsai
BBC Gardeners' World
Country Homes & Interiors
The English Garden
The Garden
Garden Answers
Garden News
Garden Trade News International
Gardens Illustrated
Good Housekeeping
Home
Homes & Gardens
Horticulture Week
House Beautiful
House & Garden
The Lady
Nurseryman and Garden Centre
Perfect Home
Woman and Home
Your Garden

Food & Drink

Asian Hotel & Caterer
Bella

Best
Chat
British Baker
Country Homes & Interiors
Essentials
Essentially America
Good Housekeeping
Highbury House Communications
Homes & Gardens
Hotel & Restaurant Magazine
House Beautiful
House & Garden
Independent Caterer
Inspirations
Prima
Pub Food
The Publican Newspaper
Scottish Licensed Trade News
Tax-Free Trader
Wine & Spirit International

Glamour

Active Magazine
Amateur Photographer
Club International
Desire Direct
Fiesta
Knave
Loaded
Mayfair
Men Only
Penthouse
Photo Answers
Practical Photography

Home Environment & Interiors

Bathrooms & Kitchens: The Magazine
Best
Build It
Country Homes & Interiors
Elle Decoration
Essentials
Good Housekeeping
Home
Homes & Gardens
Homes & Ideas
HomeStyle
House Beautiful
House & Garden
Inspirations
Perfect Home
Period Living & Traditional Homes

Perspectives on Architecture
Practical Householder
Prima
Woman
Woman Alive
Woman and Home
Woman's Journal
Woman's Realm
Woman's Weekly
World of Interiors

Industrial Scenes

Chemistry & Industry
The Director
Education in Chemistry
Food Industry News
Highbury House Communications
Industrial Diamond Review
The Journal
Management Accounting
People Management
Planning
Post Magazine
Sign World
Tin International
Urethanes Technology
Utility Week
Works Management

Landscapes

Amateur Photographer
Best of British
Bird Watching
Buckinghamshire Countryside
Camping Magazine
Catholic Gazette
Coarse Fisherman
Cotswold Life
Country
Country Homes & Interiors
Country Life
Country Walking
Country Origins
The Countryman
Cumbria & Lake District Magazine
The Dalesman
Devon & Cornish Life
Dorset
Dorset Life
Essex Countryside
The Great Outdoors
Hertfordshire Countryside

The Lady
Lancashire Life
Lincolnshire Life
Motorhome Monthly
New Christian Herald
Photo Answers
Photo Technique
Practical Caravan
Practical Photography
Rambling Today
Scots Independent
The Scots Magazine
The Somerset Magazine
Sussex Life
This England
Trail
Trout & Salmon
Waterways World
Woman Alive

Military

Airforces Monthly
Defence Helicopter
Jane's Defence Weekly
The Legion

Motor Vehicles

Auto Express
Autocar & Motor
The Automobile
Automotive Management
Cars & Car Conversions
Classic American
Classic & Sportscar
Classics
Commercial Motor
Company Car
Driving Magazine
Fleet News
International Off Roader & 4x4 Owner
Land Rover Owner
Motor Trader
Motoring & Leisure
911 & Porsche World
Off Road & Four Wheel Drive
Performance Ford
Rally Car Magazine
Revs
Street Machine
Top Gear Magazine
Touring Car World
Triumph World

Truck
Truck and Driver
VW Motoring

Motorcycles

Back Street Heroes
Bike
Classic Bike
The Classic Motor Cycle
Heavy Duty
Motor Cycle News
Motorcycle Classics
Motorcycle International
Ride
Scootering
Superbike

Performing Arts

Dance and Dancers
Radio Times
The Stage
Theatre
TV Times
The Young Dancer Magazine

Pop & Rock

Big!
Blues and Soul
Cipher
Echoes
Eternity
Future Music
J17
Kerrang!
Keyboard Player
Loaded
Melody Maker
Metal Hammer
Mojo
Muzik
New Musical Express
Q
Rhythm
Select
Sky Magazine
Smash Hits
Top of the Pops
Total Guitar
Trace
Vox

Railways

British Railway Modelling
International Railway Journal
Rail
Rail Express
Railnews
Steam Classic
Steam Railway
Steam Railway News
Traction

Ships

Containerisation International
Marine Engineers Review

Sport

Active Magazine
Athletics Weekly
Badminton
Boat International
Boxing Monthly
Cars & Car Conversions
Country
Cricket World Monthly
The Cricketer International
Cycle Sport
Cycling & Mountain Biking Today
Cycling Plus
Darts World
Esquire
FC
Fighters – The Martial Arts Magazine
First Down
First XV
Focus
Football Europe
Football Monthly
Fore!
FourFourTwo
F1 News
GQ
Goal
Golf Monthly
Golf World
Highbury House Communications
Hockey Sport
Inside Rugby
Loaded
Martial Arts Illustrated
Match
Maxim

Men's Health
Motor Boats Monthly
Motor Cycle News
Mountain Biker International
Mountain Biking UK
On the Ball
Paddles
Photo Answers
Pot Black Magazine
Rally Sport
Rangers News
Regatta
Rugby Leaguer
Rugby News
Rugby World
Rush
Shoot!
Shooting Gazette
Shooting Times & Country Magazine
Show Jumping
Ski & Snowboard
The Skier & Snowboarder Magazine
Snooker Scene
Snowboard UK
Sports Boat International
Sports in the Sky
Steve Grayston's Martial Arts
Swimming Times
Target Gun
Team Talk Magazine
Tennis World
Today's Golfer
Today's Runner
Total Football
Total Sport
Windsurf Magazine
Wisden Cricket Monthly
Yachts and Yachting
XL
Xtreme

Technology

Chemistry & Industry
Clean Air & Environmental Protection
Design Engineering
Electrical Times
The Engineer
Focus
International Railway Journal
Manufacturing Chemist
New Scientist

Process Engineering
Professional Engineering

Travel

Africa Economic Digest
British Airways News
Business Life
Business Traveller
Coach & Bus Week
Condé Nast Traveller
The Director
Essentially America
Executive Travel
France
The Geographical Magazine
Good Housekeeping
Highbury House Communications
The Lady
The Middle East
Motorhome Monthly
Motoring & Leisure
Options
Saga Magazine
Sovereign
Tax-Free Trader
The Traveller
Wanderlust
Woman and Home
Woman's Realm
Yours

Wildlife

Amateur Photographer
Animal Action
Animal Life
Bird Life
Bird Watching
Birds
Birdwatch
Country
Country Origins
The Countryman
The Lady
Natural World
Photo Technique
The Scottish Sporting Gazette
Shooting Times and Country Magazine
Wild Cat
Wildfowl & Wetlands
The Wildlife Photographer

Angling

ANGLER'S MAIL
IPC Magazines Ltd, King's Reach Tower, Stamford Street, London SE1 9LS.
Tel: 0171-261 5778. Fax: 0171-261 6016.
Editor: Roy Westwood.
Weekly publication with news and features for followers of coarse, sea and game fishing in the UK.
Illustrations: Colour only. Topical news pictures of successful anglers with their catches. Captions should give full details concerning weight and circumstances of capture. Covers: pictures of anglers with exceptional specimen fish or catches.
Text: Features on coarse, sea and game fishing topics only. Up to 800 words.
Overall freelance potential: Minimal for non-angling freelances.
Editor's tips: Most pictures and text seen from non-anglers are not acceptable because of lack of knowledge and experience on the part of the contributor.
Fees: By agreement.

ANGLING TIMES
EMAP Pursuit Publishing Ltd, PO Box 231, Bretton Court, Bretton, Peterborough PE3 8EN.
Tel: 01733 266222. Fax: 01733 265515.
Editor: John Kelly.
Weekly newspaper format publication covering all ranges of angling, i.e. coarse, sea and game. Includes news, features and general instruction.
Illustrations: General angling subjects – catches, action and scenics.
Text: Features on all aspects of the hobby. Up to 800 words.
Overall freelance potential: Very good. High percentage used each week.
Fees: By agreement.

BOAT ANGLER
EMAP Pursuit Publishing Ltd, Bretton Court, Bretton, Peterborough PE3 8DZ.
Tel: 01733 465307. Fax: 01733 465436.
Editor: Mel Russ. **Designer**: Steve Diggle.
Alternate-monthly for boat angling enthusiasts.
Illustrations: Colour only. Good stock shots of boat angling subjects. Amusing pictures also of interest for "Photo Finish" slot. Covers: anglers fishing from boats, obviously enjoying themselves.
Text: Illustrated articles, on sea angling techniques and choosing and using boats. 1,000 words.
Overall freelance potential: Good for anyone in contact with the subject.
Editor's tips: "We get flooded with pictures of proud anglers showing off their catches, but these are often of poor quality. Excellent quality will always find a market."
Fees: By negotiation.

COARSE ANGLING
IPC Magazines Ltd, King's Reach Tower, Stamford Street, London SE1 9LS.
Tel: 0171-261 5800. Fax: 0171-261 6016.
Editor: Colin Mitchell.
Broad-based monthly for coarse anglers.
Illustrations: Colour only. Speculative submissions considered, but mostly commissioned, including studio-based product photography. Photographers should be capable of high-quality close-up work, preferably using medium format equipment.
Text: Only from specialists.
Overall freelance potential: Good.
Editor's tips: A good working knowledge of angling is obviously an advantage, but any experienced photographer is likely to be capable of handling the work concerned.
Fees: By negotiation.

COARSE FISHERMAN
Metrocrest Ltd, 67 Tyrrell Street, Leicester LE3 5SB.
Tel: 01162 511277. Fax: 01162 511335
Editor: Simon Roff.
Monthly magazine covering all aspects of coarse fishing.
Illustrations: B&W and colour. Pictures of anglers in action or riverside/lakeside scenes where such angling takes place. Covers: colour pictures showing anglers displaying particularly fine catches.
Text: Articles of 1,000–2,000 words, most usually first person accounts of angling experiences.
Overall freelance potential: Excellent scope for angling specialists.
Fees: B&W pictures from £5 upwards. £10 upwards for colour, £25 per 1,000 words for text.

FLY-FISHING & FLY-TYING
Rolling River Publications Ltd, Aberfeldy Road, Kenmore, Perthshire PH15 2HF.
Tel/Fax: 01887 830526.
Editor: Mark Bowler.
Published eight times a year for the fly-fisherman and fly-tyer.
Illustrations: Colour. Shots of anglers in action, scenics of locations, flies and fly-tying, and appropriate insect pictures.
Text: Illustrated articles on all aspects of fly-fishing.
Overall freelance potential: Fairly good.
Editor's tips: Make an effort to avoid bland backgrounds, especially at water sides.
Fees: Colour from £24–£58; covers £45. Text £48 per 1,000 words.

IMPROVE YOUR COARSE FISHING
EMAP Pursuit Publishing Ltd, Bretton Court, Bretton, Peterborough PE3 8DZ.
Tel: 01733 266222. Fax: 01733 465436.
Editor: Gareth Purnell.
Monthly "hints and tips" style magazine for coarse fishing enthusiasts.
Illustrations: B&W and colour. Photographs depicting all aspects of coarse fishing.
Text: Ideas for illustrated features from experienced angling writers always considered. 2,500 words; submit a synopsis first.
Overall freelance potential: Limited; much of the editorial content is produced in-house.
Editor's tips: Always query the editor before submitting.
Fees: £50 per picture unless supplied with article; articles £100 – £200 inclusive of pictures.

SALMON, TROUT & SEA-TROUT
Scantec Publishing Ltd, Falmouth Business Park, Falmouth, Cornwall TR11 4SZ.
Tel: 01326 312619. Fax: 01326 211721.
Editor: Crawford Little.
Monthly magazine covering all aspects of game fishing, at home and abroad.
Illustrations: Colour. Pictures of fishermen in action, general angling scenes, and close-ups of flies and tackle. Covers: attractive scenic shots in colour.
Text: Articles on all aspects of game fishing, but check with the editor before submitting.
Overall freelance potential: Good.
Fees: By negotiation.

SEA ANGLER
EMAP Pursuit Publishing Ltd, Bretton Court, Bretton, Peterborough PE3 8DZ.
Tel: 01733 465307. Fax: 01733 465436.
Editor: Mel Russ. **Designer**: Steve Diggle.
Monthly magazine dealing with the sport of sea angling from both boat and beach.
Illustrations: Colour only. Good sea fishing and shore fishing pictures, and scenic coastline pictures from around the country. Covers: close-ups, usually head shots, of individual sea fish.
Text: Instructional features, fishing expeditions, match articles, etc. 1,000 words.

Overall freelance potential: 50 per cent of published material comes from freelance sources.
Fees: By negotiation; good rates for the right kind of material.

STILLWATER TROUT ANGLER
IPC Magazines Ltd, King's Reach Tower, Stamford Street, London SE1 9LS.
Tel: 0171-261 5829. Fax: 0171-261 6016.
Editor: Roy Westwood.
Monthly magazine for trout fishing enthusiasts.
Illustrations: Colour only. Mostly commissioned to a specific brief, but very high quality general shots of trout fishing action, fisheries, etc. will be considered.
Text: Only for established contributors.
Overall freelance potential: Small.
Editor's tips: Quality is the ultimate criterion.
Fees: By negotiation, according to quality.

TROUT FISHERMAN
EMAP Pursuit Publishing Ltd, Bretton Court, Bretton, Peterborough PE3 8DZ.
Tel: 01733 264666. Fax: 01733 465436.
Editor: Chris Dawn.
Monthly magazine for the trout fishing enthusiast.
Illustrations: Colour only. Photographs depicting any aspect of angling for trout – outstanding catches, angling locations, techniques, flies and equipment.
Text: Illustrated articles on all aspects of trout fishing, around 1,500 words.
Overall freelance potential: Excellent scope for top quality material.
Editor's tips: Too much angling photography is dull and uninteresting; an original and lively approach would be welcome.
Fees: On a rising scale according to size of reproduction or length of text.

TROUT AND SALMON
EMAP Pursuit Publishing Ltd, Bretton Court, Bretton Centre, Peterborough PE3 8DZ.
Tel: 01733 264666. Fax: 01733 465436.
Editor: Sandy Leventon. **Designer**: Julian Cooke.
Monthly magazine for game fishermen.
Illustrations: Colour only. Photographs of trout or salmon waters, preferably with an angler included in the picture. Close-up and action shots to illustrate particular techniques. Captioned news pictures showing anglers with outstanding catches. Covers: good colour pictures of game fishing waters, always with an angler present.
Text: Instructional illustrated articles on all aspects of game fishing.
Overall freelance potential: Excellent for those who can produce the right sort of material.
Fees: Pictures inside according to use. Cover shots, £60. Text according to length.

Animals & Wildlife

ALL ABOUT CATS
Gong Publishing Group Ltd. Editorial: 27 Lark Avenue, Moormede, Staines, Middlesex TW18 4RX.
Tel: 01784 461955.
Editor: Carina Norris.
Monthly magazine for all cat lovers.
Illustrations: Colour only. Specific, high-quality breed shots and behavioural situation pictures always of interest, but not pictures of ordinary "moggies" doing nothing in particular. Some use of outstanding single pictures that are simply attractive pictures in their own right. Also big and wild cats to illustrate occasional features.

Text: Good illustrated articles always considered, but no vet stories. Mainly interested in well-researched features about cats in unusual places or situations. Typical length 1,000–1,200 words. Submit a synopsis to the deputy editor.

Overall freelance potential: Excellent for quality material.

Editor's tips: Please don't submit contributions about "my cat".

Fees: Pictures according to size of reproduction, up to £80. Text £75 – £100 per 1,000 words.

ALL ABOUT DOGS

Gong Publishing Group Ltd. Editorial: 27 Lark Avenue, Moormede, Staines, Middlesex TW18 4RX. Tel: 01784 461955.

Editor: Carina Norris.

Alternate-monthly for dog lovers.

Illustrations: Colour. Always interested in good pictures of breeds, working dogs, training situations, etc. Send details of stock available to the picture editor. Some commissions may be available to illustrate features as below.

Text: News stories and well-illustrated features always considered, including breed profiles, training advice, working dogs and off-beat items. Around 1,000 words plus 4–5 pictures. Discuss ideas with the deputy editor first.

Overall freelance potential: Very good.

Fees: From £25 up to £70 for a full page. Text negotiable according to content.

ANIMAL ACTION

Royal Society for the Prevention of Cruelty to Animals, Causeway, Horsham, W.Sussex RH12 1HG. Tel: 01403 64181. Fax: 01403 241048.

Editor: Michaela Miller. **Photo Librarian**: Andrew Forsyth.

Youth Membership publication of the RSPCA, published ten times a year.

Illustrations: Mainly colour. Pictures relating to animal welfare and conservation, featuring both domestic and wild animals. Send lists first.

Text: All written in-house.

Overall freelance potential: Fair.

Editor's tips: Eye contact is essential.

Fees: Colour £20–£30; covers, £100.

ANIMAL LIFE

Royal Society for the Prevention of Cruelty to Animals, Causeway, Horsham, W.Sussex RH12 1HG. Tel: 01403 264181. Fax: 01403 241048.

Editor: Martin O'Halloran. **Photo Librarian**: Andrew Forsyth.

Official journal of the RSPCA, published four times a year.

Illustrations: Mainly colour. Most photography is commissioned. Please telephone before sending photographs speculatively. The RSPCA Photolibrary is always looking for new material (see separate entry in Agencies section). Subjects include wildlife, domestic animals, farming, the environment and natural history. Pictures must have accurate captions.

Text: All written in-house.

Overall freelance potential: Moderate.

Editor's tips: We prefer pictures that show real contact between animals and people. Not interested in "cutesy" pictures.

Fees: B&W pictures £15; colour £20–£50, dependent on size. Covers, £80.

BIRD LIFE

Royal Society for the Protection of Birds, The Lodge, Sandy, Bedfordshire SG19 2DL. Tel: 01767 680551. Fax: 01767 692365.

Editor: Mark Boyd. **Picture Researcher**: Jo Hadden.

Alternate-monthly magazine for members of the RSPB Young Ornithologists' Club.

Illustrations: Colour (Kodachrome 64 preferred). Good stock shots, preferably with a conservation angle; news pictures of YOC groups and individual achievements. Covers: colour close-ups of wild birds in their native habitat.
Text: Short illustrated articles on wildlife and conservation, written with children aged 7–12 in mind. Length around 600 words. Use of unsolicited material rare.
Overall freelance potential: Good.
Fees: photographs according to use; £60 per 1,000 words for text.

BIRD WATCHING
EMAP Pursuit Publishing Ltd, Bretton Court, Bretton, Peterborough PE3 8DZ.
Tel: 01733 264666. Fax: 01733 261984.
Editor: David Cromack.
Monthly magazine devoted to birdwatching and ornithology.
Illustrations: Colour only. Top quality photographs of birds in the wild, both in the UK and overseas. Prefer to use pictures that illustrate specific aspects of bird behaviour. Also, landscape shots of British birdwatching sites. Potential contributors are asked to always send a list of subjects available in the first instance.
Text: Illustrated features on all aspects of birds and birdwatching.
Overall freelance potential: Excellent scope for wildlife specialists.
Fees: By negotiation.

BIRDS
Royal Society for the Protection of Birds, The Lodge, Sandy, Bedfordshire SG19 2DL.
Tel: 01767 680551. Fax: 01767 692365.
Editor: Rob Hume.
Quarterly magazine for RSPB members. Covers ornithology and general conservation issues.
Illustrations: Colour only. Photo features on particular birds, groups of birds or bird behaviour; interesting habitat shots (throughout Europe); imaginative shots of people enjoying birdwatching and the countryside. No captive birds or domestic birds.
Text: Illustrated articles on all aspects of birds in the wild, including conservation. Length 1,000–1,500 words.
Overall freelance potential: Fair.
Fees: Photographs from £50 to £120; £120 per 1,000 words for text.

BIRDWATCH
Solo Publishing Ltd, 310 Bow House, 153-159 Bow Road, London E3 2SE.
Tel: 0181-983 1855. Fax: 0181-983 0246.
Editor: Dominic Mitchell. **Picture Editor**: Steve Young.
Monthly magazine for all birdwatchers. Includes a strong emphasis on the photographic side of the hobby.
Illustrations: B&W and colour. Good photographs of British and European birds in their natural habitat. Those with collections of such material should send lists of subjects available.
Text: Well-illustrated features on birdwatching topics, including practical articles on bird photography. 1,000–1,200 words, but send a synopsis first.
Overall freelance potential: Very good.
Fees: According to use.

CAT WORLD
Ashdown Publishing Ltd, Avalon Court, Star Road, Partridge Green, West Sussex RH13 8RY.
Tel: 01403 711511. Fax: 01403 711521.
Editor: Joan Moore.
Monthly for all cat lovers.
Illustrations: Colour. Top quality portraits of specific cat breeds (medium format preferred) and sequences illustrating typical cat behaviour. Also pictures showing cats in specific situations (i.e. on

holiday, on boats), but *not* pictures of ordinary moggies doing nothing in particular. Colour print acceptable for general material. Always contact the editor before submitting.
Text: Breed and other informed features from those with specialist knowledge.
Overall freelance potential: Good.
Editor's tips: For portrait shots cats must be pristine, with clean eyes, nose and fur.
Fees: Covers £50; up to £25 for pictures inside.

CATS
Our Dogs Publishing Co. Ltd, 5 James Leigh Street, Manchester M1 5NF.
Tel: 0161-236 0577. Fax: 0161-236 0892.
Editor: Brian Doyle.
Weekly publication aimed at the serious cat breeder and exhibitor and all cat lovers.
Illustrations: B&W only. Newsy photographs of interest to serious cat lovers. All pictures must be accompanied by informative captions.
Text: Limited scope for knowledgeable features.
Overall freelance potential: Limited to the coverage of serious cat matters.
Editor's tips: If the subject concerns cats, take a chance and submit it.
Fees: By negotiation.

DOGS TODAY
Pet Subjects Ltd, Pankhurst Farm, Bagshot Road, West End, Woking, Surrey GU24 9QR.
Tel: 01276 858880. Fax: 01276 858860.
Editor: Beverley Cuddy.
Monthly magazine for the pet dog lover.
Illustrations: Colour. News pictures, shots showing dogs in action or in specific situations, exciting or amusing photo sequences, and pictures of celebrities with their dogs. No simple dog portraits unless displaying a strong element of humour or sentiment.
Text: General illustrated features about dogs. Should be positive and have a "human interest" feel.
Overall freelance potential: Excellent for the right material.
Fees: According to use.

KENNEL GAZETTE
The Kennel Club, 1–5 Clarges Street, London W1Y 8AB.
Tel: 0171-493 6651. Fax: 0171-495 6162.
Editor: C. L. S. Colborn.
Monthly official journal of the Kennel Club. Aimed at owners and exhibitors of pedigree dogs.
Illustrations: B&W and colour. Pictures of pedigree dogs, with and without people; dog shows; working dogs. Covers: colour or B&W pictures of pedigree dogs.
Text: Articles on breeding, veterinary subjects, judging, grooming, police dogs, field trials, obedience classes etc. 500–2,000 words.
Overall freelance potential: For specialist material only.
Editor's tips: The readership is specialist. Submissions should reflect this. Pictures must illustrate relevant editorial unless they represent possible covers.
Fees: Inside: B&W, £10; colour, £25. Covers, £40. Features by agreement.

NATURAL WORLD
RSNC The Wildlife Trust Partnership, 20 Upper Ground, London SE1 9PF.
Tel: 0171-805 5555. Fax: 0171-805 5911.
Editor: Linda Bennett. **Picture Editor**: Susie Rowbottom.
The magazine of The Wildlife Trusts, concerned with all aspects of wildlife and countryside conservation in the UK. Published three times per year.
Illustrations: Colour; in particular, mammals, amphibians, insects, flowers and trees. Subjects must be wild; no pets or zoo animals.
Text: Short photo-features on wildlife or conservation topics particularly connected with local

Wildlife Trusts. Around 300 words.
Overall freelance potential: Limited.
Fees: £35 minimum for colour.

PETER PURVES' MAD ABOUT DOGS

David Hall Publishing, Temple Buildings, Railway Terrace, Rugby CV21 3EJ.
Tel: 01788 535218. Fax: 01788 541845.
Editor: Peter Purves. **Deputy Editor**: Jane Howard.
Monthly for all dog lovers, with the message that "dogs are fun".
Illustrations: Interesting and unusual single pictures and sequences always considered – news stories, humorous pictures, heroic dogs, celebrity owners, etc. The magazine has an in-house photographer but is also interested in building up a network of photographers to undertake occasional commissions around the country. Photographers must have proven experience of working with dogs and be able to show examples of previous work.
Text: News stories and longer features on topics as above. Particular interest in material about dogs that have proved inspirational to their owners – helping them get over an illness or follow a sporting ambition. Writing style should be warm and chatty.
Overall freelance potential: Excellent.
Editor's tips: Contributions should always emphasis the positive aspects of dog ownership.
Fees: variable, dependent on what is offered.

VETERINARY PRACTICE

A E Morgan Publications, c/o Burrows Design Works, Jonathan Scott Hall, Thorpe Road, Norwich NR1 1UH.
Tel/fax: 01603 623856.
Editor: Chris Cattrall.
Monthly newspaper for veterinary surgeons in general practice.
Illustrations: Pictures of veterinary surgeons engaged in activities either connected with or outside their professional work.
Text: Features particularly concerned with veterinary practice. 800–1,500 words.
Overall freelance potential: Limited.
Fees: By agreement.

WILD CAT

Cat Survival Trust, The Centre, Codicote Road, Welwyn, Hertfordshire AL6 9TU.
Tel: 01438 716873 or 716478. Fax: 01438 717535.
Editor: Terry Moore.
Published twice a year for members, patrons and friends of the Cat Survival Trust, as well as zoological institutions, museums and libraries in many countries.
Illustrations: B&W only. Pictures of wild cats, especially less common species. Pictures taken in the wild or overseas zoos or private collections are particularly welcome. No domestic pets. Covers: B&W pictures of same.
Text: Articles on any aspect of wild cats, e.g. biology, management, breeding, conservation, etc. 1,000–2,000 words.
Overall freelance potential: Limited.
Fees: Nominal, due to the publishers being a charity.

WILDFOWL & WETLANDS

The Wildfowl & Wetlands Trust, Slimbridge, Gloucestershire GL2 7BT.
Tel: 01453 890333. Fax: 01453 890827.
Editor: Nikki Straughan.
Quarterly magazine of The Wildfowl & Wetlands Trust.
Illustrations: B&W and colour. Pictures of water birds in their natural habitat, plus pictures of the wetland environment and other forms of wetland wildlife.

Text: Illustrated articles of a serious nature, concerning groups of waterfowl or particular species, or on threats to or conservation of wetland habitats. Travel features considered as long as they concentrate on the relevant subject matter.

Overall freelance potential: Good scope limited only by the frequency of the publication.

Fees: On the low side as the publisher is a charity, but open to negotiation.

YOUR CAT

EMAP Pursuit Publishing Ltd, Apex House, Oundle Road, Peterborough PE2 9NP.

Tel: 01733 898100. Fax: 01733 898487.

Editor: Sue Parslow.

Monthly magazine for all cat lovers. Covers every type of cat from the household moggie to the show pedigree.

Illustrations: Colour only. Mostly by commission to accompany features as below. Some scope for interesting, unusual or humorous single pictures.

Text: Illustrated news items and features on the widest variety of cats: famous cats, cats in the news, readers' cats, rare cats, cats that earn a living, etc. Also authoritative articles on practical matters: breeding, grooming, training, etc.

Overall freelance potential: Excellent; the magazine is heavily illustrated.

Fees: By negotiation.

YOUR DOG

EMAP Pursuit Publishing Ltd, Apex House, Oundle Road, Peterborough PE2 9NP.

Tel: 01733 898100. Fax: 01733 898487.

Editor: Sarah Wright.

Monthly magazine for "the everyday dog owner", with the emphasis on care and training.

Illustrations: Colour only. Top quality pictures showing dogs and their owners in a practical context, i.e. walking, training, grooming, etc.; dogs in the news; amusing pictures. Covers: portraits of the more popular breeds, or appealing cross-breeds/mongrels, with good eye contact. Must be of the highest technical quality.

Text: Illustrated news stories, practical features, and articles on any interesting canine subject, i.e. working dogs, dog charities, celebrities and their dogs, etc. Always contact editor before submitting.

Overall freelance potential: Very good.

Editor's tips: Make sure that pictures are recent and not just something dug up from the back of the filing cabinet!

Fees: According to size of reproduction and by negotiation.

Arts & Entertainment

BROADCAST HARDWARE INTERNATIONAL

The Hardware Magazine Company Ltd, 48 The Broadway, Maidenhead, Berkshire SL6 1PE.

Tel: 01628 773935. Fax: 01628 773537.

Editor: David Sparks.

Alternate-monthly magazine for the television broadcast industry, aimed at senior engineers.

Illustrations: B&W and colour. Photographers of television broadcast studios, control rooms, outside broadcast vehicles and operations. Covers: normally by commission.

Text: Technical aspects of television production and post-production. 2,000–2,500 words.

Overall freelance potential: Quite good.

Editor's tips: Phone with ideas in the first instance.

Fees: Negotiable.

CLUB MIRROR
Quantum Publishing Ltd, 29/31 Lower Coombe Street, Croydon, CR9 1LX.
Tel: 0181-681 2099. Fax: 0181-680 8828.
Editor: Dominic Roskrow.
Published 10 times a year for officials, committee members and stewards of registered clubs throughout the UK; proprietary club owners and managers; and discotheque owners and managers.
Illustrations: Colour. Interior pictures of new clubs, new club openings, interesting general pictures of club activities.
Text: Articles on new club openings, new clubs planned, news stories on clubs, special features on successful clubs. Also features on the club trade, i.e. catering services etc. 100–2,000 words.
Overall freelance potential: Good; 40 per cent from freelance sources.
Fees: By arrangement but normally NUJ rates.

DANCE AND DANCERS
Dance & Dancers Ltd, 214 Panther House, 38 Mount Pleasant, London WC1X 0AP.
Tel/fax: 0171-813 1049.
Editors: John Percival & Nadine Meisner.
Monthly magazine covering dance and ballet. Includes reviews, features and information on the subject.
Illustrations: B&W only inside. Pictures of current dance performances, occasionally archive and historical material. Covers: colour pictures of current performances or personalities to tie in with a major feature. Must be up to date.
Text: Reviews of current performances. General features on dance. Profiles of dancers. 500–2,000 words.
Overall freelance potential: Over 50 per cent is freelance, but mostly from regular contributors.
Editor's tips: Very specialist interest, using ballet/contemporary/ethnic dance only. No mime, pop dance or ballet school interest. Always check before submitting.
Fees: Negotiable.

INTERNATIONAL BROADCASTING
EMAP Business Publishing Ltd, 33-39 Bowling Green Lane, London EC1R 0DA.
Tel: 0171-505 8073. Fax: 0171-505 8076.
Editor: Paul Marks.
Published 11 times per year, for professionals in the television broadcasting industry.
Illustrations: Colour. Photographs of TV broadcast hardware, studios, sets, etc.
Text: Features on TV broadcast production. 600–1,500 words.
Overall freelance potential: Good.
Editor's tips: Always call with ideas.
Fees: By arrangement.

LEISURE WEEK
Centaur Communications, St Giles House, 50 Poland Street, London W1V 4AX.
Tel: 0171-287 5000. Fax: 0171-734 2741.
Editor: Michael Nutley.
Fortnightly trade news publication covering the whole leisure industry, from pubs and clubs to museums and theatres.
Illustrations: B&W and colour. News pictures covering happenings in any branch of the leisure industry.
Text: News stories and short features on leisure industry developments, profiles of individual operations etc.
Overall freelance potential: Quite good for those with access to specific leisure fields.
Fees: £150 per 1,000 words for text; photographs according to use (NUJ rates).

RADIO TIMES
BBC Worldwide Publishing, Woodlands, 80 Wood Lane, London W12 0TT.
Tel: 0181-576 2000. Fax: 0181-576 3160.
Editor: Sue Robinson. **Picture Editor**: Theresa Eagle.
Weekly magazine containing news and details of BBC radio and television, ITV, Channel 4, cable and satellite listings.
Illustrations: B&W and colour. Coverage of broadcasting events, usually by commission.
Text: Commissioned features on BBC personalities or programmes of current interest. 1,000 words.
Overall freelance potential: Fair for commissioned work.
Fees: Various.

THE STAGE
The Stage Newspaper Ltd, 47 Bermondsey Street, London SE1 3XT.
Tel: 0171-403 1818. Fax: 0171-357 9287.
Editor: Brian Attwood.
Weekly newspaper for professionals working in the performing arts and the entertainment industry.
Illustrations: B&W and colour. News pictures concerning people and events in the theatre and television worlds.
Text: Features on the theatre and light entertainment. 800 words.
Overall freelance potential: Better for writers than for photographers.
Fees: Pictures by agreement, text £100 per 1,000 words.

TV TIMES
IPC Magazines Ltd, King's Reach Tower, Stamford Street, London SE1 9LS.
Tel: 0171-261 7000. Fax: 0171-261 7777.
Editor: Liz Murphy. **Picture Editor**: Jo Laycock. **Art Director**: Terry Brown.
Weekly magazine containing listings and features on ITV, BBC, Channel 4, satellite television and radio programmes.
Illustrations: Colour. Usually commissioned or requested from specialist sources. Covers: quality colour portraits or groups specific to current programme content.
Text: Articles on personalities and programmes.
Overall freelance potential: Between 50 and 75 per cent each week is freelance, but mostly from recognised contributors.
Fees: Negotiable.

THEATRE
Repertory Publishers Ltd, 67 Eastwell House, Weston Street, London SE1 4DJ.
Tel: 0171-237 2087. Fax: 0171-378 1069.
Editor: Ann Shuttleworth.
Alternate-monthly magazine covering professional theatre in the UK. Aimed at theatregoers rather than the profession.
Illustrations: B&W and colour. Much obtained direct from theatres and agents, but always interested in hearing from photographers who can offer suitable coverage or stock. Covers: Usually a specially commissioned portrait; opportunities for photographers outside the London/South East area.
Text: Illustrated features and review coverage from outside London always considered. Topics include profiles of actors/actresses, new productions, back-stage workers, etc. Always raise suggestions with the editor in the first instance.
Overall freelance potential: Fair.
Fees: Photography by negotiation; text £150 per 1,000 words.

WHAT SATELLITE TV
WV Publications, 57–59 Rochester Place, London NW1 9JU.
Tel: 0171-485 0011. Fax: 0171-331 1242.
Editor: Geoff Bains.

Monthly magazine for satellite TV system buyers and users. Contains tests on receivers and dishes, general features, programme listings and reviews and the latest satellite news.
Illustrations: B&W and colour. Systems *in situ*, family/people shots in use. Covers: colour pictures of similar.
Text: Technical topics, plus programme reviews and personality pieces. 500–1,200 words.
Overall freelance potential: Around 50 per cent from such sources.
Fees: By agreement.

THE YOUNG DANCER MAGAZINE
Elwell House, West Buckland, Devon EX32 0SW.
Tel: 01598 760566. Fax: 01598 760577.
Editor: Ninette Hartley.
Monthly for young dancers and dance enthusiasts. Concentrates on ballet/contemporary dance but covers all forms including jazz, ballrom, disco, etc.
Illustrations: B&W and colour. Pictures of all types of dance involving young dancers (age range 10–20 years; not young children). Most interested in captioned pictures concerning successful youngsters. Some commissions available; submit samples of work in the first instance.
Text: Illustrated profiles of individual young dancers.
Overall freelance potential: Fair.
Editor's tips: Always interested in anything of genuine interest to the readership.
Fees: By negotation.

Aviation

AEROPLANE MONTHLY
Specialist Group, IPC Magazines, King's Reach Tower, Stamford Street, London SE1 9LS.
Tel: 0171-261 5849. Fax: 0171-261 5269.
Editor: Richard Riding.
Monthly aviation history magazine, specialising in the period 1909–1960. Occasional features on modern aviation.
Illustrations: B&W and colour. Photographs for use in their own right or for stock. Main interests – veteran or vintage aircraft, including those in museums; preserved airworthy aircraft; unusual pictures of modern aircraft. Action shots preferred in the case of colour material, e.g. air-to-air, ground-to-air, or air-to-ground. Covers: high quality air-to-air shots of vintage or veteran aircraft. 6x6cm minimum.
Text: Short news stories concerning preserved aircraft, new additions to museums and collections, etc. Not more than 300 words.
Overall freelance potential: Most contributions are from freelance sources, but specialised knowledge and skills are often necessary.
Editor's tips: The magazine is always in the market for sharp, good quality colour transparencies of preserved aircraft in the air.
Fees: Colour photographs: full page £80; centre spread £100; covers £90. B&W from £10 upwards.

AIR INTERNATIONAL
Key Publishing Ltd, PO Box 100, Stamford, Lincolnshire PE9 1XQ.
Tel: 01780 755131. Fax: 01780 757261.
Editor: Malcolm English.
Monthly general aviation magazine with emphasis on modern military aircraft and the civil aviation industry. Includes some historical topics. Aimed at both enthusiasts and industry professionals.
Illustrations: B&W and colour. Topical single pictures or picture stories on aviation subjects worldwide, e.g. airliners in new livery, new aircraft at Heathrow, etc. Overseas material welcomed. Air show coverage rarely required.

Text: Illustrated features on topics as above, from writers with in-depth knowledge of the subject. Length variable.
Overall freelance potential: Very good for suitable material.
Editor's tips: Remember the magazine is read by professionals and is not just for enthusiasts.
Fees: B&W from £10; colour based on page rate of £75. Covers, up to £130 for full-bleed sole reproduction. Text £50 per 1,000 words.

AIR PICTORIAL
The Hastings Printing Company Ltd, Drury Lane, St Leonards on Sea, East Sussex TN38 9BJ.
Tel: 01424 720477. Fax: 01424 443693/434086.
Editor: Barry Wheeler.
Monthly magazine covering aviation in general, both past and present. Aimed at both the industry and the enthusiast.
Illustrations: B&W and colour. Photographs of all types of aircraft, civil and military, old or new. Captioned news pictures of particular interest, but no space exploration or aircraft engineering.
Text: News items about current aviation matters. Historical contributions concerning older aircraft.
Overall freelance potential: About 45 per cent is contributed by freelances.
Fees: On a rising scale according to size of reproduction or length of text.

AIRFORCES MONTHLY
Key Publishing Ltd, PO Box 100, Stamford, Lincolnshire PE9 1XQ.
Tel: 01780 755131. Fax: 01780 757261.
Editor: David Oliver.
Monthly magazine concerned with modern military aircraft.
Illustrations: B&W and colour. Interesting up-to-date pictures of military aircraft from any country.
Text: Knowledgeable articles concerning current military aviation. No historical matter.
Overall freelance potential: Good for contributors with the necessary knowledge and access.
Fees: £25 minimum for colour; £10 minimum for B&W. Covers: £120. Text: by negotiation.

AIRPORTS INTERNATIONAL
SKC Communications Ltd, Southfields, South View Road, Wadhurst, East Sussex, TN5 6TP.
Tel: 01892 784099. Fax: 01892 784089.
Editor: Mark Pilling.
Published 10 times a year, dealing with all aspects of airport management and ground support operations worldwide.
Illustrations: Colour only. Photographs likely to be of interest are related to airport affairs. Particularly interested in high quality colour for cover use, and coverage of "exotic" overseas locations. Always contact the editor before submitting.
Text: Possible scope for overseas material, depending on region; China especially of interest at present.
Overall freelance potential: Moderate.
Fees: By negotiation.

BRITISH AIRWAYS NEWS
British Airways plc, PO Box 10, Heathrow Airport, Hounslow, Middlesex TW6 2JA.
Tel: 0181-562 2015. Fax: 0181-562 3545
Editor: David Snelling.
Weekly staff newspaper of British Airways.
Illustrations: B&W and colour. Captioned news pictures relating to commercial aviation or allied fields such as travel and tourism, especially any with specific BA connections or involving BA staff.
Text: Articles on general aviation industry topics. Only by commission, but ideas considered.
Overall freelance potential: Limited.
Fees: By negotiation.

COMMUTER WORLD
Shephard Press Ltd, 111 High Street, Burnham, Buckinghamshire SL1 7JZ.
Tel: 01628 604311. Fax: 01628 664334.
Editor: Ian Harbison.
Alternate-monthly publication dealing with civil air travel of the commuter and regional type. Aimed at industry, business, and users.
Illustrations: B&W and colour. Photographs of commuter aeroplanes. News pictures concerning the aeroplane industry and airline business in the commuter/regional field. Covers: colour photographs relating to commuter/regional airline operations.
Text: Knowledgeable articles on any aspect of the commuter airline business. 1,500–2,500 words.
Overall freelance potential: Good.
Fees: By negotiation.

DEFENCE HELICOPTER
The Shephard Press Ltd, 111 High Street, Burnham, Bucks SL1 7JZ.
Tel: 01628 604311. Fax: 01628 664334.
Editor: Ian Parker.
Quarterly publication concerned with military helicopters and their applications.
Illustrations: B&W and colour. Pictures of military helicopters anywhere in the world. Must be accurately captioned. Covers: high quality colour pictures of military helicopters. Should preferably be exclusive and in upright format. No "sterile" pictures; must be action shots.
Text: Knowledgeable articles on any aspect of military helicopter use and technology. 1,500–2,500 words.
Overall freelance potential: Good.
Fees: By negotiation.

FLIGHT INTERNATIONAL
Reed Business Publishing Ltd, Quadrant House, The Quadrant, Sutton, Surrey SM2 5AS.
Tel: 0181-652 3882. Fax: 0181-652 3840.
Editor-in-Chief: Allan Winn.
Weekly aviation magazine with worldwide circulation, aimed at aerospace professionals in all sectors of the industry.
Illustrations: B&W and colour. Weekly requirement for news pictures of aviation-related events. Feature illustrations on all aspects of aerospace, from airliners to satellites. Covers: colour pictures of aircraft – civil and military, light and business. Medium format preferred.
Text: Features by prior arrangement; ideas must first be submitted to the deputy editor, owing to the technical nature of the subject. Over 750 words.
Overall freelance potential: Approximately 10 per cent of news and 5 per cent of features comes from outside sources.
Editor's tips: News material should be submitted on spec. Pictures should be as new as possible or have a news relevance.
Fees: B&W, £19.61; colour, £56.38 up to 30 sq.in., £65.93 to £106.93 30–60 sq. in.; £223.30 for cover. News reports, minimum £7.07 per 100 words; commissioned features by negotiation.

FLYER
Seager Publishing Ltd, 3rd Floor, 3 Kingsmead Square, Bath BA1 2AB.
Tel: 01225 481440. Fax: 01225 481262.
Editor: Martin Le Poidevin.
Monthly magazine for private pilots.
Illustrations: Mostly colour. Attractive and striking photographs of light aircraft of the type commonly used by the private pilot. Details of material available should be sent first, rather than speculative submissions.
Text: News items and illustrated articles from those with proper knowledge of the subject.
Overall freelance potential: Limited – mainly written by established contributors.

Editor's tips: All contributors should have a genuine understanding of the flying scene.
Fees: By negotiation.

HELICOPTER WORLD
Shephard Press Ltd, 111 High Street, Burnham, Buckinghamshire SL1 7JZ.
Tel: 01628 604311. Fax: 01628 664334.
Editor: Ian Parker.
Monthly publication concerning civil and commercial helicopters. Aimed at both users and the helicopter industry.
Illustrations: B&W and colour. Photographs of all types of civil helicopters and related matters. Covers: good colour pictures, which should be exclusive and of upright format.
Text: Knowledgeable articles on any aspect of civil helicopter applications, and manufacture. 1,500–2,500 words.
Overall freelance potential: Good.
Fees: By negotiation.

PILOT
Pilot Publishing Co. Ltd, The Clock House, 28 Old Town, Clapham, London SW4 0LB.
Tel: 0171-498 2506. Fax: 0171-498 6920.
Editor: James Gilbert.
Monthly publication for the general aviation (i.e. business and private flying) pilot.
Illustrations: Mostly colour. Picture on topics associated with this field of flying.
Text: Features, preferably illustrated, on general aviation. 2,000–4,000 words.
Overall freelance potential: Excellent. Virtually all of the editorial matter in the magazine is contributed by freelances.
Editor's tips: Read a copy of the magazine before submitting and study style, content, subject and coverage.
Fees: £150–£800 for features. B&W and colour pictures, £26.00 each; covers, £200.

POPULAR FLYING
Popular Flying Association, Terminal Building, Shoreham Airport, Shoreham-by-Sea, West Sussex BN43 5FF.
Tel: 01273 461616. Fax: 01273 463390.
Editor: John Catchpole.
Bi-monthly for home builders of kit and plans-built aircraft.
Illustrations: B&W and colour. Pictures of vintage and home-built aircraft. Covers: colour air-to-air shots preferred.
Text: Features of any length on anything concerning home-built vintage and classic aircraft in the UK.
Overall freelance potential: Good.
Editor's tips: The editor is always interested to receive articles/photographs on homebuilt or classic and vintage recreational and sporting aircraft for consideration.
Fees: By negotiation.

Boating & Watersport

BOARDS
Yachting Press Ltd, 196 Eastern Esplanade, Southend-on-Sea, Essex SS1 3AB.
Tel: 01702 582245. Fax: 01702 588434.
Editor: Bill Dawes.
Monthly magazine devoted to boardsailing and windsurfing.
Illustrations: B&W and colour. Good clear action shots of boardsailing or windsurfing; pictures of

attractive girls in a boardsailing context; and any other visually striking material relating to the sport. Covers: good colour action shots are always needed.
Text: Articles and features on all aspects of the sport.
Overall freelance potential: Very good for high quality material.
Editor's tips: Action shots must be clean, clear and crisp.
Fees: By negotiation.

BOAT INTERNATIONAL
Edisea Ltd, Ward House, 5–7 Kingston Hill, Kingston-Upon-Thames, Surrey KT2 7PW.
Tel: 0181-547 2662. Fax: 0181-547 1201.
Editor: Amanda McCracken.
Monthly glossy magazine featuring the very top level of boating activity.
Illustrations: Almost exclusively colour. Top quality photographs of top quality boating, from world class yacht racing to luxury motor cruising. 35mm acceptable for action shots, but larger formats preferred for static subjects.
Text: Mostly staff produced or commissioned from top writers in the field.
Overall freelance potential: Excellent for the best in boating photography and marine subjects.
Editor's tips: Only the very best quality is of interest.
Fees: By negotiation.

BOATING BUSINESS
Rushton Marine Press, Woodside, Burnhams Road, Little Bookham, Surrey KT23 3BA.
Tel: 01372 453316. Fax: 01372 459974.
Editor: Peter Nash.
Monthly magazine for the leisure marine trade.
Illustrations: B&W and colour. News pictures relating to the marine trade, especially company and overseas news. Some scope for commissioned work.
Text: Features on marine trade topics; always consult the editor first.
Overall freelance potential: Limited.
Fees: Photographs from £20; text £100 per 1,000 words.

CANAL & RIVERBOAT
A E Morgan Publications, c/o Burrows Design Works, Jonathan Scott Hall, Thorpe Road, Norwich NR1 1UH.
Tel/fax: 01603 623856.
Editor: Chris Cattrall.
Monthly publication aimed at inland waterway enthusiasts and canal holidaymakers.
Illustrations: B&W and colour. Photographs of all inland waterway subjects. Covers: colour pictures of attractive waterways subjects, preferrably with an original approach.
Text: Illustrated articles on canals, rivers, boats and allied subjects.
Overall freelance potential: Good, especially for material with an original approach.
Fees: By negotiation.

CLASSIC BOAT
Boating Publications Ltd, Link House, Dingwall Avenue, Croydon CR9 2TA.
Tel: 0181-686 2599. Fax: 0181-781 6535.
Editor: Nic Compton.
Monthly magazine for the enthusiast interested in traditional or traditional-style boats from any part of the world. Emphasis on sailing boats, but also covers traditional power boats, steam vessels and modern reproductions of classic styles.
Illustrations: B&W and colour. Pictures to accompany features and articles. Single general interest pictures with 100 word captions giving full subject details. Particular interest in individual boat photo essays. Covers: spectacular sailing images, but exceptional boatbuilding shots may be used. Upright format with space for logo and coverlines.

Text: Well-illustrated articles covering particular types of boat and individual craft, combining well-researched historical background with hard practical advice about restoration and maintenance. Some scope for humorous pieces and cruising articles involving classic boats. Always send a detailed synopsis in the first instance.

Overall freelance potential: Good for those with specialist knowledge or access.

Editor's tips: Contributors' notes available on request.

Fees: £90 per page pro rata; covers £200.

INTERNATIONAL BOAT INDUSTRY

Prestige Magazines Ltd, Link House, Dingwall Avenue, Croydon CR9 2TA.
Tel: 0181-686 2599. Fax: 0181-781 6056.

Editor: Robert Greenwood.

10 issues a year; business publication dealing with the marine leisure industry worldwide.

Illustrations: Colour only. Pictures of boat building and moulding, chandlery shops, showrooms, new boats and equipment. Also marinas.

Text: News items about the boat industry are always of interest.

Overall freelance potential: Good for those in touch with the boat trade.

Editor's tips: This is strictly a trade magazine – simple pictures of cruising or racing are not required.

Fees: Linear scale – £100 per page down.

JET SKIER & PERSONAL WATERCRAFT

CSL Publishing Ltd, CSL House, 184 Histon Road, Cambridge CB4 3JP.
Tel: 01223 460490. Fax: 01223 315960.

Editor: Graham Stuart.

Monthly magazine devoted to small, powered water craft and related sports activity. Features Jet Skis, Wetbikes and other personal watercraft.

Illustrations: B&W and colour. Spectacular action shots and pictures of unusual individual craft and uses. Events coverage usually by commission.

Text: Some scope for illustrated articles from those with good knowledge of the subject. Submit ideas only in the first instance.

Overall freelance potential: Good.

Fees: By negotiation.

MOTOR BOAT & YACHTING

Specialist Group, IPC Magazines, King's Reach Tower, Stamford Street, London SE1 9LS.
Tel: 0171-261 5333. Fax: 0171-261 5419.

Editor: Alan Harper. **Art Editor**: Peter Allen.

Monthly magazine for owners and users of motor cruisers and motor sailers.

Illustrations: Colour. Pictures of motor cruisers at sea, harbour scenes, workboats. Covers: colour, mostly of people having fun on motor boats at sea. Also good harbour scenes, showing exceptional composition and/or lighting.

Text: Features on interesting, unusual or historic motor boats; first-person motor boat cruising accounts; technical motor boating topics; inland waterways topics. 1,500–2,500 words.

Overall freelance potential: Around 60 per cent of features and 40 per cent of pictures are freelance contributed.

Fees: Good; on a rising scale according to size of reproduction or length of article. Covers £175.

MOTOR BOATS MONTHLY

Boating Publications Ltd, Link House, Dingwall Avenue, Croydon CR9 2TA.
Tel: 0181-686 2599. Fax: 0181-781 6065.

Editor: Kim Hollamby.

Monthly magazine for all motorboating enthusiasts, but mainly aimed at owners of boats of up to 60 feet. Covers all aspects, from top level powerboat racing to inland waterway cruising.

Illustrations: Colour. News pictures, motor boat action, and shots of cruising locations, both in UK and overseas.
Text: Illustrated articles on any motorboat-related topic, UK and worldwide.
Overall freelance potential: Fairly good.
Fees: On a rising scale according to size of reproduction or length of text.

PRACTICAL BOAT OWNER
IPC Magazines Ltd, Westover House, West Quay Road, Poole, Dorset BH15 1JG.
Tel:01202 680593. Fax:01202 674335.
Editor: Rodger Witt.
Monthly magazine for yachtsmen, sail and power.
Illustrations: Colour only. Up to date aerial pictures of harbours and anchorages. Covers: Action shots of cruising boats up to about 38ft (preferably sail) showing people enjoying themselves. Strong colours.
Text: Features and associated illustrations of real use to the people who own boats. Subjects can cover any boating facet on which reader might take action, from raising the money to buy a boat, through insurance to navigation, seamanship, care and maintenance etc. No narrative yarns.
Overall freelance potential: About 75 per cent bought from contributors.
Fees: On a rising scale according to size of reproduction or length of feature.

RYA NEWS
Royal Yachting Association, RYA House, Romsey Road, Eastleigh, Hampshire SO50 9YA.
Tel: 01703 627400. Fax: 01703 629924.
Editor: Carol Baker.
Quarterly publication for personal members of the RYA, affiliated clubs and class associations.
Illustrations: B&W and colour. Pictures of boats, yachting events and personalities, used either in their own right or as illustrations for reports and articles. Covers: seasonal/topical colour shots of yachting subjects.
Text: Reports and articles on yachting.
Overall freelance potential: Moderate.
Fees: By arrangement.

REGATTA
Amateur Rowing Association, 6 Lower Mall, London W6 9DJ.
Tel: 0181-748 3632. Fax: 0181-741 4658.
Editor: Christopher Dodd. **Picture Editor**: John Shore.
Ten editions annually. Covers rowing and sculling – competitive, recreational and technical.
Illustrations: B&W and colour. Action pictures of rowing, and rowing in scenic settings.
Text: Short, illustrated articles on all aspects of rowing. Technical topics such as coaching, training and boat-building.
Overall freelance potential: Good.
Fees: Variable, around £25 for a short feature, £35 for cover picture.

SAILING TODAY
Future Publishing Ltd, Beauford Court, 30 Monmouth Street, Bath BA1 2BW.
Tel: 01225 442244. Fax: 01225 732248.
Editor: Philip Dunn. **Art Editor**: Julian Dace.
Practical monthly for active sail cruising enthusiasts.
Illustrations: Colour. Dynamic action shots of people involved in active sailing situations. Ideally compositions should be closely cropped in to focus on the sailor(s) involved, who should be clearly enjoying themselves. Some possibility of commissioned location work; write first with details of experience.

Text: Well-illustrated features about cruising round the British Isles. Should have a modern, upbeat and original approach.
Overall freelance potential: Good.
Fees: By negotiation.

SPORTS BOAT & WATERSKI INTERNATIONAL
CSL Publishing Ltd, CSL House, 184 Histon Road, Cambridge CB4 3JP.
Tel: 01223 460490. Fax: 01223 315960.
Editor: Graham Stuart.
Monthly publication covering sports boats from 14–30 feet.
Illustrations: B&W and colour. Top quality action shots of small sports boats. Also stylish pictures that show boats as glamorous and exciting. Commissions may be available to illustrate major features. Covers: colour action shots with plenty of impact.
Text: Illustrated articles on all aspects of sports boats and waterskiing will always be considered. 500–3,000 words.
Overall freelance potential: Excellent.
Fees: By negotiation.

SURF MAGAZINE
Top Floor, DRG Building, Longmoor Lane, Breaston, Derbyshire DE7 3BQ.
Tel: 01332 874731. Fax: 01332 874732.
Editor: Alf Anderson.
Bi-monthly surfing magazine.
Illustrations: B&W and colour. Anything relevant to surfing and the ocean environment, including events coverage. Plus lifestyle and marine life (occasionally use shots of dolphins etc).
Text: News items and general features on surfing and surf-related subjects.
Overall freelance potential: Good for those who can produce good action material.
Fees: B&W £10; colour around £25.

WATER CRAFT
Pete Greenfield Publishing, Gweek, Helston, Cornwall TR12 6UE.
Tel: 01326 221424. Fax: 01326 221728.
Editor: Pete Greenfield.
Alternate-monthly magazine devoted to traditional small boats and boatbuilding.
Illustrations: Colour. Photographs mainly required as part of complete feature packages, but interesting or unusual singles and sequences considered if accompanied by detailed caption information.
Text: Well-illustrated features on suitable subjects
Overall freelance potential: Limited at present; much is produced by regular contributors.
Fees: Around 80 per published page inclusive of pictures.

WATERWAYS WORLD
Waterways World Ltd, The Well House, High Street, Burton-on-Trent DE14 1JQ.
Tel: 01283 742951. Fax: 01283 561077.
Editor: Hugh Potter.
Monthly magazine that covers all aspects of canal and river navigations (not lakes) in Britain and abroad. Aimed at inland waterway enthusiasts and holiday boaters.
Illustrations: Colour only. Pictures of inland waterway subjects, e.g. interesting buildings; locks, preferably with boating activity if on a navigable waterway; canal scenes. No close-ups or artistic shots. Covers: canal or river scenes with boating activity prominently in the foreground; 6x6cm minimum.

Text: Features on inland waterways, 500–2,000 words. Send s.a.e. for contributors' guide.
Overall freelance potential: Around 20 per cent contributed.
Fees: Colour £15 minimum; cover £45.

WINDSURF MAGAZINE
Arcwind Ltd, The Blue Barn, Tew Lane, Wootton, Woodstock, Oxon OX7 1HA.
Tel: 01993 811181. Fax: 01993 811481.
Editor: Mark Kasprowicz.
Published ten times a year. Aimed at the enthusiast and covering all aspects of windsurfing.
Illustrations: B&W and colour. Sequences and singles of windsurfing action. Top quality shots always considered.
Text: Illustrated articles on any aspect of windsurfing.
Overall freelance potential: Excellent.
Fees: £5–£15 for B&W; up to £35 for full-page colour; £60 for centre-spread; £60 for covers.

YACHTING MONTHLY
IPC Magazines Ltd, Room 2215, King's Reach Tower, Stamford Street, London SE1 9LS.
Tel: 0171-261 6040. Fax: 0171-261 7555.
Editor: *To be appointed.* **Features Editor**: Paul Gelder.
Monthly magazine for cruising yachtsmen.
Illustrations: Colour only. News pictures for immediate use; general cruising and location pictures for stock; pictures illustrating seamanship, navigation and technical subjects. Covers: top quality shots of active cruising; people working boats; cruising boats at sea; yachts in harbour.
Text: Articles relevant to cruising yachtsmen, and short accounts of cruising experiences. 1,000–2,250 words.
Overall freelance potential: Around 40 per cent comes from outside contributors.
Fees: Dependent upon size of reproduction or length of feature. Normally around £50–£110 for colour; £200 for covers. Text from £100 per 1,000 words.

YACHTING WORLD
IPC Magazines Ltd, King's Reach Tower, Stamford Street, London SE1 9LS.
Tel: 0171-261 6800. Fax: 0171-261 6818.
Editor: Andrew Bray. **Art Editor**: Robert Owen.
Monthly magazine for informed yachtsmen, experienced and with their own boats.
Illustrations: Colour only. Pictures of general yachting techniques or types of boat; pictures of events and occasions. Covers: top quality pictures of yachts – on board, at sea or general harbour pictures. Atmosphere shots. No dinghies.
Text: Informative or narrative yachting articles; technical yachting features; short humorous articles; and news. 1,000–1,500 words and 2,000–2,500 words.
Overall freelance potential: Around 30 per cent comes from freelances.
Editor's tips: Do not exceed noted article lengths. Send for writers' guidelines.
Fees: Text, up to £130 per 1,000 words; covers, up to £310; inside pictures according to size.

YACHTS AND YACHTING
Yachting Press Ltd, 196 Eastern Esplanade, Southend-on-Sea, Essex SS1 3AB.
Tel: 01702 582245. Fax: 01702 588434.
Editor: Frazer Clark.
Fortnightly publication covering all aspects of racing, including dinghies and offshore racers.
Illustrations: B&W and colour. Pictures of racing dinghies, yachts and general sailing scenes. Covers: colour action shots of relevant subjects.
Text: Features on all aspects of the sailing scenes. 1,000–2,000 words.
Overall freelance potential: Quite good.
Fees: Negotiable.

Building & Engineering

ARCHITECTURE TODAY
Architecture Today plc, 161 Rosebery Avenue, London EC1R 4QX.
Tel: 0171-837 0143. Fax: 0171-837 0155.
Editors: Ian Latham and Dr Mark Swenarton.
Independent monthly for the architectural profession.
Illustrations: B&W and colour. Most photography is commissioned, but interesting pictures of current architectural projects are always of interest on spec.
Text: Illustrated articles of genuine interest to a professional readership; submit ideas only first. 800–2,000 words.
Overall freelance potential: Limited scope for specialists.
Editor's tips: Potential contributors must contact the editors before submitting anything.
Fees: £100 per 1,000 words; photography by arrangement.

BATHROOMS AND KITCHENS: THE MAGAZINE
EMAP Maclaren, Maclaren House, 19 Scarbrook Road, Croydon CR9 1QH.
Tel: 0181-277 5457. Fax: 0181-277 5460.
Editor: Richard Moss.
Monthly trade journal for bathroom, bedroom and kitchen specialist retailers, builders' merchants, distributors, manufacturers, installers, builders, developers, architects, etc.
Illustrations: Colour. Pictures of bathroom and kitchen units, bedroom furniture and fittings, appliances, sinks, taps, worktops, tiles, floor and wall coverings, ceilings, blinds, etc.
Text: Only after prior consultation. Up to 1,000 words usually.
Overall freelance potential: Fairly good for the contributor with a specialised knowledge of the subject.
Fees: Good; on a rising scale according to the size of reproduction or length of article.

BUILD IT
Inside Publications Ltd, 9 White Lion Street, London N1 9XJ.
Tel: 0171-837 8727. Fax: 0171-837 7124.
Editor: Rosalind Renshaw.
Monthly devoted to the self-build market – those people building a one-off home or converting old barns, chapels, etc.
Illustrations: Colour only. Medium and large format only. Commissions available to experienced photographers to cover architecture and interiors. Some interest in stock photographs of housing and interior decoration subjects.
Text: Authoritative features on building, landscaping and interior design, plus specialised articles on finance, legal issues, weatherproofing, etc.
Overall freelance potential: Excellent for the experienced contributor in the architecture and interiors field.
Fees: £120 per 1,000 words for text; good rates for photographers, commissioned shoots negotiable around £400-£800.

BUILDERS' MERCHANTS JOURNAL
Miller Freeman PLC, 30 Calderwood Street, Woolwich, London SE18 6QH
Tel: 0181-855 7777. Fax: 0181-316 3307.
Editor: Chris Pateman.
Monthly business to business magazine for the builders merchants industry – wholesale distributors of building products, including heating, bathroom and kitchen fixtures.
Illustrations: Mostly colour. Always interested in unusual photography of merchants' yards, showrooms and vehicles. Possible scope for creative still life shots of items such as bricks, blocks, timber, etc. Commissions also available, depending on geographic location – write in with details of experi-

ence and rates.

Text: Limited scope for freelance articles on suitable subjects – send business card and samples of published work in the first instance.

Overall freelance potential: Limited.

Editor's tips: Most commissions are rather boring; just going into a merchant's yard and taking general shots. A creative approach would be welcomed. We are only a small team so please write in and do not badger us with unsolicited phone calls.

Fees: Photographs by negotiation. Text around £125 per 1,000 words.

BUILDING SERVICES

Building Services Publications Ltd, Builder House, Exchange Tower, London E14 9GE.
Tel: 0171-560 4000. Fax: 0171-560 4020.

Editor: Roderic Bunn. **Art Editor**: Claire Stevens.

Monthly publication for engineers and senior management involved with installing heating, air conditioning, ventilation, lighting, lifts, hot and cold water systems etc. into buildings.

Illustrations: B&W and colour. Good quality pictures of building services. Pictures used for caption stories and for stock. Covers: colour, usually commissioned.

Text: Ideas for articles on the above subjects. 2,500 words maximum.

Overall freelance potential: Good, since very few pictures of this subject are offered.

Fees: By negotiation.

DESIGN ENGINEERING

Miller Freeman plc, 30 Calderwood Street, Woolwich, London SE18 6QH.
Tel: 0181-316 3410. Fax: 0181-316 3102.

Editor: David Wilson. **Art Editor**: Steve Lillywhite.

Monthly publication aimed at engineering designers and design management. Contains case histories, background features and data, surveys, products and news stories.

Illustrations: Colour only. Usually only to accompany specific features and news stories. Covers: colour pictures associated with editorial inside.

Text: Features on subjects such as mechanical and electrical engineering, CAD/CAM, fluid power, electronics, materials, etc. Only from experts in their fields. 500–4,000 words.

Overall freelance potential: Mainly for specialists.

Editor's tips: Send synopsis first.

Fees: Covers, up to £400; text and pictures inside by negotiation.

ENERGY IN BUILDINGS & INDUSTRY

Inside Communications Ltd, 8th Floor, Tubs Hill House, London Road, Sevenoaks, Kent TN13 1BL.
Tel: 01732 464154. Fax: 01732 464454.

Editor: Mark Thrower.

Monthly magazine concerned with the use and conservation of energy in large buildings and the industrial environment. Aimed at architects, energy managers, building services engineers and energy consultants.

Illustrations: Colour only. Pictures of relevant and interesting installations.

Text: Some scope for writer/photographers who have good knowledge of the energy business.

Overall freelance potential: Limited unless contributors have connections within the field.

Fees: £30–£40 per picture; £140 per 1,000 words for text.

THE ENGINEER

Miller Freeman plc, 30 Calderwood Street, Woolwich, London SE18 6QH.
Tel: 0181-855 7777. Fax: 0181-316 3040.

Editor: *To be appointed*. **Art Editor**: Gene Cornelius.

Magazine for engineering management, publishing 34 issues per year.

Illustrations: B&W and colour. Pictures showing new engineering technology in action – must have a news angle. Covers: colour news pictures concerning the engineering industry.

Text: News of manufacturing industries and personnel, plus articles on technology trends. Up to 800 words.
Overall freelance potential: Scope only for freelances in close contact with engineering matters.
Fees: By agreement.

ENGINEERING
Gillard Welch Associates, Chester Court, High Street, Knowle, Solihull B93 0LL.
Tel: 01564 771772. Fax: 01564 774776.
Editor: Mike Farish.
Monthly magazine dealing with all areas of manufacturing engineering from a design viewpoint.
Illustrations: B&W and colour. Photographs depicting all aspects of design in industrial engineering, from aerospace and computers to energy management and waste disposal. Much from manufacturers but some by commission. Covers: mostly graphic illustration, but may use some "artistic" photography.
Text: Short illustrated news items up to major design features. 250–2,000 words.
Overall freelance potential: Good for commissioned work.
Fees: £100 per published page for text. Covers £300–£400. Other commissioned photography around £120 per day.

H&V NEWS
EMAP Business Communications, PO Box 109, Maclaren House, 19 Scarbrook Road, Croydon CR9 1QH.
Tel: 0181-277 5000. Fax: 0181-277 5440.
Editor: Ian Vallely.
Weekly for those who purchase or specify heating, ventilating and air conditioning equipment.
Illustrations: B&W only inside. Action pictures of installations and equipment in use, preferably with human interest. Covers: colour pictures of relevant subjects.
Text: News stories, installation stories regarding heating, ventilating and air conditioning equipment, stories on companies and people. 200–300 words. Longer features by negotiation.
Overall freelance potential: Good scope for newsworthy material.
Editor's tips: The more current the information supplied the better its chance of success.
Fees: £12 per 100 words; pictures by negotiation.

HOUSE BUILDER
House Builder Publications Ltd, 82 New Cavendish Street, London W1M 8AD.
Tel: 0171-580 5588. Fax: 0171-323 0890.
Editor: Ben Roskrow.
Monthly journal of the House Builders Federation. Aimed at key decision makers, managers, technical staff, marketing executives, architects and local authorities.
Illustrations: B&W and colour. Some scope for housebuilding coverage, but only by prior consultation with the editor.
Text: Features on marketing, land and planning, government liaison, finance, materials, supplies, etc. Always to be discussed before submission. 1,000 words.
Overall freelance potential: Around 50 per cent comes from freelances.
Editor's tips: Authoritative articles and news stories only. No PR "puffs".
Fees: £130 per 1,000 words; pictures by agreement.

MARINE ENGINEERS REVIEW
Institute of Marine Engineers, 76 Mark Lane, London EC3R 7JN.
Tel: 0171-481 8493. Fax: 0171-488 1854.
Editor: John Butchers.
Monthly publication for marine engineers.
Illustrations: B&W and colour. Interesting photographs of ships and marine machinery.

Text: Articles on shipping and marine engineering, including naval and offshore topics.
Overall freelance potential: Good, but enquire before submitting.
Fees: By negotiation.

NEW CIVIL ENGINEER
EMAP Business Communications, 151 Rosebery Avenue, London EC1R 4QX.
Tel: 0171-505 6666. Fax: 0171-505 6667.
Editor: Mike Winney.
Weekly news magazine for professional civil engineers.
Illustrations: Colour. Up-to-date pictures depicting any civil engineering project. Must be well captioned and newsworthy.
Text: By commission only.
Overall freelance potential: Limited.
Fees: On a rising scale according to size of reproduction or length of text.

PERSPECTIVES ON ARCHITECTURE
Perspectives on Architecture Ltd, 2 Hinde Street, London W1M 5RH.
Tel: 0171-224 1766. Fax: 0171-224 1768.
Editor: Giles Worsley. **Art Editor**: Joan Hecktermann.
Architecture bi-monthly aimed at the interested layman rather than the professional. Covers architecture, heritage and the environment with special reference to the issues raised by the Prince of Wales over the past decade. Also offers practical information about the authentic decoration of homes, gardening and landscaping, arts and crafts.
Illustrations: Colour. By commission only. High quality coverage of buildings (interiors and exteriors) and the environment generally.
Text: Illustrated articles on architecture, planning, conservation and other environmental issues. Submit ideas or a synopsis in the first instance.
Overall freelance potential: Some opportunities for top quality material but much is supplied by owners and architects.
Fees: By negotiation.

PROFESSIONAL ENGINEERING
Institution of Mechanical Engineers, 1 Birdcage Walk, London SW1H 9JJ.
Tel: 0171-973 1299. Fax: 0171-973 0462.
Editor: John Dunn.
Fortnightly publication for members of the Institution of Mechanical Engineers and decision-makers in industry.
Illustrations: Colour only. People, locations, factories, processes, specific industries.
Text: Features with a general engineering bias at a fairly high management level, e.g. management techniques, new processes, materials applications, etc. 1,500 words maximum.
Overall freelance potential: A considerable amount of the magazine is freelance-contributed.
Fees: Not less than around £200 per 1,000 words published; pictures by agreement.

PROFESSIONAL LANDSCAPER AND GROUNDSMAN
Albatross Publications, PO Box 193, Dorking, Surrey RH5 5YF.
Tel: 01306 712712.
Editor: Carol Andrews.
Quarterly magazine for landscapers, contractors, foresters, architects, groundsmen and local authorities.
Illustrations: B&W and colour. Some scope for covers, only of subjects likely to be of interest to the magazine's professional readership.
Text: Well-illustrated articles dealing with technical or practical landscaping matters, forestry, and general environmental and conservation issues.
Overall freelance potential: Limited.
Fees: By negotiation.

RIBA JOURNAL
The Builder Group, Exchange Tower, 2 Harbour Exchange SquareLondon E14 9GE.
Tel: 0171-560 4102. Fax: 0171-560 4191.
Editor: John Welsh.
Monthly magazine of the Royal Institute of British Architects. Covers general aspects of architectural practice as well as criticisms of particular buildings, profiles and interviews.
Illustrations: B&W and colour. Pictures of buildings, old, new and refurbished. Covers: colour pictures connected with main feature inside.
Text: Features on architectural subjects and criticisms of particular buildings.
Overall freelance potential: Fair.
Fees: By arrangement.

Business

ACCOUNTANCY AGE
VNU Business Publications, 32–34 Broadwick Street, London W1A 2HG.
Tel: 0171-316 9000. Fax: 0171-316 9250.
Editor: Douglas Broom.
Weekly publication for qualified accountants.
Illustrations: Colour only. All commissioned but new photographers are always welcome.
Text: News and features coverage for accountants. Synopsis preferred in first instance. 1,200 words.
Overall freelance potential: Fairly good for commissioned photography. About 50 per cent of the features come from freelances.
Editor's tips: To gain acceptance, articles must contribute something which cannot be provided by the in-house staff.
Fees: By agreement.

AFRICA ECONOMIC DIGEST
African Concord Ltd, Aare Abiola House, 26–32 Whistler Street, Drayton Park, London N5 1NH.
Tel: 0171-359 5335. Fax: 0171-359 9173.
Editor: Jon Offei-Ansah.
Fortnightly review of African business and general economic developments. Aimed at senior executives of banks, trading and manufacturing companies, etc.
Illustrations: B&W only inside. Pictures of African economic, political and business life, including major development projects, agriculture, transport, ports, shipping, buildings, personalities and economic "events". Covers: colour pictures of similar subjects, plus more general African shots. No sunsets, lions or tribal dancers.
Text: Commissioned feature on above subjects considered. Contact editor first. Up to 1,000 words.
Overall freelance potential: A lot of material comes from AED correspondents, but freelance approaches welcome.
Fees: Negotiable.

BARCLAYS NEWS
Barclays Bank plc, Corporate Affairs, 54 Lombard Street, London EC3P 3AH.
Tel: 0171-699 2974. Fax: 0171-699 2688.
Editor: Brian Johnson.
Bi-monthly magazine for Barclays Group staff worldwide.
Illustrations: Colour. Pictures that relate to the bank, its staff, customers and history.
Text: Features with a specific interest to Barclays Bank, its customers and staff. 300–500 words.
Overall freelance potential: The magazine has its own team of journalists, but they are always on the lookout for items of interest throughout the country that might not have come to their attention.

Bright original photographs especially welcome.
Editor's tips: Always check first and a direct indication of interest will be given.
Fees: Negotiable.

BUSINESS OPPORTUNITY WORLD
Market Link Publishing, PO Box 78, Saffron Walden, Essex CB11 4YR.
Tel: 01799 544248. Fax: 01799 544200.
Editor: Barbara Orff.
Monthly magazine concerned with small businesses – those run from home or start-ups.
Illustrations: B&W and colour. Usually to accompany specific news items or stories about success-ful business people, as below. Some scope for general stock shots of typical small business situations, especially for cover use.
Text: Illustrated success stories about new businesses or those expanding/evolving, with emphasis on case studies and personalities involved. Also new business opportunities and financial matters. 300–1,800 words.
Overall freelance potential: Quite good.
Fees: By negotiation.

CA MAGAZINE
Institute of Chartered Accountants of Scotland, 27 Queen Street, Edinburgh EH2 1LA.
Tel: 0131-225 5673. Fax: 0131-225 3813.
Editor: John Hatfield. **Art Editor**: Jane Greig.
Scottish financial and management magazine incorporating monthly journal of The Institute of Chartered Accountants in Scotland.
Illustrations: B&W and colour. Creative and innovative images which attract readers' attention.
Text: Articles on accounting and auditing, company law, finance, taxation, management topics, com-pany/personal profiles, the financial and management scene in the UK and overseas, investment, computer science, etc. Length: 1,200–3,000 words.
Overall freelance potential: Fair for business specialists.
Fees: By arrangement.

COMMERCE MAGAZINE
Commerce Publications Ltd, Station House, Station Road, Newport Pagnell, Milton Keynes MK16 0AG.
Tel: 01908 614477. Fax: 01908 616441.
Group Editor: Steve Brennan.
Monthly regional business magazines aimed at "decision makers". Sold mainly by direct mail and some subscription. Editions for North Home Counties, M4/M40 Corridor, West Midlands, East Midlands, East Anglia, South West and South Wales, Yorkshire and Humberside, Central South.
Illustrations: Colour. Business and commerce subjects; faces well-known nationally and locally in the area – politicians, industrial leaders, etc. Covers: colour of similar subjects.
Text: Features on business and commerce subjects. Around 800 words. An advance features list is always available.
Overall freelance potential: Around 10 per cent comes from freelances.
Editor's tips: Always contact the magazine and talk over ideas before submission.
Fees: Negotiable.

DIRECTOR
The Director Publications Ltd, Mountbarrow House, Elizabeth Street, London SW1W 9RB.
Tel: 0171-730 8320. Fax: 0171-235 5627.
Editor: Tim Hindle. **Picture Editor**: Michael David.
Monthly journal for members of the Institute of Directors.
Illustrations: B&W and colour. Pictures showing overseas business areas (New York, Singapore,

Tokyo, etc.) for illustration of area surveys. Top quality portraits of chairmen or major business personalities. Covers: colour portraits or top quality business/industry subjects. More creative, avante garde illustrations also used.
Text: Interviews; management advice; company profiles; business controversies; EC affairs.
Overall freelance potential: Good.
Fees: By negotiation.

ENTREPRENEUR
Entrepreneur Business Publications, Portland Buildings, 127-129 Portland Street, Manchester M1 4QB.
Tel: 0161-236 2782. Fax: 0161-236 2783.
Editor: Martin Regan.
Glossy business monthly for the North West region, aimed at owner-managed companies with turnover between £0.5m–£10m. Covers Manchester, Cheshire, Merseyside, Lancs, Staffs, Cumbria and North Wales.
Illustrations: B&W and colour. Captioned news pictures about developments in private businesses as above. General business/industrial photography by commission, mainly portraiture but some general nusiness/industrial work.
Text: Topical articles of interest to business people in the region – hard-edged, readable, jargon-free. News items only.
Overall freelance potential: Quite good for the freelance with a professional and creative approach.
Editor's tips: We look for a creative, even off-the-wall, style. Happy to consider newcomers as long as they are thoroughly professional and reliable.
Fees: By negotiation.

EXPORT TIMES
Nexus House, Azalea Drive, Swanley, Kent BR8 8HY.
Tel: 01322 660070. Fax: 01322 666408.
Editor: Laura McCaffrey.
Monthly newspaper covering all aspects of UK exporting.
Illustrations: B&W and colour. Captioned news pictures covering foreign trade, overseas development, and everyday life and work overseas.
Text: News stories or short features about exporting.
Overall freelance potential: Limited; most material comes from regular contributors.
Editor's tips: Always best to write first. If going on a trip abroad, make contact beforehand not upon your return.
Fees: £140 per 1,000 words; pictures according to size of reproduction.

THE JOURNAL
Chartered Insurance Institute, 20 Aldermanbury, London EC2V 7HX.
Tel: 0171-417 4435. Fax: 0171-726 0131.
Editor: Peter Finch.
Alternate-monthly journal of the CII, covering insurance and financial services matters.
Illustrations: Mainly colour. Stock shots of business and industry subjects frequently used to illustrate features. Limited scope for commissions; write in the first instance.
Text: No scope.
Overall freelance potential: Limited.
Editor's tips: Try to avoid pictures which are obviously posed by models – we prefer to use "real" people.
Fees: By agreement.

MEED (MIDDLE EAST ECONOMIC DIGEST)

EMAP Business Communications, Meed House, 21 John Street, London WC1N 2BP.
Tel: 0171-404 5513. Fax: 0171-831 9537.
Editor: Edmund O'Sullivan. **Art Director**: Hassan Yussuf.
Weekly business journal covering the affairs of Middle Eastern countries.
Illustrations: Mainly colour. Pictures of current major construction projects in the Middle East and stock shots of important personalities (politicians, leading businessmen) in the region. Recent general views of particular locations occasionally used. Covers: colour pictures of contemporary Middle East subjects, preferably with an obvious business flavour. Also, high-quality colour abstracts.
Text: Specialist articles on relevant business matters.
Overall freelance potential: Limited.
Fees: On a rising scale according to size of reproduction or length of text.

MANAGEMENT ACCOUNTING

Chartered Institute of Management Accountants, 63 Portland Place, London W1N 4AB.
Tel: 0171-637 2311. Fax: 0171-580 6916.
Editor: John Hillary.
Monthly publication for members and students of the Institute.
Illustrations: B&W and colour. Small market for top quality general industrial/commercial subjects with a financial bias. Covers: colour pictures of industrial and commercial subjects, computers, plus some "abstracts".
Text: Occasional freelance market for articles on management/accountancy subjects.
Overall freelance potential: Limited.
Fees: Covers, up to £300; inside pictures by agreement.

MARKETING

Haymarket Business Publications Ltd, 174 Hammersmith Road, London W6 7JP.
Tel: 0171-413 4150. Fax: 0171-413 4504.
Editor: Mike Hewitt. **Art Editor**: Christian Brown.
Weekly publication for marketing management, both client and agency.
Illustrations: B&W and colour. Commissioned coverage of subjects relating to marketing. Experienced business photographers should contact the art editor.
Text: News and features with a marketing angle and objective case histories.
Overall freelance potential: Limited; for business specialists only.
Editor's tips: A synopsis in the first instance is very important.
Fees: Variable.

PEOPLE MANAGEMENT

Personnel Publications Ltd, 17 Britton Street, London EC1M 5NQ.
Tel: 0171-880 6223. Fax: 0171-336 7635.
Editor: Rob MacLachlan. **Art Director**: Mark Parry. **Picture Researcher**: Kerri Miles.
Fortnightly magazine of the Institute of Personnel and Development. Covers all aspects of staff management and training.
Illustrations: Colour only. Photographs of people at work in business and industry, particularly any depicting staff education and training. Detailed lists of subjects available welcomed. Some commissions may be available to experienced workers; contact the artdirector to show portfolio.
Text: Ideas for articles always welcome; submit a short written proposal first.
Overall freelance potential: Quite good – a lot of stock pictures are used. Contributions here might also be used in *Supply Management*, a similar title produced by the same team for the Chartered Institute of Purchasing and Supply.
Fees: By negotiation.

POST MAGAZINE
Timothy Benn Publishing Ltd, 39 Earlham St, London WC2H 9LD.
Tel: 0171-306 700. Fax: 0171-306 7101.
Editor in Chief: David Worsfold. **Designer**: Michael Moore.
Weekly publication covering insurance at home and abroad.
Illustrations: Colour. Pictures of traffic, houses, offices, building sites, damage (including fire and motoring accidents), shipwrecks or aviation losses, etc. Also political and industry personalities.
Text: News and features on insurance, including life assurance, general insurance, reinsurance, pensions, financial services, savings, unit trusts, investment, marketing, technology, offices and personnel areas.
Overall freelance potential: Most news and features are contributed by freelances.
Fees: By negotiation.

PROMOTIONS & INCENTIVES
Haymarket Marketing Publications Ltd, 174 Hammersmith Road, London W6 7JP.
Tel: 0171-413 4152. Fax: 0171-413 4509.
Editor: Stewart Derrick.
Monthly publication for brand managers, SP managers, incentive managers etc. Concerned with incentive ideas for staff motivation and sales promotion campaigns, aids and general marketing themes.
Illustrations: B&W and colour. Pictures limited to the marketing and/or promotions profession. Covers: highly creative colour pictures, usually linked to the main feature inside.
Text: Authoritatively written articles on technical aspects of the marketing and/or promotions profession. 1,500–2,000 words.
Overall freelance potential: Up to 30 per cent bought from freelances.
Editor's tips: Contact the magazine first.
Fees: By negotiation, depending on ability and subject matter.

Camping & Caravanning

CAMPING AND CARAVANNING
The Camping and Caravanning Club, Greenfields House, Westwood Way, Coventry CV4 8JH.
Tel: 01203 694995. Fax: 01203 694886.
Editor: Peter Frost.
Monthly magazine concerning camping and caravanning holidays in Britain.
Illustrations: Mainly colour. Usually only required in conjunction with feature articles.
Text: Illustrated features on camping and caravanning in Britain, around 1,200 words. Contact the editor with ideas only in the first instance.
Overall freelance potential: Fair.
Fees: By agreement.

CAMPING MAGAZINE
Garnett Dickinson Publishing Ltd. Editorial: Studio 9, Star Brewery, Lewes, East Sussex BN7 1YJ.
Tel/fax: 01273 477421.
Editor: John Lloyd.
Monthly magazine covering all aspects of camping. Emphasises the range of activities that camping makes available.
Illustrations: Mainly colour. Photographs showing campers engaged in various activities; do not

have to include a tent but must have an "outdoor" feel. Possible scope for atmospheric landscape shots. Covers: Strong images of campers obviously enjoying themselves on a family or lightweight camping holiday. Medium format preferred.

Text: Picture-led features that show camping as "a means to an end" and illustrate the range of people and lifestyles that camping embraces (500–1,500 words). Also travel features focusing on particular areas in the UK (2,000 words) or the Continent (1,500 words). Always check with the editor before submitting.

Overall freelance potential: Excellent.

Editor's tips: Pictures should not be dominated by tents and camping clutter. Not interested in general campsite shots unless they are particularly picturesque. Call first and have a chat about your ideas.

Fees: Text £90 per 1,000 words; pictures negotiable.

CARAVAN INDUSTRY

A.E.Morgan Publications Ltd, Stanley House, 9 West Street, Epsom, Surrey KT18 7RL.
Tel: 01372 741411. Fax: 01372 744493.
Editor: David Ritchie.
Monthly publication for manufacturers, traders, suppliers and park operators in the caravan industry.
Illustrations: B&W and colour. Pictures of new caravan park developments, new models, new dealer depots, etc. Covers: occasional colour shot may be used.
Text: Company profiles on park owners and their businesses, traders and manufacturers. 900–1,200 words.
Overall freelance potential: Up to 30 per cent of the content comes from freelance contributors.
Fees: By agreement.

CARAVAN LIFE

Warners Group Holdings Ltd, The Maltings, West Street, Bourne, Lincs PE10 9PH.
Tel: 01778 393313. Fax: 01778 425437.
Editor: Stuart Craig.
Monthly caravanning magazine targeted at experienced caravanners.
Illustrations: Colour only. Mostly commissioned work; scope only for photographers with experience of caravan photography.
Text: Approaches from experienced writers will be considered.
Overall freelance potential: Good; a band of regular contributors produces most of the coverage.
Fees: By negotiation.

MOTORHOME MONTHLY

Stone Leisure Ltd, Andrew House, 2A Granville Road, Sidcup, Kent DA14 4BN.
Tel: 0181-302 6150/6069 and 0181-300 2316. Fax: 0181-300 2315.
Editor: Bob Griffiths.
Monthly magazine for motorhome owners. Covers travel, lifestyle, etc.
Illustrations: B&W and colour. Photographs related to above subjects.
Text: Features on travel and motorhoming. 750–1,500 words with pix.
Overall freelance potential: Good.
Editor's tips: Preference for copy that requires a minimum of subbing or rewriting.
Fees: £15–£20 for illustrated articles.

PRACTICAL CARAVAN

Haymarket Publishing Ltd, 60 Waldegrave Road, Teddington, Middlesex TW11 8LG.
Tel: 0181-943 5629. Fax: 0181-943 5798.
Editor: Rob McCabe. **Art Editor**: Alan Muir.
Monthly magazine aimed at touring caravanners with the emphasis on caravan and product tests, the practical aspects of touring, sites and places.

Illustrations: Colour only. General distinctive travel pictures, landscapes and sights from all areas of the UK and Europe. Must be exceptional quality as they are often used across a spread. Caravan park pics only useful with full details included. Telephone before sending material.
Text: Illustrated articles about the practical aspects of touring Britain or Europe, and personal caravanning experiences. Always discuss with the editor first.
Overall freelance potential: Fair.
Fees: Variable.

Children & Teenage

BIG!
EMAP Metro Publications Ltd, 5th Floor, Mappin House, 4 Winsley Street, London W1N 7AR.
Tel: 0171-436 1515. Fax: 0171-323 0276.
Editor: Richard Galpin. **Picture Editor**: Clara Massie.
Fortnightly magazine for 8–16 year olds, concentrating on celebrities from pop music, film and TV.
Illustrations: All colour. Exclusive news pictures and pin-up shots of suitable current stars, but little accepted on spec.
Text: Little scope.
Overall freelance potential: Only for those closely involved in this scene.
Fees: By negotiation.

BROWNIE
The Guide Association, 17–19 Buckingham Palace Road, London SW1W 0PT.
Tel: 0171-834 6242. Fax: 0171-828 8317.
Editor: Marion Thompson.
Monthly publication for Brownies in the 7–10 age group.
Illustrations: Colour only. Action pictures featuring Brownie activities and subjects.
Text: Articles with Brownie themes. Also original, inexpensive craft ideas suitable for 7–10 year-olds, in step-by-step format with illustrations of each step. 500 words approx.
Overall freelance potential: Around 10 per cent is contributed.
Fees: By arrangement; tend to be on the low side.

GUIDING
The Guide Association, 17–19 Buckingham Palace Road, London SW1W 0PT.
Tel: 0171-834 6242. Fax: 0171-828 8317.
Editor: Nora Warner.
Monthly official magazine of The Guide Association.
Illustrations: B&W and colour. Action pictures of Guiding subjects. Covers: Colour shots of Rainbows, Brownies, Guides, Rangers or Young Leaders in action.
Text: Articles relating to work with young people in various fields. 650–1,200 words.
Overall freelance potential: Suitable material from freelances always welcome.
Fees: By arrangement.

J17
EMAP Elan Ltd, 189 Shaftesbury Avenue, London WC2H 8JG.
Tel: 0171-208 3408. Fax: 0171-208 3590.
Editor: Sam Baker. **Picture Editor**: Sam Ripley
Weekly magazine for teenage girls in the 13–17 age group.
Illustrations: B&W and colour. Almost entirely by commission to accompany features.
Text: Articles and features on topics of interest to fashion-conscious teenage girls, always by commission. Features on current pop music stars.
Overall freelance potential: Restricted to the experienced contributor to this field.
Fees: £150 per 1,000 words for text. Commissions £350 per day.

MIZZ
IPC Magazines Ltd, Kings Reach Tower, Stamford Street, London SE1 9LS.
Tel: 0171-261 5000. Fax: 0171-261 6032.
Editor: Lesley Johnston. **Picture Editor**: Andrew Roberts.
Fortnightly magazine aimed at young women in the 15–19 age group.
Illustrations: B&W and colour. Some scope for single captioned pictures of a humorous nature. Celebrity pictures always of interest. Most other photography by commission, to illustrate specific features.
Text: Lively illustrated features on almost any topic that could be of interest to young women in the target age group. Text should be informative as well as entertaining. A detailed synopsis should always be submitted in the first instance.
Overall freelance potential: Good for the experienced contributor to the women's press.
Fees: By negotiation.

SCOUTING
The Scout Association, Baden-Powell House, Queen's Gate, London SW7 5JS.
Tel: 0171-584 7030. Fax: 0171-590 5124.
Editor: David Easton.
Monthly publication, concerning practical programme and activity ideas for Scout Groups, plus supplements for Leaders and articles of general interest to members of the Scout Movement and its supporters.
Illustrations: B&W and colour. Pictures of Scouting activities, preferably action shots. Covers: colour action and head and shoulder shots of Beaver Scouts, Cub Scouts, Scouts, Venture Scouts.
Text: Features on activities, competitions and interesting and unusual news stories suitable for a national readership. All material should be Scouting related or relevant to Scouting.
Overall freelance potential: Very high proportion of pictures and around 60 per cent of text comes from freelances.
Editor's tips: Note that where uniform is used, it should the the correct uniform. Also, if the pictures are of adventurous or hazardous activities, the correct safety rules must be seen to be observed and the correct safety equipment and precautions must be evident.
Fees: By agreement.

SUGAR
Attic Futura (UK) Ltd, 16 Berners Street, London W1P 3DD.
Tel: 0171-636 5155. Fax: 0171-636 5055.
Editor: Marina Gask. **Art Editor**: Fay Martin. **Picture Editor**: Jo Monaghan. **Fashion Editor**: Tina Rabin.
Monthly for teenage girls.
Illustrations: B&W and colour. Fashion, beauty, still-life and portraiture, all commissioned for specific features – contact the relevant editor to show portfolio. Some scope for celebrity stock.
Text: No scope.
Overall freelance potential: Only for experienced specialists.
Fees: Basic rate £350 per day.

County & Country

BUCKINGHAMSHIRE COUNTRYSIDE
Beaumonde Publications, 4 Mill Bridge, Hertford SG14 1PY.
Tel: 01992 553571. Fax: 01992 587713.
Editor: Sandra Small.
Bi-monthly county magazine for the named area.
Illustrations: B&W and colour. People, places, and events in the county. Medium format required in the case of colour. Covers: colourful local countryside views.

Text: Topical articles, of a cultural nature, on any aspect of the county.
Overall freelance potential: Limited because much is supplied by regular freelance contributors.
Fees: By negotiation.

COTSWOLD LIFE
Beshara Press, Beshara House, Northway Lane, Tewkesbury, Gloucestershire GL20 8JH.
Tel: 01684 854410. Fax: 01684 854458.
Editor: John Drinkwater.
Monthly county magazine with emphasis on tradition and nostalgia.
Illustrations: Mainly colour. Pictures of local scenes and events, preferably with some life in them.
Covers: Medium format colour of lively local scenes, with clear space at top left for title logo.
Text: Illustrated articles of varying lengths, on local people, places, crafts, etc. Historical and nostalgic items.
Overall freelance potential: About half published material is from freelances.
Fees: Cover shots £40. Articles and other illustrations negotiable.

COUNTRY
Country Gentlemen's Association, Hill Crest Mews, London Road, Baldock, Herts SG7 6ND.
Tel: 01462 490206. Fax: 01462 893565.
Editor: Barry Turner.
Monthly magazine of the Country Gentlemen's Association.
Illustrations: B&W and colour. Good stock shots of attractive British landscapes, wildlife, farming, historic houses and gardens. Also coverage of game shooting, fishing and other field sports, but excluding hunting. Covers: striking colour of wildlife, and rural scenes.
Text: Illustrated articles on British subjects of interest to a traditional, up-market male readership.
Overall freelance potential: Excellent scope for the right type of material.
Editor's tips: Material must be of top class quality and of genuine relevance/interest to the readership.
Fees: By arrangement, according to use.

COUNTRY LIFE
IPC Magazines Ltd, Kings Reach Tower, Stamford Street, London SE1 9LS.
Tel: 0171-261 7058. Fax: 0171-261 5139.
Editor: Clive Aslet. **Picture Editor**: Michael Lyons.
Weekly magazine for a general readership.
Illustrations: Colour. Pictures of British countryside, wildlife, interiors, country pursuits. Covers: colour pictures of landscapes, rural and urban. Medium format acceptable, but 5x4in preferred.
Text: No scope.
Overall freelance potential: Limited; only around 10 per cent of the magazine comes from freelance sources.
Fees: Average; on a rising scale according to size of reproduction. Covers, £250.

COUNTRY ORIGINS
The Countrylover's Club, PO Box 4, Nairn IV12 4HU.
Tel: 01667 454441/01729 860219. Fax: 01667 454401.
Editor: Hilary Gray.
Quarterly magazine featuring nostalgia and factual pieces on "yesterday's countryside".
Illustrations: Mostly colour; prints acceptable though transparencies preferred. Good photographs and photo features depicting the "real countryside", especially pictures of country people and their traditional activities. Always interested in old colour photography of suitable subjects, accompanied by detailed and informative captions. Send details of subjects available in the first instance. Landscape pictures only acceptable if identifiable changes have taken place. Covers: good pictures with covering information always considered.
Text: Illustrated articles on any aspect of yesterday's (British) countryside, including environmental issues, but always with a positive slant. Submit a brief outline first.

Overall freelance potential: Very good, though the magazine has many regular contributors and is generally overstocked with general material.
Editor's tips: Text should be written taking an observer's standpoint, not in the first person. Contributors are asked not to telephone but to write in in all cases.
Fees: £20 per printed page.

COUNTRY WALKING
EMAP Pursuit Publications Ltd, Bretton Court, Bretton, Peterborough PE3 8DZ.
Tel: 01733 264666. Fax: 01733 465939.
Editor: Lynne Maxwell.
Monthly magazine for ramblers and hill-walkers and anyone with a love of the countryside.
Illustrations: Colour only. Pictures depicting walkers in attractive locations, preferably wearing proper outdoor gear. Also top quality landscapes of suitable parts of the country, historic locations, landscapes with elements of walking interest (eg. stile, path). Covers: seasonal pictures of walkers in very attractive landscape settings. Medium format preferred.
Text: Well-illustrated articles and features on any walking or countryside topics. Strong emphasis on entertainment and capturing the essence of why people walk.
Overall freelance potential: Fair.
Editor's tips: The emphasis is always on getting enjoyment from walking and the countryside.
Fees: Full page and covers around £70, pro rata for smaller shots.

THE COUNTRYMAN
The Countryman Ltd, Sheep Street, Burford, Oxfordshire OX18 4LH.
Tel: 01993 822258.
Editor: Tom Quinn.
Published six times a year, covering all matters of countryside interest other than blood sports.
Illustrations: B&W and colour. Sequences of pictures about particular places, crafts, customs, farming practices, kinds of wildlife, etc. Must be accompanied by ample caption material. Only limited scope for single stock pictures. Covers: colour country scenes, must fit small (120mm x 112mm) space and still be noticeable on bookstalls.
Text: Well-illustrated articles of around 1,200 words, on such subjects as mentioned above. Must be accurate, and usually based on the writer's own experience.
Overall freelance potential: Excellent; almost all photographs, and most articles, are from freelance contributors.
Fees: £10 upwards for photographs. Text according to length and merit.

CUMBRIA AND LAKE DISTRICT MAGAZINE
Dalesman Publishing Company Ltd, Stable Courtyard, Broughton Hall, Skipton, N.Yorks BD23 3AE.
Tel: 01756 701381. Fax: 01756 701326.
Editor: Terry Fletcher.
Monthly countryside magazine for Cumbria, especially the Lake District and surrounding areas.
Illustrations: Colour only. Attractive shots of landscapes, rural characters, wildlife, country pursuits and local heritage.
Text: Illustrated articles on any aspect of Lakeland country life. 800–1,200 words.
Overall freelance potential: Excellent.
Fees: By negotiation.

THE DALESMAN
Dalesman Publishing Company Ltd, Stable Courtyard, Broughton Hall, Skipton, N.Yorks BD23 3AE.
Tel: 01756 701381. Fax: 01756 701326.
Editor: Terry Fletcher.
Monthly countryside magazine for Yorkshire.
Illustrations: Colour. Attractive shots of local landscapes, rural characters, wildlife, country pursuits and heritage.

Text: Illustrated articles on any aspect of rural Yorkshire life. 800–1,200 words.
Overall freelance potential: Excellent.
Fees: By negotiation.

DORSET
Poundbury Publishing Ltd, Agriculture House, Acland Road, Dorchester, Dorset DT1 1EF.
Tel: 01305 266360. Fax: 01305 262760.
Editor: Peter Shaw.
Monthly "for people who like to explore" the Dorset region.
Illustrations: Mainly colour. Good stock photographs of the region: people, places, natural history, culture and heritage.
Text: Local news and illustrated articles on subjects as above, around 1,500 words.
Overall freelance potential: Good.
Fees: by negotiation.

DORSET LIFE
Dorset County Magazines Ltd, 95 North Street, Wareham, Dorset BH20 4AE.
Tel: 01929 551264. Fax: 01929 552099
Editor: John Newth.
Monthly magazine for the Dorset area.
Illustrations: B&W and colour. Interesting and original photographs, but usually required as part of an article, not in isolation. Covers: Medium format transparencies of local scenes, suitable for upright reproduction. Must be original.
Text: Well-illustrated articles on any topic relating to Dorset, around 1,000 words.
Overall freelance potential: Most contributions come from regular freelance contributors but new contributors always considered.
Fees: According to size of reproduction and length of text.

ESSEX COUNTRYSIDE
Market Link Publishing, "Griggs Farm", West Street, Coggeshall, Essex CO6 1NT.
Tel: 01376 562578. Fax: 01376 562581.
Editor: Andy Tilbrook.
Monthly county magazine for the named area.
Illustrations: B&W and colour. People, places, and events in the county. Covers: transparencies of local countryside views; action shots preferred.
Text: Topical articles on any aspect of the county.
Overall freelance potential: Limited; much is supplied by regular freelance contributors.
Fees: £40 for cover. B&W, inside colour and text by negotiation.

THE FIELD
IPC Magazines, King's Reach Tower, Stamford Street, London SE1 9LS.
Tel: 0171-261 5198. Fax: 0171-261 5358.
Editor: Jonathan Young.
Monthly publication concerned with all country and sporting interests.
Illustrations: Colour only. Good pictures illustrating relevant articles as below.
Text: Illustrated features on country and sporting subjects. Length according to article, in the range 1,000–2,000 words.
Overall freelance potential: Around 50 per cent comes from outside contributors, most of whom are specialists.
Fees: According to merit.

THE GREAT OUTDOORS
Caledonian Magazines, The Plaza Tower, The Plaza, East Kilbride, Glasgow G74 1LW.
Tel: 013552 46444. Fax: 013552 63013.

Editor: Cameron McNeish.
Monthly magazine for walkers in the UK. Covers hill and mountain walking, and related topics.
Illustrations: Colour only. Material required for stock – mostly landscapes; no towns or churches.
Plus pictures to illustrate features. Covers: colour pictures in upright format considered independently of internal content. Photographs of walkers, backpackers and fell walkers in landscape settings.
Must be modern, well-equipped people in photos; action shots preferred.
Text: Features on the subjects mentioned above. 2,000 words.
Overall freelance potential: Most of the magazine comes from freelance sources.
Editor's tips: Too many freelances send material which is outside the scope of the magazine – not interested in lkow level rambling.
Fees: Articles, £100–£250 depending on length and number of illustrations; covers, £200.

HERTFORDSHIRE COUNTRYSIDE
Beaumonde Publications, 4 Mill Bridge, Hertford SG14 1PY.
Tel: 01992 553571. Fax: 01992 587713.
Editor: Sandra Small.
Monthly county magazine for the named area.
Illustrations: B&W and colour. People, places, and events in the county. Medium format required in the case of colour. Covers: colourful local countryside views.
Text: Topical articles, of a cultural nature, on any aspect of the county.
Overall freelance potential: Limited because much is supplied by regular freelance contributors.
Fees: By negotiation.

LANCASHIRE LIFE
Life Magazines, Oyston Mill, Strand Road, Preston PR1 8UR.
Tel: 01772 722022. Fax: 01772 736496.
Editor: Tony Skinner.
Monthly up-market county magazine specialising in regional features.
Illustrations: B&W and (mainly) colour. Pictures of the Lancashire region, mainly to accompany features. Pictures of nationally known personalities with a Lancashire connection. Covers: top quality regional scenes; medium format preferred.
Text: Articles and features on regional topics. Always consult the editor in the first instance.
Overall freelance potential: Good; around 75 per cent is from freelance sources.
Editor's tips: The magazine is not interested in the merely parochial.
Fees: By negotiation.

LINCOLNSHIRE LIFE
County Life Ltd, PO Box 81, Lincoln LN1 1HD.
Tel: 01522 527127. Fax: 01522 560035.
Executive Editor: Jez Ashberry.
Monthly magazine, dealing with county life past and present from the Humber to the Wash.
Illustrations: B&W and colour. Pictures of people and places within the county of Lincolnshire. No current social events. Covers: portrait format colour pictures of landscapes, buildings, street scenes, etc. 35mm acceptable, but medium format preferred. Submissions for annual calendar also accepted.
Text: Features on people and places within the appropriate area. No more than 1,200 words.
Overall freelance potential: Fifty per cent of the magazine comes from freelance sources.
Fees: By agreement.

NORTH EAST TIMES COUNTY MAGAZINE
Chris Robinson (Publishing) Ltd, Tattler House, Beech Avenue, Fawdon, Newcastle-upon-Tyne NE3 2RN.
Tel: 0191-284 4495. Fax: 0191-285 9606.
Editor: Chris Robinson.
Monthly up-market county magazine.

Illustrations: B&W and colour. Any general interest pictures connected with the North East of England.
Text: Features on fashion, property, motoring, wining and dining, sport, etc. all with North East connections. Around 750 words with two pictures.
Overall freelance potential: Fully committed to freelances.
Fees: By agreement.

RAMBLING TODAY

The Ramblers' Association, 1–5 Wandsworth Road, London SW8 2XX.
Tel: 0171-339 8500. Fax: 0171-339 8501.
Editor: Annabelle Birchall.
Quarterly journal for the 116,000 members of the Ramblers' Association.
Illustrations: Colour. Scenic views of the countryside, preferably but not necessarily with ramblers. Also pictures of problems encountered when walking in the countryside, e.g. damaged bridges, locked gates, obstructed footpaths, etc.
Text: Articles on the work of the Ramblers' Association. Any issues affecting the countryside or walkers' interests.
Overall freelance potential: Quite good for pictures. Limited for text as most articles are commissioned.
Fees: By agreement.

THE SCOTS MAGAZINE

D. C. Thomson and Co. Ltd, 2 Albert Square, Dundee DD1 9QJ.
Tel: 01382 223131. Fax: 01382 322214.
Editor: John Methven.
Monthly magazine for Scots at home and abroad, concerned with Scottish subjects.
Illustrations: Mostly colour. Scottish scenes, but avoid the obvious. Non-Highland subjects particularly welcome. Scenics with one or more figures preferred to "empty pictures".
Text: Features on all aspects of Scottish life past and present. 2,000–3,500 words.
Overall freelance potential: Around 80 per cent of the magazine comes from freelances.
Editor's tips: Do not cover sport, politics, household, beauty or fashion.
Fees: Variable.

SCOTTISH FIELD

The Oban Times Ltd, Royston House, Caroline Park, Edinburgh EH5 1QY.
Tel: 0131-551 2942. Fax: 0131-551 2938.
Editor: Archie Mackenzie.
Monthly magazine reflecting the quality of life in Scotland today for Scots at home and abroad.
Illustrations: Mainly colour. Must be accompanied by appropriate text.
Text: Illustrated features with a Scottish dimension. Submit only ideas initially, rather than completed articles. 850, 1,200, 1,500 words.
Overall freelance potential: There are only limited openings for new contributors.
Editor's tips: Market study is essential.
Fees: Negotiable.

THE SOMERSET MAGAZINE

Smart Print Publications Ltd, 23 Market Street, Crewkerne, Somerset TA18 7JU.
Tel: 01460 78000. Fax: 01460 76718.
Editor: Roy Smart.
Monthly magazine for the Somerset area.
Illustrations: B&W and colour. Interesting and original photographs of the area, but usually required as part of an article. 6x6cm or larger transparencies for d.p.s. features and covers.

Text: Well-illustrated articles on any topic relating to Somerset, around 1,000 words.
Overall freelance potential: Most material comes from regular freelance contributors but new contributors always considered.
Fees: According to size of reproduction and length of text.

SUSSEX LIFE
Sussex Life Ltd, 30A Teville Road, Worthing, West Sussex BN11 1UG.
Tel: 01903 218719. Fax: 01903 820193.
Editor: Trudi Linscer.
Monthly county magazine.
Illustrations: B&W and colour. Stock photographs always welcomed, but complete illustrated articles are preferred. Covers: medium format transparencies of Sussex scenes, usually depicting landscapes, houses, activities, interiors also welcome.
Text: Well illustrated features on any topic relevant to the county. 1,000–2,000 words.
Overall freelance potential: Quite good.
Fees: 1,000-word article plus pics, £25.

THIS ENGLAND
This England International Ltd, PO Box 52, Cheltenham, Gloucestershire GL50 1YQ.
Tel: 01242 577775. Fax: 01242 222034.
Editor: Roy Faiers.
Quarterly magazine on England, mainly its people, places, customs and traditions. Aimed at those who love England and all things English.
Illustrations: B&W and colour. Town, country and village scenes, curiosities, craftsmen at work, nostalgia, patriotism. Prefer people in the picture. Dislike cars, boats, modernity, etc. Pictures for stock or use in their own right.
Text: Illustrated articles on all things traditionally English. 1,500–2,000 words.
Overall freelance potential: Around 70 per cent comes from freelance sources.
Fees: Colour page, £25; B&W, £20; covers, £70.

TRAIL
EMAP Pursuit Publishing Ltd, Bretton Court, Bretton, Peterborough PE3 8DZ.
Tel: 01733 264666. Fax: 01733 465939.
Editor: Victoria Tebbs.
Monthly magazine aimed at the more adventurous walker, plus rock climbers and mountain bikers.
Illustrations: Colour only. Well-composed pictures of walkers, backpackers, climbers and mountain bikers in suitable landscapes, UK or overseas. High viewpoints preferred. Covers: "stunning" colour shots as above.
Text: Illustrated articles on any aspect of long-distance walking and backpacking, but always discuss ideas with the editor in the first instance.
Overall freelance potential: Good.
Fees: From £15–£50; £70 for covers.

Cycling & Motorcycling

BACK STREET HEROES
Myatt McFarlane plc, PO Box 28, Altrincham, Cheshire WA15 8SH.
Tel: 0161-928 3480. Fax: 0161-929 0534.
Editor: Stu Garland.
Monthly magazine for custom bike enthusiasts.
Illustrations: Colour only. Pictures of individual customised or one-off machines, and coverage of

custom bike meetings and events. The style of photography must be tailored to fit the style of the magazine.

Text: Limited freelance market.

Overall freelance potential: Good for those who can capture the flavour and style of the custom bike scene.

Editor's tips: This is something of a "lifestyle" magazine, and it is essential that the stylistic approach be absolutely right.

Fees: By negotiation.

BIKE

EMAP National Publications Ltd, Bushfield House, Orton Centre, Peterborough PE2 5UW.
Tel: 01733 237111. Fax: 01733 231137.

Editor: Richard Fincher. **Art Editor**: Paul Lang.

Monthly motorcycling magazine aimed at all enthusiasts in the 18–80 age group.

Illustrations: B&W and colour. Interesting or unusual topical pictures always required for news section. Sporting pictures for file. Top quality action pictures, "moody" statics and shots that are strong on creative effects. Reportage/documentary shots of events/people.

Text: Interesting or unusual news items. Scope for features on touring, personalities, icons etc; 1,000–3,000 words.

Overall freelance potential: All photography comes from freelances; 20 per cent of the words.

Editor's tips: "Always looking for new photographers and styles."

Fees: By agreement.

CLASSIC BIKE

EMAP National Publications Ltd, 20-22 Station Road, Kettering, Northants NN15 7HH.
Tel: 01536 386777. Fax: 01536 386782.

Editor: Phillip Tooth.

Monthly magazine dealing with thoroughbred and classic motorcycles from 1950 to 1980.

Illustrations: Colour only. Pictures of rallies, races, restored motorcycles.

Text: Technical features, histories of particular motorcycles, restoration stories, profiles of famous riders, designers etc. 500–2,000 words.

Overall freelance potential: All photography is freelance contributed.

Editor's tips: Contact the editor before submitting.

Fees: By agreement and on merit.

THE CLASSIC MOTORCYCLE

EMAP National Publications Ltd, 20-22 Station Road, Kettering, Northants NN15 7HH.
Tel: 01536 386777. Fax: 01536 386782.

Editor: Brian Crichton.

Monthly magazine covering veteran, vintage and post-war classic motor cycles and motorcycling.

Illustrations: B&W and colour. Pictures that cover interesting restoration projects, unusual machines, personalities with a background story, etc. Covers: colour pictures, usually a well-restored and technically interesting motor cycle, always related to editorial.

Text: Features on subjects detailed above. 1,500–2,500 words.

Overall freelance potential: Around 60 per cent of the magazine comes from freelances, but much of it is commissioned.

Editor's tips: Potential contributors must have a good technical knowledge of the field.

Fees: Good; on a rising scale according to size of reproduction or length of article.

CYCLE SPORT

IPC Magazines Ltd, King's Reach Tower, Stamford Street. London SE1 9LS.
Tel: 0171-261 5588. Fax: 0171-261 5758.

Editor: Andrew Sutcliffe.

Monthly devoted to professional cycle sport, offering a British perspective on this essentially

Continental sport.
Illustrations: Colour only. High quality, topical photographs relating to professional cycle racing.
Text: Illustrated features on the professional scene, but always query the editor before submitting. 2,000–4,000 words.
Overall freelance potential: Good for those with access to the professional scene, but most coverage comes from specialists based on the Continent.
Editor's tips: Most interested in "the news behind the news".
Fees: Pictures according to nature and use. Text £100–£200 per 1,000 words.

CYCLING PLUS
Future Publishing Ltd, Beauford Court, 30 Monmouth Street, Bath BA1 2BW.
Tel: 01225 442244. Fax: 01225 732310.
Editor: Dan Joyce. **Art Editor**: Elinor Grandison.
Monthly magazine aimed at recreational cyclists, covering all aspects including top level racing.
Illustrations: Mainly colour. Photographs that capture the excitement and dynamics of cycle sport. Speculative submissions welcomed; commissions also available.
Text: Little freelance scope; most is produced by a team of regular writers.
Overall freelance potential: Very good for photographers.
Fees: By negotiation.

CYCLING & MOUNTAIN BIKING TODAY
67-71 Goswell Road, London EC1V 7EN.
Tel: 0171-410 9410. Fax: 0171-410 9415.
Editor: Roger St Pierre.
Monthly magazine covering all aspects of general and recreational cycling.
Illustrations: Colour only. Good photographs of all aspects of recreational cycling, including fitness training, travel-related material and mountain biking. Pics with a strong news story attached are especially welcome. Minimal racing coverage.
Text: Ilustrated articles on any relevant topic, including adventure cycling and expedition stories. Submit suggestions in the first instance.
Overall freelance potential: Excellent.
Editor's tips: Interesting high-quality photographs always sought: "if a picture is good enough, we'll hang a story on it!"
Fees: Depends on what is offered, but around £75 per published page for copy and pics; £35 for one-off pics.

CYCLING WEEKLY
IPC Magazines Ltd, King's Reach Tower, Stamford Street, London SE1 9LS.
Tel: 0171-261 5588. Fax: 0171-261 5758.
Editor: Andrew Sutcliffe.
News-biased weekly magazine covering all aspects of cycling; aimed at the informed cyclist.
Illustrations: B&W and colour. Good photographs of cycle racing and touring, plus any topical photographs of interest to cyclists. Covers: striking colour photographs of cycle racing; must be current.
Text: Well-illustrated articles on racing, touring and technical matters. Around 1,500 words.
Overall freelance potential: Fairly good.
Fees: According to use.

HEAVY DUTY
Stone Leisure Ltd, Andrew House, 2a Granville Road, Sidcup, Kent DA14 4BN.
Tel: 0181-302 6150. Fax: 0181-300 2315.
Editor: Bob Griffiths.
Monthly magazine for Harley-Davidson custom builders.
Illustrations: B&W and colour. Photographs of unusually interesting machines and related lifestyle material. Coverage of events throughout the Europe and America. Travel coverage involving Harley

Davidson or Triumph bikes.
Text: Some scope for those with knowledge of this scene; discuss ideas with the editor.
Overall freelance potential: Good for those in touch with the custom bike scene.
Fees: £50–£75.

MOTOR CYCLE NEWS

EMAP National Publications Ltd, 20-22 Station Road, Kettering, Northants NN15 7HH.
Tel: 01536 411111. Fax: 01536 411750.
Editor: Adam Duckworth.
Weeekly tabloid for all road-riding and recreational motorcyclists. Also covers motorcycle sport.
Illustrations: B&W and colour. Rarely use on-spec material, but frequently require freelances for assignments. Seek competent photographers with keen news sense, able to work closely to a given brief yet able to incorporate their own visual ideas. Successful applicants are added to a nationwide contact list and may be approached to cover stories at any time. Contact the deputy editor initially.
Text: Illustrated news stories on all aspects of motorcycling always considered. Lively tabloid style required.
Overall freelance potential: Good.
Editor's tips: Assignments are often at short notice and to tight deadlines – photographers who can work quickly and flexibly stand the best chance of success. Commission fees include copyright assignment to MCN, though permission to reuse by the photographer is rarely denied.
Fees: Single pictures from £50; day rate £200 plus expenses.

MOTORCYCLE CLASSICS

Trapelet Publications Ltd, Traplet House, Severn Drive, Upton-on-Severn, Worcestershire WR8 0JL.
Tel: 01684 594505. Fax: 01684 594586.
Editor: Claire Leavey.
Monthly magazine devoted to classic motorcycles of all nationalities from steam era to present day.
Illustrations: B&W and colour. High quality pictures, in full sets and ideally with words, certainly with owner contact. Single photographs accepted for news purposes with words, or stand-alone if exceptional. Action work essential for full set unless machine of particular historic value. Selected archive material without text may be bought outright. Centrespread: Medium or large format required. Spread machine always featured. Covers: Full bleed single colour shot always drawn from issue's contents. Original historic photographs used occasionally if quality suitable.
Text: Classoc racing and events coverage worldwide. Workshop features and series. Road tests of significant classic motorcycles new and old. One full colour restoration per month. Historical features and series supported by archive material. Anecdotal material from readers and history greats. In-depth knowledge of subject essential. Length: 2,500–3,500 words for principal features; 1,000–2,500 elsewhere.
Overall freelance potential: Excellent for specialists.
Fees: By negotiation.

MOTORCYCLE INTERNATIONAL

Myatt McFarlane plc, PO Box 28, Altrincham, Cheshire WA14 2FG.
Tel: 0161-928 3480. Fax: 0161-941 6897.
Editor: Roger Willis.
Monthly guide to the motorcycle market, plus general motorcycling features. Aimed at the older rider.
Illustrations: Mostly colour. Sporting action at international level; off-beat pictures; examples of motorcycles being used in an unusual or unorthodox way; coverage of world trips by motorcycle.
Text: Well-illustrated articles on any motorcycling topic – sport, world trips, etc. Around 2,000–2,500 words.
Overall freelance potential: About 25 per cent of the magazine is contributed by freelances, though most of it is commissioned.
Editor's tips: Material must be composed imaginatively and be of first class technical competence.
Fees: Photographs according to use. Text £75–£125 per 1,000 words.

MOUNTAIN BIKER INTERNATIONAL
Link House Magazines, Link House, Dingwall Avenue, Croydon CR9 2TA.
Tel: 0181-686 2599. Fax: 0181-760 0973.
Editor: Chris Porter. **Picture Editor**: Huw Williams.
Monthly covering mountain bike racing and touring in both the UK and abroad.
Illustrations: Colour only. Top quality race action, preferably with "rider large, expression strong". Some scope for dramatic landscapes incorporating mountain bikers, for use with touring features. Covers: very bright, colourful action shots – usually a stunt. Must have plenty space to left of main subject to allow for the magazine's title logo.
Text: Ideas for features considered, though much is obtained from regulars. Raise ideas with the editor in the first instance.
Overall freelance potential: Excellent for good action material; the magazine is profusely illustrated.
Fees: According to size and position; up to £100 for full page. Text £100 per 1,000 words.

MOUNTAIN BIKING UK
Future Publishing Ltd, Beauford Court, 30 Monmouth Street, Bath BA1 2BW.
Tel: 01225 442244. Fax: 01225 462986.
Editor: Tym Manley. **Art Editor**: Jo Boardman.
Monthly magazine devoted to the sport of mountain biking.
Illustrations: B&W and colour. Spectacular or unusual shots of mountain biking, action pictures that convey a sense of both movement and height. General coverage of events and individual riders may be of interest.
Text: Well-illustrated articles that show good knowledge of the sport.
Overall freelance potential: Good scope for individual and original photography.
Fees: By negotiation.

RIDE
EMAP National Publications Ltd, Bushfield House, Orton Centre, Peterborough PE2 5UW.
Tel: 01733 237111. Fax: 01733 231137.
Editor: Tim Thompson. **Art Editor**: Kar Lee.
Monthly magazine for the motorcycling enthusiast.
Illustrations: Colour only. Commissions available to produce coverage for road tests and general features, but only for those with prior experience of motor sport or similar action photography. Contact the art editor to show portfolio.
Text: Little scope.
Overall freelance potential: Limited, but increasing.
Editor's tips: "We are looking to expand our nationwide network of photographers, for reader shots, news pictures etc."
Fees: Around £250 per day.

SCOOTERING
PO Box 46, Weston-Super-Mare, North Somerset BS23 1AF.
Tel/fax: 01934 414785.
Editor: Stuart Lanning.
Monthly magazine for motor scooter enthusiasts.
Illustrations: B&W and colour. Pictures of motor scooters of the Lambretta/Vespa type – shows, meetings, "runs", racing, special paint jobs, "chopped" scooters, etc. Covers: usually staff-produced, but a good freelance shot might be used.
Text: Short illustrated articles of up to 500 words on any scootering topic. Contributors should be aware of the particular lifestyle and terminology attached to the scooter scene.
Overall freelance potential: Good scope for those who know the current scooter scene and its followers.
Editor's tips: The magazine being based in the South and able to cover events in its own locality,

contributions from the North are particularly welcome.
Fees: By negotiation.

SUPERBIKE

Link House Magazines Ltd, Dingwall Avenue, Croydon CR9 2TA.
Tel: 0181-686 2599. Fax: 0181-760 0973.
Editor: Grant Leonard.
Monthly for sports motorcycle enthusiasts. Specialising in new model tests and old model reviews, Grand Prix (motorcycle), World Superbike and UK racing scene.
Illustrations: All colour. Pictures of unusual motorcycles, road-racing, drag-racing and other sports pictures of unusual interest or impact; crash sequences; motorcycle people. Covers: colour pictures with strong motorcycle interest.
Text: Features of general or specific motorcycle interest. Editorial style is humorous, irreverent. 1,500–3,000 words.
Overall freelance potential: Around 30 per cent of the magazine is contributed from outside sources.
Fees: Dependent on size and position in magazine.

Electronics & Computing

CITIZEN'S BAND

Radio Active Publications, 1A Munster Road, North End, Portsmouth, Hampshire PO2 9BS.
Tel: 01705 613800. Fax: 01705 690626.
Editor: Elaine Richards.
Monthly magazine for CB radio enthusiasts and anyone else interested in the world of two-way communications.
Illustrations: B&W only. Pictures connected with the CB world. Prefer to commission work.
Text: Features on CB and two-way radio systems. News and reviews of equipment, clubs, etc. 1,000–2,000 words.
Overall freelance potential: Between 30 and 50 per cent comes from freelances.
Editor's tips: The magazine is always on the lookout for features on new and novel uses for CB or short news items on how CB might have been used to report accidents, crime or traffic problems, etc.
Fees: £40 per published page.

COMPUTER WEEKLY

Reed Business Publishing Ltd, Quadrant House, The Quadrant, Sutton, Surrey SM2 5AS.
Tel: 0181-652 8642. Fax: 0181-652 8979.
Editor: Helena Sturridge.
News magazine aimed at professional computer staff and managers.
Illustrations: B&W and colour. News pictures, plus general shots of people involved in computer usage situations for general illustration purposes.
Text: Illustrated features on professional and business applications and issues in information technology. Length around 1,200 words.
Overall freelance potential: Main scope is for specialists.
Fees: By negotiation.

ETI

Nexus Special Interests Ltd, Nexus House, Boundary Way, Hemel Hempstead, Herts HP2 7ST.
Tel: 01442 66551. Fax: 01442 66998.
Editor: Helen Armstrong.
Monthly magazine aimed at professional electronics engineers, advanced hobbyists, hi-fi enthusiasts and general scientific interest.

Illustrations: B&W and colour. Photographs of technical subjects, invariably tied to specific articles. Some humorous captioned photos occasionally used. Covers: Usually commissioned to tie in with leading article.
Text: Technical articles of general scientific and electronic nature, and related items of more general interest to the readership. 700–5,000 words.
Overall freelance potential: Limited; most material is supplied by working technical journalists and specialists.
Editor's tips: It is useful to have samples of work and details of specialisation, so that commissions may be offered.
Fees: Negotiable.

ELECTRONICS WORLD & WIRELESS WORLD
Reed Business Publishing Ltd, Quadrant House, The Quadrant, Sutton, Surrey SM2 5AS.
Tel: 0181-652 3128. Fax: 0181-652 8956.
Editor: Martin Eccles. **Art Editor**: Alan Kerr.
Monthly technical journal covering electronics, computing, broadcasting, audio and video at a professional level.
Illustrations: B&W and colour. Mainly for use with features. Covers: colour pictures of any subject in the area detailed above. No blatant advertising shots.
Text: Illustrated features on subjects detailed above. 4,000 words.
Overall freelance potential: Limited; mainly from professional engineers.
Fees: £90 per printed page. Covers by agreement.

INFOMATICS DIGEST
VNU Business Publications, 32–34 Broadwick Street, London W1A 2HG.
Tel: 0171-439 4242. Fax: 0171-437 8985.
Editor: David Guest. **Art Editor**: Julie Fairless.
News-driven business monthly concerned with computers, electronics and telecommunications, with the emphasis on sales and marketing.
Illustrations: Colour pictures relating to computers, electronics and telecommunications.
Text: Features and stories relating to sales of systems, careers in sales and marketing.
Overall freelance potential: Low.
Fees: Commissioned photography, £45 for half-day; £80 for full day. Other material according to use.

PRACTICAL WIRELESS
PW Publishing Ltd, Arrowsmith Court, Station Approach, Broadstone, Dorset BH18 8PW.
Tel: 01202 659910. Fax: 01202 659950.
Editor: Rob Mannion. **Art Editor**: Steve Hunt.
Monthly magazine covering all aspects of radio of interest to the radio amateur and enthusiast.
Illustrations: Colour and B&W. Usually only required to illustrate specific articles. Covers: radio-related subjects; B&W or colour.
Text: Articles on amateur radio or short wave listening, or on aspects of professional radio systems of interest to the enthusiast. 1,000–5,000 words.
Overall freelance potential: Little scope for individual photographs, but complete, illustrated articles always welcome.
Editor's tips: Free author's guide available on request.
Fees: By negotiation.

PRO SOUND NEWS
Miller Freeman Entertainment Ltd, 4th Floor, 8 Montague Close, London SE1 9UR.
Tel: 0171-620 3636. Fax: 0171-401 8036.
Editor: Philip Ward.
Monthly news magazine for professionals working in the European sound production industry. Covers recording, live sound, post-production, mastering and broadcasting.

Illustrations: Colour. News pictures on all aspects of the industry, from equipment manufacture to live sound shows and concert performances to recording studios.
Text: Illustrated news items and features (800–1,000 words) on any aspect of the industry, but always check with the editor before submitting.
Overall freelance potential: Good for those with contacts in the audio and music business.
Fees: £100–150 per 1,000 words for text; photographs according to use.

WHAT HI-FI?
Haymarket Magazines Ltd, 60 Waldegrave Road, Teddington, Middlesex TW11 8LG.
Tel: 0181-943 5000. Fax: 0181-943 5798.
Editor: Jez Ford. **Art Editor**: Frank Foster.
Monthly magazine with emphasis on equipment reviews.
Illustrations: Colour only. News pictures from hi-fi shows, providing they are submitted quickly after the show. Commissioned photography to illustrate articles. As well as photographing equipment, the magazine looks for photographers who can take pix of readers, industry figures and hi-fi dealers to illustrate appropriate features (especially outside London).
Text: No scope.
Overall freelance potential: Fair.
Editor's tips: Photographers should be able to inject life into essentially "boring" black boxes.
Fees: Commissions usually £100 per day.

Equestrian

EQUESTRIAN TRADE NEWS
Equestrian Management Consultants Ltd, Wothersome Grange, Bramham, Nr. Wetherby, West Yorkshire LS23 6LY.
Tel: 0113 2893188. Fax: 0113 2893576.
Editor: Liz Benwell.
Monthly publication for business people and trade in the equestrian world.
Illustrations: B&W and colour. Pictures covering saddlery, feedstuffs, new riding schools and business in the industry. Also people connected with the industry, e.g. people retiring, getting married, etc.
Text: Features on specialist subjects and general articles on retailing, marketing and business. 1,000 words.
Overall freelance potential: Around 50 per cent comes from freelances.
Editor's tips: Only stories with a business angle will be considered. No scope for general horsey or racing material.
Fees: Text, £25 per 1,000 words; pictures by arrangement.

GALLOP!
EMAP Pursuit Publishing Ltd, Bretton Court, Bretton, Peterborough PE3 8DZ.
Tel: 01733 264666. Fax: 01733 465939.
Editor: Alison Joy.
Monthly aimed at the female rider, emphasising the pleasure of riding and horse ownership.
Illustrations: Mainly colour; occasional B&W "for effect". Pictures of celebrities with their horses; famous horses of past or present; accidents, mishaps and horses misbehaving; humorous shots. Covers: Usually staff-produced but open to fresh ideas. Invariably depicts an attractive female rider with her horse.
Text: Mostly staff-produced.
Overall freelance potential: Limited; much is produced by regulars.
Editor's tips: Pictures should convey the feelings and the fun of horse ownership.
Fees: By negotiation.

HORSE MAGAZINE
IPC Magazines Ltd, King's Reach Tower, Stamford Street, London SE1 9LS.
Tel: 0171-261 5867. Fax: 0171-261 7979.
Editor: Amanda Stevenson.
Monthly aimed at the female rider.
Illustrations: Colour. All photography by commission only to illustrate specific features.
Experienced workers should send an introductory letter with examples of previously published work.
Text: No scope.
Overall freelance potential: Limited and only for the experienced equestrian specialist.
Fees: By negotiation.

HORSE AND PONY
EMAP Pursuit Publications Ltd, Bretton Court, Bretton, Peterborough PE3 8DZ.
Tel: 01733 264666. Fax: 01733 465939.
Editor: Andrea Oakes.
Fortnightly magazine reflecting the dedication and enthusiasm of children who love horses.
Illustrations: Colour only. Amusing or unusual pictures of horses at work and play.
Text: Picture caption articles on the practical side of the subject.
Overall freelance potential: Around 10 per cent is contributed from outside.
Editor's tips: Possible news stories – check with office (by telephone) beforehand if possible or immediately after event. Awareness of the magazine's style and needs is advantageous.
Fees: Negotiable.

HORSE AND RIDER
D. J. Murphy (Publishers) Ltd, Haslemere House, Lower Street, Haslemere, Surrey GU27 2PE.
Tel: 01428 651551. Fax: 01428 653888.
Editor: Alison Bridge.
Monthly magazine aimed at adult horse-riders.
Illustrations: Colour. Off-beat personality shots and pictures for photo stories illustrating equestrian subjects, e.g. plaiting up, clipping, etc. Also general yard pictures, riding pictures, people and horses. Covers: horse's heads.
Text: Illustrated instructional features on stable management, grooming, etc. 1,500 words.
Overall freelance potential: Good for freelances who show an understanding of the market.
Editor's tips: Material must be technically accurate, i.e. riders must be shown wearing the correct clothes, especially hats; horses must be fit and correctly tacked.
Fees: B&W pictures, £15; colour, £25–£60. Text £65 per 1,000 words.

PONY
D. J. Murphy (Publishers) Ltd, Haslemere House, Lower Street, Haslemere, Surrey GU27 2PE.
Tel: 01428 651551. Fax: 01428 653888.
Editor: Janet Rising.
Monthly magazine about horses, ponies and riding. Aimed at the 8–16 age group.
Illustrations: Mainly colour – transparencies and prints. High quality, close-up shots to illustrate features on ponies, stable management and riding. Must be technically accurate. Inside colour poster spreads: "pretty" pictures and atmospheric shots; medium format preferred. Covers: striking close-up colour shots of ponies.
Text: Short picture stories on ponies. Illustrated features about horses and the care of them. 800 words.
Overall freelance potential: Good quality freelance work is always welcome.
Fees: B&W pictures, £15; covers, £50; text around £65 per 1,000 words.

Are you working from the latest edition of The Freelance Photographer's Market Handbook? It's published on 1 October each year. Markets are constantly changing, so it pays to have the latest edition

---

RIDING
GreenShires Creative Colour Ltd. Editorial offices: Suite B, Barber House, Storeys Bar Road, Fengate, Peterborough PE1 5YS.
Tel: 01733 555830. Fax: 01733 555831.
Editor: Steve Moore.
A monthly, non-practical magazine covering equestrian disciplines and topics across the board.
Illustrations: Mainly colour (prints acceptable), occasional black and white. News pictures and good stock illustration of all equestrian subjects, especially behind the scenes coverage and candids at major events.
Text: Concentrating heavily on people-orientated features with in-depth interviews, general interest articles. Around 1,500 words depending on subject matter.
Overall freelance potential: Some freelance work is used each month.
Fees: On a rising scale, according to quality and size of reproduction or length of feature.

SHOW JUMPING
Cecile Park Publishing Ltd, 55-63 Goswell Road, London EC1V 7EN.
Tel: 0171-490 3398. Fax: 0171-490 3394.
Editor: Lewis Carnie.
Popular monthly for all show jumping enthusiasts.
Illustrations: Mainly colour. Coverage of show jumping at all levels. Must be colourful, original, up-to-date and accompanied by accurate and detailed captions. Must also be clearly presented; anything not immediately easy to look at and identify will be returned unseen. Commissions may be available to cover specific events, but only to those who have already provided evidence of their competence.
Text: Competition reports, rider profiles, illustrated articles and feature ideas always considered. 1,000–1,500 words. Write to the editor with suggestions before submitting.
Overall freelance potential: Very good for quality material.
Editor's tips: "We look for original shots – not just the same old horses going over fences routine. Stunning horses, unusual fences, interesting faces, behind the scenes work, background and atmosphere. Show a sense of humour, imagination, enthusiasm and above all, promote a positive image of the sport."
Fees: Photographs according to subject matter and use. Text £75 per 1,000 words.

Farming

CROPS
Reed Farmers Publishing Group, Quadrant House, The Quadrant, Sutton, Surrey SM2 5AS.
Tel: 0181-652 4080. Fax: 0181-652 8928.
Editor: Debbie Beaton.
Fortnightly magazine catering exclusively for the arable farmer.
Illustrations: Colour only. News pictures depicting anything of topical, unusual or technical interest concerning crop farming and production. Captions must be precise and detailed.
Text: Limited scope for short topical articles written by specialists.
Overall freelance potential: Good for farming specialists.
Fees: By negotiation.

DAIRY FARMER
Miller Freeman Professional Ltd, Wharfedale Road, Ipswich IP1 4LG.
Tel: 01473 241122. Fax: 01473 240501.
Editor: Graeme Kirk.
Monthly technical journal for dairy farmers.
Illustrations: Mainly colour. Captioned pictures for use as fillers. Pictures of a positive interest, technical or maybe historical.

Text: Features on technical advances and other notable achievements in dairying.
Overall freelance potential: About 20 per cent comes from outside sources, but that includes several regular contributors.
Fees: By arrangement.

FARMERS WEEKLY
Reed Business Publishing, Quadrant House, The Quadrant, Sutton, Surrey SM2 5AS.
Tel: 0181-652 4911. Fax: 0181-652 4005.
Editor: Stephen Howe. **Picture Library Manager**: Barry Dixon.
Weekly publication covering all matters of interest to farmers.
Illustrations: Colour only. News pictures relating to the world of farming. Picture stories on technical aspects.
Text: Tight, well-written copy on farming matters and anything that will help the farmer to run his business more efficiently.
Overall freelance potential: Fair.
Fees: By negotiation.

INTERNATIONAL MILLING FLOUR AND FEED
Turret Group plc, Armstrong House, 38 Market Square, Uxbridge, Middx UB8 1TG.
Tel: 01895 454545. Fax: 01895 454647.
Editor: Susan Fraser.
Monthly international business journal for the flour milling and feed compounding industries. Covers news, marketing, products, government policies and market reports on flour, wheat and animal feeds, new technology.
Illustrations: B&W and colour. Explosions/fires in milling plants, etc.
Text: Market reports, opinion polls, articles, new milling technology. Off-beat features which will create discussion. 1,500 words.
Overall freelance potential: The magazine uses a lot of freelance work. Especially of interest are articles on new mills (incl. Third Word countries) and innovative technology.
Editor's tips: Phone before submission, or send synopsis.
Fees: Pictures by negotiation. Text £55 per 1,000 words.

THE LANDWORKER
Transport & General Workers Union, Transport House, Palace Street, London SW1E 5JD.
Tel: 0171-828 7788. Fax: 0171-963 4440.
Editor: Bridget Henderson.
Journal of the Rural, Agricultural and Allied Workers National Trade Group. Six issues per year, dealing with politics and agriculture. Aimed mainly at rural workers.
Illustrations: B&W and colour. Pictures of all types of farm work, forestry, food processing, rural employment and union activity.
Text: Features on subjects detailed above. Up to 800 words.
Overall freelance potential: Limited.
Fees: On a rising scale according to size of reproduction or length of article. NUJ rates.

PIG FARMING
Miller Freeman Professional Ltd, 2 Wharfedale Road, Ipswich, Suffolk IP1 4LG.
Tel: 01473 241122. Fax: 01473 240501.
Editor: Roger Abbott.
Monthly publication for pig farmers.
Illustrations: Colour. Pictures showing specific points of pig production, new ideas, systems, etc.

Occasional off-beat pictures of pigs used.
Text: Well-illustrated technical and practical articles on modern pig production, covering the industry from breeding through to products ready for the shop. Some general interest features. Maximum 1,200 words.
Overall freelance potential: Limited.
Fees: By arrangement.

POULTRY WORLD
Reed Business Publishing, Quadrant House, Sutton, Surrey SM2 5AS.
Tel: 0181-652 4021. Fax: 0181-652 4748.
Editor: John Farrant.
Monthly publication aimed at the UK, EC and worldwide commercial poultry industries. Covers egg production as well as chickens, turkeys, ducks and geese. Includes Pure Breeds section.
Illustrations: Colour only, prints preferred. News pictures and good general stock relating to the poultry industry, both in UK and overseas.
Text: News stories and ideas for features always considered; breeding, processing, packing, marketing, etc.
Overall freelance potential: Limited.
Fees: By negotiation.

TRACTOR AND FARM MACHINERY TRADER
Richard Lee Magazines, 88 Main Road, Romford, Essex RM2 5JB.
Tel/fax: 01708 743626.
Editor: Richard Lee.
Monthly publication for farm machinery dealers.
Illustrations: B&W only. Pictures of farm machinery dealers standing, with a few of their key staff members, in front of their premises, to illustrate short reports on the people involved.
Text: Short reports (100 words) on above pictures detailing the dealer's main agencies and the situation with current trade. Illustrated short features (300 words) on dealers at county shows.
Overall freelance potential: Over 50 per cent comes from freelances.
Fees: Short reports with picture, £20; illustrated features with 5/6 pictures, £40. Other features by arrangement.

Food & Drink

ASIAN HOTEL & CATERER
Asian Trade Publications Ltd, Garavi Gujarat House, 1 Silex Street, London SE1 0DW.
Tel: 0171-928 1234. Fax: 0171-261 0055.
Editor: Ramniklal Solanki.
Monthly covering the Indian, Chinese and other Asian catering and hotel trade.
Illustrations: B&W and colour. Captioned news pictures concerning Asian restaurateurs and hotel-keepers (openings, success stories, etc). Possible scope for commissions, dependent on location.
Text: Illustrated profiles of individual establishments, entrepreneurs, chefs, etc, and general features on catering topics. Write first enclosing samples of previous work.
Overall freelance potential: Fair opportunities for anyone in touch with the Asian catering trade.
Fees: Negotiable; depends upon the work involved.

HOTEL & RESTAURANT MAGAZINE
Quantum Publishing Ltd, 29/31 Lower Coombe Street, Croydon CR9 1LX.
Tel: 0181-681 2099. Fax: 0181-680 8828.
Editor: Mark Hayes. **Art Director**: David Foster.
Monthly magazine for the UK hotel and restaurant trade.

Illustrations: Mainly colour. Mostly commissioned to accompany specific features. Much emphasis on design and "creative" photography.
Text: Illustrated features on areas of development, profiles of individual restaurateurs, hoteliers and their establishments. Coverage from outside London particularly welcome, but always contact the art director first.
Overall freelance potential: Good for the more experienced worker.
Editor's tips: The magazine deals with restaurants and hotels from the medium to the top end of the market and there is no interest in fast food outlets etc.
Fees: By negotiation.

INDEPENDENT CATERER
Datateam Publishing, Fairmeadow, Maidstone, Kent ME14 1NG.
Tel: 01622 687031. Fax: 01622 757646.
Editor: Rowena Blackford.
Monthly magazine for the independent catering sector.
Illustrations: Mainly colour. News, products and specific feature pictures with stories relating to independent caterers in mainly medium-sized restaurants in hotels, restaurants and pubs.
Text: Illustrated articles that would interest caterers, i.e. new products for their businesses and practical advice that would assist in the successful running of such operations.
Overall freelance potential: Quite good.
Fees: By negotiation.

THE JEWISH VEGETARIAN
The International Jewish Vegetarian Society, 853/855 Finchley Road, London NW11 8LX.
Tel/fax: 0181-455 0692.
Editorial contact: Shirley Labelda.
Quarterly concerned with vegetarianism, its ethics, nutritional value and health benefits.
Illustrations: B&W only inside. Pictures showing ecology, animal welfare and proper land use. Pictures with an emotional interest between man (especially children) and animals. Covers: colour pictures of same.
Text: No freelance market.
Overall freelance potential: Limited.
Fees: By negotiation.

PUB FOOD
Quantum Publishing Ltd, 29/31 Lower Coombe Street, Croydon CR9 1LX.
Tel: 0181-681 2099. Fax: 0181-680 8828.
Editor: Mathew Moggridge.
Monthly magazine which aims to help publicans increase their profits through catering.
Illustrations: Colour only. By commission only. Top quality food and interiors photography to illustrate main features. Submit samples of previous work in the first instance.
Text: Illustrated short features and case studies concerning pub food, service, training and general trends. Style informal and accessible but must contain hard and specific business information, i.e. turnovers, profits, costings, etc. 500–1,000 words.
Overall freelance potential: Good, but limited.
Fees: Covers, £250; other photography by negotiation; £130 per 1,000 words for text.

THE PUBLICAN NEWSPAPER (and magazines)
Quantum Publishing Ltd, 29/31 Lower Coombe Street, Croydon CR9 1LX.
Tel: 0181-681 2099. Fax: 0181-680 2389.
Editor: Lorna Harrison.
Weekly independent newspaper for publicans throughout the UK, and allied monthly magazines – *Rural & Village, Community Pub, Town & City* – each targeting a different sector of the market.
Illustrations: Colour only. Topical pictures concerning pubs and publicans, brewery management

and the drinks trade generally. Must be newsworthy or have some point of unusual interest, and preferably include people.
Text: News items and picture stories about publicans – humorous, unusual, or controversial. Stories that have implications for the whole pub trade, or that illustrate a problem. Original ways of increasing trade. News items up to 250 words; features around 500–800 words.
Overall freelance potential: Good for original material, especially from outside London and the South East.
Editor's tips: Forget charity bottle smashes and pub openings, and forget pictures of people pulling or holding pints – hundreds of these are received already.
Fees: On a rising scale according to size of reproduction or length of text.

SCOTTISH LICENSED TRADE NEWS
Peebles Publishing Group, Berguis House, Clifton Street, Glasgow G3 7LA.
Tel: 0141-331 1022. Fax: 0141-331 1395.
Editor: Patrick Duffy.
Fortnightly publication for Scottish publicans, off-licensees, hoteliers, caterers, restaurateurs, drinks executives, drinks companies.
Illustrations: B&W only. News pictures connected with the above subjects.
Text: News and features of specific interest to the Scottish trade.
Overall freelance potential: Limited.
Fees: By agreement.

WINE AND SPIRIT INTERNATIONAL
Quest Magazines Ltd, Publishing House, 652 Victoria Road, South Ruislip, Middlesex HA4 0SX.
Tel: 0181-842 1010. Fax: 0181-841 2557.
Editor: B. Cormie.
Monthly trade magazine for the international wine and spirit industry. Aimed at buyers, importers, producers and retailers.
Illustrations: Colour and B&W. Pictures relevant to the industry. Covers: vertical format shots of wine and spirit subjects.
Text: Features on marketing and production in the wine and spirits industry worldwide, interviews with producers. 1,000–2,000 words. By commission only but ideas welcome; submit a synopsis first.
Overall freelance potential: Good; around 60 per cent comes from freelance sources.
Editor's tips: Telephone before submitting.
Fees: Negotiable for pictures; text around £150 per 1,000 words.

Gardening

AMATEUR GARDENING
IPC Magazines Ltd, Westover House, West Quay Road, Poole, Dorset BH15 1JG.
Tel: 01202 680586. Fax: 01202 674335.
Editor: Graham Clarke.
Weekly magazine for the amateur gardener.
Illustrations: Colour only. Little scope for speculative submissions, but the editor is always interested in receiving lists of subjects available from freelances.
Text: Illustrated out-of-the-ordinary features from contributors with a good knowledge of the subject.
Overall freelance potential: Limited to the specialist contributor.
Fees: By arrangement.

BBC GARDENERS' WORLD MAGAZINE
BBC Worldwide Ltd, Room AG185, 80 Wood Lane, London W12 0TT.
Tel: 0181-576 3959. Fax: 0181-576 3986.
Editor: Adam Pasco. **Art Director**: Abigail Dodd.

Monthly magazine for gardeners at all levels of expertise.
Illustrations: Colour only. No speculative submissions. Photographers with specialist gardening collections should send lists of material available. Commissions may be available to photograph individual gardens; the editor will always be pleased to hear from photographers who can bring potential subjects to his attention.
Text: All text is commissioned..
Overall freelance potential: Mainly for specialists.
Editor's tips: Always looking for interesting "real" gardens for possible coverage. Small gardens, patios and container gardening of particular interest.
Fees: By negotiation.

THE ENGLISH GARDEN

Romsey Publishing Group, Glen House, Stag Place, London SW1E 5AQ.
Tel: 0171-233 9191. Fax: 0171-630 8084.
Editor: Vanessa Berridge.
Heavily-illustrated monthly featuring the most attractive gardens in Britain, from cottage gardens to stately homes.
Illustrations: Colour. Pictures mainly required as part of complete feature packages as below. Some scope for good stock shots illustrating specific types of garden, plant or tree – send lists of subjects available. Medium format transparencies preferred.
Text: High-quality, exclusive features on individual gardens accompanied by a good selection of pictures (8–10 published within each feature). Can be considered on spec but best to discuss with the editor first.
Overall freelance potential: Very good for top quality material.
Editor's tips: Most interested in beautiful, idyllic gardens that readers can either visit or just fantasise about.
Fees: By negotiation and according to use.

THE GARDEN

EMAP Apex Publications Ltd, Apex House, Oundle Road, Peterborough PE2 9NP.
Tel: 01733 898100. Fax: 01733 890657.
Editor: Ian Hodgson.
Monthly Journal of the Royal Horticultural Society. Publishes articles on plants and specialist aspects and techniques of horticulture.
Illustrations: Colour. Top quality photographs of identified plants, general horticultural subjects and specific gardens.
Text: Some freelance market; submit suggestions first.
Overall freelance potential: Some potential opportunities.
Fees: £40–£100, according to size of reproduction; cover £150.

GARDEN ANSWERS

EMAP Apex Publications Ltd, Apex House, Oundle Road, Peterborough PE2 9NP.
Tel: 01733 898100. Fax: 01733 315984.
Managing Editor: Adrienne Wild.
Monthly magazine for the enthusiastic amateur gardener.
Illustrations: Colour only. Little scope for speculative submissions, but the editor is always interested in receiving lists of subjects available from photographers, accompanied by up to 20 transparencies.
Text: Experienced gardening writers may be able to obtain commissions.
Overall freelance potential: Limited to the experienced gardening contributor.
Editor's tips: Practical gardening pictures are required, rather than simple shots of plants. Must be accompanied by detailed and accurate captions.
Fees: By arrangement.

GARDEN NEWS
EMAP Apex Publications Ltd, Apex House, Oundle Road, Peterborough PE2 9NP.
Tel: 01733 898100. Fax: 01733 898433.
Editor: Jim Ward.
Weekly consumer newspaper for gardeners.
Illustrations: Colour only. Pictures of general horticultural subjects. Practical photographs to illustrate gardening techniques, top quality colour portraits of trees, shrubs, flowers and vegetables, and coverage of quality small/medium sized gardens. Medium format material preferred.
Text: Short practical features of interest to gardeners. 600–800 words.
Overall freelance potential: Fair.
Fees: By agreement.

GARDEN TRADE NEWS
Trade Promotion Services, Exhibition House, Warren Lane, London SE18 6BW.
Tel: 01733 703690. Fax: 01733 703691.
Editor: Mike Wyatt.
Monthly trade publication containing news, features and advice for wholesalers, manufacturers and distributors of horticultural products.
Illustrations: B&W and colour. Pictures for illustrated features.
Text: Articles about, or of interest to, garden centres and garden shops. Maximum 600 words.
Overall freelance potential: Limited.
Editor's tips: Remember this is a trade magazine, not a consumer publication.
Fees: £8 per 100 words; pictures on a rising scale according to size of reproduction.

GARDENS ILLUSTRATED
John Brown Publishing Ltd, 136-142 Bramley Road, London W10.
Tel: 0171-470 2400. Fax: 0171-381 3930.
Editor: Rosie Atkins. **Art Director**: Claudia Zeff.
Alternate-monthly, heavily-illustrated magazine with a practical and inspirational approach.
Illustrations: Colour only. Usually commissioned, but high quality submissions may be considered on spec. Photography should have a narrative and journalistic slant rather than just pretty pictures of gardens. The gardens should be depicted in relation to the landscape, houses and the people who own or work them. Coverage from outside UK welcome.
Text: Scope for experienced gardening writers – submit samples of previously published work first.
Overall freelance potential: Very good for the right material.
Editor's tips: Material previously featured elsewhere is not of interest.
Fees: By negotiation.

HORTICULTURE WEEK
Haymarket Publishing Ltd, 174 Hammersmith Road, London W6 4JP.
Tel: 0171-413 4595. Fax: 0171-413 4518.
Editor: Vicky Browning.
Weekly aimed at commercial growers of ornamental plants and those employed in landscape work, garden centres, public parks and gardens.
Illustrations: B&W and colour. Captioned news and feature pictures relating to commercial horticulture, landscaping, public parks, garden centres.
Text: Short news items about happenings affecting the trade. Longer articles may be considered – discuss ideas with the editor. 500–1,500 words.

As a member of the Bureau of Freelance Photographers, you'll be kept up-to-date with markets through the BFP Market Newsletter, published monthly. For details of membership, turn to page 9

Overall freelance potential: Limited.
Editor's tips: Contact the news or features editor first.
Fees: By arrangement.

NURSERYMAN & GARDEN CENTRE
Nexus Media, Nexus House, Swanley, Kent BR8 8HY
Tel: 01322 660070. Fax: 01322 667633.
Editor: Peter Dawson.
Fortnightly publication for nurserymen, garden centre operators, manufacturers of garden products, gardening journalists, educational establishments in the field, landscape designers and contractors, groundsmen, etc.
Illustrations: B&W and colour. Fully captioned single pictures of subjects of genuine interest to the readership.
Text: Features on all aspects of garden centre and nursery work, and the equipment used. New developments at home and abroad. 1,000–1,500 words.
Overall freelance potential: Fair.
Fees: By negotiation.

YOUR GARDEN
IPC Magazines Ltd, Westover House, West Quay Road, Poole, Dorset BH15 1JG.
Tel: 01202 680603. Fax: 01202 674335.
Editor: Mike Pilcher. **Art Editor**: John Bickerton.
Monthly practical magazine for the new and enthusiastic gardener.
Illustrations: Colour only. Mainly supplied by a range of regular contributors, but material from anyone who can offer a fresh approach or new ideas always welcome.
Text: Illustrated features from contributors with sound horticultural knowledge and experience. 800–2,000 words.
Overall freelance potential: Only for specialists.
Fees: By arrangement; around £100 per 1,000 words for text on All Rights basis.

General Interest

ACTIVE LIFE
Aspen Specialist Media, Christ Church, Cosway Street, London NW1 5NJ.
Tel: 0171-262 2622. Fax: 0171-706 4811.
Editor: Helene Hodge.
Bi-monthly general interest magazine for the over-50s.
Illustrations: Mainly colour. Positive images of older people; usually to accompany specific articles but some scope for stock material.
Text: Illustrated articles on a wide range of topics, offering a positive view of the retired lifestyle. Should contain plenty of informative details. Style should be simple and punchy, running from 500–1,000 words.
Overall freelance potential: Fair.
Editor's tips: "Try not to write as though readers are only fit for the knackers yard!"
Fees: £100 per 1,000 words for text; pictures by negotiation.

THE AMERICAN
British American Newspapers Ltd, 114–115 West Street, Farnham, Surrey GU9 7HL.
Tel: 01252 713366. Fax: 01252 724951.
Associate Editor: David J Williams.
Fortnightly publication for American residents in the UK and short-term US visitors.
Illustrations: B&W and colour, prints only (no transparencies). Pictures of Americans or American

activities in the UK, as below.
Text: Features on Americans or American activities in the UK. Human interest and "people" stories work best, particularly if they involve business, education, arts or sports.
Overall freelance potential: Good. Always looking to increase the number of stories.
Editor's tips: Phone queries are OK, but should be followed by a query letter and manuscript within two weeks. Seasonal material should be submitted two months in advance.
Fees: 50p per column centimetre printed; pictures from £15.

BEST OF BRITISH
Ian Beacham Publishing, 200 Eastgate, Deeping St James, Peterborough PE6 8RD
Tel/Fax: 01778 347003.
Editor: Ian Beacham.
Alternate-monthly magazine covering all aspects of British heritage, but with a strong focus on people.
Illustrations: Mainly colour. Top quality coverage of all British heritage subjects, from landscapes and museums to craftspeople and collectors; send details of material available in the first instance. Also seasonal scenes incorporating older people (50+) in the shot, though they should occupy no more than 20% of image area.
Text: Illustrated articles offering a positive view of aspects of Britain, past and present. Also profiles of people with unusual passions, humorous pieces about the British people and interviews with celebrities about aspects of Britain they love. Submit ideas or an outline first.
Overall freelance potential: Excellent.
Editor's tips: Pictures with good captions are always more interesting than those without. Material should always reflect a positive view of Britain. Nostalgic pictures always welcome.
Fees: Fees for inside use range between £20 - £50 according to size.

BIZARRE
John Brown Publishing Ltd, The Boathouse, Crabtree Lane, Fulham, London SW6 6LU.
Tel: 0171-470 2400. Fax: 0171-610 1931.
Editor: Fiona Jerome. **Art Editor**: Tim Harrison.
Monthly devoted to strange phenomena, weird behaviour, unusual experiences, cults and conspiracies, bizarre humour. Heavily illustrated, including special 10-page photo section.
Illustrations: Mostly colour. Will consider pictures depicting anything that broadly falls within the above parameters, "the more unique the better". Prefer material that has not been previously published.
Text: Little freelance scope unless the contributor is a genuine expert in a specific subject.
Overall freelance potential: Very good.
Editor's tips: Always call first with details of what you have to offer.
Fees: By negotiation and dependent on what is being offered.

CHOICE
Choice Publications Ltd, Apex House, Oundle Road, Peterborough PE2 9NP.
Tel: 01733 555123. Fax: 01733 898487.
Editor: Sue Dobson. **Art Editor**: Gill Shaw.
General interest monthly for the over-50s.
Illustrations: Colour. Photographs mainly used to illustrate specific features. Top quality stock shots of people 50+ enjoying various activities may be of interest, but send lists of material available in the first instance.
Text: Ideas for articles on any suitable topic always welcome, especially when accompanied by relevant photos.
Overall freelance potential: Excellent
Fees: By negotiation.

DESIRE DIRECT
Moondance Media Ltd, 192 Clapham High Street, London SW4 7UD.
Tel: 0171-627 5155. Fax: 0171-627 5808.
Editor: Ian Jackson.
Alternate-monthly magazine providing erotic entertainment for both men and women.
Illustrations: B&W and colour. Quality erotic photography of all kinds, especially portraying couples. Both single pictures and sets. Must be tasteful not crude.
Text: Features celebrating sex and sensuality as a mutual, shared experience; study the magazine before submitting.
Overall freelance potential: Good.
Editor's tips: We look for material that is a cut above the usual standard of the more explicit top shelf.
Fees: Negotiable, but "competitive".

FORUM
Northern & Shell plc, Northern & Shell Tower, PO Box 381, City Harbour, London E14 9GL.
Tel: 0171-308 5090. Fax: 0171-308 5075.
Editor: Elizabeth Coldwell. **Art Director**: Mark Chambers.
Monthly magazine dealing with all aspects of sex, i.e. social, medical, problematical, political, relationships, etc. Aimed at intelligent, aware, educated men and women.
Illustrations: B&W only. Pictures are taken only to illustrate articles. Must be tasteful despite the subject matter, which can be anything from fetishes to problems with love and marriage.
Text: Factual, social and medical features with a keen sex relevance. No porn.
Overall freelance potential: Nearly all material comes from freelance sources.
Editor's tips: Study recent issues and submit only a synopsis or outline in the first instance.
Fees: By arrangement, but reasonably good.

HERITAGE
Bulldog Magazines Ltd, 4 The Courtyard, Denmark Street, Wokingham, Berkshire RG40 2AZ.
Tel: 01189 771677. Fax: 01189 772903.
Editor: Sian Ellis.
Bi-monthly magazine devoted to British history, culture and travel.
Illustrations: Colour. Pictures of British landscapes, places of cultural or historic interest, monuments, etc., but send only lists of subjects available in the first instance. Some commissioned work available.
Text: Well-illustrated articles on British subjects and events. Profiles of places and people with a strong "heritage" connection.
Overall freelance potential: Excellent.
Fees: Photographic fees based on a page rate of £60. Covers around £150.

HIGHBURY HOUSE COMMUNICATIONS
The Publishing House, Highbury Station Road, Islington, London N1 1SE.
Tel: 0171-226 2222. Fax: 0171-359 5225.
Picture Editor: Becky Morris.
Large magazine publishing group, producing around 80 titles per annum. Publications include specialist European and international business magazines, consumer magazines on a wide range of subjects and specialist annuals.
Illustrations: Mostly colour; some B&W. Colour pictures to illustrate the whole range of the company's products. Major subjects of interest: babies, food, healthcare, agriculture, industry, conservation, pollution, travel and royalty. Sports coverage of special interest. B&W archive material of foreign countries, royalty and politicians. Send a few samples plus lists of subjects available, or make an

appointment to show portfolio.
Text: No scope.
Overall freelance potential: Good.
Fees: Variable according to use, from £35 upwards.

LEGION
The Royal British Legion, 48 Pall Mall, London SW1Y 5JY.
Tel: 0171-973 7200. Fax: 0171-973 7239.
Editor: Sandra Pruski.
Alternate-monthly journal of The Royal British Legion.
Illustrations: B&W and colour. News pictures concerned with The Royal British Legion or retired people within the ex-service community.
Text: Articles on health, music, gardening, sport, personal finance, and events and exhibitions.
Overall freelance potential: Limited.
Fees: On a rising scale according to size of reproduction or length of article.

OK! WEEKLY
Northern & Shell plc, Northern & Shell Tower, City Harbour, London E14 9GL.
Tel: 0171-308 5391. Fax: 0171-308 5082.
Editor: Sharon Ring. **Art Director**: Amanda Hamblyn. **Picture Editor**: Mette Johnson.
Weekly, picture-led magazine devoted to celebrity features and news pictures.
Illustrations: Colour only. Shots of celebrities of all kinds considered on spec – submit to the picture editor. Commissions available to experienced photographers – contact the art director.
Text: Exclusive stories/interviews with celebrities always of interest.
Overall freelance potential: Excellent for the right type of material.
Fees: Negotiable; depends on nature of the material or assignment.

READER'S DIGEST (British Edition)
The Reader's Digest Association Ltd, 11 Westferry Circus, Canary Wharf, London E14 4HE.
Tel: 0171-715 8000. Fax: 0171-408 0748.
Editor: Russell Twisk. **Picture Researcher**: Sarah Anderson.
Monthly magazine for a general interest readership.
Illustrations: Mostly colour. Pictures to illustrate specific general interest features; photographers with good stock collections should send detailed lists. Some commission possibilities for experienced specialist workers.
Text: High quality features on all topics.
Overall freelance potential: Limited opportunities for new freelance contributors.
Fees: By agreement.

SAGA MAGAZINE
Saga Publishing Ltd, The Saga Building, Middelburg Square, Folkestone, Kent CT20 1AZ.
Tel: 01303 711523. Fax: 01303 712699.
Editor: Paul Bach.
Monthly general interest magazine aimed at retired people.
Illustrations: Colour only. Usually required to illustrate articles or as part of a complete feature package. Picture features on hobbies or collecting of nostalgic items, heritage, nostalgia, crafts and natural history and celebrities/achievers of interest/relevance to the age group.
Text: Illustrated articles with general appeal to 50+ readership. Suggestions are always welcome.
Overall freelance potential: Good scope for top quality photo features.
Fees: By negotiation.

SKY MAGAZINE
Emap Metro Ltd, 5th Floor, Mappin House, 4 Winsley Street, London W1N 7AR.
Tel: 0171-436 1515. Fax: 0171-637 0948.

Editor: Mark Frith. **Art Director**: Sean Cook.
Monthly youth culture magazine aimed at both sexes in the 18–24 age group. Major subjects covered include music, films, fashion, style, news stories and sport.
Illustrations: Mostly colour. Pictures to illustrate articles and features. Mainly commissioned work in the fields of music, fashion, still life and portraiture. Top quality speculative submissions always considered.
Text: Lively and very topical articles on any subject of interest to an intelligent young readership, invariably by commission. Ideas are always welcome.
Overall freelance potential: Good for top quality work.
Fees: Photographic fees based on a page rate of £150. Covers around £250; colour spreads around £300. Text by arrangement.

YOURS
Yours Publishing Co Ltd, Apex House, Oundle Road, Peterborough PE2 9NP.
Tel: 01733 555123. Fax: 01733 898487.
Editor: Neil Patrick.
Monthly publication aimed at the over-sixties. Aims to be entertaining as well as informing the retired generation of their rights and entitlements. It also campaigns on behalf of retired people.
Illustrations: B&W and colour. News pictures showing older people's achievements. Good stock shots of elderly people engaged in a variety of activities, or depicted in varying moods (happy, worried, thoughtful, etc), always needed for general illustration purposes. The latter should be model-released. Send list of subjects and a few samples first.
Text: Positive stories about older people's achievements and general features likely to be of particular interest to an older readership. 750–1,000 words.
Overall freelance potential: Good.
Fees: By negotiation.

Health & Medical

ACTIVE
Artonia Ltd, 41 Overstone Road, Hammersmith, London W6 0AD.
Tel: 0181-741 0215. Fax: 0181-748 7812.
Editor: Lydia Campbell.
Alternate-monthly covering health, fitness and beauty. Aimed at fitness professionals as well as a (mainly female) general readership.
Illustrations: Mostly colour. Stock shots of healthy, attractive models taking part in sport or fitness exercise. A touch of glamour or sexiness is appreciated. Covers: as above, or glamorous portraits.
Text: Illustrated articles on exercise, nutrition, general health, sports fashion, etc. Length 500 words or 1,000–1,200 words.
Overall freelance potential: Good.
Fees: By negotiation.

GENERAL PRACTITIONER
Medical Publications Ltd, 174 Hammersmith Road, London W6 7JP.
Tel: 0171-413 4032. Fax: 0171-413 4513.
Editor: Carol Lewis. **Art Editor:** Shantu Douglas.
Weekly newspaper for family doctors.
Illustrations: Colour. Pictures of general practitioners involved in news stories, and clinical/scientific pictures for features.
Text: News stories, up to 400 words, preferably by prior arrangement with the news editor; features, always by prior arrangement with the features editor.
Overall freelance potential: The paper uses a lot of pictures from freelances.
Fees: By negotiation, but around £120 per 1,000 words, and £80 for half-day photographic session.

HEALTH & EFFICIENCY (H+E)
New Freedom Publications Ltd, Bow House Business Centre, 153-159 Bow Road, London E3 2SE.
Tel: 0181-983 3011. Fax: 0181-983 6322.
Editor: Helen Ludbrook.
Monthly naturist/nudist magazine. Also quarterly and bi-annual editions.
Illustrations: B&W and colour. Attractive photos of naturists. Male and female nudes, single or groups, young (18+) to mature. Also travel and scenic shots used.
Text: Short illustrated articles about naturists, resorts, human relationships.
Overall freelance potential: Very good.
Editor's tips: Contributors' guidelines are available on request.
Fees: £20+ per page and pro rata for colour; £10 per page and pro rata for black and white. Higher rates negotiable for top quality submissions.

HEALTH & FITNESS MAGAZINE
Nexus Media Ltd, Nexus House, Azalea Drive, Swanley, Kent BR8 8HY.
Tel: 0171-405 2055. Fax: 0171-405 6528.
Editor: Sharon Walker.
Glossy monthly covering all aspects of fitness, health and nutrition, aimed at women.
Illustrations: Mostly colour; some B&W. Captioned news pictures, and photographs for use in illustrating articles and features. Covers: outstanding and striking colour shots, usually featuring an obviously healthy young woman in close-up, or a young, healthy male and female couple.
Text: Articles and features on suitable topics, with an appeal to women generally. Always query the editor before submitting.
Overall freelance potential: Good.
Fees: By negotiation.

HERE'S HEALTH
EMAP Elan, Endeavour House, 189 Shaftesbury Avenue, London WC2H 8JG.
Tel: 0171-437 9011. Fax: 0171-434 0656.
Editor: Sheena Miller. **Art Editor**: Cathy Constable.
Monthly publication covering anything that relates to alternative health, from vitamin and mineral supplements to ecology and conservation. Accent is on the practical. Aimed at people who want to help themselves to total health: physical, mental and spiritual.
Illustrations: Colour. Mainly commissioned to illustrate specific features; send examples of work to art editor.
Text: Features on all forms of alternative medicine, therapies, travel, food.
Overall freelance potential: Good.
Editor's tips: "Have a look at a recent issue to see if your work is appropriate".
Fees: On a rising scale, according to quality and size.

PULSE and FINANCIAL PULSE
Miller Freeman PLC, 30 Calderwood Street, London SE18 6QH.
Tel: 0181-855 7777. Fax: 0181-855 2406.
Group Editor: Howard Griffiths. **Picture Researcher**: Marie Louise Collard.
Weekly newspaper for family doctors and fortnightly sister publication concerned with the financial and management side of general practice medicine.
Illustrations: Colour only. Pictures with captions, involving family doctors. Commissions available for high quality portraiture, especially outside the London area.
Text: News and topical features about family doctors.
Overall freelance potential: Good, especially for portrait specialists.
Editor's tips: Most interested in photographers who can produce original and creative portrait work.
Fees: Negotiable. Around £150 per day for commissions.

Hobbies & Crafts

THE AQUARIST AND PONDKEEPER
MJ Publications Ltd, Caxton House, Wellesley Road, Ashford, Kent TN24 8ET.
Tel: 01233 636349. Fax: 01233 631239.
Editor: Dick Mills.
Monthly fishkeeping magazine dealing with tropical, freshwater, marine and coldwater fish; water gardening, aquarium keeping and allied subjects, e.g. reptiles, amphibians, conservation, etc.
Illustrations: B&W and colour. Any picture connected with indoor or outdoor keeping of pet fish, reptiles and amphibians, and water gardening. *Not* fishing or angling.
Text: Features on the keeping of indoor or outdoor fish, aquatic plants, expeditions, conservation and herpetological subjects. All articles should be illustrated, either by photographs or with line drawings. 1,200–1,500 words.
Overall freelance potential: Reasonable; over 50 per cent comes from outside contributors.
Fees: By arrangement.

THE ART OF BONSAI
Freestyle Publications Ltd, Alexander House, Ling Road, Tower Park, Poole, Dorset BH12 4NZ.
Tel: 01202 735090. Fax: 01202 733969.
Editor: Rachel Darke.
Alternate-monthly devoted to the Japanese art of growing and maintaining bonsai trees.
Illustrations: Mainly colour; some B&W. High quality pictures of bonsai trees and related Japanese-style garden settings, always accompanied by detailed captions. Photographers who can show the requisite skill may be able to obtain commissions.
Text: Specialist articles always considered.
Overall freelance potential: Good for anyone with access to this highly-specialised subject.
Editor's tips: Great care must always be taken with lighting and backgrounds, since shadows can ruin the all-important outline of a tree.
Fees: According to use and the nature of the material.

BIRD KEEPER
IPC Magazines, King's Reach Tower, Stamford Street, London SE1 9LS.
Tel: 0171-261 6128. Fax: 0171-261 7851.
Editor: Peter Moss.
Monthly magazine for bird keepers and breeders, particularly aimed at the newcomer to the hobby.
Illustrations: B&W and colour. Good pictures of foreign birds, budgerigars, canaries and parrots, plus any more general pictures illustrating news or developments in aviculture. Covers: top quality colour of individual birds.
Text: Most contributed by known experts, but some scope for photo features of about 1,500 words.
Overall freelance potential: Quite good.
Fees: By negotiation.

BRITISH RAILWAY MODELLING
Warner Group Holdings plc, The Maltings, West Street, Bourne, Lincs PE10 9PH.
Tel: 01778 393313.
Editor: David Brown.
Monthly magazine for model railway enthusiasts at all levels. Covers only British railway subjects.
Illustrations: Mostly colour. Top quality coverage of "serious" model railway layouts and interesting or unusual models. Also good archive pictures of real railway subjects to back up modelling features. Some commissions may be available to those who can show real competence in this field. 35mm acceptable but larger formats preferred.
Text: Well-illustrated features on layouts or single models, which incorporate a very high standard of

both modelling and photography.

Overall freelance potential: Excellent for those with suitable expertise; the magazine is always open to freelance approaches and uses a lot of pictures.

Editor's tips: Photographers must be able to shoot small items in detail whilst maintaining perfect sharpness and depth of field.

Fees: £15–£30 per picture depending on size of reproduction. Text around £25–£35 per published page (most pages carry only a small amount of text since pictures dominate).

CAGE & AVIARY BIRDS

IPC Magazines Ltd, King's Reach Tower, Stamford Street, London SE1 9LS.
Tel: 0171-261 6116. Fax: 0171-261 6095.
Editor: Peter Moss.
Weekly journal covering all aspects of birdkeeping and breeding, aimed at enthusiasts of all ages.
Illustrations: B&W and colour. Mostly as illustrations to features. Others should cover avicultural subjects in general. Covers: good colour shots of birds mentioned below.
Text: Features on all aspects of breeding birds such as British birds, budgerigars, canaries, pheasants, foreign birds, waterfowl and birds of prey. Any reasonable length.
Overall freelance potential: Very good. Most material comes from freelances.
Fees: Good; on a rising scale according to size of reproduction or length of feature.

CLOCKS

Nexus Special Interests Ltd, Nexus House, Boundary Way, Hemel Hempstead, Herts HP2 7ST.
Tel: 01442 66551. Fax: 01442 66998.
Editor: John Hunter.
Monthly magazine for clock enthusiasts generally, i.e. people interested in building, repairing, restoring and collecting clocks as well as watches.
Illustrations: B&W and colour. Pictures of anything concerned with clocks, e.g. public clocks, clocks in private collections or museums, clock movements and parts, people involved in clock making, repairing or restoration. Detailed captions essential. Covers: colour as detailed above.
Text: Features on clockmakers, repairers or restorers; museums and collections; clock companies. 1,000–2,000 words.
Overall freelance potential: Around 90 per cent of the magazine is contributed by freelances.
Editor's tips: Pictures unaccompanied by textual descriptions of the clocks, or articles about them, are rarely used.
Fees: By arrangement.

COLLECT IT!

Collect it! Ltd, PO Box 3658, Bracknell, Berkshire RG12 7XZ.
Tel: 01344 891922. Fax: 10344 868284.
Editors: Gwyn Jones, Lorne Spicer.
Monthly for collectors in all fields, concentrating on "affordable" collectible objects ranging from Royal Doulton to toys and labels.
Illustrations: Colour. Mostly by commission to illustrate specific collections around the country, with most opportunities for photographers outside the South East Region.
Text: Original ideas always considered. Submit an outline and a sample picture or to in the first instance.
Overall freelance potential: Fair.
Fees: By negotiation.

CRAFTS BEAUTIFUL

Maze Media Ltd, Castle House, 97 High Street, Colchester, Essex CO1 1TH.
Tel: 01206 578690. Fax: 01206 571607.
Editor: Helen Stuttle.
Glossy monthly covering all types of arts and crafts. Aimed primarily at women, beginners to experts.

Illustrations: Colour only. Commissions available to illustrate specific features. Medium or larger format equipment essential. Send samples of work in the first instance.
Text: Step-by-step illustrated features dealing with crafts which appeal to women, i.e. cross stitch, decoupage, silk painting, etc. 1,500–2,000 words.
Overall freelance potential: Good for those with suitable expertise.
Fees: Photography by negotiation. Features around £80 per 1,000 words.

ENGINEERING IN MINIATURE
TEE Publishing, The Fosse, Fosse Way, Radford Semele, Leamington Spa, Warks, CV31 1XN.
Tel: 01926 614101. Fax: 01926 614293.
Managing Editor: C. L. Deith.
Monthly magazine concerned with model engineering and working steam models.
Illustrations: B&W only inside. Photographs only used in conjunction with specific news items or articles. No stock photos required. Covers: colour of model steam locomotives, engines or other model engineering subjects. 6x6cm minimum.
Text: Well-illustrated articles and features on all aspects of model engineering and serious modelling, and on full size railways and steam road vehicles. Must be of a serious and technical nature.
Overall freelance potential: Some 80 per cent of contributions come from freelances.
Editor's tips: Ideally engines depicted should be true steam-operated, not electric steam outline. There is no coverage of model railways below '0' gauge, or of plastic models.
Fees: Negotiable.

FURNITURE & CABINETMAKING
GMC Publications Ltd, 86 High Street, Lewes, East Sussex BN7 1XN.
Tel: 01273 477374. Fax: 01273 486300.
Editor: Paul Richardson.
Monthly magazine for the serious furniture maker.
Illustrations: Colour. Mostly by commission to illustrate step-by-step projects and features on individual craftsmen – write with details of experience and samples of work. Good stock shots of fine furniture often required to illustrate specific styles. Topical single pictures may be considered if accompanied by detailed supporting text.
Text: Ideas for illustrated features always welcome. Submit a synopsis and one sample picture in the first instance.
Overall freelance potential: Good for experienced workers.
Fees: £25 per single picture inside; illustrated articles £50 per page.

GIBBONS STAMP MONTHLY
Stanley Gibbons Ltd, 5 Parkside, Christchurch Road, Ringwood, Hampshire BH24 3SH.
Tel: 01425 472363. Fax: 01425 470247.
Editor: Hugh Jefferies.
Monthly magazine for stamp collectors.
Illustrations: B&W and colour. Pictures inside only as illustrations for articles. Covers: colour pictures of interesting or unusual stamps relating to editorial features.
Text: Features on stamp collecting. 500–3,000 words.
Overall freelance potential: Most of the editorial comes from freelance contributors.
Fees: From £25 per 1,000 words.

GOOD WOODWORKING
Future Publishing Ltd, Beauford Court, 30 Monmouth Street, Bath BA1 2BW.
Tel: 01225 442244. Fax: 01225 446023.
Editor: Phil Davy. **Art Editor**: Ollie Alderton.
Monthly magazine for the serious amateur woodworker.
Illustrations: Mostly colour. By commission only. Assignments available to cover specific projects – contact the art editor.

Text: Ideas and suggestions welcome, but writers must have good technical knowledge of the subject. Commissions available to interview individual woodworkers.
Overall freelance potential: Good for those with knowledge of the subject.
Fees: Photography by negotiation. Text around £150 per 1,000 words.

JUST PARROTS

Key Publications Ltd, 53 High Street, Steyning, West Sussex BN44 3RE.
Tel: 01903 816600. Fax: 01903 816900.
Editor: John Catchpole.
Alternate-monthly for the parrot enthusiast.
Illustrations: Colour only. High quality photographs of specific types of parrots and parakeets. Must be well-posed and well lit, showing clear details of plumage. Full and accurate caption information (preferably including scientific names) also essential. Limited scope for amusing pictures involving parrots.
Text: Illustrated articles, written by experts only. Amusing parrot stories.
Overall freelance potential: Good for top-quality material.
Editor's tips: *Do not* submit unidentified generic pictures of the "parrot on a branch" variety, or shots taken from long distances in zoos or bird parks. Only properly thought out, close-up shots will be considered.
Fees: Dependent on quality, up to £100.

KOI CARP

Freestyle Publications Ltd, Alexander House, Ling Road, Poole, Dorset BH12 4NZ.
Tel: 01202 735090. Fax: 01202 733969.
Editor: Rachel Darke.
Monthly magazine for Koi carp enthusiasts.
Illustrations: Colour. Good, well-captioned stock photographs of individual fish (including close-ups and disease shots), ponds and water gardens.
Text: Illustrated features of around 1,500 words on any aspect of Koi keeping or water gardening, including travel articles and relevant company profiles.
Overall freelance potential: Very good for specialist material.
Editor's tips: This is a specialist magazine so don't just submit generic shots of "carp in a pond"; fish must be properly identified.
Fees: According to size of reproduction and nature of the material.

MODEL BOATS

Nexus Special Interests Ltd, Nexus House, Boundary Way, Hemel Hempstead, Herts HP2 4ST.
Tel: 01442 66551. Fax: 01442 66998.
Editor: John Cundell.
Monthly magazine that covers any facet of model boating plus occasional material on full-size subjects of interest to modellers.
Illustrations: B&W and colour. All model boating subjects, including regattas. Sharp colour prints preferred. Covers: colour transparencies of model boating subjects. Medium format preferred, but will consider 35mm if vertical format.
Text: News items, illustrated articles and plans on wide range of ship and boat modelling, e.g. scale, electric, internal combustion, steam, sail, etc. Other maritime subjects considered if there is some connection with modelling. Up to 3,000 words.
Overall freelance potential: Good; 30 per cent bought from outside contributors.
Editor's tips: Send SAE with a request for a contributor's guide before submitting. Prints should be well captioned.
Fees: Approximately £20 per published page.

MODEL ENGINEER
Nexus Special Interests Ltd, Nexus House, Boundary Way, Hemel Hempstead, Herts HP2 7ST.
Tel: 01442 66551. Fax: 01442 66998.
Editor: E. J. Jolliffe.
Twice monthly magazine aimed at the serious model engineering enthusiast.
Illustrations: B&W and limited colour. No stock shots required; all pictures must be part of an article. Covers: medium format transparencies depicting models of steam locomotives and traction engines; metalworking equipment and home workshop scenes; some full size vintage vehicles.
Text: Well-illustrated articles from specialists.
Overall freelance potential: Considerable for the specialist.
Fees: Negotiable.

POPULAR CRAFTS
Nexus Special Interests Ltd, Nexus House, Boundary Way, Hemel Hempstead, Herts HP2 7ST.
Tel: 01442 66551. Fax: 01442 66998.
Editor: Carolyn Schulz.
Monthly magazine for everyone interested in crafts.
Illustrations: B&W and colour. Pictures used as illustrations for features, or with news items. Covers: colour pictures linked with feature inside.
Text: Illustrated articles on all types of crafts. Should have a strong practical bias, helped by step-by-step pictures, or should be interesting profiles of craftspeople. 500–2,000 words. Also 100-word news items.
Overall freelance potential: Around 85 per cent of the magazine is contributed.
Fees: Approximately £40 per published page.

PRACTICAL CRAFT
Magmaker Ltd, Cromwell Court, New Road, St Ives, Cambridge PE17 4BG.
Tel: 01480 496130. Fax: 01480 495514.
Editor: Frank Ward.
Monthly "how to do it" crafts magazine with the emphasis on useful or money-making projects.
Illustrations: Mainly colour. Invariably in conjunction with specific articles as below.
Text: Well-illustrated "how to" crafts projects. Submit suggestions and/or examples of previous work in the first instance.
Overall freelance potential: Good for the experienced worker in this field.
Fees: By negotiation.

PRACTICAL FISHKEEPING
EMAP Apex National Publications Ltd, Apex House, Oundle Road, Peterborough PE2 9NP.
Tel: 01733 898100. Fax: 01733 898487.
Editor: Steve Windsor.
Monthly magazine for all tropical freshwater, marine, pond and coldwater fishkeepers, aimed at every level from hobbyist to expert.
Illustrations: Colour. Pictures of all species of tropical, marine and coldwater fish, plants, tanks, ponds and water gardens. Prefer to hold material on file for possible future use.
Text: Emphasis on instructional articles on the subject. 1,000–1,500 words.
Overall freelance potential: Most is supplied by contributors with a specific knowledge of the hobby, but freelance material is considered on its merit at all times.
Editor's tips: Telephone first to give a brief on the intended copy and/or photographs available. Caption all fish clearly and get names right.
Fees: Negotiable.

SCALE MODELS INTERNATIONAL
Nexus Special Interests Ltd, Nexus House, Boundary Way, Hemel Hempstead, Herts HP2 7ST.
Tel: 01442 66551. Fax: 01442 66998.
Editor: Kelvin Barber.

Monthly magazine for serious modellers of any type of scale model.
Illustrations: B&W and colour. Pictures of unusual and original scale models, but usually only as part of an article.
Text: Well-illustrated articles written for serious and experienced modellers. A style sheet is available for potential contributors.
Overall freelance potential: Good for those in touch with the modelling scene.
Editor's tips: Contributors should have good working knowledge of the field.
Fees: By negotiation.

TEDDY BEAR SCENE

EMF Publishing, The Old Barn, Ferringham Lane, Ferring, West Sussex BN12 5LL.
Tel: 01903 244900. Fax: 01903 506626.
Editor: Jennie Alexander
Monthly for collectors of teddy bears and other "furry friends".
Illustrations: Colour only. Pictures of interesting individual bears or of specialist collectors, supported by detailed captions or a story.
Text: Well-illustrated features on notable bear makers or collectors. Raise ideas with the editor in the first instance.
Overall freelance potential: Fair.
Editor's tips: Always on the lookout for fresh and original contributions.
Fees: From £25 per page; negotiable for special material.

TOYMAKING

GMC Publications Ltd, Castle Place, 86 High Street, Lewes, East Sussex BN7 1XN.
Tel: 01273 477374. Fax: 01273 486300.
Editor: Bernard C Cooper.
Alternate-monthly magazine devoted to the making of toys from traditional craft materials – wood, fabric, etc.
Illustrations: Colour. Photographs only used within complete project features as below.
Text: Profusely-illustrated, step-by-step features detailing the making of individual toys. Suggestions always welcomed.
Overall freelance potential: Good for suitable material of high quality.
Editor's tips: Project features should include as many photographs as are necessary to make the techniques and procedures crystal clear.
Fees: £25 per single picture inside; illustrated articles £50 per page.

TREASURE HUNTING

Greenlight Publishing, The Publishing House, Hatfield Peverel, Chelmsford, Essex CM3 2HF.
Tel: 01245 381011. Fax: 01245 381950.
Editor: Greg Payne.
Monthly magazine for metal detecting and local history enthusiasts.
Illustrations: Colour prints preferred. Usually only as illustrations for features detailed below, but captioned news pictures may be of interest. Covers: colour pictures of people using metal detectors in a countryside or seaside setting.
Text: Illustrated news stories and features on individual finds, club treasure hunts, lost property recovery, local history, etc. News, 300–1,000 words; features, 1,000–3,000 words.
Overall freelance potential: Approximately 50 per cent of the magazine comes from freelances.
Editor's tips: Advisable to telephone the magazine before attempting a cover.
Fees: Covers, £55; news items £10 per 1,000 words; features £15 per 1,000 words.

WOODCARVING

Guild of Master Craftsman Publications Ltd, 86 High Street, Lewes, East Sussex BN7 1XN.
Tel: 01273 477374. Fax: 01273 487692.
Editor: Nick Hough.

Magazine published six times per year and aimed at both amateur and professional woodcarvers. **Illustrations**: Colour only. Mostly to illustrate specific articles, but some scope for news pictures and shots of interesting pieces of work accompanied by detailed captions. Covers: striking colour shots of exceptional woodcarvings or woodcarvers in action, relating to article inside.
Text: Illustrated articles on all aspects of serious woodcarving, including profiles of individual craftsmen.
Overall freelance potential: Good for the right material.
Fees: £25 for one-off reproductions inside. £50 per published page for articles, including photos.

WOODTURNING
Guild of Master Craftsman Publications Ltd, 86 High Street, Lewes, East Sussex BN7 1XN.
Tel: 01273 477374. Fax: 01273 486300.
Editor: Neil Bell.
Monthly magazine aimed at both amateur and professional woodturners.
Illustrations: Colour only. Mostly to illustrate specific articles, but some scope for unusual or interesting single pictures with full captions. Covers: striking colour shots of turned items, relating to article inside.
Text: Illustrated articles on all aspects of woodturning, including profiles of individual craftsmen.
Overall freelance potential: Good for the right material.
Fees: £25 for one-off reproductions inside. £50 per published page for articles, including photos.

WOODWORKER
Nexus Special Interests Ltd, Nexus House, Boundary Way, Hemel Hempstead, Herts HP2 7ST.
Tel: 01442 66551. Fax: 01442 66998.
Editor: Mark Ramuz.
Monthly magazine for all craftspeople in wood. Readership includes schools and woodworking businesses, as well as individual hobbyists.
Illustrations: Colour. Pictures relating to wood and wood crafts, mostly as illustrations for features. Covers: colour pictures of fine furniture. 35mm acceptable but medium format preferred.
Text: Illustrated features on all facets of woodworking crafts. 1,500 words.
Overall freelance potential: Good, about 75 per cent bought from outside contributors.
Editor's tips: Clear, concise authoritative writing in readable, modern style essential.
Fees: Negotiable, but around £50–55 per published page.

Home Interest

COUNTRY HOMES AND INTERIORS
Southbank Publishing Group, King's Reach Tower, Stamford Street, London SE1 9LS.
Tel: 0171-261 6451. Fax: 0171-261 6895.
Editor: Katherine Hadley. **Art Editor**: Peter Davis.
Monthly magazine concerning up-market country homes, interiors, and allied subjects.
Illustrations: Colour only. Top quality coverage of architecture, interiors, gardens, landscapes, food, and personalities. Mostly by commission, but speculative submissions of picture features on specific country houses or gardens, or other country-based topics, may be considered if of the highest quality. No market for single pictures. Covers: always related to a major feature inside.
Text: Top level coverage of country lifestyle subjects and personality profiles, only by commission.
Overall freelance potential: Excellent for photographers who can provide the right sort of material.
Fees: Negotiable from a minimum of £100.

ELLE DECORATION
Hachette/EMAP Magazines Ltd, Endeavour House, 189 Shaftesbury Avenue, London WC2H 8JG.
Tel: 0171-437 9011. Fax: 0171-434 0656.
Editor: Ilse Crawford. **Picture Editor**: Shelly Mason.
Glossy interior decoration magazine aimed at a youthful readership (25–40). Published 10 times per year.
Illustrations: Mostly colour. By commission only, but always interested in hearing from photographers experienced in this field.
Text: Ideas for features always of interest.
Overall freelance potential: Plenty of scope for the experienced freelance.
Editor's tips: Particular projects must always be discussed in detail beforehand to ensure that the magazine's specific styling requirements are observed.
Fees: £100 per page for photography; £250 per 1,000 words/page for text.

HOME
Portcullis Publications Ltd, 4 The Linen Yard, South Street, Crewkerne, Somerset TA18 8AB.
Tel: 01460 77727. Fax: 01460 77747.
Editor: Caroline Foster.
Glossy monthly concentrating on individual homes and interior design, but also covering all home interest topics.
Illustrations: Colour only. By commission only to illustrate features – mainly houses/interiors work and still life/product photography. The magazine has photographers based in London and Somerset, so most opportunities are outside those regions. Possible scope for celebrity portraiture.
Text: Well-illustrated features on individual homes and decorating possibilities. Most interested in homes that have been decorated in very personal, creative style by the occupants. Write in with suggestions first.
Overall freelance potential: Very good; all contributions are freelance.
Fees: By negotiation.

HOMESTYLE
RAP Publishing Ltd, 120 Wilton Road, London SW1V 1JZ.
Tel: 0171-834 8534. Fax: 0171-873 8557.
Editorial Director: Barbara Raine-Allen. **Art Editor**: Stewart Heath.
Monthly magazine concerned with home and home improvement projects.
Illustrations: Colour only. Commissions available for experienced workers in the home or DIY fields.
Text: Scope for contributors who can write knowledgeably and enjoyably on specific subjects, i.e. crafts, home, interior design, etc. Illustrated features on one particular project are required for regular "Open House" feature, but submit ideas only in the first instance. Celebrity features also considered.
Overall freelance potential: Very good for those with some experience in the field.
Fees: By negotiation.

HOMES & GARDENS
IPC Magazines Ltd, King's Reach Tower, Stamford Street, London SE1 9LS.
Tel: 0171-261 5000. Fax: 0171-261 6247.
Editor: Matthew Line. **Art Editor**: Claire Wood.
Monthly glossy magazine devoted to quality interior design and related matters.
Illustrations: Colour only. High quality commissioned coverage of interior decoration, design, architecture, gardens, furnishings and food. Emphasis on homes decorated in a youthful modern style, up-market and attractive rather than wacky. Ideas for coverage always welcome.
Text: Heavily-illustrated features as above.
Overall freelance potential: Good for really top quality work.
Editor's tips: Out of London material particularly welcome.
Fees: By negotiation.

HOMES AND IDEAS
IPC Magazines Ltd, King's Reach Tower, Stamford Street, London SE1 9LS.
Tel: 0171-261 5000. Fax: 0171-261 7495.
Editor: Debbie Djordjevic. **Art Director:** Sharon Johnston. **Art Editor**: Julian Barrett.
Monthly home interest magazine aimed at young home-owners with limited finance.
Illustrations: Colour only. By commission only, to illustrate individual home profiles and improvement features. Those experienced in the field should contact the art editor.
Text: No scope.
Overall freelance potential: Good scope for experienced home interest workers.
Fees: By negotiation.

HOUSE BEAUTIFUL
National Magazine Company Ltd, 72 Broadwick Street, London W1V 2BP.
Tel: 0171-439 5000. Fax: 0171-439 5595.
Editor: Caroline Atkins. **Art Director**: Lucy Allnutt.
Monthly magazine with the emphasis on practical home decorating ideas.
Illustrations: All colour. Usually by commission. Photographs of houses, interior decoration, furnishings, cookery and gardens. Complete picture features depicting houses and interiors of interest.
Text: Features on subjects as above, invariably commissioned, but possible scope for speculative features on suitable subjects.
Overall freelance potential: Quite good for experienced contributors in the home interest and interiors field.
Fees: By negotiation.

HOUSE & GARDEN
Condé Nast Publications Ltd, Vogue House, Hanover Square, London W1R OAD.
Tel: 0171-499 9080. Fax: 0171-493 1345.
Editor: Susan Crewe.
Monthly glossy magazine devoted to high quality homes and associated subjects.
Illustrations: Colour only. Almost entirely by commission. Photographs of interior decoration, architecture, furnishings, food and wine, and gardens. Complete picture features depicting a house or apartment of interest and quality.
Text: Features on subjects as above, invariably commissioned.
Overall freelance potential: Reasonable scope for experienced architectural and interiors photographers to obtain commissions. Some scope for non-commissioned features on houses, gardens and food.
Fees: By negotiation.

INSPIRATIONS
GE Magazines Ltd, Elme House, 133 Long Acre, London WC2E 9AW.
Tel: 0171-836 0519. Fax: 0171- 497 2364.
Editor: Deborah Barker. **Art Editor**: Jude Curle.
Monthly creative homes magazine covering interior design, gardens and food.
Illustrations: Colour only. By commission only; studio and location assignments available to experienced photographers.
Text: No freelance scope.
Overall freelance potential: Good for the experienced worker in this field.
Fees: By negotiation.

PERFECT HOME
DMG Home Interest Magazines, Times House, Station Approach, Ruislip, Middx HA4 8NB.
Tel: 01895 677677. Fax: 01895 676027.
Editor: Julia Smith.
Monthly magazine for anyone interested in home improvements.

Illustrations: Colour only. Pictures to accompany articles and features on interior decoration, home improvements, gardens, etc. Usually comissioned.
Text: Suggestions from experienced contributors always considered.
Overall freelance potential: Good for experienced contributors in this field.
Fees: By negotiation.

PERIOD LIVING & TRADITIONAL HOMES
EMAP Elan, Endeavour House, 189 Shaftesbury Avenue, London WC2H 8JG.
Tel: 0171-208 3507. Fax: 0171-208 3597.
Editor: Clare Weatherall. **Art Director**: Kevan Westbury.
Monthly magazine featuring homes from any period pre-1939.
Illustrations: Colour only. Commissions available to experienced interiors photographers, who should show portfolios in the first instance.
Text: No scope.
Overall freelance potential: Good for interior decoration specialists only.
Fees: By negotiation.

PRACTICAL HOUSEHOLDER
Nexus Media Ltd, Boundary Way, Hemel Hempstead, Herts HP2 4STY.
Tel: 01442 66551. Fax: 01442 66998.
Editor: John McGowan.
Monthly magazine concerned with DIY and practical home improvements.
Illustrations: B&W and colour. Pictures to accompany articles and features on interior decoration and home improvement projects.
Text: Practical articles on home projects and interior design ideas. Technical and building matters discussed in a simple and straightforward manner. Basic DIY projects and personal experiences are sometimes of interest.
Overall freelance potential: Good for experienced contributors in this field.
Editor's tips: "Look carefully at the magazine before submitting – it will save your time and mine."
Fees: By negotiation.

THE WORLD OF INTERIORS
The Condé Nast Publications Ltd, Vogue House, Hanover Square, London W1R 0AD.
Tel: 0171-499 9080. Fax: 0171-493 4013.
Editor-in-Chief: Min Hogg. **Art Editor**: Malgosia Szemberg.
Monthly magazine showing the best interior decoration of all periods and in all countries.
Illustrations: Mainly colour, occasional B&W. Subjects as above. Extra high standard of work required.
Text: Complete coverage of interesting houses; occasionally public buildings, churches, shops, etc. 1,000–2,000 words.
Overall freelance potential: Much of the work in the magazine comes from freelances.
Fees: Negotiable.

Industry

APPAREL INTERNATIONAL
Cowise International Publishing Group, Abbey House, 2 Southgate Road, Potters Bar, Hertfordshire EN6 5DU.
Tel: 01707 656828. Fax: 01707 645322.
Editor: Ken Clark.
Monthly publication for clothing and footwear manufacturers.
Illustrations: Mainly colour. News pictures and coverage of individual processes in the trade.

Text: Features on manufacturing and marketing of clothing and footwear. 1,000 words.
Overall freelance potential: Limited, owing to specialist nature of the subject matter.
Fees: News pictures, £15; other pictures and words by arrangement.

BT TODAY
BT, A233, BT Centre, 81 Newgate Street, London EC1A 7AJ.
Tel: 0171-356 5276. Fax: 0171-356 6546.
Editor: Ken Runicles.
Monthly publication for all BT employees, plus pensioners, opinion formers, MPs, the media, etc.
Illustrations: Colour only. Pictures of all Telecom subjects, usually by commission.
Text: Stories related to BT. About 300 words.
Overall freelance potential: Limited.
Fees: By agreement.

ELECTRICAL TIMES
Reed Business Publishing Ltd, Quadrant House, The Quadrant, Sutton, Surrey SM2 5AS.
Tel: 0181-652 3115. Fax: 0181-652 8972.
Editor: Chris Bennett.
Monthly publication for electrical contractors in the public and private sectors, wholesalers, architects, commercial and industrial users of electricity and the electricity supply industry.
Illustrations: Colour only. Pictures of new technical products, site installation work, electrical-related exhibitions, personalities, equipment, etc.
Text: Technical articles are usually commissioned. Some openings for business-related articles on the electrical industry. 750–1,000 words.
Overall freelance potential: Limited.
Fees: By negotiation.

EUROPEAN RUBBER JOURNAL
Crain Communications Ltd, New Garden House, 78 Hatton Garden, London EC1N 8JQ.
Tel: 0171-457 1400. Fax: 0171-457 1440.
Editor: David Shaw.
Published 11 times per year for the rubber producing, processing and using industries.
Illustrations: B&W and occasional colour inside. Pictures of rubber and rubber applications of a technical nature, e.g. tyres, belting, etc. Also news and people pictures. Covers: graphically striking colour pictures of rubber-related subjects. Human interest would help as well as technical content. Vertical format.
Text: Features on new applications of rubber and new product stories; new equipment, materials, processes information; business, marketing, personnel and technical news. Features up to 2,000 words.
Overall freelance potential: Limited, but around 5 to 10 per cent of the publication comes from freelances.
Editor's tips: All contributions must have a high news value or have sound technical content.
Fees: By arrangement.

FOOD INDUSTRY NEWS
Beacon Publishing Ltd, 95 Bridger Way, Crowborough, East Sussex TN6 2XD.
Tel: 01892 668172. Fax: 01892 668173.
Editor: Stephen Blake.
Monthly publication covering the food production industry, aimed at managers and technologists.
Illustrations: Mainly colour (transparencies preferred; good quality prints acceptable). News pictures, which must be up-to-date and fully captioned. Some interest in stock pictures depicting specialist areas of food processing and technology. Commissions sometimes available to illustrate company profiles and special features.
Text: Features or news items welcomed on spec. Otherwise by commission, only from specialists.

Overall freelance potential: Limited.
Fees: News pix from £10; news stories 15p per per word published (max 500 words). Features from £120 per published page.

GLASS AGE & WINDOW CONSTRUCTION

Miller Freeman Entertainment Ltd, 8th Floor, Ludgate House, 245 Blackfriars Road, London SE1 9UR.
Tel: 0171-620 3636. Fax: 0171-401 8035.
Editor: Richard Schwarz.
Monthly magazine for the flat glass and allied industries. Aimed at builders, architects, double glazing producers, shopfitters, glass merchants, stained glass artists and all glass-related workers.
Illustrations: B&W only. Particularly interested in pictures of glass in new buildings. Detailed captions essential.
Text: Features on glass in construction.
Overall freelance potential: Good opportunities for high quality architectural photography.
Editor's tips: Make contact before submitting any material.
Fees: On a rising scale according to the size of reproduction or length of feature.

INDUSTRIAL DIAMOND REVIEW

De Beers Industrial Diamond Division (UK) Ltd, Charters, Sunninghill, Ascot, Berks SL5 9PX.
Tel: 01344 23456. Fax: 01344 28188.
Editor: Chris Barrett.
Quarterly publication designed to promote a wider and more efficient use of diamond tools, i.e. grinding wheels, drill bits, saw blades, etc. in all branches of engineering.
Illustrations: B&W and colour. Pictures of any type of diamond tool in action.
Text: Case histories on the use of diamond tools in engineering, mining, etc. Up to 2,000 words for finished feature.
Overall freelance potential: Excellent but highly specialised.
Editor's tips: Technical case histories are welcome, but check acceptance with editor before submitting material. Potential contributors are requested to consult the editor before pursuing any possible editorial leads.
Fees: Excellent; by arrangement.

INDUSTRIAL FIRE JOURNAL

Kennedy Communications Ltd, Unit 8, The Old Yarn Mills, Westbury, Sherborne, Dorset DT9 3RG.
Tel: 01935 816030. Fax: 01935 817200.
Editor: Aidan Turnbull.
Quarterly magazine concerning firefighting in the industrial sector.
Illustrations: Mostly B&W. Pictures of anything involving firefighting services in an industrial context, including firefighting personnel in action. Covers: powerful colour images of the same.
Text: No scope for non-specialists.
Overall freelance potential: Fair.
Editor's tips: Please seek the editor's agreement before sending in specific photographs for consideration. We don't want to see contact sheets. No photos of ordinary car fires or firefighters/engines at domestic home/high street fires. We look for racy, exciting and explicit shots to interest and educate a readership of trained fire professionals who've "seen it all before".
Fees: Negotiable, but generally good. Up to £200 for a really good cover picture.

INK AND PRINT

Batiste Publications Ltd, Pembroke House, Campsbourne Road, Hornsey, London N8 7PE.
Tel: 0181-340 3291. Fax: 0181-341 4840.
Editor: Jackie Gibson.
Quarterly publication for all involved in the manufacture of ink and development of ink technology: manufacturers and suppliers of printing companies, inplant printers, industry and commerce, adver-

tising companies, government and local authorities, research establishments.
Illustrations: B&W and colour. Pictures of all printing subjects, i.e. machinery, ink, paper, raw materials, personalities etc. Covers: interesting or unusual shots of printing processes; medium format.
Text: Technical articles on the ink and print business. 1,500–2,500 words.
Overall freelance potential: Growing.
Fees: By agreement.

MANUFACTURING CHEMIST
Miller Freeman PLC, 30 Calderwood Street, Woolwich, London SE18 6QH.
Tel: 0181-855 7777. Fax: 0181-316 3017.
Editor: Gerry Duggin.
Monthly journal for the chemical industry. Read by senior management involved in research, development, reproduction and marketing of general chemicals, drugs, household products, cosmetics, toiletries and aerosol products.
Illustrations: B&W and (mostly) colour. Pictures of any aspect of the fine chemical industry from general chemicals to drugs and cosmetics. Covers: good colour of same. 35mm acceptable, but medium format preferred.
Text: Features on any aspect of the chemical industry as detailed above. 1,000–2,000 words.
Overall freelance potential: Approximately 30 per cent is contributed by freelances.
Fees: Text, £120 per 1,000 words for features, £15 per 100 words for news stories; pictures by agreement.

ROUSTABOUT MAGAZINE
Roustabout Publications, Suite 5, International Base, Greenwell Road, East Tullos, Aberdeen AB1 4AX.
Tel: 01224 876582. Fax: 01224 879757.
Editor: Ann Duguid.
Monthly for oil industry personnel working on and off shore in the North Sea. Also covers Houston, Norway & business news.
Illustrations: Colour. All pictures must be directly related to the international oil and gas industry. Minimum transparency size: 6x6cm.
Text: Articles related to the international oil and gas industry. 600–1,000 words.
Overall freelance potential: Limited because of extremely specialised subject.
Fees: By arrangement.

SIGN WORLD
A. E. Morgan Publication Ltd, Stanley House, 9 West Street, Epsom, Surrey KT18 7RL.
Tel: 01372 741411. Fax: 01372 744493.
Editor: Mike Connolly.
Monthly publication dealing with sign manufacturing and allied industries. Aimed at architects, town planners, surveyors, traffic and design engineers, shopfitters, sign manufacturers, trade suppliers, designers, advertising agents, exhibition organisers and specifiers in major organisations.
Illustrations: Mainly B&W (also colour by arrangement). Only as illustrations to features.
Text: Features on new technological developments in the sign manufacturing industry. Information on relevant contracts at home and abroad. Usually 1,000–1,500 words, or by arrangement.
Overall freelance potential: Open to development for freelances with the right specialist knowledge
Editor's tips: Sample copies available – phone for details.
Fees: About £100 per 1,000 words; pictures by agreement.

STEEL TIMES
Argus Business Media Ltd, Queensway House, 2 Queensway, Redhill RH1 1QS.
Tel: 01737 768611. Fax: 01737 761685.
Editor: Tim Smith.

Monthly publication for all those interested in the iron and steel industry.
Illustrations: B&W and colour. Topical pictures related to the industry, usually to illustrate specific features.
Text: Articles on new products, processes and contracts in the industry plus economic and review articles on the steel industry.
Overall freelance potential: Limited.
Fees: By negotiation.

TIMBER GROWER
Timber Growers Association Ltd. Editorial: 64 Church Road, Fleet, Hampshire GU13 8LB.
Tel: 01252 622301. Fax: 01252 627298.
Editor: David Steers.
Quarterly publication for woodland owners, agents and managers, contractors and those interested in forestry as a land use and as an industry.
Illustrations: B&W and some colour. Pictures of forestry activity and people, relevant to articles and content.
Text: Features on forestry. 750 words.
Overall freelance potential: Limited.
Fees: By agreement.

TIN INTERNATIONAL
Market Information and Industrial Data, PO Box 244, Redhill, RH1 5YS.
Tel/fax: 01342 844988.
Editor: Robin Amlot.
Monthly publication covering all aspects of the production and consumption of tin, including can manufacturing, canning, soldering, chemicals and alloys.
Illustrations: B&W only. Pictures illustrating any aspects of the mining of tin and its application in end uses.
Text: Features on subject detailed above. 1,000–2,000 words.
Overall freelance potential: Limited.
Fees: £100 per 1,000 words; pictures by agreement.

URETHANES TECHNOLOGY
Crain Communications Ltd, 4th Floor, New Garden House, 78 Hatton Garden, London EC1N 8JQ.
Tel: 0171-457 1400. Fax: 0171-457 1440.
Editor: David Reed.
Alternate-monthly publication for the polyurethane producing, processing, and using industries.
Illustrations: B&W and occasional colour. Pictures of production, equipment, and application of polyurethane materials. Also news pictures and shots of trade personalities. Covers: top quality and graphically striking medium format colour of polyurethane-related subjects.
Text: Features on new applications of polyurethanes; new products; new equipment and processing. Business, marketing, personnel and technical news items. Features, up to 2,000 words.
Overall freelance potential: Good scope for those with access to the industries involved.
Fees: By arrangement.

UTILITY WEEK
Reed Business Publishing Ltd, Quadrant House, The Quadrant, Sutton, Surrey SM2 5AS.
Tel: 0181-652 3805. Fax: 0181-652 8906.
Editor: Paul Garrett. **Picture Editor**: Naomi Russell.
Weekly business magazine for the four major supply utilities: electricity, gas, telecommunications and water.
Illustrations: Colour. News pictures concerning the major utilities. Possible scope for good stock coverage of industry subjects. Commissions available to experienced portrait and business/industry workers.

Text: Contributors with expert knowledge always welcomed. Submit details of experience in the first instance.
Overall freelance potential: Very good for industrial specialists.
Fees: By negotiation.

WORKS MANAGEMENT
Hadlow House, 9 High Street, Green Street Green, Orpington, Kent BR6 6BG.
Tel: 01689 862562. Fax: 01689 857735.
Editor: Adam Lawrence. **Art Editor**: Roland Davies.
Monthly publication for managers and engineers who directly control or perform the works management function in selected manufacturing concerns.
Illustrations: B&W and colour. Occasional need for regional coverage of managers and workers in realistic work situations in factories. Mostly pictures are used only to illustrate features.
Text: Illustrated features of interest to management, e.g. productivity, automation in factories, industrial relations, employment law, finance, energy, maintenance, handling and storage, safety and welfare. Around 1,500 words.
Overall freelance potential: Up to 30 per cent is contributed by freelances.
Fees: By agreement.

WORLD TOBACCO
International Trade Publications Ltd, Queensway House, 2 Queensway, Redhill, Surrey RH1 1QS.
Tel: 01737 855221. Fax: 01737 855470.
Editor: George Gay.
Alternate-monthly aimed at international manufacturers, dealers and suppliers to the tobacco processing and manufacturing industries.
Illustrations: B&W and colour. Pictures of tobacco growing, processing or manufacture from any part of the world.
Text: Limited scope depending on the country.
Overall freelance potential: Fair.
Editor's tips: Pictures from remote parts of the world are particularly welcome.
Fees: By arrangement.

Local Government & Services

FIRE PREVENTION
Fire Protection Association, Melrose Avenue, Borehamwood, Hertfordshire WD6 2BJ.
Tel: 0181-207 2345. Fax: 0181-236 9701.
Editor: Anna Hayes.
Technical publication on fire safety, produced 10 times a year (monthly, but Jan/Feb, Jul/Aug issues combined). Aimed at fire brigades, fire equipment manufacturers, architects, insurance companies, and those with responsibility for fire safety in public sector bodies, commerce and industry.
Illustrations: B&W and colour. Pictures of large and small fires to illustrate reports. Pictures showing different types of occupancy (offices, commercial premises, warehouses, etc) also welcome.
Text: Technical articles and news items on fire prevention and protection. Features 1,000–2,000 words.
Overall freelance potential: Good pictures of fires and unusual fire safety experiences are always welcome.
Fees: Pictures, negotiable from £15. Text, negotiable from £110 per 1,000 words.

FIRE AND RESCUE
Kennedy Communications Ltd, Unit 8, The Old Yarn Mills, Sherborne, Dorset DT9 3RG.
Tel: 01935 816030. Fax: 01935 817200.
Editor: Aidan Turnbull.

Quarterly magazine for all involved in municipal firefighting and emergency services.
Illustrations: Mostly B&W. Good shots of firefighting and emergency services personnel in action. Also pictures of major fires, accidents, vehicle crashes, extrications, fire and accident victims. Pics of paramedic intervention, specific injuries and unusual rescues also appreciated but discuss these with the editor first. Covers: powerful colour images of the same.
Text: Scope only for those with expert knowledge of the subject.
Overall freelance potential: Fair.
Editor's tips: Please seek the editor's agreement before sending in photographs for consideration. We don't want to see contact sheets, photos of ordinary car fires, or boring, dull and conventional shots of firefighters/engines at domestic home/high street fires. Require racy, exciting and explicit shots to interest and educate trained fire professionals who've "seen it all before".
Fees: Negotiable, but generally good. Up to £200 for a really good cover picture.

JUNIOR EDUCATION
Scholastic Ltd, Villiers House, Clarendon Avenue, Leamington Spa, Warwickshire CV32 5PR.
Tel: 01926 887799. Fax: 01926 883331.
Editor: Mrs Terry Saunders.
Monthly publication for teachers in primary education.
Illustrations: Mostly B&W. News pictures and good, unposed pictures of junior schoolchildren in the 7–12 age range in classroom and other school situations. Covers: colour pictures as above, but often commissioned.
Text: Will consider good practical curriculum ideas for work in the junior classroom. 1,000 words.
Overall freelance potential: Good, though the magazine is often overstocked.
Fees: By agreement.

LEGAL ACTION
The Legal Action Group, 242 Pentonville Road, London N1 9UN.
Tel: 0171-833 2931. Fax: 0171-837 6094.
Editor: Lesley Exton.
Monthly publication for lawyers, advice workers, law students and academics.
Illustrations: B&W only. Pictures of lawyers, judges, especially other than the standard head and shoulders shot. Courts. Plus stock pictures to illustrate features covering a wide range of subjects (e.g. housing, police, immigration, advice services).
Text: Features on legal services and professional issues, including the courts. High technical detail required. Also information for news and feature material that can be written in-house.
Overall freelance potential: Always interested in knowing of photographers holding suitable material.
Fees: By negotiation.

LOCAL GOVERNMENT NEWS
B&M Publications (London) Ltd, PO Box 13, Hereford House, Bridle Path, Croydon CR9 4NL.
Tel: 0181-680 4200. Fax: 0181-681 5049.
Editor: Phillip Cooper.
Monthly news magazine for professional officers, middle to higher grade, in technical departments of local authorities, officers in water authorities and professional civil servants in relevant government departments.
Illustrations: B&W only. Pictures of architectural and building projects, road schemes, housing projects, national and local politicians and news pictures with local government angle.

Are you working from the latest edition of The Freelance Photographer's Market Handbook? It's published on 1 October each year. Markets are constantly changing, so it pays to have the latest edition

---

Text: Features on any local government related story with exception of those dealing with education or social service policy matters. 750–1,000 words.
Overall freelance potential: More than 50 per cent of material comes from freelance sources.
Fees: By negotiation.

MUNICIPAL JOURNAL
Hemming Group Ltd, 32 Vauxhall Bridge Road, London SW1V 2SS.
Tel: 0171-973 6400. Fax: 0171-233 5051.
Editor: Michael Burton.
Weekly publication for senior local government officers, councillors, Whitehall departments and academic and other institutions.
Illustrations: B&W and colour. Relevant personalities, vehicles, buildings, etc; general stock shots of local government subjects and situations to illustrate features.
Text: Features on local government issues. 750–1,000 words.
Overall freelance potential: Very good.
Fees: Good; on a rising scale according to the size of reproduction or length of feature.

PLANNING
Haymarket Business Publications Ltd, 174 Hammersmith Road, London W6 7JP
Tel: 0171-413 4328. Fax: 0171-413 4013.
Editor: Jackie Buist.
Weekly news magazine for all involved with town and country planning and related issues. Official journal of the Royal Town Planning Institute.
Illustrations: B&W and colour. News pictures always of interest, on specific planning issues. Also good generic shots of subjects planning touches on, e.g. conservation, transport, rivers, waste disposal, housing, energy, industry, retailing, etc. Some commissions available to illustrate major features.
Text: Illustrated news stories and longer features from contributors with good knowledge of planning issues, up to 1,500 words. Must be relevant to planners. Always contact the editor before submitting.
Overall freelance potential: Good for genuinely relevant topical material.
Editor's tips: Photos can be of general or specific interest.
Fees: Photography according to use or assignment; text £100 per 1,000 words.

POLICE REVIEW
Police Review Publishing Company Ltd, Calcon House, 5th floor, 289-293 High Holborn, London WC1V 7HU.
Tel: 0171-440 4700. Fax: 0171-405 7163.
Editor: Gary Mason.
Weekly news magazine for the police service.
Illustrations: B&W and colour. All aspects of the police service. Particular interest in up-to-date news pictures covering the previous seven days. Some commissioned work available, with a need for more photographers to carry out regional work. Contact first to show portfolio.
Text: Limited scope because of specialist subject matter, but will consider any subject of contemporary interest to police officers, 1,000–1,500 words.
Overall freelance potential: Good.
Editor's tips: The magazine is published on Wednesdays with a Tuesday morning deadline for news pictures. Photographs for features should be good photojournalism and reportage; not interested in "publicity style" photos.
Fees: Negotiable, minimum £50.

SAFETY EDUCATION
The Royal Society for the Prevention of Accidents, Edgbaston Park, 353 Briston Road, Birmingham B5 7ST.
Tel: 0121-248 2000. Fax: 0121-248 2001.
Editor: Jackie Steenson. **Design Editor**: Stephen Bunce.

Published three times per year and aimed at teachers and educationalists in local authorities.
Illustrations: B&W and colour. Pictures depicting road safety, home safety, playground safety, industrial safety and water safety subjects; predominantly aimed at children. Covers: colour of similar subjects.
Text: Features on topics detailed above. 1,000–3,000 words.
Overall freelance potential: Pictures, 10 per cent of the magazine; articles, 60–70 per cent.
Fees: On a rising scale according to the size of reproduction or length of article.

SPECIAL BEAT
Police Review Publishing Company Ltd, Calcon House, 5th floor, 289-293 High Holborn, London WC1V 7HU.
Tel: 0171-440 4700. Fax: 0171-405 7163.
Editor: Gary Mason.
Quarterly publication of the Special Constabulary, the volunteer reserve police force.
Illustrations: Colour preferred; prints acceptable. Pictures of members of the Special Constabulary in action at special events, engaged in public order or involved in any other newsworthy activities. Should be fully captioned with officer's name, force, location and role in the event depicted.
Text: No freelance scope.
Overall freelance potential: Very good. Looking to establish a roster of reliable and imaginative photographers around the country. Will often use good speculative news pictures.
Editor's tips: Specials can be identified by their flat caps and shoulder flash stating "Special Constabulary", although those in the Metropolitan Police and some other forces wear identical uniforms to regulars (including helmets) and are only identified by a small "SC" on their epaulettes. Interested in good photojournalism, not publicity/recruiting style material.
Fees: Reproduction fees from £30. Commission fees negotiable.

THE TEACHER
National Union of Teachers, Hamilton House, Mabledon Place, London WC1H 9BD.
Tel: 0171-380 4708. Fax: 0171-387 8458.
Editor: Mitch Howard.
Official magazine of the National Union of Teachers. Published eight times a year.
Illustrations: B&W and colour. News pictures concerning any educational topic, especially those taken in schools and colleges. Coverage of union activities, personalities, demonstrations, etc.
Text: Short articles and news items on educational matters.
Overall freelance potential: Limited; interested in good pics though.
Editor's tips: Consult the editor before submitting.
Fees: Acording to use.

YOUNG PEOPLE NOW
National Youth Agency, 17–23 Albion Street, Leicester LE1 6GD.
Tel: 0116 285 6789. Fax: 0116 247 1043.
Editor: Mary Durkin.
Monthly publication for youth workers, social workers, careers officers, teachers, youth counsellors and others working in the youth affairs field.
Illustrations: B&W and colour. Pictures of young people aged 13–21, involved in group activities of a formal or informal nature, street activities, relationships with police, inter-generational groups, positive images of young people. Lists of specialities welcomed.
Text: Small proportion of copy is from freelance contributors.
Overall freelance potential: Occasional news pictures and two or three features using freelance photos per issue.
Fees: From £10 per picture used. From £45 per 1,000 words.

Male Interest

ARENA
Wagadon Ltd, 3rd Floor, Block A, Exmouth House, Pine Street, London EC1R 0JL.
Tel: 0171-689 9999. Fax: 0171-689 0901.
Editor: Ekow Eshuan. **Art Editor**: Martin Farren-Lee.
Monthly general interest magazine for fashion-conscious men in the 20–40 age group.
Illustrations: Mainly colour; plus high-quality B&W. By commission only, to illustrate features on fashion, design, sport, travel, etc. Photographers with an original approach always welcome.
Text: Features and profiles aimed at the intelligent and style-conscious man. Up to 3,000 words.
Overall freelance potential: Fairly good, but only for the experienced contributor.
Fees: Photography by negotiation; text around £200 per 1,000 words.

ATTITUDE
Northern & Shell PLC, Northern & Shell Tower, City Harbour, London E14 9GL.
Tel: 0171-308 5090. Fax: 0171-308 5075.
Editor: James Collard. **Art Director**: Nigel Truswell.
Monthly style magazine for both gay and straight men.
Illustrations: Colour and B&W. Mostly by commission to illustrate specific features. Some opportunities for experienced fashion and style workers. Also some scope for travel, reportage and popular culture material.
Text: Ideas for features always considered; submit an outline first. Should appeal to a gay readership even if written from a "straight" perspective.
Overall freelance potential: Fair.
Fees: By negotiation.

CLUB INTERNATIONAL
Paul Raymond Publications Ltd, 2 Archer Street, London W1V 8JJ.
Tel: 0171-292 8000. Fax: 0171-734 5030.
Editor: Robert Swift.
Popular monthly for men.
Illustrations: Colour only; 35mm Kodachrome preferred. Requires top quality glamour sets of very attractive girls.
Text: Articles on sexual or humorous topics, or factual/investigative pieces. 1,000–2,000 words.
Overall freelance potential: Most of the published glamour material comes from freelances, but they are normally experienced glamour photographers.
Editor's tips: Study the magazine to appreciate style. As well as being very attractive girls featured must look contemporary and fashionable.
Fees: £650 for glamour sets. Text up to £200 per 1,000 words.

ESCORT
Paul Raymond Publications Ltd, 2 Archer Street, London W1V 8JJ.
Tel: 0171-292 8000. Fax: 0171-292 8042.
Editor: Rebecca Eden.
Monthly for men; less sophisticated than the other Paul Raymond publications, *Men Only* and *Club International*.
Illustrations: Colour only; 35mm Kodachrome preferred. Looks for glamour sets of "normal, healthy, girl-next-door" types. Each issue contains about 10 glamour sets running to 2–5 pages each.
Text: Purely "readers' contributions".
Overall freelance potential: Good.
Fees: £400 for glamour sets. Articles: £50–£100.

ESQUIRE
The National Magazine Company Ltd, 72 Broadwick Street, London W1V 2BP.
Tel: 0171-439 5000. Fax: 0171-312 3920.
Editor: Peter Howarth. **Picture Editor**: Henny Manley. **Art Director**: Christophe Gowans.
Up-market general interest monthly for intelligent and affluent men in the 25–44 age group.
Illustrations: Mainly colour. Top-quality material only, invariably by commission. Mostly portrait or fashion work with some photojournalism.
Text: Scope for "name" writers only.
Overall freelance potential: Good for photographers, but restricted to those experienced at the highest level of magazine work.
Fees: By negotiation.

FHM
EMAP Metro Ltd, Mappin House, 4 Winsley Street, London W1N 7AR.
Tel: 0171-312 1515. Fax: 0171-312 8191.
Editor: Ed Needham. **Art Editor**: Jennie Ecclestone. **Picture Editor**: Laura Carlile.
Monthly lifestyle and fashion magazine for young men.
Illustrations: Mainly colour. Main feature and fashion photography always by commission. Stock images relating to subjects of major interest (sports, travel, adventure, cars, sex) often required – send details of coverage available.
Text: Will consider interesting short items of interest to a young male readership, and feature ideas from experienced workers.
Overall freelance potential:Good for the experienced contributor.
Fees: By negotiation.

FIESTA
Galaxy Publications Ltd, PO Box 312, Witham, Essex CM8 3SZ.
Tel: 01376 510555. Fax: 01376 510680.
Editor in Chief: Ross Gilfillan.
Monthly men's magazine, actually aimed at both men and women for whom nudity and sex are not too problematic.
Illustrations: Colour. Glamour photo sets – colourful, interesting settings in which a girl strips. Other picture subjects have included Soho strippers, the Alternative Miss World competition, girls who get wet/muddy, girls in uniform, sexy lingerie, etc.
Text: Features on all aspects of sex, humour, and related topics and what turns men and women on. 1,700–2,000 words. Fillers: 500–1,000 words.
Overall freelance potential: Freelances contribute a major part of the magazine.
Editor's tips: Girl sets which include sheets of cover shots especially welcomed.
Fees: Photo sets, by negotiation up to £600; Features by negotiation.

GQ
Condé Nast Publications Ltd, Vogue House, Hanover Square, London W1R 0AD.
Tel: 0171-499 9080. Fax: 0171-495 1679.
Editor: James Brown. **Art Director**: Tony Chambers. **Picture Editor**: Luisa Nitrato-Izzo.
Up-market general interest magazine for men in the 20–45 age group.
Illustrations: Mainly colour. Top-quality illustrations for articles on a range of topics, invariably by commission.
Text: Top level investigative, personality, fashion and style features, plus articles on other subjects likely to be of interest to successful and affluent men.

As a member of the Bureau of Freelance Photographers, you'll be kept up-to-date with markets through the BFP Market Newsletter, published monthly. For details of membership, turn to page 9

Overall freelance potential: Only for the contributor experienced at the top level of magazine work.
Editor's tips: People can see from the magazine itself what sort of style and quality is required.
Fees: By negotiation.

KNAVE

Galaxy Publications Ltd, PO Box 312, Witham, Essex CM8 3SZ.
Tel: 01376 510555. Fax: 01376 510680.
Editor: Ruth Davis. **Picture Editor**: Andy Morgan.
Monthly magazine for men.
Illustrations: Mostly colour. Glamour girl sets (minimum 200 transparencies). Also feature illustrations, by commission only.
Text: Sexy, humorous, factual articles. Plus pieces of general male interest.
Overall freelance potential: Most of the magazine comes from freelances.
Fees: Glamour sets, £600; articles without pictures £200; articles with accompanying illustrations £300–£400.

LOADED

IPC Magazines Ltd, King's Reach Tower, Stamford Street, London SE1 9LS.
Tel: 0171-261 5480. Fax: 0171-261 5640.
Editor: Derek Harbinson.
General interest monthly for men in their twenties. Covers music, sport, humour, fashion and popular culture in a down-to-earth and irreverent manner.
Illustrations: Mainly colour. Mostly by commission to accompany features, but speculative submissions always considered. Submit only dupes or photocopies in the first instance.
Text: Fashion features, reportage (clubs, drugs, crime, etc), interviews, humour and "anything off the wall".
Overall freelance potential: Always open to fresh and original photography and ideas.
Fees: By negotiation.

MAXIM

Dennis Publishing Ltd, 19 Bolsover Street, London W1P 7HJ.
Tel: 0171-631 1433. Fax: 0171-917 7663.
Editor: Nigel Ambrose. **Art Director**: Peter Green.
General interest lifestyle magazine aimed at sophisticated men in the 25–44 age group. More practical and less "aspirational" than other men's magazines.
Illustrations: Mostly colour. Commissioned coverage of male fashion, grooming, sport, cars, etc. – make appointment to show portfolio. Also some high quality reportage work on topical issues, colour or B&W.
Text: Limited scope, but ideas from experienced contributors always considered.
Overall freelance potential: Good for the experienced worker.
Editor's tips: An original approach could pay off.
Fees: Variable according the nature of the work.

MAYFAIR

Paul Raymond Publications Ltd, 2 Archer Street, London W1V 8JJ.
Tel: 0171-292 8000. Fax: 0171-437 8788.
Editor: Steve Shields.
Sophisticated monthly for men.
Illustrations: Colour only; 35mm preferred. Glamour sets taken in up-market surroundings. Only top quality material can be accepted. Backgrounds should be real-life locations, such as a luxury furnished flat. Outdoor material needs strong sunlight. Also interested in photos/photo features covering "extreme" sports. Covers: always feature a girl, partly nude (nipples not shown); sexy, provocative, natural and head-turning.

Text: Articles on general male interests.
Overall freelance potential: Very good; all the photographs and major features are the work of freelance contributors.
Editor's tips: Thought should be given to the erotic use of clothing and suggestion of sex appeal or sexual situation, together with striking but simple colour co-ordination.
Fees: £250–£1,000 for glamour sets. Covers: £150 and up.

MEN ONLY
Paul Raymond Publications Ltd, 2 Archer Street, London W1V 7HF.
Tel: 0171-734 9191. Fax: 0171-734 5030.
Editor: Mike Collier.
Sophisticated monthly for men.
Illustrations: Colour only; 35mm Kodachrome preferred. Imaginative glamour sets featuring "the most beautiful women". Picture-led supporting features.
Text: Laid-back humour, sport, male interests etc.
Overall freelance potential: Excellent – "new ideas and faces always welcome".
Editor's tips: "Men Only models are young, fresh, athletic and natural. We welcome sets from new photographers as well as our established contributors. Attention to detail in clothes and make-up, a wide variety of poses and imaginative locations will always set you apart. Don't be afraid to call us!"
Fees: £500–£1,000 for glamour sets. Other pictures by negotiation.

MEN'S HEALTH
Rodale Press Ltd, 7-10 Chandos Street, London W1M 0AD.
Tel: 0171-291 6000. Fax: 0171-291 6060.
Editor: Phil Hilton. **Art Director**: Katherine Carnegie.
Magazine published 10 times per year and covering sports, fitness, grooming and other aspects of male lifestyle.
Illustrations: Mainly colour. Mostly by commission, though possible scope for good generic stock shots of fitness etc. subjects.
Text: Articles on male lifestyle subjects, especially health and fitness. Write with ideas and details of experience in the first instance.
Overall freelance potential: Only for the experienced contributor.
Fees: By negotiation.

PENTHOUSE
Lancaster Publications Ltd, 6 White Horse Street, London W1Y 7LA.
Tel: 07000 740255. Fax: 07000 740256.
Editor: Tom Hilditch.
Sophisticated monthly devoted to erotic photography and the subject of sex.
Illustrations: Mainly colour. Very high-quality erotic photography of all kinds considered, sets or singles, in all formats. Images should be positive, intelligent and not demeaning to women. Some scope for reportage work on sex-based subjects.
Text: Little scope.
Overall freelance potential: Very good for the right material.
Editor's tips: Think about fresh ways of depicting sex and eroticism for grown-ups. This is no longer a typical "top shelf" title.
Fees: Negotiable dependent on what is offered.

Are you working from the latest edition of The Freelance Photographer's Market Handbook? It's published on 1 October each year. Markets are constantly changing, so it pays to have the latest edition

---

Motoring

AUTO EXPRESS
Dennis Publishing, 19 Bolsover Street, London W1P 7HJ
Tel: 0171-631 1433. Fax: 0171-917 5556.
Editor: David Johns. **Picture Editor**: Lewis Durham.
Popular weekly magazine, aimed at the average motorist rather than the car enthusiast.
Illustrations: Colour only. Hard news pictures and topical motoring subjects with impact may be considered on spec, but most is by commission.
Text: Features on any motoring topic, to appeal to a general readership. May be practical but should not be too technical. 1,000–2,000 words. Always submit a synopsis in the first instance.
Overall freelance potential: Limited for the non-specialist.
Editor's tips: Although a popular non-technical title, accuracy is essential.
Fees: Photographs according to size of reproduction. Text usually £200 per 1,000 words.

AUTOCAR
Haymarket Publishing Ltd, 38–42 Hampton Road, Teddington, Middlesex TW11 0JE.
Tel: 0181-943 5013. Fax: 0181-943 5853.
Editor: Patrick Fuller.
High quality general interest motoring weekly. Includes road tests, new car descriptions, international motor sport, motor shows, etc.
Illustrations: B&W and colour. Top quality car coverage, pre-production models under test, performance cars, picture stories, portraits. Mostly by commission.
Text: Illustrated features on motoring subjects. 1,000–2,000 words.
Overall freelance potential: Around 20 per cent of features and pictures come from freelance sources.
Editor's tips: Technical accuracy is essential. Full information on the cars featured must be detailed. Feature, news and photographic ideas welcome.
Fees: Features by negotiation.

THE AUTOMOBILE
Enthusiast Publishing Ltd. Editorial: Spring Cottage, 20 High Street, Milford-on-Sea, Lymington SO41 0QD.
Tel/fax: 01590 645900.
Editor: Brian Heath.
Monthly publication featuring veteran, vintage, and pre-1950s motor vehicles.
Illustrations: Colour. Not much scope for single pictures unless of particular interest. The main requirement is for well-illustrated articles concerning any pre-1950s motor vehicle; not only cars but also commercial vehicles. Also limited room for coverage of race meetings, exhibitions or other events at which old motor vehicles are present.
Text: Informative illustrated articles as above. Of particular interest are good restoration features, with both "before" and "after" pictures showing what can be achieved.
Overall freelance potential: Although limited there is scope for illustrated features – consult the editor before starting on feature.
Editor's tips: There is absolutely no point in submitting material concerning post-1950s vehicles.
Fees: By negotiation.

AUTOMOTIVE MANAGEMENT
Leading Edge Publishing Ltd, 2 Oxted Chambers, 185-187 Station Road East, Oxted, Surrey RH8 0QE.
Tel: 01883 732000. Fax: 01883 730933.
Editor: Tony Willard.
Fortnightly publication for the retail motor trade (both car and commercial vehicle) concentrating on

franchised dealers.
Illustrations: B&W and colour. News photographs covering the motor trade generally. Some scope for commissions to photograph industry figures and premises.
Text: Regional news items and good "grass roots" features about the franchised dealer scene.
Overall freelance potential: Good for those with contacts in the trade and local freelances.
Fees: By negotiation.

CAR AND ACCESSORY TRADER
Haymarket Magazines Ltd, 38-42 Hampton Road, Teddington, Middlesex TW11 0JE.
Tel: 0181-943 5906. Fax: 0181-943 5993.
Editor: Robin Shute.
Monthly magazine for traders involved in the selling of car parts and accessories.
Illustrations: B&W and colour. Captioned news pictures concerning new products, openings of new premises, handover of sales awards, etc. Much is commissioned. Covers: excellent relevant photographs considered.
Text: Varied subjects of interest to the trade, by commission only.
Overall freelance potential: About 50 per cent of contributions are from freelance sources.
Fees: £100 per £1,000 words. Photographs negotiable.

CARS AND CAR CONVERSIONS
Link House Magazines (Croydon) Ltd, Link House, Dingwall Avenue, Croydon CR9 2TA.
Tel: 0181-686 2599. Fax: 0181-781 6042.
Editor: Steve Bennett.
Monthly magazine concentrating on technical matters, performance tuning and motor sport.
Illustrations: B&W and colour. Coverage of motor sport events involving both saloon and sports cars, such as saloon car racing, rallying, etc. Picture stories concerning interesting or unusual car modifications. Covers: good colour action shots.
Text: General or technical articles about high performance cars, modification, and racing. 1,500 words upwards.
Overall freelance potential: Around 20 per cent is contributed by freelances.
Fees: Negotiable.

CLASSIC AMERICAN
Myatt McFarlane plc, Trident House, Heath Road, Hale, Altrincham, Cheshire WA14 2UD.
Tel: 0161-928 3480. Fax: 0161-941 6897.
Editor: Paul Guinness.
Monthly magazine concerning American cars mainly of the '50s, '60s and '70s.
Illustrations: Mainly colour. Striking or unusual pictures of classic US vehicles. However, much of the photography is commissioned from regulars or staff-produced.
Text: Illustrated articles on specific cars or bikes and their owners, plus features on other aspects of American-style youth culture such as clothing, music, sport, etc. 1,000–2,000 words. Always check with the editor before submitting.
Overall freelance potential: Car coverage welcome, but best scope is for lifestyle features.
Fees: Pictures by negotiation. £100 per 1,000 words for text.

CLASSIC AND SPORTSCAR
Haymarket Magazines Ltd, 38-42 Hampton Road, Teddington, Middlesex TW11 0JE.
Tel: 0181-943 5000. Fax: 0181-943 5844.
Editor: Gavin Conway.
Monthly magazine covering mainly post-1945 classic cars, generally of a sporting nature. Strong coverage of the owners scene.
Illustrations: B&W and colour. Mainly interested in coverage of club or historic car gatherings, unless staff photographer is present. Feature photography always commissioned.
Text: Articles of interest to the classic car enthusiast and collector, up to 2,500 words.

Overall freelance potential: Small, as much material is staff produced.
Editor's tips: Always get in touch before submitting.
Fees: According to merit.

CLASSICS
Security Publications Ltd, Berwick House, 8–10 Knoll Rise, Orpington, Kent BR6 0PS.
Tel: 01689 874025. Fax: 01689 876438.
Editor: Andrew Noakes.
Monthly practical magazine for classic car owners.
Illustrations: Colour only. Captioned pictures of newsworthy cars and events, including relevant motorsport coverage, always considered on spec. Also scope for commissions to do photo shoots of featured cars; send samples of previous work in the first instance.
Text: Well-illustrated features about individual cars or events considered on spec.
Overall freelance potential: Good.
Editor's tips: Look at mag carefully before submitting work, particularly the editorial profile and style. Always interested in hearing about cars which might make a good feature subject. Send a sample shot with some details about the car and a commission to shoot may be offered.
Fees: Pictures, £30 per page; commissioned photography, £180 per day.

COMPANY CAR
International Trade Publications Ltd, Queensway House, 2 Queensway, Redhill, Surrey RH1 1QS.
Tel: 01737 768611. Fax: 01737 855462.
Editor: Curtis Hutchinson.
Monthly magazine for companies running in excess of ten cars. Aimed at main board directors and senior executives/managers.
Illustrations: Colour only. Exclusive and newsworthy pictures relating to fleet sales or fleet cars. Covers: topical colour pictures, including new car launches; medium format required.
Text: Features on car management or cost. Exclusive material only. 1,000–1,500 words plus 2/3 pictures.
Overall freelance potential: Most photography supplied by PR sources.
Fees: Negotiable.

DRIVING MAGAZINE
Safety House, Beddington Farm Road, Croydon CR0 4XZ.
Tel: 0181-665 5151. Fax: 0181-665 5565.
Editor: Graham Fryer.
Bi-monthly road safety publication for advanced drivers, road safety educationists and driving instructors.
Illustrations: Colour (prints preferred). Pictures of home or overseas motorists/driving school vehicles in unusual surroundings or circumstances. Humorous incidents, i.e. traffic accidents of an unusual nature, unusual road signs, humorous signs or those in extraordinary positions. Covers: colour.
Text: Features on road safety, driver training occasionally accepted. 500–2,000 words.
Overall freelance potential: Modest.
Fees: Photographs: £10–£15, variable, according to subject and quality.

FLEET NEWS
EMAP Automotive Ltd, Wentworth House, Wentworth Street, Peterborough PE1 1DS.
Tel: 01733 467076. Fax: 01733 467100.
Editor: Ashley Martin.
Weekly newspaper aimed at those responsible for running company car and light commercial vehicle fleets.
Illustrations: Colour. Captioned news pictures concerning company car operations, handover of car fleets to companies, appointments in the trade, etc.
Text: News, articles on business car management and related subjects.

Overall freelance potential: Excellent.
Editor's tips: Always telephone first.
Fees: Negotiable.

INTERNATIONAL OFF-ROADER

Milebrook Ltd, 120 Queens Road, Bury St Edmunds, Suffolk IP33 3ES.
Tel: 01284 752340. Fax: 01284 752343.
Managing Editor: Richard Howell-Thomas.
Monthly magazine for four-wheel-drive enthusiasts.
Illustrations: All colour. Little scope for individual photographs unless accompanied by extended captions or background text.
Text: Well-illustrated articles on all aspects of the four-wheel-drive scene; travel/adventure stories, features on interesting individual vehicles and off-roading personalities, competition and club event reports. Limited scope for vehicle test reports.
Overall freelance potential: Excellent for those who can add words to their pictures.
Fees: By negotiation.

LAND ROVER OWNER

EMAP National Publications plc, Bushfield House, Orton Centre, Peterborough PE2 5UW.
Tel: 01733 237111. Fax: 01733 465876.
Editor: Carl Rodgerson.
Monthly magazine for Land Rover owners and enthusiasts.
Illustrations: B&W and colour. Interesting or unusual pictures of Land Rovers and Range Rovers. Celebrities pictured with such vehicles.
Text: Illustrated articles on overland expeditions using Land Rovers. Length: 1,000 words, plus around six pictures.
Overall freelance potential: Good.
Fees: Text, £100 per 1,000 words; pictures by negotiation.

MOTOR TRADER

Reed Business Publishing, Quadrant House, The Quadrant, Sutton, Surrey SM2 5AS.
Tel: 0181-652 3276. Fax: 0181-652 8962.
Editor: Murdo Morrison.
Weekly trade newspaper, controlled circulation and subscription, read by dealers & manufacturers in the car and component industries, garage owners, body shop workers.
Illustrations: B&W and colour. News pictures on anything connected with the motor trade.
Text: News and features relevant to the motor trade and industry. 300–1,000 words.
Overall freelance potential: Good for those in touch with the trade.
Editor's tips: This is the trade's only weekly newspaper; it is particularly interested in hard news. Call to discuss with editor or deputy before submitting material.
Fees: Negotiable.

MOTORING AND LEISURE

CSMA Ltd, Britannia House, 95 Queens Road, Brighton, East Sussex BN1 3WY.
Tel: 01273 321921. Fax: 01273 323990.
Editor: David Arnold.
Monthly journal of the Civil Service Motoring Association, covering motoring, travel and leisure activities.
Illustrations: Mainly colour. General car-related subjects and Continental travel.
Text: Illustrated articles on motoring, travel, camping and caravanning. 750–1,000 words.
Overall freelance potential: Limited.
Fees: By arrangement.

911 & PORSCHE WORLD
CH Publications Ltd, PO Box 75, Tadworth, Surrey KT20 7XF.
Tel: 01737 814311. Fax: 01737 814591.
Editor: Chris Horton.
Magazine published nine times a year and devoted to Porsche or Porsche-derived cars.
Illustrations: B&W and colour. All commissioned, but good opportunities for those who have original ideas and can produce top quality car photography.
Text: Ideas for articles always of interest; write with details in the first instance.
Overall freelance potential: Very good for specialist coverage.
Fees: Photography by arrangement; around £100 per 1,000 words.

OFF ROAD AND FOUR WHEEL DRIVE
Link House Magazines Ltd, Link House, Dingwall Avenue, Croydon CR9 2TA.
Tel: 0181-686 2599. Fax: 0181-781 6042.
Editor: Bob Cooke.
Monthly magazine devoted to four-wheel-drive vehicles.
Illustrations: Colour. Pictures of new vehicles, travel and other "off road" events. Must be captioned with full details of driver, event, and location.
Text: Illustrated articles concerning four-wheel-drive vehicles and off-road activities. 1,000–2,000 words.
Overall freelance potential: There is room for new contributors.
Fees: By negotiation.

PERFORMANCE FORD
Unity Media Communications Ltd, Stakes House, Quebec Square, Westerham, Kent TN16 1TD.
Tel: 01959 565690. Fax: 01959 564390.
Editor: Greg Emmerson.
Monthly magazine devoted to Ford and Ford-based vehicles, with the emphasis on high-performance road use.
Illustrations: Colour only. Pictures to illustrate features, or topical single pictures of particular quality, i.e. prototypes, one-offs, etc. Medium format transparencies preferred.
Text: Illustrated articles on maintenance and modification of Ford-based cars. Personality profiles with a direct relevance to Ford products.
Overall freelance potential: Fair.
Editor's tips: Always raise ideas with the editor before submitting material.
Fees: Pictures according to size of reproduction; text £120 per 1,000 words.

RALLY SPORT
A&S Publishing, Messenger House, 33-35 St Michael's Square, Gloucester GL1 1HX.
Tel: 01952 825078. Fax: 01952 825001.
Editor: Neil Perkins.
Monthly magazine covering the sport of motor rallying and all matters of interest to rally enthusiasts.
Illustrations: Colour. Pictures of, or connected with, rallying or high-performance road cars. Covers: dramatic colour shots of rallying.
Text: Articles, of varying lengths, about rallying or high-performance cars.
Overall freelance potential: About a third of the magazine is contributed by freelances.
Fees: (Minimum) B&W pictures £7.50; colour £20; covers £50. Articles up to £250 by negotiation.

REVS
EMAP National Publications Ltd, Bushfield House, Orton Centre, Peterborough PE2 0UW.
Tel: 01733 237111. Fax: 01733 465522.
Editor: Jim Blackstock.
Lively monthly aimed at car modification enthusiasts on a budget.

Illustrations: Colour only. Mostly by commission to a tight brief. Happy to hear from photographers who are prepared to experiment with the magazine to produce something different. The odd on-spec shot may be considered if it is absolutely right for the target market.

Text: Always interested in hearing from writers who understand the field and its ethos, and who can produce good entertaining copy.

Overall freelance potential: Very good for those who can produce exciting, top quality work.

Editor's tips: Photographers need to be able to produce exciting action as well as having a good eye for statics and details.

Fees: By negotiation.

SOVEREIGN

Sovereign Magazines Ltd, 45 Blondvil Street, Coventry CV3 5QX.
Tel: 01203 505339. Fax: 01203 503135.
Editor: John Lowe.
Glossy general interest magazine for owners of Jaguar and Daimler cars. Published three times a year.

Illustrations: Colour only. High quality commissoned photography of cars, travel and general lifestyle subjects. Only for experienced workers with medium format equipment.

Text: Strongly-illustrated articles on travel and lifestyle subjects considered on spec, but check with the editor before submitting. Around 1,500 words.

Overall freelance potential: Good for experienced workers, though somewhat limited by the publishing frequency.

Fees: Photography by negotiation. Articles around £300 including pictures.

STREET MACHINE

CH Publications Ltd, PO Box 75, Tadworth, Surrey KT20 7XF.
Tel: 01737 812030. Fax: 01737 814591.
Editor: Richard Nicholls.
Monthly magazine covering custom cars and hot rods based on pre-1975 vehicles, British or American.

Illustrations: Colour only. Newsy and well-captioned single pictures depicting happenings on the UK custom car scene. Other pictures usually as part of a story/picture package on subjects detailed below. Prefers British-sourced material.

Text: Well-illustrated features on completed cars, step-by-step illustrated material on how to do it, track tests of modified cars and coverage of shows and events. Always phone or write first to discuss ideas.

Overall freelance potential: Good for the right sort of material.

Editor's tips: Not interested in front-wheel drive or post-1980 vehicles.

Fees: £20–£50 for news items; text £120 per 1,000 words.

TOP GEAR MAGAZINE

BBC Magazines, Room A1136, Woodlands, 80 Wood Lane, London W12 0TT.
Tel: 0181-576 2000. Fax: 0181-576 3754.
Editor: Kevin Blick. **Art Director**: Marcel Ashby.
General interest motoring magazine designed to complement the BBC TV programme of the same name.

Illustrations: Colour only. Invariably by commission from known specialists, but photographers with a fresh approach and a good portfolio are welcomed.

Text: No scope.

Overall freelance potential: Limited.

Fees: By negotiation.

TRIUMPH WORLD
CH Publications Ltd, PO Box 75, Tadworth, Surrey KT20 7XF.
Tel: 01895 623612. Fax: 01895 623613.
Editor: Tony Beadle.
Alternate-monthly for Triumph car (*not* motorcycle) enthusiasts.
Illustrations: B&W and colour. Photographs of newsworthy or unusual Triumph cars, especially the "classics" such as Heralds, TRs, Spitfires and Stags. Some opportunities for experienced photographers to produce commissioned work for major features.
Text: Illustrated articles likely to appeal to the dedicated enthusiast. Phone first to discuss ideas.
Overall freelance potential: Good.
Fees: Pictures by negotiation and according to use. Text £100 per 1,000 words.

VW MOTORING
Warners Group Holdings plc, The Maltings, West Street, Bourne, Lincs PE10 9PH.
Tel: 01778 391000 ext 2157. Fax: 01778 394748.
Editor: Neil Birkitt.
Monthly magazine for owners and enthusiasts of Volkswagen Audi, new and old, classic and custom, plus coverage of SEAT, Skoda and Porsche.
Illustrations: B&W and colour. Relevant photo features, motorsport photography. Covers: full bleed A4 format of VW Audi vehicles in interesting settings.
Text: Features of interest to VW and Audi enthusiasts, especially DIY, rebuild projects, historical and technical subjects. In-depth knowledge of the subject more important than slick writing style, but must be accompanied by relevant photographic or illustrative material to publication standards.
Overall freelance potential: Mostly use regular contributors, but always open to appropriate material from freelance sources.
Editor's tips: Good quality 35mm 100ASA trans OK for A4 and A3 bleed, crisp 6x4 colour prints OK for detail pics.
Fees: By agreement, on sight of material.

Music

BLUES AND SOUL
Blues & Soul Ltd, 153 Praed Street, London W2 1RL.
Tel: 0171-402 6869. Fax: 0171-224 8227.
Editor: Bob Kilbourn.
Fortnightly publication devoted to soul, R&B, funk, fusion, jazz, Afro, Soca, Salsa, Latin, dance/electro. All forms of black music *excepting* reggae.
Illustrations: Mostly B&W; colour used on front and back covers and centre spread. Original and exclusive pictures of black music performers.
Text: Small amount of scope for exclusive articles or interviews.
Overall freelance potential: Limited.
Editor's tips: Think of the readership, and the format, in order to produce something really striking and eye-catching.
Fees: By negotiation.

CIPHER
Cipher Publishing, 184 Bridgewater Road, Alperton, Middlesex HA0 1AR.
Tel: 0181-903 6530. Fax: 0181-795 0502.
Editor: Joan L Smith.
Alternate-monthly "survivors' guide" aimed at helping young people who aspire to enter the music business. Focuses on black popular music, from dance through rap to jazz.
Illustrations: Some colour, but a strong emphasis on black and white photography. Original por-

traits of artists and personalities in black music and reportage covering urban/street life.
Text: Articles on black music and urban culture always considered. Prefer to hear from experienced writers who can supply cuttings of previous work.
Overall freelance potential: Provides a good showcase for up-and-coming photographers.
Editor's tips: Fresh ideas are encouraged.
Fees: By negotiation.

CLASSIC CD
Future Publishing Ltd, Beauford Court, Monmouth Street, Bath BA1 2BW.
Tel: 01225 442244. Fax: 01255 732396.
Editor: Neil Evans. **Art Editor**: David Eachus.
Monthly classical music magazine with large review section.
Illustrations: Mostly colour. Good classical music images, especially of contemporary composers and performers. Stock material always considered; commissions available to experienced workers. Send a few samples initially, or make an appointment to show portfolio.
Text: No scope.
Overall freelance potential: Good for those with an original approach.
Editor's tips: We seek photographers who can supply a more personal touch than found in run-of-the-mill library images; photographers who have a major interest in the subject and can thus get closer to the artist.
Fees: Standard reproductions £30–£90 depending on size. Day rate £250–£350 depending on circumstances of the shoot; half-day £150.

CLASSICAL MUSIC
Rhinegold Publishing Ltd, 241 Shaftesbury Avenue, London WC2H 8EH.
Tel: 0171-333 1742. Fax: 0171-333 1769.
Editor: Keith Clarke. **Art Editor**: Sarah Davies.
Fortnightly news and feature magazine for classical music professionals and the interested general public.
Illustrations: B&W only. Very limited scope as most pictures are supplied by record companies, promoters, etc, but always happy to look at portfolios, subject to appointment. Occasional urgent need for a musician or group in the news – most easily met if freelances can supply lists of photographs they hold.
Text: Short news items and news stories about events in the music/arts world, including politics and performance, up to 800 words. Longer background features about musicians, usually relating to a forthcoming event, up to 1,500 words. All work is commissioned.
Overall freelance potential: Limited for photographers, but some 65 per cent of text is from commissioned freelance sources.
Fees: Pictures by negotiation; text from £85 per 1,000 words.

ECHOES
Black Echoes Ltd, 7/9 Charlotte Street, London W1 1HD.
Tel: 0171-323 0178. Fax: 0171-436 4573.
Editor: Chris Wells.
Weekly publication devoted to all aspects of black popular music.
Illustrations: Mostly colour. Outstanding photographs of popular black music performers, for immediate publication or for file.
Text: Little scope.
Overall freelance potential: Fair.
Fees: By negotiation.

ETERNITY
Eternity Management Ltd, PO Box 156, Robin Hood, Wakefield, West Yorks WF1 5YY.
Tel: 01924 291670. Fax: 01924 291671.
Editor: Paul Boote.

Monthly magazine devoted to dance music and youth culture.
Illustrations: Mainly colour; B&W considered. Always interested in DJ and artist/band shots in the contemporary dance music field. Also crowd and event shots at specific venues, usually by prior arrangement. Send samples of work initially.
Text: Features on dance music and any topic that concerns the youth of today; always open to ideas.
Overall freelance potential: Growing.
Fees: By agreement, but commissions around £50–£100; articles £50 plus expenses.

FOLK ROOTS
Southern Rag Ltd, PO Box 337, London N4 1TW.
Tel: 0181-340 9651. Fax: 0181-348 5626.
Editor: Ian Anderson.
Monthly publication concerned with folk music.
Illustrations: B&W only. Pictures to be used in conjunction with interviews, reviews of records or reports on events. Mostly commissioned. Covers: colour pictures of artists covered editorially.
Text: Interviews and reviews concerned with folk music.
Overall freelance potential: Very small for the contributor unknown in this field. The magazine favours its regular contributors.
Fees: By agreement.

FUTURE MUSIC
Future Publishing Ltd, Beauford Court, 30 Monmouth Street, Bath BA1 2BW.
Tel: 01225 442244. Fax: 01225 732353.
Editor: Andrew Jones. **Art Editor**: Katie Taylor.
Monthly magazine covering developments in modern music technology, aimed at both amateur and professional musicians.
Illustrations: B&W and colour. Opportunities for commissions to cover trade shows, studio profiles, etc.
Text: Articles from writers who are fully familiar with the technology and can write in an entertaining and informative manner. Always query the editor in the first instance.
Overall freelance potential: Limited.
Fees: Photography negotiable. Text £80 per 1,000 words.

KERRANG!
EMAP Metro Ltd, Mappin House, 4 Winsley Street, London W1N 7AR.
Tel: 0171-436 1515. Fax: 0171-312 8910.
Editor: Phil Alexander.
Weekly magazine covering a wide range of hard rock.
Illustrations: Mainly colour. Pictures of relevant bands. On-stage performance shots preferred, with the emphasis on action. Some posed shots and portraits of top performers also used.
Text: Little freelance market.
Overall freelance potential: Very good. The magazine is heavily illustrated.
Fees: According to size of reproduction.

KEYBOARD PLAYER
Bookrose Ltd, 27 Russell Road, Enfield, Middlesex EN1 4TN.
Tel: 0181-367 2938. Fax: 0181-367 2359.
Editor: Steve Miller.
Monthly magazine for players of all types of keyboard instrument. Covers pianos, organs, keyboards and synthesisers; and all forms of music, from pop to classical.
Illustrations: Mainly B&W; some colour. Photographs of keyboard instruments and their players, preferably accompanied by a newsy caption. Covers: striking colour pictures of keyboard instruments.
Text: Articles of around 1,000 words on any topic of interest to keyboard players.
Overall freelance potential: Fairly limited, but scope is there for the right type of material.

Editor's tips: Run-of-the-mill pictures of players seated at their instruments will not be met with much enthusiasm – a strikingly different approach is required.
Fees: By negotiation.

MELODY MAKER
IPC Magazines Ltd, 26th Floor, King's Reach Tower, Stamford Street, London SE1 9LS.
Tel: 0171-261 6229. Fax: 0171-261 6706.
Editor: Mark Sutherland. **Picture Editor**: Maria Jeffries.
Weekly music paper for the 15–24 age group.
Illustrations: B&W and colour. Contemporary rock music subjects.
Text: Features, news and reviews relevant to pop and rock music. Around 300 words.
Overall freelance potential: Occasional use of outside contributors, but mostly staff-produced.
Fees: Pictures from £21.78, according to size of reproduction. Text £94.74 per 1,000 words.

METAL HAMMER
Dennis Publishing Ltd, 19 Bolsover Street, London W1P 7HJ.
Tel: 0171-631 1433. Fax: 0171-917 7655.
Editor: Robyn Doreian.
Monthly for heavy metal and hard rock fans.
Illustrations: Mostly colour. Good action and group portrait photographs of hard rock or heavy metal performers – send lists of subjects available. Commissions available to experienced rock photographers.
Text: Illustrated articles, interviews and reviews. Submit suggestions only in the first instance.
Overall freelance potential: Excellent for those in touch with this scene.
Fees: By negotiation.

MOJO
EMAP Metro Ltd, Mappin House, 4 Winsley Street, London W1N 1AR.
Tel: 0171-436 1515. Fax: 0171-312 8296.
Editor: Mat Snow. **Picture Editor**: Susie Hudson.
Monthly rock music magazine aimed at the older fan.
Illustrations: B&W and colour. Photographs of leading rock artists, both contemporary and from earlier eras. Archive material from the '50s, '60s and '70s always of interest. Limited scope for commissioned work.
Text: In-depth profiles of individual artists and bands, but scope mainly for established writers.
Overall freelance potential: Good for archive material.
Editor's tips: Previously unpublished photographs, or those that have not been used for some years, are of particular interest.
Fees: According to use.

MUZIK
IPC Magazines Ltd, King's Reach Tower, Stamford Street, London SE1 9LS.
Tel: 0171-261 5993. Fax: 0171-261 7100.
Editor: Push. **Art Editor**: Brett Lewis.
Monthly covering the contemporary dance music scene and club culture.
Illustrations: Mostly colour. Visually exciting photographs of the dance and club scene always considered. Commissions also available; contact art editor to show portfolio.
Text: Mostly staff-produced.
Overall freelance potential: Very good for photographers in touch with the scene. New talent is encouraged.
Editor's tips: Always keen to see an exciting and original approach.
Fees: By negotiation, but similar to other IPC music titles.

NEW MUSICAL EXPRESS
IPC Magazines Ltd, 25th Floor, King's Reach Tower, Stamford Street, London SE1 9LS.
Tel: 0171-261 6472. Fax: 0171-261 5185.
Editor: Steve Sutherland. **Art Editor**: Marc Pechart.
Weekly tabloid covering all aspects of popular music and allied youth culture.
Illustrations: B&W and colour. All aspects of contemporary popular music, but see below.
Text: Scope for exclusive news stories or interviews with rock musicians, film stars, or other personalities of interest to a young and aware readership. Always write or phone with suggestions first.
Overall freelance potential: Good, but very dependent on subject matter.
Editor's tips: NME only covers those parts of the music scene considered worthwhile by the editorial team – study recent issues.
Fees: On a rising scale according to size of reproduction.

Q
EMAP Metro Ltd, Mappin House, 4 Winsley Street, London W1N 7AR.
Tel: 0171-436 1515. Fax: 0171-312 8247.
Editor: David Davies. **Picture Editor**: Kimberley Kriete.
Monthly rock music magazine aimed at the 18–35 age group.
Illustrations: B&W and colour. Most pictures staff-produced or commissioned from a pool of regular contributors, but suitable stock pictures of relevant personalities will always be considered.
Text: Top quality profiles, interviews and feature articles of interest to a rock-oriented readership, invariably by commission.
Overall freelance potential: Very limited for commissions; good for library/stock shots.
Fees: By negotiation.

RHYTHM
Future Publishing Ltd, Beauford Court, 30 Monmouth Street, Bath BA1 2BW.
Tel: 01225 442244. Fax: 01225 446019.
Editor: Ronan Macdonald.
Monthly magazine for drummers and percussionists in the rock and pop music field.
Illustrations: B&W and colour. Interesting photographs relating to contemporary percussion instruments and their players, including the use of electronic and computer-aided equipment.
Text: Illustrated profiles, interviews and features about leading contemporary drummers and percussionists. Articles on technique and programming from knowledgeable contributors.
Overall freelance potential: Limited.
Fees: £75 per 1,000 words for text; photographs according to use.

SELECT
EMAP Metro Ltd, Mappin House, 4 Winsley Street, London W1N 5AR.
Tel: 0171-436 1515. Fax: 0171-312 8250.
Editor: John Harris. **Picture Editor**: Claire Blake.
Monthly youth music magazine covering the rock, dance and indie scenes.
Illustrations: B&W and colour. Good photographs of current bands and performers, preferably with a strong "creative" edge. Commissions available for the more experienced worker.
Text: Limited freelance scope, but ideas always considered.
Overall freelance potential: Good.
Fees: Pictures according to use.

SMASH HITS
EMAP Metro Ltd, 2nd Floor, Mappin House, 4 Winsley Street, London W1N 7AR.
Tel: 0171-436 1515. Fax: 0171-636 5792.
Editor: Gavin Reeve. **Picture Editor**: Sue Miles.
Fortnightly popular music magazine aimed at 11–19 year olds.
Illustrations: Some B&W; mostly colour. Posed, pin-up style photographs of performers who current-

ly have a record in the charts, usually studio shots. Faces should be clearly shown. Covers: usually commissioned.
Overall freelance potential: Very good for photographers in touch with the current pop music scene.
Fees: £40 upwards for any picture. £110-£150 for full page. Covers: £400 upwards.

TOP OF THE POPS
BBC Worldwide Ltd, Woodlands, 80 Wood Lane, London W12 0TT.
Tel: 0181-576 3025. Fax: 0181-576 3267.
Editor: Peter Lorraine. **Art Editor**: Simeon Jenices. **Picture Editor**: Jane Channon.
Monthly pop music magazine linked to the BBC TV programme of the same name.
Illustrations: Colour only. Good opportunities for portraiture and performance coverage, invariably by commission. Exclusive news pictures or picture stories considered on spec.
Text: Little scope, though exclusive stories/interviews always of interest.
Overall freelance potential: Good for the experienced contributor, but new talent also encouraged.
Fees: By negotiation.

TOTAL GUITAR
Future Publishing Ltd, Beauford House, Monmouth Street, Bath BA1 2BW.
Tel: 01225 442244. Fax: 01225 732285.
Editor: Tim Tucker. **Art Editor**: Ian Miller.
Monthly magazine for guitar players at all levels, concentrating on practical advice.
Illustrations: Mainly colour. Mostly commissioned to accompany features and reviews. Stock shots of well-known players and individual instruments always of interest; send lists first.
Text: Profiles and interviews with leading guitarists, and practical articles. Submit ideas only in the first instance.
Overall freelance potential: Limited.
Fees: By negotiation.

TRACE
Still True Ltd, 65 Clerkenwell Road, London EC1R 5BH.
Tel: 0171-831 5006. Fax: 0171-831 5007.
Editor: Claude Grunitzky. **Art Director**: Graham Roundthwaite.
Urban style magazine focusing on black music and culture.
Illustrations: B&W and colour. Music, fashion, and some reportage. Mostly by commission. Write to the art director in the first instance enclosing samples of work.
Text: Stylish and serious features on black music and youth culture, especially anything with an international perspective. Submit ideas to the editor in the first instance.
Overall freelance potential: Very good for those involved in black culture and offering an original approach.
Editor's tips: Study the magazine for style pointers before submitting.
Fees: By negotiation.

VOX
IPC Magazines Ltd, King's Reach Tower, Stamford Street, London SE1 9LS.
Tel: 0171-261 6312. Fax: 0171-261 5627.
Editor: Everett True. **Art Editor**: Marc Pechart.
Monthly magazine for adult rock fans in the 20–30 age group.
Illustrations: Mainly colour. Scope for experienced music photographers to undertake commissions. Few openings for speculative work unless of an exclusive and highly original nature.
Text: Mainly staff-produced but some scope for established music press contributors.
Overall freelance potential: Good for specialists.
Fees: By negotiation.

Parenting

BABYCARE & PREGNANCY
D.C.Thomson & Co Ltd, 80 Kingsway East, Dundee DD4 8SL.
Tel: 01382 223131. Fax: 01382 225511.
Editor: Irene Duncan.
Monthly magazine for "the modern mum". Covers pregnancy, birth and childcare up to two years of age.
Illustrations: B&W and (mainly) colour. Situation pictures, mother and baby shots, atmosphere work as well as more practical pictures. Commissions available for experienced workers; submit samples of previously published work first.
Text: Illustrated articles on practical health and childcare subjects, and on motherhood in its own right. Up to 2,000 words.
Overall freelance potential: Excellent for high quality material.
Editor's tips: Situation pictures are much more useful than simple "mother and baby" shots. Writing style should be down-to-earth and broken into short sentences and paras.
Fees: By negotiation.

FUN FOR KIDS
DMG Home Interest Magazines Ltd, Times House, Station Approach, Ruislip, Middlesex HA4 8NB.
Tel: 01895 677677. Fax: 01885 676027.
Editor: Julia Sugdon. **Art Editor**: Gary Batchelor.
Alternate-monthly for parents with children in the 4–12 age group, providing features and listings to help them make the most of their leisure time.
Illustrations: Colour. Some opportunities for commissioned work to illustrate features on such subjects as education, travel, health, food and home interests. Also high quality, stock "family" images. Covers: top quality pictures of family groups, usually the "ideal" standard image of mum, dad and two kids though any combination of at least two family members (including a child) will be considered. Subjects must look healthy and happy and children must be within the age range specified above.
Text: Illustrated features on topics as above. Ideas and suggestions always welcomed.
Overall freelance potential: Quite good.
Editor's tips: Remember the emphasis is always on enjoyable family activity.
Fees: By negotiation.

MOTHER & BABY
EMAP Elan Ltd, Endeavour House, 189 Shafestbury Avenue, London WC2H 8JG.
Tel: 0171-437 9011. Fax: 0171-434 0656.
Editor: Sharon Parsons. **Art Director**: Natalie Williams.
Monthly aimed at pregnant women and mothers of young children.
Illustrations: Mostly colour. High quality photographs of mothers with babies, or babies (under one year) on their own. Medium format preferred.
Text: Articles on all subjects related to pregnancy, birth, baby care and the early years.
Overall freelance potential: Limited, since the magazine is frequently overstocked.
Editor's tips: Only top quality pictures will be considered.
Fees: From £30 upwards for single pictures.

NURSERY WORLD
Fifth Floor, Lector Court, 151-153 Farrindon Road, London EC1R 3AD.
Tel: 0171-278 7441. Fax: 0171-278 3896.
Editor: Liz Roberts. **Art Director**: Tim Noonan.
Weekly publication on child care. Aimed at professional baby and child care workers such as teachers, nursery nurses and nannies.
Illustrations: B&W and colour. Pictures of babies and young children (up to 5 years old) involved in various activities, also photographs of babies in general. Covers: colour pictures of nursery workers,

children in work situations, playing outside, etc.
Text: Features on child care, education, health, and any aspect of bringing up children, e.g. physical, intellectual, emotional etc. Ideas for nurseries and playgroups.
Overall freelance potential: Many features come from freelance contributors.
Editor's tips: Material must have authority.
Fees: By arrangement.

OUR BABY

IPC Magazines Ltd, King's Reach Tower, Stamford Street, London SE1 9LS.
Tel: 0171-261 5238. Fax: 0171-261 6542.
Editor: Jayne Marsden. **Art Editor**: Richard Gadsby.
Practical monthly concerned with pregnancy, health, and child development up to 1 year old.
Illustrations: Colour only. Mostly by commission to illustrate specific features. Covers: Possible scope, but these are normally shot in-house. 6x6cm for cover. Ideally baby that is 3-4 months old, looking to camera and very, very cute.
Text: No freelance scope.
Overall freelance potential: Plenty of scope for experienced photographers who can shoot good stock material.
Fees: Around £250 – £300 per shoot; extra for cover material.

PARENTS

EMAP Elan Ltd, Endeavour House, 189 Shafestbury Avenue, London WC2H 8JG.
Tel: 0171-437 9011. Fax: 0171-434 0656.
Editor: Ruth Beaty. **Art Director**: Naomi Lowe.
Monthly magazine for parents with children up to around 6 years old. Covers pregnancy, birth, babies, children, health, education, schools, child development, food, relationships, nutrition, medicine and fashion.
Illustrations: Mainly colour. Mostly used as illustrations for features on above topics.
Text: Features on the above subjects.
Overall freelance potential: Approximately 75 per cent of the magazine is commissioned from outside.
Fees: £65 per half-page, £90 per page. Covers £200.

RIGHT START

Needmarsh Publishing Ltd, 71 Newcomen Street, London SE1 1YT.
Tel: 0171-403 0840. Fax: 0171-378 6883.
Editor: Lynette Lowthian. **Art Editor**: Carolyne Sibley.
Alternate-monthly magazine for parents of pre-school and primary school age children, covering health, behaviour and education.
Illustrations: B&W and colour. Mostly by commission. Some scope for good stock coverage of children in educational and learning situations; send only lists or details of coverage available in the first instance.
Text: Opportunities for education and child care specialists. Approach with details of ideas and previous experience.
Overall freelance potential: Limited.
Fees: By negotiation.

YOU & YOUR BABY

Baby Publications Ltd, Windsor House, Station Court, Station Road, Great Shelford, Cambridge CB2 5LR.
Tel: 01223 846696. Fax: 01223 841491.
Editor: Alison Mackonochie. **Art Editor**: Alan Edwards.
Quarterly guide to "pregnancy, birth and your baby".
Illustrations: Colour only. Bright, clear photographs of mothers and babies, preferably illustrating

some specific aspect of birth or baby care, e.g. breast feeding, exercising, playing, etc.
Text: Illustrated articles always considered, written with the first-time parent in mind. Always contact the editor with suggestions in the first instance.
Overall freelance potential: Good, though limited by the magazine's frequency.
Editor's tips: Ensure that pictures are not too obviously posed.
Fees: Photographs by negotiation. Text £100 per 1,000 words.

Photography & Video

AMATEUR PHOTOGRAPHER
IPC Specialist Group, King's Reach Tower, Stamford Street, London SE1 9LS.
Tel: 0171-261 5100. Fax: 0171-261 5404.
Editor: Keith Wilson.
Weekly magazine for all photographers, from beginners to experienced enthusiasts.
Illustrations: B&W and colour. Pictures to illustrate specific photo techniques and general photo features. Series ideas welcomed. General portfolios in B&W and colour. Send no more than 20 pictures, prints unmounted, slides in a plastic slide wallet. No glass mounts. Covers: upright colour and black & white pictures, various strong subjects. Sometimes linked with portfolio inside. Always leave space for logo and coverlines.
Text: Technique articles on all types of photography. Picture captions on a separate sheet. 1,000–1,500 words.
Overall freelance potential: Good. Around half of photography comes from freelance sources.
Fees: £100 per full page colour and pro rata; £100 per page black and white. Covers £120–£150. Text: £90 per 1,000 words.

AUDIO VISUAL
EMAP Media Ltd, 33-39 Bowling Green Lane, London EC1R 0DA.
Tel: 0171-505 8190. Fax: 0171-505 8198.
Editor: Peter Lloyd.
Monthly magazine for managers in industry and commerce, public services, government etc who use audi-visual communication techniques, eg slides, film, video, overhead projection and filmstrips, plus the new technologies of computer graphics and telecommunication.
Illustrations: B&W and colour. Pictures of programmes being shown to audiences, preferably supported by case history details; relevant news; new products or location shooting pictures. All must be backed with solid information. Covers: colour pictures of same, but check before submitting.
Text: Case histories of either shows, conferences or studies of a particular company's use of AV techniques. Good location/conference stories always welcome. 1,000–2,500 words.
Overall freelance potential: Up to 25 per cent comes from freelances.
Fees: Text, £150-£160 per 1,000 words; pictures by agreement.

THE BRITISH JOURNAL OF PHOTOGRAPHY
Timothy Benn Publishing, 39 Earlham Street, London WC1H 9LD.
Tel: 0171-306 7000. Fax: 0171-306 7017.
Editor: Reuel Golden.
Weekly publication for professional and semi-professional photographers, technicians, etc., and all those engaged in professional photography.
Illustrations: B&W and colour. Portfolios along with some biographical notes about the photographer concerned.
Text: Interested in anything related to professional photography, particularly the more unusual aspects.
Overall freelance potential: Good for bringing freelances to the attention of potential clients.

Editor's tips: Remember the magazine is aimed at those engaged in professional and semi-professional photography, and does not use the type of how-to-do-it material used in magazines aimed at amateur photographers.

Fees: Portfolios not normally paid for; exposure in the magazine frequently leads to commissions elsewhere. Negotiable for text.

BUYING CAMERAS

EMAP Apex Publications Ltd, Apex House, Oundle Road, Peterborough PE2 9NP.
Tel: 01733 898100. Fax: 01733 894472.
Editor: Peter Bargh.
Monthly magazine aimed at the photographic equipment buyer.
Illustrations: Mainly colour. Photographs to illustrate equipment-based features, showing applications of equipment, i.e. illustrating the difference between focal lengths of a zoom lens, before and after effects of filters, portraits using different focal length lenses, etc. Write first with details of suitable images which are available or which you are prepared to shoot at short notice.
Text: Informative features on the use and choice of photographic equipment, ideally with a fresh approach. Write first with an outline of ideas and with examples of previously published work.
Overall freelance potential: Good.
Editor's tips: Always write first, please don't phone.
Fees: Pictures from £10–£30; text £100 per 1,000 words.

CAMCORDER USER

WV Publications, 57–59 Rochester Place, London NW1 9JU.
Tel: 0171-331 1000. Fax: 0171-331 1242.
Editor: Christine Morgan. **Art Editor**: Marlon Richards.
Monthly magazine for buyers and users of camcorders, with a practical bias.
Illustrations: B&W and colour. General shots of camcorders in use, shots to illustrate technique and advice features. Good colour pictures of camcorders in use at various locations especially welcomed, e.g. on the beach, at sports events, at social occasions, on expeditions. Also pictures of editing and post-production equipment in use. Spectacular location shots may also be considered.
Text: Technique articless on producing better video movies, tests on machines and accessories, action and application features, equipment reviews and personality interviews.
Overall freelance potential: Excellent. Around 50 per cent from such sources.
Fees: By agreement.

DARKROOM USER

Foto Format Publications, PO Box 4, Machynlleth, Powys SY20 8WB.
Tel: 01654 703752.
Editor: Ed Buziak.
Specialist bi-monthly with a high technical content, covering all aspects of darkroom work.
Illustrations: Mostly B&W, some colour. Little scope for single photographs, but portfolios are considered. Will consider high-quality work, on any subject except glamour, that shows evidence of printing techniques and style. Pictures should be accompanied by extended captions explaining the techniques used.
Text: Well-researched articles that illustrate a darkroom process or a specialised photographic tech-

nique that depends on access to a darkroom. Must be accompanied by a full set of pictures illustrating the techique or process concerned. 2,500–4,500 words. Send an outline first.
Overall freelance potential: Good for the specialist, though much is contributed by regulars.
Editor's tips: Always study the magazine first; contributor's guidelines available on request.
Fees: Based on £50 per published page. Annual print competition offers £2,500 in prize money.

EOS MAGAZINE
Robert Scott Associates, The Old Barn, Ball Lane, Tackley, Kidlington, Oxon OX5 3AG.
Tel: 01869 331741. Fax: 01869 331641.
Editor: Philip Raby.
Quarterly magazine for users of Canon EOS cameras.
Illustrations: Mostly colour, but B&W considered. Top quality photographs of any subject taken with Canon SLR cameras. Should demonstrate some aspect of photographic technique or the use of equipment. Comparision shots always of interest.
Text: Contributions are welcomed.
Overall freelance potential: Very good.
Editor's tips: Up-to-date details of photo requirements available on request. Phone to discuss ideas for written contributions.
Fees: Text: £90–£150 per 1,000 words (higher rates are for technique material which is comprehensive and well researched). Minimum fee for pictures is £10, but most are paid at between £15 and £50 depending on usage. Cover and dps, £100.

PHOTO ANSWERS
EMAP Apex Publications Ltd, Apex House, Oundle Road, Peterborough PE2 9NP.
Tel: 01733 898100. Fax: 01733 894472.
Editor: Roger Payne.
Monthly photographic magazine with the emphasis on practical information presented in an informal style.
Illustrations: Mainly colour. Good quality photographs, slide or print, of any subject. Comparison pictures and technique pictures to illustrate specific "answers" and step-by-step features. Readers' pictures particularly welcome.
Text: Suggestions always welcome; submit a synopsis first highlighting the main points of the article and including an introductory paragraph.
Overall freelance potential: Excellent.
Editor's tips: Always supply informative captions and full technical details about how a picture was taken, and include suggestions as to how you see the pictures being used. Study a recent issue first.
Fees: From £20–£100 (full page).

PHOTO TECHNIQUE
IPC Magazines Ltd, King's Reach Tower, Stamford Street, London SE1 9LS.
Tel: 0171-261 5100. Fax: 0171-261 5404.
Editor: Liz Walker.
Monthly magazine with emphasis on techniques for taking better pictures.
Illustrations: Some B&W, mostly colour. Top quality landscape, wildlife and portrait photographs, some sport, plus brief captions explaining how photograph was taken including lens and exposure details. Demonstrations of good studio lighting and darkroom work accepted, technique sequences and sets of comparison pictures very welcome. Seasonal material preferred.
Text: Illustrated photo technique and step-by-step features.
Overall freelance potential: Excellent; more editorial pages than any other photo magazine.
Editor's tips: We don't just want to see the picture that succeeded; we want to see the others taken at the same time that didn't quite work. Restrict submissions to 20 transparencies/prints max, and nothing larger than 10x8in.
Fees: From £15 minimum to £90 (full page), £180 (full DPS). Covers: £150. Text £90 per 1,000 words. Word and picture packages £200–£250.

THE PHOTOGRAPHER

British Institute of Professional Photography. Editorial: PO Box 369, Peterborough, Cambs PE3 6EG.
Tel: 01733 343093. Fax: 01733 352513.
Editor: Steve Bavister.
Monthly official journal of the BIPP. Aimed at professional photographers in general practice.
Illustrations: B&W and colour. Photographs only required in conjunction with features as below.
Text: Photo-feature material describing specific professional techniques. Also interviews and profiles concerning individual BIPP members or companies with BIPP connections. Around 1,600 words.
Overall freelance potential: Only for material of genuine interest to the practising professional.
Editor's tips: There is definitely no scope here for amateur photo press type material (e.g. travel features), no matter how good the photographs.
Fees: Negotiable, but budget is limited.

PHOTON

Icon Publications Ltd, Maxwell Lane, Kelso, Roxburghshire TD5 7BB.
Tel: 01573 226032. Fax: 01573 26000.
Editor: David Kilpatrick.
Monthly magazine for all involved in professional, semi-professional or creative photography.
Illustrations: B&W and colour. Mostly required to accompany and illustrate specific articles. Limited scope for outstanding single pictures and portfolios. Covers: exceptional and striking images preferably with strong eye contact. 5x4in preferred.
Text: Articles and features on all aspects of serious amateur and professional photography.
Overall freelance potential: Most of the content is freelance produced.
Editor's tips: Always make contact before submitting.
Fees: Features £60 per page. Covers: £75.

PRACTICAL PHOTOGRAPHY

EMAP Apex Publications Ltd, Apex House, Oundle Road, Peterborough PE2 9NP.
Tel: 01733 898100. Fax: 01733 894472.
Editor: Martyn Moore.
Monthly magazine offering practical information to amateur photographers, plus news, interviews, equipment tests and general interest items on related topics.
Illustrations: B&W and colour. Pictures on any subject considered for the magazine's files – any shots showing some aspect of photographic technique. Colour and black & white portfolios are used regularly. Covers: glamour, fashion or female portraits in colour. 35mm acceptable, but medium format preferred.
Text: Any feature on a practical aspect of photography will be considered, although most basic techniques are covered by staff writers. Contact with ideas only in the first instance.
Overall freelance potential: Relatively little scope for written material, but many published pictures are from freelances.
Fees: From a minimum of £10 per picture and at least £80 per 1,000 words. Negotiable for outstanding material.

PROFESSIONAL PHOTOGRAPHER

Market Link Publishing, PO Box 78, Saffron Walden, Essex CB11 4YR.
Tel: 01799 544248. Fax: 01799 544205.
Editor: Steve Hynes.
Monthly magazine for professional photographers.
Illustrations: B&W and colour. Only with features as below.
Text: Techniques, equipment, business skills and general issues of interest to professional photographers. Chech with the editor before submitting.

Overall freelance potential: Good – for the right material appropriately written.
Editor's tips: The magazine appeals to readers who find other magazines too superficial. It is therefore more important than ever that potential contributors study recent issues.
Fees: From £75 per page, for both words and pictures.

WHAT DIGITAL CAMERA
Top Events and Publications Ltd, 43 Strutton Ground, London SW1P 2HY.
Tel: 0171-799 1442. Fax: 0171-976 0435.
Editor: Simon Joinson.
Alternate-monthly consumer magazine for newcomers to digital photography.
Illustrations: Mostly colour. Will consider original, creative, digital images, preferably digitally originated rather than manipulations from conventional film.
Text: Illustrated features about the techniques and applications of digital cameras, especially the use of the technology in work contexts.
Overall freelance potential: Fair.
Fees: Pictures by negotiation and according to use. Text £100 per 1,000 words.

WHAT VIDEO & TV
WV Publications Ltd, 57–59 Rochester Place, London NW1 9JU.
Tel: 0171-331 1000. Fax: 0171-331 1242.
Editor: Kulwinder Singh Rai.
Monthly video magazine for newcomers and enthusiasts. Contains test reports, buyers' guide, general features and news of new films on video and laserdisc.
Illustrations: B&W and colour. Pictures of video recorders, TVs, cameras and "ordinary people" using them. Covers: colour pictures of similar.
Text: Technical subjects easily explained, plus interviews and showbusiness pieces – stars with interest in video photography. 850–1,000 words.
Overall freelance potential: Around 70 per cent is from freelance sources.
Fees: By agreement.

WIDESCREEN INTERNATIONAL
The Widescreen Centre, 48 Dorset Street, London W1H 3FH.
Tel: 0171-935 2580. Fax: 0171-486 1272.
Editor: Tony Shapps.
Quarterly publication for audio-visual and cine photography with a bias towards all forms of panoramic presentation and three-dimensional photography.
Illustrations: B&W only. Pictures relating to audio-visual, panoramic and three-dimensional photography.
Text: Features on audio-visual subjects, CinemaScope, widescreen filming and prints, plus other sound subjects.
Overall freelance potential: Most of the contents comes from freelances.
Fees: By agreement.

THE WILDLIFE PHOTOGRAPHER
Aquila Photographics, PO Box 1, Studley, Warwickshire B80 7AN.
Tel: 01527 852357. Fax: 01527 857507.
Editor: Mike Wilkes.
Quarterly magazine devoted to wildlife photography.
Illustrations: Mainly colour. Top quality wildlife photography always considered, single pictures or portfolios. Accurate and detailed captions essential.
Text: Illustrated articles on specific aspects of wildlife photography, including hints and tips on techniques used. Also photographers' personal experiences in the field.
Overall freelance potential: Very good, though limited by publication frequency.
Fees: Negotiable and dependent on subject matter.

Politics & Current Affairs

THE ECONOMIST
The Economist Newspaper Ltd, 25 St James's Street, London SW1A 1HG.
Tel: 0171-830 7000. Fax: 0171-839 2968.
Editor: Bill Emmott. **Picture Editor**: Celina Dunlop.
Weekly publication covering world political, business and scientific affairs.
Illustrations: B&W only inside. Pictures of politicians, businessmen, social conditions (housing, health service, etc), major industries (coal, steel, oil, motor, agriculture, etc). Always prepared to keep pictures for stock. Covers: colour pictures of a topical and political nature.
Text: All staff-produced.
Overall freelance potential: Only for serious and experienced photojournalists.
Editor's tips: Telephone picture editor in the first instance.
Fees: On a rising scale according to size of reproduction inside. No commissioning.

THE EUROPEAN
200 Gray's Inn Road, London WC1X 8NE.
Tel: 0171-418 7777. Fax: 0171-713 1840.
Editor-in-Chief: Andrew Neil. **Picture Editor**: Jeannette Downing.
Weekly current affairs and business magazine covering the pan-European scene.
Illustrations: B&W and colour. Major news pictures, plus stock shots illustrating contemporary issues and personalities in the worlds of European business, politics, the arts and sport.
Text: Little scope other than for experienced specialists.
Overall freelance potential: Limited; most is sourced from agencies.
Fees: According to use.

GPMU JOURNAL
Graphical, Paper & Media Union, Keys House, 63–67 Bromham Road, Bedford MK40 2AG.
Tel: 01234 351521. Fax: 01234 270580.
Editor: Tony Dubbins.
Published ten times per year for members of the union. Gives information on union policies and activities, political and social issues plus personalities and sports news.
Illustrations: Colour. Pictures involving the trade union and labour movement, printing and paper-making industries, plus some general pictures, i.e. sport, personalities, travel, etc.
Text: Features on subjects mentioned above. 300–500 words.
Overall freelance potential: Limited.
Fees: By agreement.

JANE'S DEFENCE WEEKLY
Jane's Information Group, Sentinel House, 163 Brighton Road, Coulsdon, Surrey CR5 2NH.
Tel: 0181-700 3700. Fax: 0181-763 1007.
Editor: Carol Reed.
News magazine concentrating on developments in all military fields.
Illustrations: B&W and colour. News pictures of defence subjects worldwide.
Text: News items and informed articles on the military, industrial and political aspects of global defence.
Overall freelance potential: Limited for those without contacts in the forces or defence industry, but work submitted here may also be published in the various annuals produced by the Jane's Information Group.
Fees: Photographs by negotiation; text from £100 per 1,000 words.

JEWISH CHRONICLE
Jewish Chronicle Newspapers Ltd, 25 Furnival Street, London EC4A 1JT.
Tel: 0171-405 9252. Fax: 0171-405 9040.
Editor: Edward J. Temko.
Weekly newspaper publishing news and features concerning, and of interest to, the British Jewish community.
Illustrations: B&W and colour. Any topical pictures related to the purpose stated above. Also material for the paper's wide range of supplements that deal with subjects such as holidays, fashion, interior decoration, regional development, etc.
Text: Features on topics detailed above. 600–2,500 words.
Overall freelance potential: At least 30 per cent of the content comes from freelance sources.
Fees: By negotiation.

PTC JOURNAL
The Public Services Tax and Commerce Union, 5 Great Suffolk Street, London SE1 0NS.
Tel: 0171-960 2004. Fax: 0171-960 2001.
Editor: Nick Wright.
Monthly publication for members of the PTC Union (formerly NUCPS), the biggest civil service union. Also has large private sector membership.
Illustrations: Colour. News pictures of trade union activity, especially involving members of PTC. Other topical pictures of current affairs that may impinge on Union members may also be of interest.
Text: No scope.
Overall freelance potential: Good, 75 per cent of pictures come from outside contributors.
Fees: Good; on a rising scale according to size of reproduction.

LIBERAL DEMOCRAT NEWS
Liberal Democrats, 4 Cowley Street, London SW1P 3NB.
Tel: 0171-222 7999. Fax: 0171-222 7904.
Editor: David Boyle.
Weekly tabloid newspaper of the Liberal Democrats.
Illustrations: B&W and colour. Prints only (no transparencies). Pictures of Liberal Democrat activities around the country and general political news pictures.
Text: News and features: politics, current affairs.
Overall freelance potential: Limited.
Fees: By negotiation.

THE MIDDLE EAST
IC Publications Ltd, 7 Coldbath Square, London EC1R 4LQ.
Tel: 0171-713 7711. Fax: 0171-713 7970.
Editor: Mrs Pat Lancaster.
Monthly publication directed at senior management, governmental personnel and universities. Covers Middle Eastern current affairs of a political, cultural and economic nature.
Illustrations: B&W and colour. Pictures of all topical Middle Eastern subjects, personalities and scenes.
Text: Features on Middle Eastern subjects or world subjects that relate to the area. 1,000–3,000 words.
Overall freelance potential: Most of the pictures come from freelances and around 50 per cent of the overall editorial.
Fees: B&W pictures £15–£35; covers by agreement. Text, £80 per 1,000 words.

MILAP WEEKLY and NAVIN WEEKLY
Mushro Centre, 87 Mushro Road, London W14 0LR.
Tel: 0171-385 8966.
Editors: R. Soni and R. Kumar.

Weekly news publications for Indian, Pakistani and Bangladeshi people. Published in Hindi (*Navin*) and Urdu (*Milap*).
Illustrations: B&W only. News pictures concerning topical immigrant matters, pictures of leading Asian personalities.
Text: News stories; all matters of interest to immigrant Asian communities.
Overall freelance potential: Good for those in touch with the immigrant community.
Fees: By negotiation.

NEW STATESMAN
The Statesman and Nation Publishing Co Ltd, 7th Floor, Victoria Station House, 191 Victoria Street, London SW1E 5NE.
Tel: 0171-828 1232. Fax: 0171-828 1881.
Editor: Ian Hargreaves. **Art Editor**: Andrew Chapman.
Independent political and current affairs weekly, with large arts review section.
Illustrations: B&W and colour. Major news pictures of all kinds – political events, politicians, marches, demonstrations, etc. Coverage of major foreign political events, wars, etc. Also social reportage coverage, the environment, technology, etc. Covers: colour shots of major politicians or hot news stories.
Text: Short captions with pictures, or short news stories up to 500 words. Original and well-researched features will be considered – around 1,200 words.
Overall freelance potential: Most contributions are from freelance sources.
Fees: Variable.

PEOPLE & THE PLANET
Planet 21, 1 Woburn Walk, London WC1H 0JJ.
Tel: 0171-383 4388. Fax: 0171-388 2398.
Editor: John Rowley. **Picture Editor**: Maya Pastakia.
Quarterly publication concerned with population, environment and development topics.
Illustrations: Mainly colour inside. Pictures showing environment and family planning projects, family life, rural and urban living conditions, mothers and children. Covers: always related to features.
Text: Freelance material accepted, but usually only on commission.
Overall freelance potential: Good for quality material on the Third World.
Fees: Full page pictures, £80-£100; half page, £60-£75.

Railways

INTERNATIONAL RAILWAY JOURNAL
Simmons-Boardman Publishing Corporation, PO Box 8, Falmouth, Cornwall TR11 4RJ.
Tel: 01326 313945. Fax: 01326 211576.
Editor: Mike Knutton.
Monthly publication for the principal officers of the railways of the world (including metro and light rail systems), ministers and commissioners of transport, railway equipment manufacturers and suppliers.
Illustrations: B&W and colour. Pictures of new line construction projects, electrification projects, track or signalling improvements, new locomotives, passenger coaches and freight wagons. Interesting pictures of railway operations from far-flung corners of the world. No steam or nostalgia material. Covers: colour shots tied in with the theme of a particular issue.
Text: Features on any sizeable contracts for railway equipment; plans for railway developments, i.e. new line construction, track or signalling improvements; almost anything which involves a railway spending money or making improvements and techniques. No padding or speculation.
Overall freelance potential: Quite good for the right business-oriented material.
Fees: Rising scale according to size of pictures; text, £120 per 1,000 words.

RAIL
EMAP Apex Publications, Apex House, Oundle Road, Peterborough PE2 9NP.
Tel: 01733 898100. Fax: 01733 894472.
Editor: Nigel Harris.
Fortnightly magazine dealing with modern railways.
Illustrations: Mostly colour, some black and white. Single photographs and up-to-date news pictures on any interesting railway topic in Britain, particularly accidents and incidents of all kinds.
Covers: Colour shots with strong impact.
Text: Illustrated articles of up to 1,500 words on any railway topic. Check recent issues for style, tone, content.
Overall freelance potential: Excellent.
Editor's tips: Topicality is everything in our news coverage. For other pictures try to get away from straightforward shots of trains; be imaginative. We are always looking for something different.
Fees: Pictures from £20 to £50; illustrated articles around £90–£150. Will pay more for high-impact special pics that give the magazine a commercial advantage.

RAIL EXPRESS
Foursight Publishing, 20 Park Street, King's Cliffe, Peterborough PE8 6XN.
Tel: 01780 470086. Fax: 01780 470060.
Editors: Murray Brown, Philip Sutton.
Monthly magazine for modern railway enthusiasts.
Illustrations: Mainly colour (prints acceptable). Any good or unusual photographs of the contemporary railway scene, but really need to be of current and newsworthy interest (new locomotives, new liveries, etc). Some scope for historic diesel/electric coverage.
Text: Suggestions for articles welcome, from anyone with good background knowledge of the subject, especially traction. Consult with the editor first.
Overall freelance potential: The magazine features lots of photography and always needs more.
Editor's tips: Topicality is the key.
Fees: Basic rate £15 per picture; higher rates for covers, spreads and special or rare material.

RAILNEWS
Railnews Ltd, East Side Offices, King's Cross Station, London N1 9AP.
Tel: 0171-314 4198. Fax: 0171-314 4107.
Editor: Robin Etherington.
Monthly newspaper covering the modern railway scene.
Illustrations: B&W and colour prints. Railway news pictures, unusual pictures with good captions.
Text: No scope.
Overall freelance potential: Good.
Editor's tips: Approach before submitting.
Fees: By negotiation.

STEAM CLASSIC
Ebony Ltd. Editorial Office: Trevithick House, Moorswater, Liskeard, Cornwall PL14 4LH.
Tel: 01579 340100. Fax: 01579 340200.
Editor: John Huxley.
Bi-monthly magazine for steam railway enthusiasts, inter-relating current activity with nostalgia.
Illustrations: B&W and colour. Top quality coverage of active steam trains, including close-up detail and atmospheric shots. Newsy pictures accepted on spec, but portfolio submissions should be discussed with the editor before submitting. Details of relevant collections/archive material always of interest.
Text: Well-illustrated articles on suitable subjects, which must follow the magazine's well-defined style.
Overall freelance potential: Good.
Fees: By negotiation.

STEAM RAILWAY
EMAP Apex Publications Ltd, Apex House, Oundle Road, Peterborough PE2 9NP.
Tel: 01733 898100. Fax: 01733 894472.
Editor: Peter Kelly.
Monthly magazine for the steam railway enthusiast. Closely concerned with railway preservation.
Illustrations: B&W and colour. Accurately captioned photographs depicting steam trains and railways past and present, preserved railway lines, and railway museums (topical subjects especially welcomed).
Text: Illustrated articles on relevant subjects.
Overall freelance potential: Most of the content is contributed by freelances.
Editor's tips: Material should be lively, topical and newsworthy, although some nostalgic or historic material is accepted.
Fees: By arrangement.

STEAM RAILWAY NEWS
Lancashire Publications Ltd, Martland Mill, Martland Mill Lane, Wigan WN5 0LX.
Tel: 01942 228000. Fax: 01942 214004.
Editor: Richard Bean.
Weekly tabloid covering the contemporary steam railway scene.
Illustrations: Mostly B&W; colour used on the front page only. Newsy photographs of steam locomotives and steam-hauled trains operating on private railways or British Rail. No transparencies.
Text: Topical articles of 1,000–1,500 words on suitable subjects.
Overall freelance potential: By arrangement.
Fees: According to use and the nature of the material.

TRACTION
Warners Group Holdings plc, The Maltings, West Street, Bourne, Lincs PE10 9PH..
Tel: 01778 391160. Fax: 01778 391167.
Editor: David Brown.
Monthly magazine dedicated to diesel and electric locomotives past and present.
Illustrations: B&W and colour. Photographs of classic diesels and electrics operating on British railways from the 1940s to the present day. Particular interest in archive shots from the earlier eras up to the early 1970s. More contemporary material should have a newsworthy angle.
Text: Nostalgic features, which should ideally include some technical interest, always considered.
Overall freelance potential: Good.
Fees: From £15–£30 according to size of reproduction.

Religion

CATHOLIC GAZETTE
114 West Heath Road, London NW3 7TX.
Tel: 0181-458 3316. Fax: 0181-905 5780.
Editor: Father Paul Daly.
Monthly publication concerned essentially with evangelisation.
Illustrations: B&W only. Pictures of nature or the countryside, plus people with natural or unusual expressions to illustrate points in articles, religious sculptures and architecture, religious, human themes.
Text: Well researched articles on religious topics and human interest stories based on personal experience. 1,500–2,500 words.
Overall freelance potential: Around 80 per cent is contributed by freelances.
Editor's tips: Articles should not be over-written and the human element should be kept to the forefront. Don't preach.
Fees: By agreement.

CATHOLIC HERALD

Herald House, Lamb's Passage, Bunhill Row, London EC1Y 8TQ.
Tel: 0171-588 3101. Fax: 0171-256 9728.
Editor: Deborah Jones. **Picture Editor**: Joe Jenkins.
Weekly newspaper reflecting on Catholicism/Christianity and its place in the wider world, plus church news.
Illustrations: B&W only inside, colour on the front page. Principal need for news photographs of events involving churches, clerics or prominent Catholics.
Text: Articles of up to 1,200 words on the social, economic and political significance of the church domestically and internationally, plus spiritual and reflective writings.
Overall freelance potential: Better for features than other material.
Fees: By arrangement but not high.

CATHOLIC TIMES

First Floor, St James Buildings, Oxford Street, Manchester M1 6FP.
Tel: 0161-236 8856. Fax: 0161-236 8530.
Editor: Greg Murphy.
Weekly newspaper covering Catholic affairs.
Illustrations: B&W and colour. Topical pictures of Catholic interest. Also off-beat devotional shots.
Text: News stories and short features. 900 words maximum.
Overall freelance potential: Very good; all pictures are from freelance sources.
Fees: £60 per published picture; text around £40 per 1,000 words.

CHURCH TIMES

G.J.Palmer & Sons Ltd, 33 Upper Street, London N1 0PN.
Tel: 0171-359 4570. Fax: 0171-226 3073.
Editor: Paul Handley.
Weekly newspaper covering Church of England affairs.
Illustrations: B&W and colour. Up-to-the-minute news pictures of Anglican events and personalities. Detailed captions essential.
Text: Short articles on current religious topics; up to 1,000 words.
Overall freelance potential: Fair.
Editor's tips: It is preferred that people in pictures are engaged in activities rather than just looking at the camera.
Fees: Photographs according to use; text £100 per 1,000 words.

NEW CHRISTIAN HERALD

Herald House Ltd, 96 Dominion Road, Worthing, West Sussex BN14 8JP.
Tel: 01903 821082. Fax: 01903 821081.
Editor: Russ Bravo.
Weekly tabloid aimed at evangelical Christians.
Illustrations: B&W preferred. news events, people shots.
Text: Guidelines for contributors available.
Overall freelance potential: Several freelance pictures and articles used every week.
Fees: Negotiable, but usually £5–£40.

PARENTWISE

37 Elm Road, New Malden, Surrey KT3 3HB.
Tel: 0181-942 9761. Fax: 0181-949 6991.
Editor: Jill Worth.

Monthly Christian magazine for parents with a concern for family issues.
Illustrations: B&W and colour. Pictures mainly for use with features, depicting couples, parent(s) with children, children alone.
Text: Articles on parenting and family issues. Up to 1,800 words.
Overall freelance potential: Good; many contributed articles used each month, though most are commissioned.
Fees: Up to £90 for 1,000–1,800 words.

WOMAN ALIVE
Herald House Ltd, 96 Dominion Road, Worthing, West Sussex BN14 8JP.
Tel: 01903 821082. Fax: 01903 821081.
Editor: Elizabeth Proctor.
Monthly publication for women with church links.
Illustrations: B&W and colour. Stock pictures of family life, nature, scenic views, people in various situations (holidays, jobs, festive occasions), news events, novelty and fun items.
Text: Limited freelance market.
Overall freelance potential: Several freelance pictures used each month.
Fees: Variable.

Science & Technology

CHEMISTRY AND INDUSTRY
Society of Chemical Industry, 15 Belgrave Square, London SW1X 8PS.
Tel: 0171-235 3681. Fax: 0171-235 9410.
Editor: Maria Burke.
Fortnightly science and business magazine covering chemistry and related sciences, and the chemical, food, biotech, environment and water industries.
Illustrations: B&W and colour. Photographs of chemical factories, chemistry research and environmental pollution, food, plants, water, and places.
Text: News stories and articles from contributors with the requisite technical background.
Overall freelance potential: Limited.
Editor's tips: Always contact the editor before preparing any submission.
Fees: £200 per 1,000 words for text; photographs by negotiation.

CLEAN AIR & ENVIRONMENTAL PROTECTION
National Society for Clean Air and Environmental Protection, 136 North Street, Brighton BN1 1RG.
Tel: 01273 326313. Fax: 01273 735802.
Editor: Ms Loveday Murley.
Bi-monthly publication for professionals in the field of air and noise pollution and environmental control; selected representatives of local authorities, researchers and anyone generally interested in the subject.
Illustrations: B&W only. Pictures of air pollution, environment and conservation.
Text: Features on air pollution, noise, water pollution control, waste, conservation and energy issues. 4,000–8,000 words.
Overall freelance potential: Limited.
Fees: By negotiation.

EDUCATION IN CHEMISTRY
The Royal Society of Chemistry, Burlington House, Piccadilly, London W1V 0BN.
Tel: 0171-437 8656. Fax: 0171-437 8883.
Editor: Kathryn Roberts.
Alternate-monthly publication for teachers, lecturers in schools, and universities, concerning all aspects of chemical education.
Illustrations: B&W only. Pictures that deal with chemistry in the classroom, laboratories or the chemical industry. Covers: B&W pictures relating to specific articles inside.
Text: Features concerned with chemistry or the teaching of it. Under 2,500 words.
Overall freelance potential: Moderate.
Fees: By agreement.

FOCUS
G+J of the UK Ltd, Portland House, Stag Place, London SW1 5AU.
Tel: 0171-245 8845. Fax: 0171-931 8388.
Editor: Paul Colbert. **Art Director**: Andrew Beswick.
General interest monthly covering popular science, technology, medicine, sport and the environment. Aimed at young, upmarket men.
Illustrations: Mainly colour. Will consider colour photo essays on subjects as above. Also contributions for "In Focus" double-page spread, depicting an interesting or unusual aspect of contemporary life.
Text: Interesting features on subjects above always considered. Submit a synopsis in the first instance.
Overall freelance potential: Fair.
Editor's tips: Only top quality material is considered; study the magazine before submitting.
Fees: Negotiable; generally good.

THE GEOGRAPHICAL MAGAZINE
Campion Interactive Publications Ltd, 47c Kensington Court, London W8 5DA.
Tel: 0171-938 4011. Fax: 0171-938 4022.
Editor-in-Chief: Alan Armsden. **Features Editor**: Claire Hutchings.
Monthly magazine of the Royal Geographical Society. Covers topical geographical subjects from an academic and scientific point of view whilst still appealing to the general reader.
Illustrations: Colour. Sets of pictures linked to geographical topics – human, political, ecological, economic and physical subjects. Interesting single pictures relevant to current geographical issues. Ideas for picture stories always considered.
Text: Well-illustrated articles on any geographical subject, written from a scientific perspective but with popular appeal. Length variable.
Overall freelance potential: Excellent for the right type of material.
Fees: Negotiable, but in the region of £100 per published page. Single pictures according to use.

NEW SCIENTIST
IPC Specialist Group, King's Reach Tower, Stamford Street, London SE1 9LS.
Tel: 0171-261 5000. Fax: 0171-261 6464.
Editor: Alun Anderson. **Picture Editor**: Adam Goff.
Weekly magazine about science and technology for people with some scientific or technical education and also for the intelligent layman.
Illustrations: B&W and colour. Pictures on any topic that can be loosely allied to science and technology. Particularly interested in news photographs related to scientific phenomena and events. Covers: usually connected with a feature inside.
Text: News and features on scientific/technical subjects that might appeal to a wide audience.
Overall freelance potential: A lot of freelance work used, but best to consult the magazine before submitting.
Fees: Photographs on a rising scale according to size of reproduction. Text £150 per 1,000 words.

Sport

AIR GUNNER
Romsey Publishing Company, 4 The Courtyard, Denmark Street, Wokingham, Berkshire RG40 2AZ.
Tel: 011897 71677. Fax: 011897 72903.
Managing Editor: Nigel Allen.
Monthly magazine for all airgun enthusiasts.
Illustrations: B&W & colour. Illustrated news items, and stock shots of small field animals (rats, rabbits) and pest species of birds (pigeons, magpies, crows). Covers: colour, usually commissioned, but a speculative picture might be used.
Text: Articles on any aspect of airgun use, 700–1,000 words, and accompanied by a good selection of B&W prints or colour transparencies.
Overall freelance potential: Good for file photos and well illustrated articles.
Fees: In the region of £50 per published page.

ATHLETICS WEEKLY
EMAP Pursuit Publishing Ltd, Bretton Court, Bretton, Peterborough PE3 8DZ.
Tel: 01733 261144. Fax: 01733 465206/267198.
Editor: Nigel Walsh.
Weekly news magazine for the competitive and aspiring athlete. Focuses on events and results.
Illustrations: B&W and colour. Coverage of athletics events at grass roots level, such as area championships, rather than top events (the latter are supplied by agency photographers). Always interested in anything out of the ordinary, such as well-known athletes off the track or in unusual situations.
Text: No scope.
Overall freelance potential: Fair.
Editor's tips: Freelances aware of what is happening locally can often obtain coverage missed by the nationals and agencies – top athletes "dropping in" to take part in local events etc.
Fees: According to size of reproduction, from £15–£50. Published pictures frequently gain extra sales via reader requests.

BADMINTON
Connect Sports Ltd, 14 Woking Road, Cheadle Hulme, Cheshire SK8 6NZ.
Tel: 0161-486 6159. Fax: 0161-485 2728.
Editor: William Kings.
The only magazine in the UK devoted to badminton. Published six times a year.
Illustrations: B&W and colour. Will consider good action coverage, sports fashion, health material.
Text: Little scope for writing on the sport itself, but will consider articles on sports fashion, health, fitness and diet. 750–1,000 words.
Overall freelance potential: Limited.
Fees: £25 for B&W; £50 for colour. Text by agreement.

BOXING MONTHLY
40 Morpeth Road, London E9 7LD.
Tel: 0181-986 4141. Fax: 0181-986 4145.
Editor: Glyn Leach.
Heavily illustrated publication for boxing enthusiasts, covering both professional and amateur boxing.
Illustrations: B&W and colour. Coverage of boxing at all levels, including the amateur scene.
Text: Knowledgeable articles, features, interviews, etc. on any aspect of the boxing scene. Always contact the editor in the first instance.
Overall freelance potential: Excellent scope for boxing specialists, and for good amateur boxing coverage.
Fees: By negotiation.

CLIMBER
Caledonian Magazines Ltd, Plaza Tower, East Kilbride, Glasgow G74 1LW.
Tel: 01355 246444. Fax: 01355 263013.
Editor: Tom Prentice.
Monthly magazine dealing with world-wide mountain climbing from Lakeland fells to Everest. Highly literate readership. Contributors range from "unknowns" to top climbers like Chris Bonington.
Illustrations: B&W and colour. First ascents and newsworthy events but, in the main, used only with text. Covers: action shots of climbers or dramatic mountain pictures.
Text: Features on hill walking, trekking, rock climbing, Alpinism, high altitude climbing, cross-country and mountain skiing (*not* downhill racing). 1,500–2,000 words.
Overall freelance potential: Good; 90 per cent of articles and 100 per cent of pictures come from freelances, but many are regulars.
Editor's tips: This is a specialist field and is full of good writer/photographers. There is potential for the freelance to break in, but the magazine is usually well stocked with material.
Fees: Variable.

THE CRICKETER INTERNATIONAL
The Cricketer Ltd, Third Street, Langton Green, Tunbridge Wells, Kent TN3 0EN.
Tel: 01892 862551. Fax: 01892 863755.
Editor: Peter Perchard.
Monthly publication for cricket enthusiasts of all ages. Covers all aspects of the sport.
Illustrations: B&W and colour. Pictures of less fashionable players needed, plus historical pictures. Covers: colour pictures of cricketing subjects, usually supplied by staff photographers, but occasionally bought from freelances.
Text: Features taking an original look at the subject. Up to 1,000 words.
Overall freelance potential: A high percentage comes from freelances, but usually commissioned. Ideas in writing only.
Fees: Inside pictures and text by agreement, but on average £16 per B&W picture; £30 per colour picture; £50 per 1,000 words. Covers £60.

DARTS WORLD
World Magazines Ltd, 9 Kelsey Park Road, Beckenham, Kent BR3 6LH.
Tel: 0181-650 6580. Fax: 0181-650 2534.
Editor: A. J. Wood.
Monthly magazine for darts players and organisers.
Illustrations: B&W only inside. Pictures on any darts theme, action shots and portraits of leading players. Covers: colour shots, usually of star players. Good colour also required for the annual *Darts Player*.
Text: Features on all darts subjects.
Overall freelance potential: Most of the copy and pictures comes from freelances.
Editor's tips: The darts-playing environment is often dim and smoky, which can make it difficult to produce bright, interesting pictures. Photographers who can come up with colourful shots that catch the eye are welcomed.
Fees: Good, on a rising scale according to size of reproduction or length of feature.

FC
Nash Corporation, Nash House, 322 Kensal Road, London W10 5BZ.
Tel: 0181-969 2232.
Editor: Peter Freedman.
Alternate-monthly published on behalf of the Football Association. Aimed at club secretaries and players at all levels, from Premier League down to amateur clubs.
Illustrations: Mainly colour. Stock pictures of players and good action, but behind-the-scenes coverage especially of interest.
Text: Features on topical and practical issues in the game; send suggestions with samples of previous

work in the first instance.
Overall freelance potential: Good for those in touch with the game at grass roots level.
Editor's tips: Contributions from outside London particularly welcome.
Fees: By negotiation.

F1 NEWS
Peakcourt Ltd, 116–118 Liscombe, Birch Hill, Bracknell, Berks RG12 7DE.
Tel: 01344 427846. Fax: 01344 484918.
Editor: Derek Wright. **Picture Editor**: Andrew Cocking.
News magazine devoted exclusively to Formula 1 motor racing. Published fortnightly only during the nine month racing season.
Illustrations: Mainly colour. Very up-to-date news pictures depicting anything relevant to the Formula 1 scene.
Text: Little freelance scope for non-specialists.
Overall freelance potential: Limited; most material is obtained from professional motor racing photographers and agencies.
Editor's tips: Always contact the picture editor to establish interest before submitting.
Fees: By negotiation.

FIGHTERS – THE MARTIAL ARTS MAGAZINE
Peterson Publications Ltd, Peterson House, Northbank, Berryhill Industrial Estate, Droitwich, Worcestershire WR9 9BL.
Tel: 01905 795564. Fax: 01905 795905.
Editor: Tim Ayling.
Monthly magazine for martial arts and similar disciplines.
Illustrations: B&W only inside. Coverage of events, clubs and individuals and any general martial arts interests. Covers: action shots in colour; 6x6cm minimum.
Text: Features on martial arts events, profiles of clubs and individuals and any other martial arts interests. 500–3,500 words.
Overall freelance potential: Quite good.
Fees: By negotiation.

FIRST DOWN
Independent Magazines Ltd, 7-9 Rathbone Street, London W1P 1AF.
Tel: 0171-323 1988. Fax: 0171-323 1942.
Editor: Richard Davies.
Weekly newspaper covering American football, in the UK, Europe and USA.
Illustrations: B&W and colour. Main requirement is for news pictures and personality portraits from the British scene.
Text: Short news items, match reports, and profiles or interview features.
Overall freelance potential: Quite good.
Fees: According to use.

FOOTBALL EUROPE
Poundbury Publishing Ltd, Agriculture House, Acland Road, Dorchester, Dorset DT1 1EF.
Tel/Fax: 01305 266360.
Editor: Dan Goldstein.
Monthly magazine covering the soccer scene on mainland Europe, at both club and international level.
Illustrations: Mainly colour. Up-to-date pictures of leading European footballers, portraits or action. Also stock and archive material – send lists of subjects available.
Text: Some scope for illustrated news stories. Suggestions for features always considered.
Overall freelance potential: Very good for those in touch with the Continental scene.
Fees: Photographs according to use, from a minimum of £15. Text, £50 per 1,000 words.

FOOTBALL MONTHLY
Chelsea Communications. Editorial: Mediawatch Ltd, Spendlove Centre, Charlbury, Oxford OX7 3PQ.
Tel: 01608 811266. Fax: 01608 811380.
Editor: Tony Evans.
Britain's oldest soccer magazine, covering all aspects of the game from a historical perspective.
Illustrations: Mainly colour. Top quality pictures of current football players and action, especially at the lower and non-League level. Also interested in good archive photographs, especially from the '60s and '70s.
Text: Always interested in hearing from experienced football journalists with good ideas.
Overall freelance potential: Good.
Fees: By negotiation.

FORE!
EMAP Pursuit Publishing Ltd, Bretton Court, Bretton, Peterborough PE3 8DZ.
Tel: 01733 264666. Fax: 01733 465221.
Editor: Paul Hamblin. **Art Editor**: Karen Booth.
Monthly golfing magazine with an aspirational and youthful approach.
Illustrations: Colour only. Top quality photographs of golf courses around the country, not so much the well-known ones but the "hidden gems" that will spark interest amongst golfers looking for fresh courses to play. Off-beat shots always of interest. No tournament coverage required.
Text: Little scope.
Overall freelance potential: Very good for those who can provide suitable quality coverage.
Editor's tips: "The keyword is aspirational; we look for photographs of courses that make the reader think: 'I'd really like to play that course'. Most suitable shots are likely to be taken in either early morning or late afternoon, when courses are less busy and at their most attractive."
Fees: Negotiable, according to use.

FOURFOURTWO
Haymarket Leisure Magazines Ltd, 60 Waldegrave Road, Teddington, Middlesex TW11 8LG.
Tel: 0181-943 5000. Fax: 0181-943 5668.
Editor: Christian Smyth. **Art Editor**: Paul Yelland.
Monthly magazine aimed at the adult soccer fan.
Illustrations: Mainly colour. Always interested to know of good stock collections, both current and historic. Especially interested in anything exclusive or unusual. Commissions available to photographers with at least some sports experience.
Text: Reasonable scope for football and humour specialists.
Overall freelance potential: Quite good for specialists.
Fees: According to use and size of reproduction. Text £100–£175 per 1,000 words.

GOAL
IPC Magazines Ltd, King's Reach Tower, Stamford Street, London SE1 9LS.
Tel: 0171-261 5596. Fax: 0171-261 5666.
Editor: Dave Cottrell. **Art Editor**: Tom Sayer. **Picture Editor**: Mark Ranaldi.
Monthly informed and occasional irreverent football magazine aimed at adult market.
Illustrations: Colour only. Mostly by commission to illustrate main features – contact the art editor to show portfolio. Genuinely stunning one-off pictures may be used on spec.
Text: No scope.
Overall freelance potential: Limited; most is produced by regulars or supplied by agencies.
Fees: By negotiation.

GOLF MONTHLY
IPC Magazines, King's Reach Tower, Stamford Street, London SE1 9LS.
Tel: 0171-261 7237. Fax: 0171-261 7240.
Editor: Colin Callander. **Art Editor**: Keith Jones.

Monthly international consumer magazine for golfers.

Illustrations: B&W and colour. Mainly for use as illustrations to articles. Small market for one-off pictures from golf tournaments of golf-related events.

Text: Illustrated features on instruction and other golf-related topics. Also in-depth profiles of leading world players. Around 2,000 words, but not critical.

Overall freelance potential: Most of the magazine is commissioned. Room for more material of the right type from freelances.

Editor's tips: This is an international magazine so material must have a wide appeal. No features of a parochial nature.

Fees: By agreement.

GOLF WORLD

Golf World Ltd, Mappin House, 4 Winsley Street, London W1N 7AR.

Tel: 0171-817 9641. Fax: 0171-817 9630.

Editor: David Clarke. **Art Editor**: Paul Crawford.

Monthly publication for golfers, covering all aspects of the sport.

Illustrations: B&W and colour. Unusual golfing pictures always of interest.

Text: Profiles of leading golfers and general or instructional features. 1,500–2,000 words.

Overall freelance potential: Around 20 per cent comes from freelance sources.

Fees: By agreement.

HARPERS SPORTS & LEISURE

47A High Street, Bushey, Watford, Herts WD2 1BD.

Tel: 0181-950 9522. Fax: 0181-950 7998.

Editor: Neil Hartnell.

Magazine aimed at the UK sports retail trade. 18 issues per year.

Illustrations: B&W and colour. Topical pictures concerning the retail trade, usually to illustrate specific news stories, features and new products.

Text: Illustrated features and news stories on anything to do with the sports retail industry, including manufacturer and retailer profiles etc.

Overall freelance potential: Limited.

Fees: Text, £120 per 1,000 words; pictures by negotiation.

HOCKEY SPORT

PB Publications, Unit E6, Aladdin Workspace, 426 Long Drive, Greenford, Middlesex UB6 8UH.

Tel: 0181-575 3121/0171-437 6437. Fax: 0181-575 1320/0171-734 7545.

Editor: Peter Luck.

Monthly covering all levels of hockey.

Illustrations: Always interested in news pictures and good action coverage at all levels, but especially county championships. Submit 12–20 pictures to enable a good selection, but always best to check with the editor before covering an event.

Text: News items, and longer features from contributors who really know the sport.

Overall freelance potential: Modest.

Fees: By negotiation.

INSIDE RUGBY

Brackenbury Publishing Ltd, The Quadrangle, Atalanta Street, London SW6 6TR.

Tel: 0171-386 9938. Fax: 0171-386 9722.

Editor: Richard Pembroke.

Monthly covering rugby at all levels, but with special emphasis on the "grass roots".

Illustrations: Colour. Little scope for top level coverage but always interested in good regional, local and junior material.

Text: Match reports, club or player profiles, and general features always considered, but call before

preparing or submitting.
Overall freelance potential: Good for grass roots coverage.
Editor's tips: All contributions will be considered on their merits, but always check with the editorial team before covering a specific event.
Fees: By negotiation.

MARTIAL ARTS ILLUSTRATED
Martial Arts Ltd, 8 Revenue Chambers, St Peter Street, Huddersfield, West Yorkshire HD1 1EL.
Tel: 01484 435011. Fax: 01484 422177.
Editor: Bob Sykes.
Monthly magazine covering all forms of Oriental fighting and self-defence techniques.
Illustrations: B&W and colour. Single pictures or sets depicting well-known martial artists, club events, tournament action and aspects of technique.
Text: Well-illustrated articles on any relevant subject – profiles of leading figures and individual clubs, interviews, technique sequences and self-defence features.
Overall freelance potential: Excellent for those with access to the martial arts scene.
Editor's tips: Always write in the first instance with suggestions.
Fees: Should be negotiated before submission, as many contributions are supplied free of charge.

MATCH
EMAP Pursuit Publishing Ltd, Bretton Court, Bretton Centre, Bretton, Peterborough PE3 8DZ.
Tel: 01733 260333. Fax: 01733 465206.
Managing Editor: Chris Hunt.
Weekly publication looking at the whole spectrum of soccer. Aimed at readers in the 9–15 age group.
Illustrations: Colour only. Good soccer action shots. Usually bought only after consultation with the editor. Covers: top quality colour action.
Text: Profiles and interviews concerning personalities in the soccer field. Length by arrangement.
Overall freelance potential: Few opportunities.
Fees: By agreement.

ON THE BALL
Moondance Publications, The Design Works, William Street, Gateshead NE10 0JP.
Tel: 0191-420 8383. Fax: 0191-420 4950.
Editor: Pippa Turnbull.
Monthly magazine devoted entirely to women's football.
Illustrations: Colour only. Will consider coverage of all aspects of the women's game, including good action; portraits of players and other personalities; general atmosphere shots with fans, crowds, officials, etc.
Text: Illustrated news items, profiles and interviews with leading players, plus more general features, including humorous pieces. Typical feature length 1,000 words.
Overall freelance potential: Very good.
Fees: By negotiation.

PADDLES
Freestyle Publications Ltd, Alexander House, Ling Road, Tower Park, Poole, Dorset BH12 4NZ.
Tel: 01202 735090. Fax: 01202 733969.
Editor: Kellie Parsons.
Monthly magazine for canoeing enthusiasts.
Illustrations: Colour only. Top quality action shots of all forms of canoe sport, from slalom to wild water racing, polo to sprint racing. May be used in their own right or to illustrate features.
Text: Well-illustrated features on the above, written with fellow enthusiasts in mind but with jargon kept to a minimum. Regular features on all aspects including training and education, holidays and expeditions, safety, and personality profiles. Length 1,500-2,000 words.
Overall freelance potential: Very good for those who can capture the sport well.

Fees: £100 for cover shots; other pictures according to use, but best rates paid for really top quality material. Text from £40–£100 depending on quality and content.

POT BLACK MAGAZINE
On The Ball Publications, 20-26 Market Road, Islington, London N7 9PW.
Tel: 0171-607 8585. Fax: 0171-700 1408.
Editor: Mr Chris Mills.
Monthly magazine for snooker enthusiasts, including coverage of billiards, pool (American and English) and bar billiards.
Illustrations: B&W and colour. Top quality material depicting leading snooker players in action or at leisure, and any other pictures with a snooker connection.
Text: In-depth interviews with leading players, and humorous or offbeat items.
Overall freelance potential: Limited, as most material comes from regular contributors.
Editor's tips: The magazine takes an informal and colourful view of the game.
Fees: By negotiation.

RACING PIGEON PICTORIAL INTERNATIONAL
The Racing Pigeon Publishing Co. Ltd, 13 Guilford Street, London WC1N 1DX.
Tel: 0171-831 4050. Fax: 0171-831 3766.
Editor: Rick Osman.
Monthly magazine for pigeon fanciers. Provides in-depth articles on methods, successful fanciers, scientific information, etc.
Illustrations: B&W and colour. Pictures to illustrate features, plus some one-off pictures of pigeons. Covers: colour pictures of pigeons, pigeon lofts, pigeon fanciers and related subjects.
Text: Features on pigeons, pigeon lofts, pigeon fanciers and related subjects. 1,500 words.
Overall freelance potential: Around 10–15 per cent of the pictures come from freelance photographers. Articles are mostly by specialist writers.
Editor's tips: Short, colourful, exotic articles with good illustrations stand a reasonable chance.
Fees: £20 per published page minimum.

RANGERS NEWS
Argyle House, Ibrox Stadium, Glasgow G51 2XD.
Tel: 0141-427 8844. Fax: 0141-427 0406.
Editor: Douglas Cumming.
Weekly newspaper of Rangers Football Club. Aimed at Rangers supporters but also has substantial coverage of Scottish, European and world football.
Illustrations: Colour. General action pictures of Scottish, European and world football.
Text: Little freelance market.
Overall freelance potential: Around 20 per cent is supplied by freelance photographers.
Fees: By arrangement.

RUGBY LEAGUER
Lancashire Publications Ltd, Martland Mill, Martland Mill Lane, Wigan WN5 0LX.
Tel: 01942 228000. Fax: 01942 214004.
Editor: Steve Brady.
Weekly paper covering rugby league football at home and abroad.
Illustrations: B&W and colour. Match coverage, stock pictures of individual players, and coverage of any other events relating to rugby league. Covers: good colour action focused on a single player.
Text: Little scope.
Overall freelance potential: Limited.
Fees: By arrangement with editor.

RUGBY NEWS
Independent Magazines Ltd, 7–9 Rathbone Street, London W1P 1AF.
Tel: 0171-323 1944. Fax: 0171-323 1942.
Editor: Graeme Gillespie.
Monthly rugby magazine covering all levels of the sport.
Illustrations: Almost exclusively colour. Coverage at the top level is usually obtained from agency sources, so scope for the freelance is mostly at local and "grass roots" level, including school tournaments.
Text: Articles and local match reports may be considered, but always query the editor first.
Overall freelance potential: Fair.
Editor's tips: The different picture with really good action, at whatever level, will always be of interest.
Fees: By negotiation.

RUGBY WORLD
IPC Magazines Ltd, King's Reach Tower, Stamford Street, London SE1 9LS.
Tel: 0171-261 6830. Fax: 0171-261 5419.
Editor: Alison Kervin.
Britain's biggest selling monthly rugby magazine giving general coverage of Rugby Union.
Illustrations: B&W and colour. Main scope is for regional/local coverage, since the top level matches are covered by regulars. Photographs of Cup matches, County championships, personalities, off-beat shots, etc. Covers: colour action shots of top players. Enclose s.a.e. for return of material.
Text: Dependent on quality and appeal.
Overall freelance potential: Good articles with different angles are always of interest.
Fees: On a rising scale according to size of reproduction or length of text.

RUNNER'S WORLD
Rodale Press Ltd, 7-10 Chandos Street, London W1M 0AD.
Tel: 0171-291 6000. Fax: 0171-291 6080.
Editor: Steven Seaton. **Art Editor**: Russell Fairbrother.
Monthly publication for running enthusiasts.
Illustrations: B&W and colour. Pictures relating to sports, recreational and fitness running. Consult art editor before submitting.
Text: Feature material considered, but only by prior consultation with the editor.
Overall freelance potential: Fair.
Fees: By agreement.

THE SCOTTISH SPORTING GAZETTE
Ormiston Enterprises Ltd, 22 Market Brae, Inverness IV2 3AB.
Tel: 01463 232104. Fax: 01463 225182.
Editor: John Ormiston.
Annual publication to market Scottish shooting, fishing, stalking and allied services. Aimed at the upper income bracket in the UK, Europe and America.
Illustrations: B&W and colour. Pictures of shooting, fishing, stalking, live game animals, whisky production, antique Scottish weapons, tartans, castles and hunting lodges. Covers: exceptional colour pictures of game animals or action sporting shots.
Text: Features on shooting, fishing and stalking in Scotland or articles on other topics that are particularly Scottish, as above. 600–2,000 words.
Overall freelance potential: Good.
Editor's tips: Pictures and text must be unusual, not the normal anecdotes associated with this field. Material should have a good Scottish flavour. It does not have to be essentially sporting, but should be allied in some way.
Fees: Open to negotiation.

SCUBA WORLD

Freestyle Publications Ltd, Alexander House, Ling Road, Tower Park, Poole, Dorset BH12 4NZ.
Tel: 01202 735090. Fax: 01202 733969.
Editor: Richard Chumbley.
Monthly for recreational scuba divers, diving clubs, underwater photographers.
Illustrations: Colour only. To accompany features as below. Covers: interesting shots showing a diver either underwater or on surface, or wrecks and marine life.
Text: Illustrated articles on UK diving and wreck sites, holiday destinations, aquatic life, underwater photography, equipment and topical subjects. 1,500–2,000 words, written in a light style.
Overall freelance potential: Very good; all contributions are freelance.
Fees: Between £40 and £100 per feature. Covers £50.

SHOOT!

IPC Magazines Ltd, King's Reach Tower, Stamford Street, London SE1 9LS.
Tel: 0171-261 6287. Fax: 0171-261 6019.
Editor: *To Be Announced*. **Picture Editor**: Duncan Bond.
Weekly football magazine aimed primarily at the youth market.
Illustrations: All colour. Stock material covering all English divisions, Scottish cup matches, European and International games. Offbeat pictures of national teams. Team groups from The Premier League, First Division and leading Scottish clubs. International games featuring home countries and Republic of Ireland. All cup games and European matches. Covers: pictures of top players from The Premier League, and Internationals, particularly those from UK and Ireland.
Text: Topical newsworthy articles on and by players in the limelight. In-depth features on clubs and all aspects of the game. Usual length either one-page (450–500 words) or two-page (800–1,000 words).
Overall freelance potential: Excellent, virtually 100 per cent of photographic content comes from freelances.
Editor's tips: Picture choice is selective with only top quality material from the top levels of the game being used.
Fees: According to size of reproduction or length of text.

THE SHOOTING GAZETTE

BPG (Bourne) Ltd, 2 West Street, Bourne, Lincolnshire PE10 9NE.
Tel: 01778 393747. Fax: 01778 425453.
Editor: Mike Barnes.
Britain's only monthly magazine covering exclusively game and rough shooting.
Illustrations: Colour. Pictures for general illustration and stock depicting any aspect of game shooting.
Text: Well-illustrated articles from those with specialist knowledge, and profiles or interviews. Up to 1,000 words.
Overall freelance potential: Fair.
Fees: By negotiation.

SHOOTING TIMES & COUNTRY MAGAZINE

IPC Magazines Ltd, King's Reach Tower, Stamford Street, London SE1 9LS.
Tel: 0171-261 6180. Fax: 0171-261 7179.
Editor: John Gregson. **Art Editor**: Simon Fevyer.
Weekly magazine concentrating on all aspects of quarry shooting (game, pigeon, rough shooting, wildfowling and stalking). Also covers clay shooting, other fieldsports and general country topics.
Illustrations: Mostly colour. Good photographs of shooting subjects plus gundogs, wildlife, rural crafts, country food. Some scope for good generic photographs of British counties, showing known landmarks. B&W news pictures. Covers: shots should be vertical in shape with room for title at the top – medium format preferred but *sharp* 35mm acceptable.
Text: Illustrated features on all aspects of quarry shooting and general country topics as above. In the region of 900 words.

Overall freelance potential: Excellent; plenty of scope for new contributors.
Editor's tips: The magazine likes to keep pictures on file as it is not always possible to know in advance when a picture can be used. For features, remember that the readers are real country people.
Fees: Colour inside £10–£60 according to size; covers £70–£90. Features £40 per 500 words.

SKI & SNOWBOARD
The Ski Club of Great Britain, The White House, 57-63 Church Road, Wimbledon Village, London SW19 4DQ.
Tel: 0181-410 2000. Fax: 0181-410 2001.
Editor: Gill Williams.
Published five times a year. Official journal of the Ski Club of Great Britain, covering the sport at all levels.
Illustrations: Colour only. Pictures of holiday skiing, ski-touring, racing, and equipment. Shots illustrating snowcraft and particular techniques. Good, attractive pictures of ski resorts and ski slopes in season. Covers: good colour action with the skier taking up at least two-thirds of the pictures. 35mm acceptable but larger formats preferred.
Text: Some scope for general articles about skiing, and on techniques.
Overall freelance potential: Quite good.
Fees: By arrangement.

THE SKIER AND SNOWBOARDER MAGAZINE
Mountain Marketing Ltd, 48 London Road, Sevenoaks, Kent TN13 1JR.
Tel: 01732 743644. Fax: 01732 743647.
Editor: Frank Baldwin.
Published five times a year: Oct, Nov, Dec, Winter (Jan/Feb), Spring (Mar/Apr). Covers all aspects of skiing and snowboarding.
Illustrations: B&W and colour. Good action pictures and anything spectacular, odd or humorous that summons up the spirit of skiing. Also a special "Photo File" section in which photographers can submit up to three favourite shots backed by text which tells the reader about the set-ups/techniques used, linked with a short biog of the photographer.
Text: Original ideas for illustrated features always welcome. Possible scope for resort reports and news items.
Overall freelance potential: Very good.
Fees: By negotiation.

SNOOKER SCENE
Cavalier House, 202 Hagley Road, Edgbaston, Birmingham B16 9PQ.
Tel: 0121-454 2931. Fax: 0121-452 1822.
Editor: Clive Everton.
Monthly publication for snooker players and enthusiasts.
Illustrations: B&W and colour. Snooker action pictures and coverage related to tournaments, or material of historical interest. Covers: Colour pictures on similar themes.
Text: Features on snooker and billiards. 250–1,000 words.
Overall freelance potential: Small.
Fees: By arrangement.

SNOWBOARD UK
Air Publications Ltd, Unit 1A, Franchise Street, Kidderminster, Worcs DY11 6RE.
Tel: 01562 827744. Fax: 01562 755705.
Editor: Ian Sansom.
Magazine covering the sport of snowboarding. Published six times a year during the winter sports season and once in the summer.
Illustrations: Colour. Good action coverage of the sport always required; should be colourful and stylish. Interested in any freestyle or alpine shots from anywhere in the world.

Text: Short, heavily-illustrated articles on any aspect of the sport.
Overall freelance potential: Excellent; the magazine is very photo-based.
Editor's tips: The magazine is keen to build up a pool of photographers who can be relied upon to produce quality coverage of the sport. We also supply shots to other publications.
Fees: Variable; according to use and nature of material.

SPORTS IN THE SKY
Freestyle Publications Ltd, Alexander House, Ling Road, Tower Park, Poole, Dorset BH12 4NZ.
Tel: 01202 735090. Fax: 01202 733969.
Editor: Gethin James.
Monthly magazine dedicated to aerial sports.
Illustrations: Colour only. Top quality action photography of hang gliding, ballooning, paragliding, parachuting and microlighting. Covers: usually relate to an article inside, but outstanding individual shots may be used.
Text: Well-illustrated articles on training, safety, navigation, holidays and expeditions, personality profiles, memorable flights and specialist areas. 1,500 words written in a light but informative style.
Overall freelance potential: Excellent for quality material.
Editor's tips: Too many of the photographs we receive are poor both technically and aesthetically; only really top quality material is used.
Fees: Pictures according to size of reproduction; covers £60. Articles up to £100.

SPORTS TRADER
Nexus Media, Nexus House, Swanley, Kent BR8 8HY.
Tel: 01322 660070. Fax: 01322 667633.
Editor: Alistair Phillips.
Monthly publication for retailers, manufacturers, importers and exporters in the sports clothing and equipment trade.
Illustrations: B&W and colour. General sporting pictures, sporting events linked to sponsorship by manufacturers, sponsorships, sports product pictures.
Text: General news stories linked to the sports industry, usually concerning manufacturers, retailers, importers and exporters. General features concerning the sports industry. In-depth features on trends, legal articles on legislation. News stories, 250 words; features 750–1,000 words.
Overall freelance potential: Good market for the right type of material.
Editor's tips: Always telephone first.
Fees: Pictures £10–£20. Text, £100 per 1,000 words.

STEVE GRAYSTON'S MARTIAL ARTS
Grayston Graphics Co Ltd, PO Box 100, Dagenham, Essex RM8 1BH.
Tel: 0181-270 8479/8480. Fax: 0181- 517 5458.
Editor: Steve Grayston.
Monthly for the serious martial artist. Aimed at teachers and senior grades as well as novices.
Illustrations: B&W only inside. High quality martial arts pictures, but only if accompanied by text. Covers: top quality colour of senior masters, teachers, etc.
Text: Contributions considered, but in-depth specialist knowledge essential.
Overall freelance potential: Very good.
Editor's tips: Avoid flash use (except studio) as participants normally wearing white suits! Look at past covers to get an idea of the type of shot that appeals. We are happy to offer accreditation for events, etc.
Fees: Variable according to importance of material and quality.

SWIMMING TIMES
18 Derby Square, Loughborough, Leicestershire LE11 5AL.
Tel: 01509 618743. Fax: 01509 618746.
Editor: Peter Hassall.

Official monthly magazine of the Amateur Swimming Association and Institute of Swimming Teachers and Coaches. Covers all aspects of swimming including diving, synchro-swimming, water polo, etc.
Illustrations: B&W and colour. News pictures of swimmers at major events and any off-beat or particularly interesting shots of swimming-related activity.
Text: Human interest stories about individual swimmers.
Overall freelance potential: Limited.
Fees: Negotiable.

TARGET GUN
Peterson Publications Ltd, Peterson House, Northbank, Berryhill Industrial Estate, Droitwich, Worcestershire WR9 9BL.
Tel: 01905 795564. Fax: 01905 795905.
Editor: Richard Atkins.
Monthly publication for all target shooters (fullbore and smallbore, pistols and rifles, airweapons).
Illustrations: B&W and colour. Pictures of weapons, events, technical/engineering matters and pictures of general interest in the sport. Some opportunities for colour covers.
Text: General and technical instructional articles; reports of meetings. 500–2,500 words.
Overall freelance potential: Quite good.
Fees: By negotiation.

TEAM TALK MAGAZINE
Tony Williams Publications, Helland, North Curry, Taunton, Somerset TA3 6DU.
Tel: 01823 490684. Fax: 01823 490281.
Editor: Tony Williams.
Monthly magazine covering all levels of football below the Premier and Endsleigh Leagues. Also annual yearbook.
Illustrations: B&W and colour. Football action, player portraits and team shots considered on spec. Commissions may be available.
Text: Will always consider ideas; anyone interested should phone for a chat.
Overall freelance potential: Excellent, but budget is limited.
Fees: By negotiation.

TENNIS WORLD
Mediawatch Ltd, The Spendlove Centre, Enstone Road, Charlbury, Oxon OX7 3PQ.
Tel: 01608 811266. Fax: 01608 811380.
Acting Editor: Paul Larkins.
Monthly for tennis enthusiasts, covering both the British and international scene.
Illustrations: B&W and colour. Top quality tournament coverage always considered. Also action shots and portraits of leading individual players.
Text: Tournament reports, profiles of individual players and technique features, 500–1,500 words.
Overall freelance potential: Fair.
Fees: By negotiation.

TODAY'S GOLFER
EMAP Pursuit Publishing Ltd, Bretton Court, Bretton, Peterborough PE3 8DZ.
Tel: 01733 264666. Fax: 01733 465221.
Editor: Neil Pope.
Monthly for golfing enthusiasts.
Illustrations: B&W and colour. Stock shots of leading players and courses, and anything off-beat,

considered on spec.
Text: Instructional material; player profiles; equipment.
Overall freelance potential: Limited.
Fees: By negotiation.

TODAY'S RUNNER

EMAP Pursuit Publishing Ltd, Bretton Court, Bretton, Peterborough PE3 8DZ.
Tel: 01733 264666. Fax: 01733 267198/465206.
Editor: Victoria Tebbs.
Monthly magazine for active running enthusiasts, those who run for health or recreation.
Illustrations: Colour only. Coverage of competitions and running events at local or regional level, off-beat pictures, and general stock shots of runners. Both racing and training pictures are welcome. Some scope for general atmospheric pictures incorporating runners and athletic-looking subjects in picturesque and inspirational settings. Possible commission scope for "fashion" features. Covers: usually by commission – interested in hearing from photographers who can bring a creative approach to the subject.
Text: Illustrated articles of a practical nature, giving advice on training, diet, etc., and on unusual or exciting running events worldwide 1,000–1,500 words. Features of an inspirational nature also welcome – well-written and illustrated pieces on elite athletes, or other sportspeople who run as part of their training. Discuss ideas with the editor first.
Overall freelance potential: Good.
Fees: From a minimum of £20 up to £80 for a full page; text £70 per 1,000 words.

TOTAL FOOTBALL

Future Publishing Ltd, Beauford Court, 30 Monmouth Street, Bath BA1 2BW.
Tel: 01225 442244. Fax: 01225 732248.
Editor: Richard Jones. **Art Editor**: Nick Moyle.
Monthly aimed at male soccer fans in their 20s, featuring the fan lifestyle as well as the game.
Illustrations: Colour only. Mostly commissioned. Good action coverage from the lower divisions, plus "lifestyle" material. Contact the art editor with suggestions in the first instance.
Text: Little scope, but original ideas considered.
Overall freelance potential: Fair.
Editor's tips: The aim is to make the magazine as different as possible from its rivals, so a genuinely original approach could pay dividends.
Fees: By negotiation.

TOTAL SPORT

EMAP Metro Ltd, Mappin House, 4 Winsley Street, London W1N 1AR.
Tel: 0171-436 1515. Fax: 0171-312 8936.
Editor: Danny Kelly. **Picture Editor**: Simon Vinall.
Glossy, heavily-illustrated general sports monthly concentrating on the major sports.
Illustrations: Mainly colour. Commissioned photography of sporting personalities and top sporting events. Stock material usually obtained via agencies.
Text: Profiles of sports celebrities and features on major events. Usually commissioned from top names.
Overall freelance potential: For experienced specialists only.
Fees: By negotiation.

TOURING CAR WORLD

Pro-Activ Publications, 3 High Street, Chislehurst, Kent BR7 5AB.
Tel: 0181-295 1414. Fax: 0181-295 1401.
Editor: Andrew Charman.
Monthly covering the touring car racing scene.

Illustrations: Colour. Coverage of the touring car scene worldwide, with the emphasis on pictures that are excellent photographs in their own right rather than standard stock shots. Not just shots of cars racing but also atmosphere, people, details, etc. Assignments may be available to those who can show original talent.
Text: Little scope.
Overall freelance potential: Excellent; the editor encourages fresh and original talent.
Editor's tips: "If you have touring car shots that might arouse the interest of a photographic magazine... I will be interested too. Material should be original but not gimmicky."
Fees: By negotiation, dependent on what is offered.

WISDEN CRICKET MONTHLY
Wisden Cricket Magazines Ltd. Editorial: The Boathouse, Crabtree Lane, Fulham, London SW6 6LU. Tel: 0171-470 2400. Fax: 0171-381 6903.
Editor: Tim de Lisle.
Monthly publication aimed at all cricket lovers. Concentrates on the game at first-class and especially international level.
Illustrations: B&W and colour. Exceptional photographs of the above always considered.
Text: Scope for exclusive news stories and features. But check first before submitting. 400–2,500 words.
Overall freelance potential: Much increased following recent change of editorship.
Fees: On a rising scale according to size of pictures or length and significance of article.

XL
EMAP Metro Ltd, Mappin House, 4 Winsley Street, London W1N 7AR.
Tel: 0171-436 1515. Fax: 0171-312 8787.
Editor: John Westlake. **Art Editor**: Duncan Spires. **Picture Editor**: Krissy Hodgkinson.
Monthly magazine covering sport, health and fitness and aimed at an up-market male readership.
Illustrations: Mainly colour, but exceptional B&W work also of interest. Most sports coverage obtained through picture agencies, but top quality pictures of major sporting activity always considered. Some opportunities for commissioned work covering health/fitness subjects.
Text: No scope.
Overall freelance potential: Limited.
Editor's tips: Do not submit run-of-the-mill photographs; only top quality material is of interest.
Fees: Negotiable.

XTREME
Xtreme Publications, 132 Buckingham Palace Road, London SW1W 9SA.
Tel: 0171-259 9229. Fax: 0171-259 9258.
Editor: Jerome Smail.
Lifestyle monthly covering all forms of extreme sports as well as more mainstream activities. Aimed at 18-30 year old males.
Illustrations: Colour. Top quality action photographs of all types of extreme sport, plus mainstream sports such as climbing, mountain biking, surfing, etc, and pictures depicting other forms of dangerous or wacky behaviour. Either shots that have great impact in themselves, or which have an interesting or unusual story attached.
Text: Well-illustrated features on extreme sports or risk lifestyles or anything that could be described as "extreme living". Write first with proposals.
Overall freelance potential: Very good.
Editor's tips: To be successful material should have a genuinely extreme angle – the more extreme the better.
Fees: Negotiable, but up to around £90 for single pictures.

Trade

THE BOOKSELLER

J. Whitaker and Sons Ltd, 12 Dyott Street, London WC1A 1DF.
Tel: 0171-420 6000. Fax: 0171-420 6103.
Editor: Louis Baum. **Production Editors**: Mark Guest, Brian Payne.
Weekly trade paper aimed at librarians, booksellers, publishers, agents, authors and anyone interested in the book industry. Covers trade trends and events, authors, etc.
Illustrations: Colour and B&W. Pictures of bookshops and book-related activities outside London. Busy book fairs, busy book shops, etc. Portraits of authors and book trade figures.
Text: Serious, humorous, analytical, descriptive articles connected with the book trade, plus author interviews.
Overall freelance potential: Only for those freelances who have good access to the book trade.
Fees: Variable; depends on material.

BRITISH BAKER

Quantum Publishing Ltd, Maclaren House, 19 Scarbrook Road, Croydon CR9 1QH.
Tel: 0181-277 5318. Fax: 0181-277 5302.
Editor: Garry Parker.
Weekly business-to-business magazine covering the entire baking industry.
Illustrations: Colour only. Interesting photographs relating to working bakeries, especially news items such as shop openings, promotions, charity events, etc. Also good stock shots of bakery products.
Text: Short news stories (300 words) or features (500–1,000 words) on any baking industry topic.
Overall freelance potential: Fair, for those who can supply relevant material.
Fees: £115 per 1,000 words for text; photographs by negotiation.

CABINET MAKER

Miller Freeman plc, Miller Freeman House, Sovereign Way, Tonbridge, Kent TN9 1RW.
Tel: 01732 364422. Fax: 01732 361534.
Editor: Sandra Danby.
Weekly publication for all those in the furniture and furnishing trade and industry.
Illustrations: Colour. Freelances commissioned to cover news assignments in the trade. Some scope for pictures to illustrate features.
Text: Features about companies making furniture for sale to retailers and interior designers. Length from one to four pages (1,000 words plus three pictures makes two pages).
Overall freelance potential: Around 10 per cent contributed, including news coverage.
Editor's tips: Please approach the editor, features editor or news editor for a brief before submitting.
Fees: By agreement.

CATERER & HOTELKEEPER

Reed Business Information Ltd, Room H415, Quadrant House, The Quadrant, Sutton, Surrey SM2 5AS.
Tel: 0181-652 8538. Fax: 0181-652 8973.
Editor: Forbes Mutch. **Art Editor**: Sarah Thompson.
Weekly magazine for the hotel and catering trade.
Illustrations: B&W and colour. News pictures relevant to hotel and catering establishments – openings, extensions, refurbishments, people, etc. Special interest in regional material. Commissions possible to cover establishments, equipment and food.
Text: Specialist articles of interest to the trade, by commission only.
Overall freelance potential: Mainly limited to those with connections within the trade.
Editor's tips: "We welcome tip-offs concerning the industry, for which we will pay £15–£25."
Fees: On a rising scale according to size of reproduction or length of text.

CHEMIST AND DRUGGIST
Miller Freeman PLC, Miller Freeman House, Sovereign Way, Tonbridge, Kent TN9 1RW.
Tel: 01732 364422. Fax: 01732 361534.
Editor: Patrick Grice.
Weekly news publication for retail pharmacists; the pharmaceutical, toiletries and cosmetics industries; pharmaceutical wholesalers, etc.
Illustrations: B&W and colour. News pictures concerning individual retailers and retailing related events, plus industry events relating to pharmaceutical companies.
Text: Local news stories relating to community pharmacy.
Overall freelance potential: Limited.
Fees: On a rising scale, according to contribution.

CONVENIENCE STORE
William Reed Ltd, Broadfield Park, Crawley, West Sussex RH11 9RT.
Tel: 01293 613400. Fax: 01293 613206.
Editor: Christian Davis.
Fortnightly magazine for small independent retailers and convenience stores, and their wholesale suppliers.
Illustrations: Colour. Photographs usually to illustrate specific features; little scope for pictures on their own.
Text: Illustrated features or stories concerning late-night, local, food-based stores. Should ideally feature a retailer who is doing something a bit different, or who has been highly successful in some way.
Overall freelance potential: Modest, but the editor will be pleased to hear from freelances who can produce an interesting illustrated feature in this field.
Fees: By negotiation.

DRAPERS RECORD
EMAP Business Communications, Angel House, 338-346 Goswell Road, London EC1V 7QP.
Tel: 0171-520 1509. Fax: 0171-520 1511.
Editor: *To Be Appointed*. **Art Editor**: Lorna Wood.
Weekly news publication for clothing and textile retailers.
Illustrations: B&W and colour. News pictures of interest to the trade. Commissioned coverage for fashion and major trade stories.
Text: Features and news items of relevance to retailers in the fashion and textile fields.
Overall freelance potential: Limited for news; fair for commissioned work.
Editor's tips: Please do not send unsolicited material – call the editor first.
Fees: Good; on a rising scale according to size of illustration or length of feature.

EUROFRUIT MAGAZINE
Market Intelligence Ltd, 4th Floor, Market Towers, One Nine Elms Lane, London SW8 5NQ.
Tel: 0171-498 6711. Fax: 0171-498 6472.
Editor: Chris White.
Monthly magazine of the European fresh fruit and vegetable trade, published in five languages. Aimed at producers, exporters, importers, merchants and buyers.
Illustrations: B&W and colour. Subjects such as harvesting fruit, loading on to ships or lorries, quality checks on fruit, packing etc. Photographs accepted mostly forthe magazine's own picture library.
Text: Topical features on fruit and vegetables, e.g. Chilean apples in Europe, French Iceberg lettuce, Egypt's expanding export range, Norway as an alternative market, etc. 1,250–2,000 words.
Overall freelance potential: Quite good. Some regular contributors, but scope for the freelance writer who can also supply pictures.
Editor's tips: It is best to work in close contact with the editorial department to get names of people who would be of interest to the publication.
Fees: Negotiable.

FX
ETP Ltd, 2 Legg Street, Chelmsford, Essex CM1 1AH.
Tel: 01245 491717. Fax: 01245 499110.
Editor: Aidan Walker. **Art Editor**: Patrick Myles.
Interior design business magazine for the retail, hotel and commercial sectors. Aimed at architects, designers and their clients. Published 10 times per year.
Illustrations: Mainly colour. By commission only; experienced architectural and interiors photographers with fresh ideas always welcome.
Text: Articles on commercial design matters and related business issues, only from those with real expertise in these areas.
Overall freelance potential: Good for the experienced worker.
Editor's tips: We are very receptive to original ideas. Articles should be hard-hitting and possibly contentious.
Fees: Photography around £200–£250 per day. £160 per 1,000 words.

FW
EMAP Business Communications Ltd, Angel House, 338 Goswell Road, London EC1V 7QP.
Tel: 0171-520 1500. Fax: 0171-520 1646.
Editor: William Drew.
Retail trade magazine published eight times per year, covering women's and men's fashion, denim and sportswear.
Illustrations: B&W and colour. News pictures concerning the fashion, textile and related trades. Main fashion coverage always commissioned.
Text: Little scope.
Overall freelance potential: Good for the specialist freelance in touch with the fashion scene.
Fees: Negotiable.

FASHION EXTRAS
Reflex Publishing Ltd, 177A High Street, Tonbridge, Kent TN9 1BX.
Tel: 01732 362445. Fax: 01732 362447.
Editor: Bridget Gill.
Monthly trade publication dealing with fashion accessories such as gloves, scarves, jewellery, hosiery and shoes, and including leathergoods, i.e. handbags, luggage.
Illustrations: B&W and colour. Interested in stock fashion pictures or fashion show coverage.
Text: Features on the legal, insurance and cash side of the business. Specialist articles on all aspects of selling to the consumer. Retail trends. Fashion articles. Up to 1,000 words.
Overall freelance potential: Small but regular income possible for outside contributors. About 20 per cent is contributed.
Editor's tips: New approaches and thoughts on still-life photography always welcome.
Fees: Negotiable.

FISHING MONTHLY
Special Publications, Royston House, Caroline Park, Edinburgh EH5 1QJ.
Tel: 0131-551 2942. Fax: 0131-551 2938.
Editor: Keith Broomfield.
Monthly tabloid for the the Scottish fishing industry, but with coverage extending to the rest of Britain and Europe.
Illustrations: B&W and colour. Captioned news pictures covering any subject relating to the Scottish and European fishing industry, including fish farming, processing, etc.
Text: Short illustrated news items, and longer features from contributors with suitable knowledge of the industry.
Overall freelance potential: Good, especially for those with connections in the fishing industry.
Fees: By negotiation.

THE FLORIST TRADE MAGAZINE

Florist Trade Magazine Ltd, The Vineyard, 39 Ham Common, Richmond, Surrey TW10 7JG.
Tel: 0181-332 6655. Fax: 0181-332 9377.
Editor: Caroline Marshall-Foster.
Publication for retail florists, published 10 times a year.
Illustrations: Mainly colour. News pictures about the trade and other interesting pictures of floristry in the retail context, i.e. special displays, promotions, etc.
Text: Features on anything relating to floristry and retailing, shop profiles, practical aspects, advertising and promotion, etc.
Overall freelance potential: Limited.
Fees: Text, £100 per 1,000 words published; pictures by agreement.

FORECOURT TRADER

William Reed Publishing Ltd, Broadfield Park, Crawley, West Sussex RH11 9RT.
Tel: 01293 613400. Fax: 01293 610330.
Editor: Merril Boulton.
Monthly magazine for petrol station operators.
Illustrations: Colour only. News pictures relating to petrol stations and the petrol sales business generally.
Text: News and features relating to all areas of petrol retailing.
Overall freelance potential: Fair.
Fees: Text, £120 per 1,000 words; pictures according to use.

HARDWARE & GARDEN REVIEW

Faversham House Group Ltd, Faversham House, 232A Addington Road, South Croydon CR2 8LE.
Tel: 0181-651 7100. Fax: 0181-651 7117.
Editor: Liam O'Brien.
Monthly magazine for the independent hardware, housewares, garden centre and DIY trade.
Illustrations: B&W and colour. Trade news pictures and picture stories concerning particular stores and outlets.
Text: Illustrated articles on store redesign, and retailer profiles. Around 1,000 words.
Overall freelance potential: Fair.
Editor's tips: Articles should be exclusive in this field. Always send an outline in the first instance.
Fees: On a rising scale according to size of reproduction or length of text.

INDEPENDENT RETAIL NEWS

Reed Business Publishing, Quadrant House, The Quadrant, Sutton, Surrey SM2 5AS.
Tel: 0181-652 8754. Fax: 0181-652 8936.
Editor: Keely Harrison.
Fortnightly publication for independent, convenience, licensed and CTN retailers. Assists them in being more profitable and aware of new products and campaigns.
Illustrations: Colour only. Captioned news pictures and picture stories of interest to independent grocery and convenience store traders. Medium format preferred.
Text: Articles and stories about successful small retailers fighting off the giants, unfair trading, warnings of unscrupulous dealings and novelty and business ideas. 650 words minimum.
Overall freelance potential: Obtain 50 per cent of news pictures from freelances and about 20 per cent of stories either from freelance writers or from freelance tip-offs.
Editor's tips: A sample copy of the magazine is available to potential contributors. Always ring first with ideas.
Fees: Photographs according to size of reproduction, but around £40–£50. £80 per 1,000 words for commissioned features; 20p per line for news stories.

MEAT & POULTRY NEWS
Yandell Publishing Ltd, 8 Vermont Place, Tongwell, Milton Keynes, Bucks MK15 6JA.
Tel: 01908 613323. Fax: 01908 210656.
Editor: Pam Brook.
Monthly journal for the whole meat and poultry trade.
Illustrations: B&W and colour. Pictures relating to any current meat trade issue, including legislation, food scares, court cases, etc.
Text: Stories on current issues as above. Illustrated features of around 1,000 words on current food issues, research, technology, and profiles of individual businesses.
Overall freelance potential: Very good for those in a position to cover this industry.
Editor's tips: It is much preferred if material offered is exclusive.
Fees: £15 for B&W reproductions; £25 for colour. £110 per 1,000 words for text. Higher rates may be payable for material of special interest.

MEAT TRADER
National Federation of Meat & Food Traders, 1 Belgrove, Tunbridge Wells, Kent TN1 1YW.
Tel: 01892 541412. Fax: 01892 535462.
Editor: Graham Bidston.
Official magazine of the National Federation of Meat & Food Traders. Published 10 times a year covering news and issues in the meat trade.
Illustrations: B&W and colour. Topical pictures related to the meat trade.
Text: Topical features on the meat and livestock trade. Up to 2,000 words.
Overall freelance potential: Fair for those in close contact with the trade.
Editor's tips: To be considered, material must be exclusive.
Fees: By negotiation.

MENSWEAR
EMAP Fashion, Angel House, 338-346 Goswell Road, London EC1V 7QP.
Tel: 0171-520 1662. Fax: 0171-520 1663.
Editor: Chris Scott-Gray.
Fortnightly publication for retailers and buyers of men's clothing.
Illustrations: Colour. News pictures concerning the men's clothing retail trade. Pictures to illustrate merchandise features, usually comissioned.
Text: Illustrated news and features on the industry.
Overall freelance potential: Limited. Best scope is for news from outside London.
Editor's tips: Always interested in new retail openings, especially outside London.
Fees: Negotiable.

PRESTIGE INTERIORS
(Three separate titles covering **CORPORATE**, **HIGH STREET**, and **HOTEL AND RESTAURANT** interiors)
Albatross Publications, PO Box 193, Dorking, Surrey RH5 5YF.
Tel: 01306 712712.
Editor: Carol Andrews.
Alternate-monthly publications covering interior design in the three commercial sectors specified above. Aimed at managers concerned with interiors in the fields of hotels and restaurants, office administration, retail and catering, and the designers serving them.
Illustrations: Colour only. News pictures or good stock shots of interesting new interiors and developments, especially striking examples of good (or bad) design and decor, lighting, and specific problems encountered.
Text: News stories, and profiles of relevant individual companies or projects, but always contact the editor with suggestions first.
Overall freelance potential: Fair.

Editor's tips: Remember that these are professional publications for business people and interior designers.
Fees: By negotiation.

SHOE AND LEATHER NEWS
EMAP Fashion, Angel House, 338-346 Goswell Road, London EC1V 7QP.
Tel: 0171-520 1657. Fax: 0171-520 1501.
Editor: Joshua Sims.
Monthly trade publication for specialist footwear retailers, manufacturers and designers to the footwear industry.
Illustrations: Colour only. News pictures relating to the market and items of interest to the trade in general. Portraits of trade personalities.
Text: Features on all aspects of the trade, especially on footwear retailing and fashion. Manufacturing of footwear or allied products also of interest. 500–1,500 words.
Overall freelance potential: Average.
Fees: By agreement.

THE SUBPOSTMASTER
National Federation of Subpostmasters, Weston Post Office, 7 High Street, Weston, Bath BA1 4BX.
Tel/fax: 01225 423083.
Editor: D. T. Broadwith.
Monthly journal of the Federation of Subpostmasters, with strong news content concerning individual members.
Illustrations: B&W, or colour prints. Pictures of any subpostmaster in the news for any reason, with captions.
Text: No freelance market.
Overall freelance potential: Small.
Editor's tips: More interested in subjects with unusual hobbies, histories, etc. than in attack stories.
Fees: On a rising scale, according to the size of reproduction.

TAX-FREE TRADER
Argus Business Media, Queensway House, 2 Queensway, Redhill, Surrey RH1 1QS.
Tel: 01737 768611. Fax: 01737 761989.
Editor: Peter Tipthorp.
Monthly publication for executives in duty-free trade worldwide, in airports, airlines, cruise ships, ferry services, etc, and suppliers of duty-free goods in all fields, e.g. alcohol, tobacco, cosmetics, toiletries, watches, luxury gifts.
Illustrations: B&W and colour. Specially interested in pictures which illustrate locations and displays at duty-free shops – general views, and especially close-ups of customers, individual displays and individual products. Covers: colourful and attractive pictures of duty-free shops.
Text: Features on products, shops and personalities in the international duty-free trade. 2,000–2,500 words.
Overall freelance potential: Around 40 per cent comes from freelances.
Editor's tips: Send an outline of ideas in the first instance.
Fees: £130 per 1,000 words; pictures by agreement.

WORLD FISHING
Nexus Media Ltd, Nexus House, Azalea Drive, Swanley, Kent BR8 8HY.
Tel: 01322 660070. Fax: 01322 666408.
Editor: Mark Say.
Monthly journal for the commercial fishing industry. Covers fisheries and related industries from an international perspective.
Illustrations: B&W and colour. Mainly to accompany specific articles, but some scope for scene-set-

ting shots of commercial fishing activity in specific locations worldwide.
Text: Illustrated articles on any commercial fishing topic. Should always contain some international interest. Maximum 1,800 words.
Overall freelance potential: Good for those with connections in the industry.
Fees: Photographs by negotiation.Text £75 per 1,000 words.

Transport

COACH AND BUS WEEK
EMAP Automotive Publishing Ltd, Wentworth House, Wentworth Street, Peterborough PE1 1DS.
Tel: 01733 467139. Fax: 01733 467154.
Editor: Mike Morgan.
Weekly news magazine covering coach and bus operations. Aimed at licensed coach, bus and tour operators.
Illustrations: Colour. Pictures as illustrations to features mentioned below; coach and bus related news items. Places of interest to coach parties.
Text: Features on coach and bus operators, hotels, ferry operations, resorts and venues, anything that would be of interest to a coach party or an operator. Articles on subjects that an operator might find useful in his day to day business. Up to 2,000 words.
Overall freelance potential: Always interested in seeing work from freelances.
Fees: By negotiation.

COMMERCIAL MOTOR
Reed Business Publishing Ltd, Quadrant House, The Quadrant, Sutton, Surrey SM2 5AS.
Tel: 0181-652 3302. Fax: 0181-652 8969.
Editor: Brian Weatherley. **Art Editor**: Steve Gale.
Weekly publication devoted to the road haulage industry. Aimed at vehicle enthusiasts as well as industry readers.
Illustrations: Colour only. Mostly commissioned; arrange to show portfolio to the art editor first. Stock photographs of commercial vehicles and all aspects of road haulage and road usage may be of interest – send lists of subjects available.
Text: Technical articles on road haulage topics, from expert contributors only.
Overall freelance potential: Very good.
Fees: Day rate around £150–£200 plus expenses. Other material by negotiation.

CONTAINERISATION INTERNATIONAL
EMAP, 1st Floor, 151 Rosebery Avenue, London EC1R 4QX.
Tel: 0171-505 3530. Fax: 0171-505 3535.
Editor: Jane R.C.Boyes. **Art Editor**: Damian Le Bargy.
Monthly business-oriented magazine on issues facing the international container transport industry.
Illustrations: Colour. Unusual pictures of container shipping activities, especially in exotic locations overseas, or interesting uses for containers inland.
Text: Well-researched and *exclusive* articles, preferably on some aspect of the container transport business not covered by staff writers. Around 2,000 words.
Overall freelance potential: Limited.
Fees: By agreement.

OLD GLORY
CMS Publishing, Bullimores House, Church Lane, Cranleigh, Surrey GU6 8AR.
Tel: 01483 274004. Fax: 01483 274144.
Editor: Brian Gooding.
Monthly devoted to industrial heritage and vintage restoration including traction engines, tractors, etc.

Illustrations: B&W and colour. Pictures of all forms of traction engines, tractors, buses, commercial vehicles, fairground machinery and maritime subjects such as old steamboats. News pictures of individual machines, restoration projects, etc. Detailed captions necessary including where and when picture taken. Covers: colour pictures of traction engines in attractive settings.
Text: Illustrated articles on subjects as above.
Overall freelance potential: Excellent. A lot of scope for good colour material.
Fees: Generally £5–£15 for B&W; £10–£25 for colour; text, £40 per 1,000 words.

ROADWAY

Road Haulage Association Ltd, Roadway House, 35 Monument Hill, Weybridge, Surrey KT13 8RN.
Tel: 01932 841515. Fax: 01932 852516.
Editor: Steve Gray.
Monthly news magazine for the road haulage industry.
Illustrations: Colour. Pictures of trucks on motorways, at depots etc. Should be newsworthy or of unusual interest.
Text: Articles on any aspect of the road haulage industry. Length by prior agrement with the editor.
Overall freelance potential: Limited.
Fees: By arrangement.

TRUCK

Reed Business Information, Quadrant House, The Quadrant, Sutton, Surrey SM2 5AS.
Tel: 0181-652 3664. Fax: 0181-652 8988.
Editor: Dean Stiles. **Art Director**: Emma Sayers.
Monthly magazine for truck operators and lorry drivers.
Illustrations: B&W and colour. Pictures of interesting individual trucks, unusual situations involving trucks and their drivers, humorous situations, and news items.
Text: Commissioned features on any topic of relevance to truck drivers. Looks for freelances with ideas.
Overall freelance potential: Good.
Fees: By negotiation.

TRUCK & DRIVER

Reed Business Information, Quadrant House, The Quadrant, Sutton, Surrey SM2 5AS.
Tel: 0181-652 3500. Fax: 0181-652 8988.
Editor: Dave Young. **Art Director**: Emma Sayers.
Monthly magazine for truck drivers.
Illustrations: Colour only. Interesting individual trucks, unusual situations involving drivers and their vehicles, news items and some studio work.
Text: Commissioned features on anything of interest to truck drivers. Looks for freelances with ideas.
Overall freelance potential: Very good.
Fees: By negotiation.

Travel

BUSINESS LIFE

Premier Magazines Ltd, Haymarket House, 1 Oxendon Street, London SW1Y 4EE.
Tel: 0171-925 2544. Fax: 0171-839 4508.
Editor: Sandra Harris.
Monthly business travel magazine distributed on British Airways flights within Europe.
Illustrations: Colour only. All aspects of business travel within Europe. Send details of specialities and coverage available in the first instance. Covers: colourful, graphic shots with a "different" angle.

Text: Little scope, but original ideas on European business travel always considered.
Overall freelance potential: Fair.
Fees: According to the nature of material and use.

BUSINESS TRAVELLER

Perry Motorpress Ltd, Compass House, 22 Redan Place, London W2 4SZ.
Tel: 0171-229 7799. Fax: 0171-229 9441.
Editor: Julia Brookes. **Picture Editor**: Deborah Miller-Umpelby.
Monthly consumer publication aimed at the frequently travelling international business executive.
Illustrations: Colour only. Pictures to illustrate destination report articles on a wide variety of cities around the world – request features list of upcoming destinations. No photo features used.
Text: Features on business travel, but only by consultation with the editor.
Overall freelance potential: Around 65 per cent of the magazine is contributed by freelances.
Editor's tips: Prefer and recommend the submission of dupes rather than originals.
Fees: Pictures from £50 up to £180 for a full page; covers £250. Text, £150 per 1,000 words.

CONDÉ NAST TRAVELLER

The Condé Nast Publications Ltd, Vogue House, Hanover Square, London W1R 0AD.
Tel: 0171-629 5393. Fax: 0171-493 3758.
Editor: Sarah Miller. **Picture Editor**: Caroline Metcalfe.
Heavily-illustrated glossy monthly for the more affluent traveller.
Illustrations: Colour and occasional B&W. Top quality photo-feature material covering all aspects of travel, not just the luxury end of the market but including adventure travel, ecological issues, archeology, etc. Very stylish and striking black and white photography also sought. Always interested in hearing from experienced photographers who are planning specific trips.
Text: Mostly commissioned from top name writers.
Overall freelance potential: Very good for material of the highest quality.
Editor's tips: The magazine seeks to use material with an original approach. Particularly interested in hearing from photographers who can produce excellent work but who are not necessarily travel specialists.
Fees: Variable depending on what is offered, but top rates paid for suitable material.

ESSENTIALLY AMERICA

Phoenix Publishing & Media Ltd, 18-20 Scrutton Street, London EC2A 4RJ.
Tel: 0171-247 0537. Fax: 0171-377 2741.
Editor: Mary Moore Mason.
Alternate-monthly magazine covering North American travel and lifestyle for a British and Irish readership.
Illustrations: Colour only. Pictures of a wide variety of US and Canadian subjects required to illustrate features on places, people, cuisine, history, native Americans, sports, etc. As interested in lifestyle material as in scenics and landmarks. Send details of material available, or request forthcoming features list for which pictures may be required.
Text: Illustrated articles on subjects as above. Submit suggestions only in the first instance.
Overall freelance potential: Very good.
Fees: By negotiation.

EXECUTIVE TRAVEL

Reed Travel Group, Church Street, Dunstable, Bedfordshire LU5 4HB.
Tel: 01582 600111. Fax: 01582 695095.
Editor: Mike Toynbee. **Picture Editor**: Catherine Miller.
Monthly magazine for the frequent traveller.
Illustrations: Colour only. High quality photographs of destinations worldwide. The emphasis is on business rather than pleasure, although some leisure pursuits are covered. Features list on request.

Text: Only by commission, but ideas are always welcome.
Overall freelance potential: Good, for genuinely suitable material.
Fees: by negotiation.

FRANCE

Central Haven Ltd, France House, Digbeth Street, Stow-on-the-Wold, Gloucestershire GL54 1BN.
Tel: 01451 831398. Fax: 01451 830869.
Editor: Philip Faiers. **Picture Researcher**: Alison Hughes.
Quarterly magazine for Francophiles, with the emphasis on the real France.
Illustrations: Colour only. Picture stories, and top quality individual pictures to illustrate articles, on French regions, annual events, cuisine, travel, arts, history, shopping, fashion and sport. Especially interested in character and human interest shots, and mood pictures. Covers: pictures that capture the essence of France.
Text: Lively and colourful illustrated features on the life, culture and history of France. Normally around 800–1,200 words, but up to 2,000 words considered. Factual accuracy essential.
Overall freelance potential: Excellent for top quality material.
Editor's tips: Regular "wants" lists and contributors' notes will be sent on request. Not much interested in accounts of family holidays or of setting up home in France.
Fees: Photographs from £25 up to £100 for cover or DPS. £1 per 62 characters of printed text.

LONDON 2000

Talisman Publishing Ltd, Woodcock House, Gibbard Mews, 37 High Street, Wimbledon Village, London SW19 5BY.
Tel: 0181-944 6622. Fax: 0181-944 7798.
Editor: *To be appointed.*
Bi-monthly magazine for travellers arriving at London Heathrow Airport. Primarily a business publication, with general features on health, travel and celebrities.
Illustrations: Mainly colour. Will consider high quality and original photo essays on London themes, B&W or colour. Contact the editor with suggestions.
Text: No scope.
Overall freelance potential: Mainly uses regular contributors.
Fees: By negotiation.

TRAVELLER

WEXAS International Ltd, 45 Brompton Road, London SW3 1DE.
Tel: 0171-581 4130. Fax: 0171-581 1357.
Editor: Miranda Haines.
Quarterly publication containing informative and entertaining articles on travel, and travel-related subjects of an "ethnographic" nature, usually in the developing countries of the world. Aimed at the independent traveller who prefers to travel off the beaten track and with minimal cultural impact.
Illustrations: Mainly colour. High quality documentary travel pictures, invariably from developing countries, rarely Europe or North America, but usually required as an integral part of illustrated articles as below. No "tourist brochure" shots.
Text: Well-illustrated travel articles from contributors with in-depth knowledge of the area/subject covered. Around 1,500 words, plus 4–10 pictures. Unusual subject matter preferred, including coverage of world hot spots. Send synopsis first.
Overall freelance potential: Good, but limited by the magazine's frequency.
Editor's tips: Excellent photographic work is essential. For text, a topical approach helps.
Fees: Photographs, £25; £50 for cover. Text, £150 per 1,000 words.

WANDERLUST

Wanderlust Publications Ltd, PO Box 1832, Windsor, Berks SL4 6YP.
Tel: 01753 620426. Fax: 01753 620474.
Editor: Lyn Hughes.

Alternate-monthly for the "independent-minded" traveller. Aims to promote awareness of other cultures and the environment.

Illustrations: Mainly colour. Little scope for pictures on their own; most required for use in conjunction with features. Send a summary stocklist in the first instance. Covers: always looking for simple, bold images that say "Wanderlust", preferably faces. Should be vertical or croppable to vertical.

Text: Well-illustrated features on independent travel at any level and in any part of the world, from day-trips to cross-continent expeditions. Contributors must have in-depth knowledge of their subject area and be prepared to cover both good and bad aspects. Short pieces up to 750 words; longer articles from 1,800–2,500 words.

Overall freelance potential: Excellent for complete packages of words and pictures.

Editor's tips: Don't send unsolicited originals; photocopies or prints will do as samples. Detailed "Notes for Contributors" and "Guidelines for Photographers" are available on receipt of a sae.

Fees: Photographs by negotiation and according to use; text £100 per 1,000 words.

Women's Interest

BELLA
H. Bauer Publishing Ltd, Shirley House, 25–27 Camden Road, London NW1 9LL.
Tel: 0171-284 0909. Fax: 0171-485 3774.
Editor: Jackie Highe.
Weekly magazine for women, covering human interest stories, fashion, cookery and celebrities.

Illustrations: B&W and colour. Pictures of celebrities, Royalty, off-beat pictures and curiosities. Fashion and food, mostly commissioned.

Text: Some scope for exclusive human interest features and celebrity interviews. Always check with the editor first.

Overall freelance potential: Limited for speculative work.

Fees: By negotiation.

BEST
G&J of the UK, Portland House, Stag Place, London SW1E 5AU.
Tel: 0171-245 8700. Fax: 0171-245 8825.
Editor: Julie Akhurst. **Picture Editor**: Alison Thurston.
Weekly magazine for women, covering affordable fashion, health matters, cookery, home improvements, features etc.

Illustrations: B&W and colour. Scope for off-beat, general human interest and curiosity shots. Commissioned coverage of fashion, food, features, etc.

Text: Articles with a practical slant, aimed at working women.

Overall freelance potential: Quite good.

Fees: Commissioned photography by negotiation; other material according to use.

CHAT
IPC Magazines, King's Reach Tower, Stamford Street, London SE1 9LS.
Tel: 0171-261 6565. Fax: 0171-261 6534.
Editor: Keith Kendtrick. **Picture Editor**: John Kilpatrick.
Weekly magazine of general interest to 25–50 year old women.

Illustrations: B&W and colour. Fashion, beauty, food, etc. Coverage all produced by freelances on commission.

Text: Short, chatty features written in a high-calibre style. Must be human interest and of appeal to the average woman.

Overall freelance potential: Very good for experienced contributors to the women's press.

Editor's tips: The magazine uses a huge amount of material each week, so always keen to receive fresh ideas.

Fees: By negotiation.

COMPANY
National Magazine Company Ltd, 72 Broadwick Street, London W1V 2BP.
Tel: 0171-439 5000. Fax: 0171-439 5117.
Editor: Fiona McIntosh. **Art Editor**: Ellen Erickson.
Monthly magazine aimed at up-market young women in their twenties.
Illustrations: B&W and colour. Photographs to illustrate features on fashion, beauty, relationships, careers, travel and personalities, invariably by commission.
Text: Articles on the above topics, of varying lengths. Also, more topical and "newsy" features.
Overall freelance potential: Fair scope for experienced contributors.
Fees: By negotiation.

COSMOPOLITAN
National Magazine Company Ltd, 72 Broadwick Street, London W1V 2BP.
Tel: 0171-439 5000. Fax: 0171-439 5016.
Editor: Mandi Norwood. **Art Editor**: Fiona Hayes. **Picture Editor**: Joan Tinney.
Monthly magazine for women in the 18–34 age group.
Illustrations: Colour. Photographs to illustrate features on fashion, style and beauty, by commission only. Some top quality stock situation pictures may be used to illustrate more general features on emotional, sexual or social issues.
Text: Articles of interest to sophisticated young women. Always query the editor in the first instance.
Overall freelance potential: Only for the experienced contributor to the women's press.
Fees: By negotiation.

ELLE
Hachette-EMAP Magazines Ltd, Endeavour House, 189 Shafestbury Avenue, London WC2H 8JG.
Tel: 0171-437 9011. Fax: 0171-208 3599.
Editor: Marie O'Riordan. **Picture Editor**: Jenny Kirby.
Up-market monthly magazine with the emphasis on fashion.
Illustrations: Mainly colour. Top quality coverage of fashion and style subjects, portraiture and still life, always by commission.
Text: Some scope for top quality feature articles and photojournalism, usually by commission and from established contributors.
Overall freelance potential: Good for contributors experienced at the top level of magazine journalism.
Fees: By negotiation.

ESSENTIALS
IPC Magazines Ltd, King's Reach Tower, Stamford Street, London SE1 9LS.
Tel: 0171-261 6970. Fax: 0171-261 5262.
Editor: Karen Livermore. **Art Editor**: Liz Austin.
Monthly mass-market magazine for women with the emphasis on practical matters.
Illustrations: B&W and colour. Health, interior decoration, travel, food, etc. Some commissioned work available.
Text: Practical articles, health, features of interest to women. Synopsis essential in the first instance.
Overall freelance potential: Good for experienced contributors to quality women's magazines.
Fees: By negotiation.

EVA
IPC Magazines Ltd, King's Reach Tower, Stamford Street, London SE1 9LS.
Tel: 0171-261 5857. Fax: 0171-261 6442.
Editor: Eve Finlay-Dawson. **Picture Editor**: Vanessa Colls.
General entertainment weekly for women, focusing on true-life human interest stories and celebrity gossip.
Illustrations: Colour only. Pictures mostly used alongside a story, but photographers who don't feel

159

up to writing can simply submit pictures and a story outline. Some scope for single humorous or curiosity pictures with long caption, including animal material. Also good celebrity shots.
Text: Short, picture-led stories of around 100–300 words; dramatic, amusing, scandalous, touching, etc. Must be real-life stories about real people.
Overall freelance potential: Excellent for the right kind of material; around 50 picture-based stories used each week.
Fees: Depends on the nature and "importance" of the material.

GOOD HOUSEKEEPING
National Magazine Company Ltd, National Magazine House, 72 Broadwick Street, London W1V 2BP.
Tel: 0171-439 5000. Fax: 0171-439 5591.
Editor-in-Chief: Pat Roberts Cairns. **Picture Researcher**: Tess Weightman. **Creative Director**: Denise Barnes.
General interest magazine for up-market women. Concentrates on home and family life.
Illustrations: B&W and colour. Interiors, gardening, food, fashion, travel and reportage. Usually by commission to illustrate specific articles.
Text: Articles of interest to up-market women – interesting homes (with photos), gardening, personality profiles, emotional features, humorous articles, etc.
Overall freelance potential: Good scope for the highest quality material.
Fees: By negotiation.

HARPERS & QUEEN
National Magazine Company Ltd, 72 Broadwick Street, London W1V 2BP.
Tel: 0171-439 5000. Fax: 0171-439 5506.
Editor: Fiona Macpherson. **Picture Editor**: Haydn Wood. **Art Director**: Sheila Jack.
Monthly glossy magazine featuring fashion, design, travel, interiors, beauty and health.
Illustrations: B&W and colour. Top quality photography to illustrate subjects as above, only by commission.
Text: General interest features of very high quality. 1,500–3,000 words. Only by commission.
Overall freelance potential: Good for those who can produce the right material.
Fees: Good; on a rising scale according to length of feature.

HELLO!
Hello Ltd, Wellington House, 69/71 Upper Ground, London SE1 9PQ.
Tel: 0171-667 8700. Fax: 0171-667 8716.
Editor: Maggie Koumi. **Picture Editor**: Chris Hewitt.
Weekly magazine for women covering people and current events.
Illustrations: Mainly colour. Pictures and picture stories on personalities and celebrities of all kinds. People in the news and current news events. Off-beat pictures. Dramatic picture stories of bravery, courage or rescue.
Text: Interviews and/or reports to accompany photos.
Overall freelance potential: Excellent for quality material.
Editor's tips: "We have short lead times and this is something we wish to exploit to the full. We can include late stories in colour up to the Thursday of the week before publication."
Fees: By negotiation.

HOME AND COUNTRY
NFWI, 104 New Kings Road, Fulham, London SW6 4LY.
Tel: 0171-731 5777. Fax: 0171-736 4061.
Editor: Amber Tokeley. **Designer**: Diane Gibb.
Monthly publication for Women's Institute members. Includes WI news and features, plus general articles of interest to women.
Illustrations: B&W and colour. Pictures of WI events etc.
Text: Features of general women's interest and rural conservation issues, commissioned in advance;

ideas welcomed. 800–1,200 words.
Overall freelance potential: A small but regular amount bought each month.
Editor's tips: Always consult the editor before submitting.
Fees: By agreement.

THE LADY
The Lady, 39–40 Bedford Street, Strand, London WC2E 9ER.
Tel: 0171-379 4717. Fax: 0171-497 2137.
Editor: Arline Usden. **Picture Researcher**: Sarah Fox.
Weekly general interest magazine for women.
Illustrations: Colour and B&W. Pictures only required to accompany particular articles. Covers: colour pictures depicting traditional British scenes, still life, some animals, paintings.
Text: Illustrated articles on British and foreign travel, the countryside, human interest, wildlife, pets, cookery, gardening, fashion, beauty, British history and commemorative subjects. 800–1,000 words.
Overall freelance potential: Excellent for complete illustrated articles.
Fees: B&W reproductions, £14–£18. Text from £60 per 1,000 words.

LOOKS
EMAP Women's Group Ltd, Endeavour House, 189 Shafestbury Avenue, London WC2H 8JG.
Tel: 0171-437 9011. Fax: 0171-208 3586.
Editor: Wendy Rigg. **Art Editor**: Nicholas Sang.
Monthly aimed at young women, 16–25, covering every subject relating to their appearance.
Illustrations: Mainly colour. Commissioned coverage of fashion and beauty subjects.
Text: Little scope.
Overall freelance potential: Excellent scope for experienced photographers to obtain commissions.
Fees: By negotiation.

MARIE CLAIRE
European Magazines Ltd, 2 Hatfields, London SE1 9PG.
Tel: 0171-261 5240. Fax: 0171-261 5277.
Editor: Juliet Warkentin. **Art Director**: Suzanne Sykes. **Picture Researcher**: Andrew Roberts.
Fashion and general interest monthly for sophisticated women in the 20–35 age group.
Illustrations: Mainly colour. Top quality fashion, beauty, portraits, interiors, still life, etc., always be commission.
Text: In-depth articles, features and profiles aimed at an intelligent readership. Up to 4,000 words.
Overall freelance potential: Very good for experienced contributors in this field.
Fees: By negotiation.

MINX
Endeavour House, 189 Shaftesbury Avenue, London WC2H 8JG.
Tel: 0171-437 9011. Fax: 0171-437 0656.
Editor: Toni Rodgers. **Art Editor**: Steven Whitchurch.
Monthly designed for assertive and independent young women in the 22–25 age group.
Illustrations: Mostly colour. All by commission for the usual women's interest topics: beauty, fashion, product news, etc. Will also consider picture-led features on more general subjects.
Text: Features on any subject that could interest the target readership. Submit an outline in the first instance.
Overall freelance potential: Good for those with original ideas; the magazine likes to encourage new talent.
Fees: Variable according the nature of the work.

MORE!

EMAP Elan Ltd, Endeavour House, 189 Shafestbury Avenue, London WC2H 8JG.
Tel: 0171-437 9011. Fax: 0171-208 3595.
Editor: Tammy Butt. **Picture Editor**: Holly Coles.
Fortnightly magazine for young women in the 18–24 age group.
Illustrations: Mainly colour. Up-to-date news pictures featuring celebrities. Fashion, beauty, health and pictures to illustrate specific articles, always by commission.
Text: Articles and features, often with a practical slant, of general interest to young women. Submit ideas only in the first instance.
Overall freelance potential: Quite good for quality material.
Editor's tips: "No unsolicited features please – commissions only."
Fees: By negotiation.

MS LONDON WEEKLY

Independent Magazines, 7–9 Rathbone Street, London W1P 1AF.
Tel: 0171-636 6651. Fax: 0171-255 2352.
Editor: Bill Williamson. **Art Editor**: Claudia Branston.
Weekly magazine for young, independent women working in London.
Illustrations: B&W and colour. Mostly fashion and portraits, some still life and reportage work. Covers: colour fashion and general interest subjects; medium format preferred.
Text: Off-beat, sharply-written features of interest to young, aware, working Londoners. 800–1,500 words.
Overall freelance potential: Around 90 per cent of the magazine comes from freelances.
Editor's tips: Best to send copies of recently-published work plus list of ideas before actual submission.
Fees: Approximately £120 per 1,000 words; pictures by agreement.

19

IPC Magazines Ltd, King's Reach Tower, Stamford Street, London SE1 9LS.
Tel: 0171-261 6410. Fax: 0171-261 7478.
Editor: Lee Kynaston. **Art Editor**: Philippa Williams.
Popular young women's magazine aimed at the 17–24 age group, covering topical issues, fashion and beauty.
Illustrations: B&W and colour. Pictures to illustrate fashion and beauty features, always by commission. Some scope for still-life, celebrity or reportage material.
Text: Articles on general topics of interest to young women, ranging from the amusing and entertaining to more serious social matters. Length variable according to importance of subject, up to around 3,000 words.
Overall freelance potential: Good.
Fees: By arrangement.

NOW

IPC Magazines Ltd, King's Reach Tower, Stamford Street, London SE1 9LS.
Tel: 0171-261 7366. Fax: 0171-261 6789.
Editor: Jane Ennis. **Picture Editor**: Michael Butcher.
Weekly entertainment for women with the focus on celebrities and "true-life" stories.
Illustrations: Colour only. Topical coverage of current film and TV stars, both formal and informal shots. Some commissions available to illustrate true-life stories and general features.
Text: Ideas for stories and interviews always considered.
Overall freelance potential: Limited.
Fees: Variable according to the material or assignment; top rates paid for good exclusives.

As a member of the Bureau of Freelance Photographers, you'll be kept up-to-date with markets through the BFP Market Newsletter, published monthly. For details of membership, turn to page 9

OPTIONS
IPC Magazines Ltd, King's Reach Tower, Stamford Street, London SE1 9LS.
Tel: 0171-261 5000. Fax: 0171-261 7344.
Editor: Maureen Rice. **Art Editor**: Jackie Hampsey.
Monthly for women in the 25–40 age group, those who have grown out of the younger magazines and want a magazine relevant to their lifestyle now. Modern "thirty-something" attitude.
Illustrations: B&W and colour. Small shots required for "Informer" section. Stylish/glamorous shots required for features, health and beauty etc. Some personalities. Covers: good quality headshots, commissions only.
Text: Features of interest to readership mainly composed of modern career women in a settled relationship, with or without children. Fashion, health, cookery, travel, entertaining articles, plus strong individual general features – personality profiles, investigative, sociological.
Overall freelance potential: Very good; a lot of outside contributors are used.
Fees: By negotiation.

PRIMA
G+J of the UK, Portland House, Stag Place, London SW1E 5AU.
Tel: 0171-245 8700. Fax: 0171-630 5509.
Editor: Lindsay Nicholson. **Art Director**: Chris Thurston.
General interest women's monthly with a strong emphasis on practical subjects. Major topics covered include cookery, gardening, crafts, health, fashion and homecare.
Illustrations: B&W and colour. Top quality work in the fields of food, fashion, still-life, interiors and portraiture, usually by commission. Some scope for good stock shots of family and domestic situations, food, pets, etc. that could be used for general illustration purposes.
Text: Short, illustrated practical features with a "how-to-do-it" approach.
Overall freelance potential: The magazine relies heavily on freelances.
Fees: Commissioned photography in the region of £410 per day. Other fees by negotiation.

SHE
National Magazine Company, National Magazine House, 72 Broadwick Street, London W1V 2BP.
Tel: 0171-439 5000. Fax: 0171-439 5350.
Editor: Alison Pylkkanen. **Picture Editor**: Aimee Blumsom. **Art Director**: Brian Saffer.
Monthly magazine offering "a great balance for modern women".
Illustrations: B&W and colour. Most material by commission for specific articles; anything else only considered by appointment.
Text: Top quality features of interest to intelligent women; always query the editor first.
Overall freelance potential: Little unsolicited material used, but quite good for commissions.
Editor's tips: Please study the format before contacting magazine.
Fees: By arrangement.

THAT'S LIFE!
H.Bauer Publishing Ltd, 2nd Floor, 1-5 Maple Place London W1P 5FX.
Tel: 0171-388 6268. Fax: 0171-388 6112.
Editor: Janice Turner. **Features Editor**: Karen Jones. **Picture Editor**: Jim Taylor.
Popular women's weekly concentrating on true-life stories and confessions.
Illustrations: Colour only. Mostly commissioned shots of people to accompany stories; photographers who can produce good informal portrait work should write to the picture editor enclosing a couple of samples. Also limited opportunities in fashion, food and still life. Quirky and amusing "readers' pictures" always considered on spec – should be accompanied by a brief story or anecdote.
Text: Personal true-life stories always of interest – shocking, scandalous, embarrassing, tear-jerking, etc. Around 300 words. Contact the features editor with suggestions first.
Overall freelance potential: Good.
Fees: Story shoots around £150; readers' pictures £25; other photography by negotiation. £200 for true stories.

WOMAN

IPC Magazines Ltd, King's Reach Tower, Stamford Street, London SE1 9LS.
Tel: 0171-261 6395. Fax: 0171-261 5997.
Editor: Carole Russell. **Picture Editor**: Emma Smith.
Weekly magazine devoted to all women's interests.
Illustrations: B&W and colour. Most pictures commissioned to illustrate specific features. Some scope for human interest shots which are dramatic, off-beat or unusual.
Text: Interviews with leading personalities, human interest stories, campaigns. Other features mostly staff-produced. Submit a synopsis in the first instance.
Overall freelance potential: Only for experienced contributors in the field.
Fees: Good; on a rising scale according to size of reproduction or length of articles.

WOMAN AND HOME

IPC Magazines Ltd, King's Reach Tower, Stamford Street, London SE1 9LS.
Tel: 0171-261 5423. Fax: 0171-261 7346.
Editor: Jan Henderson. **Picture Editor**: Jayne Biggs.
Monthly magazine for all women concerned with family and home. Subjects covered include cookery, fashion, beauty, interior design, DIY, gardening, travel, topical issues and personality articles.
Illustrations: B&W and colour. All photography on above subjects commissioned from experienced freelances.
Text: Articles on personalities, either well-known or who lead interesting lives. 1,500 words.
Overall freelance potential: Very good for the experienced worker. Including regular contributors, about 50 per cent of the magazine is contributed by freelances.
Fees: £120 per 1,000 words. Pictures by negotiation.

WOMAN'S JOURNAL

IPC Magazines Ltd, King's Reach Tower, Stamford Street, London SE1 9LS.
Tel: 0171-261 6622. Fax: 0171-261 7061.
Editor: *To be appointed.* **Picture Editor**: Natalie Huke.
Monthly glossy magazine for women.
Illustrations: B&W and colour. Commissioned coverage for fashion, portraits, home, beauty, cookery, travel and general features.
Text: Features of general interest to women and on subjects detailed above. 2,000 words maximum.
Overall freelance potential: Good for commissioned work.
Fees: Negotiable.

WOMAN'S OWN

IPC Magazines Ltd, King's Reach Tower, Stamford Street, London SE1 9LS.
Tel: 0171-261 5474. Fax: 0171-261 5346.
Editor: Keith McNeill. **Picture Editor**: Peter Gray. **Art Editor**: Ms Sina Capaldo.
Weekly publishing articles and practical features of interest to women.
Illustrations: B&W and colour. Mostly commissioned to illustrate features on fashion, interior design, crafts, etc.
Text: Mostly staff-produced. Send a brief outline of any proposed feature in the first instance to the features editor.
Overall freelance potential: Fair for commissioned work, but much is produced by regulars.
Fees: Good; on a rising scale according to size of reproduction or length of article.

WOMAN'S REALM

IPC Magazines Ltd, King's Reach Tower, Stamford Street, London SE1 9LS.
Tel: 0171-261 5000. Fax: 0171-261 7678.
Editor: Kathy Watson. **Picture Editor**: Corrinne Peebles.
General interest women's weekly, with the emphasis on short features and human interest stories.
Illustrations: Colour. Some opportunities for commissioned work in the usual women's interest

fields – fashion, beauty, cookery, home and garden, human interest, personalities, travel, etc.
Text: Some scope for short features on subjects of general women's interest as above, and illustrated romantic or dramatic true-life stories.
Overall freelance potential: Limited; although some opportunities.
Fees: According to use and nature of material.

WOMAN'S WEEKLY
IPC Magazines Ltd, King's Reach Tower, Stamford Street, London SE1 9LS.
Tel: 0171-261 5000. Fax: 0171-261 6322.
Editor: Olwen Rice. **Art Editor**: Susan Wilkins.
General interest family-oriented magazine for women in the 35+ age group.
Illustrations: Colour only. Mostly by commission to illustrate features on fashion, beauty, cookery, decoration, etc.
Text: Practical features on general women's topics, plus human interest stories and celebrity pieces.
Overall freelance potential: Fairly good for the experienced contributor.
Fees: By negotiation.

NEWSPAPERS

In this section we list the national daily and Sunday newspapers, and their associated magazine supplements. While the supplements may publish a wide range of general interest subject matter, the parent papers are obviously only likely to be interested in hard news pictures and stories of genuine interest to a nationwide readership.

News pictures

Despite the heavy presence of staff and agency photographers at major events, it is still perfectly possible for an independent freelance to get the shot that makes the front page. And when it comes to the unexpected, the freelance is often the only one on the spot to capture the drama.

If you think you have obtained a "hot" news picture or story, don't wait to get the film processed and see the results; the best procedure is to telephone the papers most likely to be interested as soon as possible and let them know what you have to offer. If interested, they will either make arrangements to have the pictures or undeveloped film collected, or will ask you to send it by the fastest convenient method.

Most of the major papers now prefer – or even insist – that material be supplied "down-line" electronically. This can be a problem for freelances who do not have access to suitable facilities, so if you think you may be supplying newspapers on a fairly regular basis you will need to consider investing in suitable equipment, or find someone (a colleague or local news agency perhaps) whose facilities you can use.

In the listings that follow you will find direct line telephone numbers which bypass the main switchboard and take you directly through to the picture desk of the paper concerned, except in a few cases where such lines are not available.

In the case of fax numbers it is advisable to always check the correct number for the department you want. Most newspapers offices have numerous fax machines; the numbers listed here are necessarily general editorial numbers and if used without checking might delay your message getting through to the specific department you need.

Other material

There is some scope for other material apart from hard news in most of the papers. Some use the occasional oddity or human interest item as a "filler", while in the tabloids there is always a good market for celebrity pictures.

Finally, of course, there is a market for top quality glamour material of the "Page 3" variety in several of the tabloids.

The supplements operate much like any other general interest magazine. Most of their content is commissioned from well-established photographers and writers, though some will accept exceptional photojournalistic features or exclusives on spec.

Fees

Fees paid by newspapers can vary tremendously according to what is offered and how it is used. However, it can be taken for granted that rates paid by the leading papers listed here are good. Generally, picture fees are calculated on standard rates based on the size of the reproduction.

However, for material that is exclusive or exceptional the sky is almost literally the limit. If you think you have something very special and are prepared to offer it as an exclusive, make sure you negotiate a fee, and perhaps get several offers, before committing the material to anyone.

National Daily Newspapers

DAILY MAIL
The Daily Mail Ltd, Northcliffe House, Derry Street, London W8 5TT.
Tel: 0171-938 6000. Picture desk: 0171-938 6373. Fax: 0171-937 5560.
Editor: Paul Dacre. **Picture Editor**: Geoff Webster.

DAILY MIRROR
Mirror Group Newspapers Ltd, Canary Wharf Tower, 1 Canada Square, London E14 5AP.
Tel: 0171-293 3000. Picture desk: 0171-293 3851. Fax: 0171-293 3983.
Editor: Piers Morgan. **Picture Editor**: Ron Morgans.

DAILY RECORD
The Scottish Daily Record and Sunday Mail Ltd, Anderston Quay, Glasgow G3 8DA.
Tel: 0141-248 7000. Picture desk: 0141-242 3248. Fax: 0141-242 3835.
Editor: Terry Quinn. **Picture Editor**: Stuart Nicol.

DAILY SPORT
19 Great Ancoats Street, Manchester M60 4BT.
Tel: 0161-236 4466. Fax: 0161-236 4535.
Editor: Jeff McGowan. **Picture Editor**: Paul Currie.

DAILY STAR
Express Newspapers, Ludgate House, 245 Blackfriars Road, London SE1 9UX.
Tel: 0171-928 8000. Picture desk: 0171-922 7353. Fax: 0171-922 7960.
Editor: Phil Walker. **Picture Editor**: Mark Moylan.

THE DAILY TELEGRAPH
The Daily Telegraph Plc, 1 Canada Square, Canary Wharf, London E14 5DT.
Tel: 0171-538 5000. Picture desk: 0171-538 6369. Fax: 0171-538 7640.
Editor: Charles Moore. **Picture Editor**: Robert Bodman.
TELEGRAPH MAGAZINE
Editor: Emma Soames. **Picture Editor**: Maryse Vassalo.

EXPRESS
Express Newspapers, Ludgate House, 245 Blackfriars Road, London SE1 9UX.
Tel: 0171-928 8000. Picture desk: 0171-922 7171. Fax: 0171-922 7976.
Editor: Richard Addis. **Picture Editor**: Chris Djukanovic.
SATURDAY
Editor: Catherine Ostler. **Picture Editor**: Yvonne Irwin.

FINANCIAL TIMES
The Financial Times Ltd, Number One Southwark Bridge, London SE1 9HL.
Tel: 0171-873 3000. Picture desk: 0171-873 3466. Fax: 0171-873 3073.
Editor: Andrew Gowers. **News Picture Editor**: Chris Lawson.

Are you working from the latest edition of The Freelance Photographer's Market Handbook? It's published on 1 October each year. Markets are constantly changing, so it pays to have the latest edition

---

THE GUARDIAN
119 Farringdon Road, London EC1R 3ER.
Tel: 0171-278 2332. Picture desk: 0171-239 9585. Fax: 0171-239 9951.
Editor: Alan Rusbridger. **Picture Editor**: Eamonn McCabe.
WEEKEND GUARDIAN
Editor: Deborah Orr. **Picture Editor**: Eamonn McCabe.

THE HERALD
195 Albion Street, Glasgow, Scotland G1 1QP.
Tel: 0141-552 6255. Fax: 0141-552 2288.
Editor: Harry Reis. **Picture Editor**: James Connor.

THE INDEPENDENT
Newspaper Publishing Plc, 1 Canada Square, Canary Wharf, London E14 5DL.
Tel: 0171-293 2000. Picture desk: 0171-293 2428. Fax: 0171-293 2086.
Editor: Andrew Marr. **Picture Editor**: David Swanborough.
THE INDEPENDENT MAGAZINE
Editor: David Robson.

THE SCOTSMAN
The Scotsman Publications Ltd, 20 North Bridge, Edinburgh EH1 1YT.
Tel: 0131-225 2468. Picture desk: 0131-243 3389. Fax: 0131-226 7420.
Editor: Martin Clarke. **Picture Editor**: Steve Walker.

THE SUN
News Group Newspapers Ltd, 1 Virginia Street, London E1 9XP.
Tel: 0171-782 4000. Picture desk: 0171-782 4110-4116. Fax: 0171-782 4108.
Editor: Stuart Higgins. **Picture Editor**: Ken Lennox.

THE TIMES
Times Newspapers Ltd, 1 Virginia Street, London E1 9XN.
Tel: 0171-782 7000. Picture desk: 0171-782 5877. Fax: 0171-782 5449.
Editor: Peter Stothard. **Picture Editor**: Andrew Moger.
THE TIMES MAGAZINE
Editor: Nicholas Wapshott. **Picture Editor**: Graham Wood.

National Sunday Newspapers

EXPRESS ON SUNDAY
Express Newspapers, Ludgate House, 245 Blackfriars Road, London SE1 9UX.
Tel: 0171-928 8000. Picture desk: 0171-922 7171. Fax: 0171-922 7976.
Editor: Richard Addis. **Picture Editor**: Chris Djukanovic.
EXPRESS ON SUNDAY MAGAZINE
Editor: Kate Bowen-Bravery. **Picture Editor**: Denise Glyn.

THE INDEPENDENT ON SUNDAY
Newspaper Publishing Plc, 1 Canada Square, Canary Wharf, London E14 5DL.
Tel: 0171-293 2000. Picture desk: 0171-293 2837/2888. Fax: 0171-293 2086.
Editor: Rosie Boycott. **Picture Editor**: David Sandison.

THE MAIL ON SUNDAY
Northcliffe House, 2 Derry Street, Kensington, London W8 5TS.
Tel: 0171-938 6000. Picture desk: 0171-938 7016. Fax: 0171-937 3829.
Editor: Jonathan Holborow. **Picture Editor**: Andy Kyle.
YOU MAGAZINE
Editor: Dee Nolan. **Picture Editor**: Eve George.
NIGHT & DAY
Editor: Simon Kelner. **Picture Editor**: Tim Leith.

NEWS OF THE WORLD
News Group Newspapers Ltd, Virginia Street, London E1 9XR.
Tel: 0171-782 4000. Picture desk: 0171-782 7927/7557. Fax: 0171-782 7474.
Editor: Phillip Hall. **Picture Editor**: Lynn Cullen.
SUNDAY MAGAZINE
Editor: Judy McGuire. **Picture Editor**: Caroline Jeffrey.

THE OBSERVER
The Observer Ltd, 119 Farringdon Road, London EC1R 3ER.
Tel: 0171-278 2332. Picture desk: 0171-713 4304. Fax: 0171-713 4250.
Editor: Will Hutton. **Picture Editor**: Greg Whitmore.
OBSERVER LIFE
Editor: Justine Picardie. **Picture Editor:** Jenny Ricketts.

THE PEOPLE
Mirror Group plc, 1 Canada Square, Canary Wharf, London E14 5AP.
Tel: 0171-293 3000. Picture desk: 0171-293 3901. Fax: 0171-293 3810.
Editor: Len Gould. **Picture Editor**: Martin Spaven.
YES MAGAZINE!
Editors: As above.

SCOTLAND ON SUNDAY
The Scotsman Publications Ltd, 20 North Bridge, Edinburgh EH1 1YT.
Tel: 0131-225 2468. Fax: 0131-220 2443.
Editor: John McGurk. **Picture Editor**: Neil Hanna.

THE SUNDAY MAIL
The Scottish Daily Record and Sunday Mail Ltd, Anderston Quay, Glasgow G3 8DA.
Tel: 0141-248 7000. Picture desk: 0141-242 3434. Fax: 0141-242 3587.
Editor: Jim Cassidy. **Picture Editor**: David McNeil.

SUNDAY MIRROR
Mirror Group plc, 1 Canada Square, Canary Wharf, London E14 5AP.
Tel: 0171-293 3000. Picture desk: 0171-293 3335/6. Fax: 0171-293 3939.
Editor: Bridget Rowe. **Picture Editor**: Paul Bennett.
PERSONAL MAGAZINE
Picture Editor: Jo Lockwood.

As a member of the Bureau of Freelance Photographers, you'll be kept up-to-date with markets through the BFP Market Newsletter, published monthly. For details of membership, turn to page 9

SUNDAY POST
D. C. Thomson & Co Ltd, Courier Place, Dundee DD1 9QJ.
Tel: 01382 223131. Fax: 01382 201064.
Editor: Russell Reid. **Picture Editor**: Iain MacKinnon.

SUNDAY SPORT
Sport Newspapers Ltd, 19 Great Ancoats Street, Manchester M60 0DB.
Tel: 0161-238 8183. Picture desk: Ext: 8415. Fax: 0161-236 2418.
Editor: Mark Harris. **Picture Editor**: Paul Currie.

THE SUNDAY TELEGRAPH
The Telegraph Plc, 1 Canada Square, Canary Wharf, London E14 5AR.
Tel: 0171-538 5000. Picture desk: 0171-538 7369. Fax: 0171-538 7918.
Editor: Dominic Lawson. **Picture Editor**: Nigel Skelsey.
SUNDAY TELEGRAPH MAGAZINE
Editor: Rebecca Tyrrell. **Picture Editor**: Hilary Kirby.

THE SUNDAY TIMES
Times Newspapers Ltd, 1 Pennington Street, London E1 9XW.
Tel: 0171-782 5000. Picture desk: 0171-782 5666. Fax: 0171-782 5563.
Editor: John Witherow. **Picture Editor**: Ray Wells.
THE SUNDAY TIMES MAGAZINE
Editor: Robin Morgan. **Picture Editor**: Aidan Sullivan.

BOOKS

Books represent a substantial and growing market for the photographer. In an increasingly visual age the market for heavily illustrated books continues to expand, with hundreds of new titles being published every year. Book publishers are also now moving into the new electronic media with CD-ROM publishing, a field which also has a growing appetite for photographs.

In this section we list major book publishers, and specifically those companies that make considerable use of photographic material.

As well as regular publishers, also listed here are book packagers, marked (P). These are companies that offer a complete editorial production service and specialise in producing books that can be sold as finished packages to publishers internationally. The majority of their products are of the heavily illustrated type, and thus these companies often present a greater potential market for photographic material than do the mainstream publishers.

Making an approach

In this field the difficulty for the individual freelance is that there is no easy way of knowing who wants what and when.

Obviously book publishers only require pictures of specific subjects when they are currently working on a project requiring such material. Much of the time they will rely heavily on known sources such as picture libraries, but this does not mean that there is not good scope for the individual photographer who has a good collection of material on particular subjects, or who can produce suitable work to order. The solution for the photographer, therefore, is to get details of what he or she has to offer in front of all those companies that might conceivably require material of that type.

The initial approach is simply to send an introductory letter outlining the sort of material that you can supply. A detailed list of subjects can be attached where appropriate.

There is little point however, in sending any photographs at this stage, unless it be one or two samples to indicate a particular style. And one should not expect an immediate response requesting that work be submitted; most likely the publisher will simply keep your details on file for future reference.

Preceding the listings of book publishers is a subject index that should assist in identifying the most promising markets for those areas in which you have good coverage.

In the listings that follow, the major areas of activity for each publisher are detailed under "Subjects". Of course, the larger companies publish on the widest range of subjects and therefore their coverage may be stated as "general", but in most entries you will find a list of specific subject areas. These are by no means a complete list of all the subjects handled by each publisher, but indicate those areas where the company is most active and therefore most likely to be in need of photographic material.

In some entries a "Contact" name is given. However in most cases it is not possible to give a specific name as book publishers usually have large numbers of editorial personnel with constantly shifting responsibilities for individual projects. In addition, many companies frequently use the services of freelance picture researchers. A general approach should therefore simply be addressed to the editorial director.

Rights and fees

Whereas the rights sold in the magazine world are invariably for UK use only, book publishers – and especially packagers – make a good deal of their profit from selling their products to other publishers in overseas markets.

It is therefore quite likely that when work is chosen for use in a particular book the publisher may at some stage request, in addition to British publishing rights, rights for other areas such as "Commonwealth", "North American", "French language", etc. These differing rights will, of course, affect the fees that the photographer receives – the more areas the book sells into, the higher the fees.

Other major factors affecting fees are the size of reproduction on the page and the quantity of the print-run. Thus there is no easy way to generalise about the sort of fees paid in this field. On the whole, however, fees in book publishing are quite good and comparable with good magazine rates. For packages destined for the international co-edition market they can be substantially higher.

A word about names and imprints

The use by large publishers of a multiplicity of names for different divisions can be quite confusing.

Many famous publishing names, though still in existence, now belong to huge publishing conglomerates. Some are still run as separate companies, but others have effectively become "imprints".

Imprints are the names used by large publishers for specific sections of their list. Only relevant, illustrated imprints are listed here, and are generally cross-referenced to their parent company. Note, however, that in many cases an imprint may operate as a completely separate company.

Subject Index

ulture**

Addison Wesley Longman
Farming Press Books

Antiques

Antique Collectors Club Ltd
Barrie & Jenkins Ltd
Conran Octopus Ltd

Archaeology

B. T. Batsford Ltd
Cambridge University Press
Manchester University Press
Sutton Publishing Ltd
Thames & Hudson Ltd

Architecture

Academy Editions
Addison Wesley Longman
Antique Collectors Club Ltd
B. T. Batsford Ltd
Calmann & King Ltd
Cambridge University Press
Cameron Books (Production) Ltd
Robert Hale Ltd
Manchester University Press
John Murray (Publishers) Ltd
Phaidon Press Ltd
Sheldrake Press Ltd
Sutton Publishing Ltd
Thames & Hudson Ltd
Philip Wilson Publishers Ltd
Yale University Press

Arts & Crafts

Academy Editions
Albion Press Ltd
Antique Collectors Club Ltd
The Apple Press
Aurum Press Ltd
B. T. Batsford Ltd
Barrie & Jenkins Ltd
A & C Black (Publishers) Ltd
Breslich & Foss
Brown Packaging Ltd
Calmann & King Ltd

Cambridge University Press
Cameron Books (Production) Ltd
Cassell plc
Richard Cohen Books
Conran Octopus Ltd
David & Charles Publishing plc
W. Foulsham & Co Ltd
Robert Hale Ltd
Frances Lincoln Ltd
The Lutterworth Press
Macmillan General Books
Marshall Cavendish Books
Marshall Editions Ltd
John Murray (Publishers) Ltd
New Holland Publishers
Nexus Special Interests Ltd
Phaidon Press Ltd
Quarto Publishing plc
The Reader's Digest Association Ltd
Salamander Books Ltd
Savitri Books Ltd
Thames & Hudson Ltd
Usborne Publishing
Virgin Publishing Ltd
Philip Wilson (Publishers) Ltd
Yale University Press

Aviation

Airlife Publishing Ltd
Ian Allan Publishing
Brown Packaging Ltd
Grub Street
Nexus Special Interests Ltd
Patrick Stephens Ltd
Sutton Publishing

Countryside

Airlife Publishing Ltd
Farming Press Books
Headline Book Publishing Ltd
Sutton Publishing Ltd

DIY

W. Foulsham & Co Ltd
Haynes Publishing
Marshall Cavendish Books
The Reader's Digest Association Ltd

Equestrian

J A Allen & Co Ltd
B. T. Batsford Ltd
Cassell plc
David & Charles Publishing plc
The Kenilworth Press Ltd

Fashion

Ebury Press
Marshall Cavendish Books
Piatkus Books
Plexus Publishing Ltd
Thames & Hudson Ltd

Food & Drink

Albion Press Ltd
The Apple Press
BBC Books
Bantam Press
Boxtree Ltd
Brown Packaging Ltd
Cassell plc
Chatto & Windus Ltd
Conran Octopus Ltd
Ebury Press
W. Foulsham & Co Ltd
Grub Street
Robert Hale Ltd
Headline Book Publishing plc
Hodder Headline plc
Frances Lincoln Ltd
Macmillan General Books
Marshall Cavendish Books
Marshall Editions Ltd
New Holland Publishers
Pavilion Books
Piatkus Books
Prion
Quarto Publishing plc
The Reader's Digest Association Ltd
Salamander Books Ltd
Sheldrake Press
Smith Gryphon Ltd
Souvenir Press Ltd
Sunburst Books
Weidenfeld & Nicholson Ltd

Gardening

Antique Collectors' Club Ltd
The Apple Press

BBC Books
B. T. Batsford Ltd
Boxtree Ltd
Breslich & Foss
Cassell plc
Conran Octopus Ltd
David & Charles Publishing plc
W. Foulsham & Co Ltd
Headline Book Publishing plc
Frances Lincoln Ltd
Macmillan General Books
Marshall Cavendish Books
Marshall Editions Ltd
New Holland Publishers
Pavilion Books
The Reader's Digest Association Ltd
Salamander Books Ltd
Souvenir Press Ltd
Sunburst Books

Health & Medical

The Apple Press
Bantam Press
Breslich & Foss
Cambridge University Press
Conran Octopus Ltd
Ebury Press
W. Foulsham & Co Ltd
Grub Street
Frances Lincoln Ltd
John Murray (Publishers) Ltd
Piatkus Books
Robinson Publishing
Smith Gryphon Ltd
Souvenir Press Ltd
Thorsons

Interior Design

Conran Octopus Ltd
Frances Lincoln Ltd
New Holland Publishers
Pavilion Books
Thames & Hudson

Military

Airlife Publishing Ltd
Ian Allan Publishing
Brown Packaging Ltd
Cassell plc
Constable & Co Ltd
Robert Hale Ltd

Haynes Publishing
Nexus Special Interests Ltd
Osprey Publishing
Salamander Books Ltd
Spellmount Ltd
Patrick Stephens Ltd
Sutton Publishing Ltd

Motoring

Ian Allan Publishing
Haynes Publishing
Osprey Publishing Ltd
Patrick Stephens Ltd
Sunburst Books
Sutton Publishing Ltd

Music

Bantam Press
A & C Black (Publishers) Ltd
Boxtree Ltd
Brown Packaging Ltd
Cambridge University Press
Cassell plc
Faber & Faber Ltd
Victor Gollancz
Guinness Publishing Ltd
Robert Hale Ltd
Headline Book Publishing plc
Hodder Healine plc
Omnibus Press/Book Sales Ltd
Pavilion Books
Plexus Publishing Ltd
Quartet Books
Salamander Books Ltd
Sheldrake Press
Sidgwick & Jackson
Smith Gryphon Ltd
Thames & Hudson
Virgin Publishing Ltd
Ward Lock Educational Co Ltd

Natural History

Airlife Publishing Ltd
A & C Black (Publishers) Ltd
Cambridge University Press
Cameron Books (Production) Ltd
Cassell plc
David & Charles Publishing plc

Robert Hale Ltd
Christopher Helm Publishers Ltd
Larousse Kingfisher plc
Marshall Editions Ltd
New Holland Publishers
Prion
The Reader's Digest Association Ltd
Salamander Books Ltd
Savitri Books Ltd
Sunburst Books
The Templar Company
Usborne Publishing

Politics & Current Affairs

Addison Wesley Longman
BBC Books
Bantam Press
Blackwell Publishers
Bloomsbury Publishing Ltd
Century
Chatto & Windus Ltd
Richard Cohen Books
Constable & Co Ltd
Faber & Faber Ltd
Fourth Estate Ltd
Victor Gollancz
Hamish Hamilton Ltd
Hutchinson
Macmillan General Books
Manchester University Press
Secker & Warburg Ltd
Sidgwick & Jackson
Virgin Publishing Ltd
Yale University Press

Railways

Addison Wesley Longman
Ian Allan Publishing
Haynes Publishing
Milepost 92½
Nexus Special Interests Ltd
Patrick Stephens Ltd
Sutton Publishing Ltd
Unicorn Books

Science

Addison Wesley Longman
Bantam Press

Cambridge University Press
Fourth Estate Ltd
The Lutterworth Press
John Murray Publishers
The Templar Company
Virgin Publishing Ltd
Ward Lock Educational Co Ltd

Sport

A & C Black (Publishers) Ltd
Boxtree Ltd
Brown Packaging Ltd
Cassell plc
Richard Cohen Books
Ebury Press
W. Foulsham & Co Ltd
Victor Gollancz
Guinness Publishing Ltd
Robert Hale Ltd
Hodder Headline plc
Marshall Cavendish Books
Partridge Press
Pavilion Books
Sidgwick & Jackson
Sunburst Books
Virgin Publishing Ltd

Travel

AA Publishing
Aurum Press Ltd
BBC Books
Bantam Press
A & C Black (Publishers) Ltd
Bloomsbury Publishing Ltd
Cambridge University Press
Chatto & Windus Ltd
Constable & Co Ltd
W. Foulsham & Co Ltd
Victor Gollancz
Robert Hale Ltd
Hamish Hamilton Ltd
Hodder Headline plc
Hutchinson
Macmillan General Books
John Murray (Publishers) Ltd
New Holland Publishers
Pavilion Books
Prion
George Philip Ltd
Quarto Publishing plc
Secker & Warburg Ltd
Sheldrake Press
Thames & Hudson Ltd

Book Publishers

AA PUBLISHING
Automobile Association, Fanum House, Basingstoke, Hampshire RG21 2EA.
Tel: 01256 491588. Fax: 01256 492440.
Contact: W Voysey, Picture Researcher.
Subjects: Guide books, travel and leisure.

ACADEMY EDITIONS
42 Leinster Gardens, London W2 3AN.
Tel: 0171-402 2141. Fax: 0171-723 9540.
Subjects: Art, architecture, design.

ADDISON WESLEY LONGMAN
5 Bentinck Street, London W1M 5RN.
Tel: 0171-935 0121. Fax: 0171-486 4204.
Subjects: General academic and professional; agriculture, building, engineering, geography, history, politics, science and technology.

ADLARD COLES – see A & C BLACK

AIRLIFE PUBLISHING LTD
101 Longden Road, Shrewsbury, Shropshire SY3 9EB.
Tel: 01743 235651. Fax: 01743 232944.
Imprint: Swan Hill Press.
Contact: Peter Coles, Managing Editor.
Subjects: Aviation, country pursuits, military, natural history, photography, yachting.

ALBION PRESS LTD (P)
Spring Hill, Idbury, Oxfordshire OX7 6RU.
Tel: 01993 831094. Fax: 01993 831982.
Subjects: Children's, cookery, fine arts, social history.

IAN ALLAN PUBLISHING
Coombelands House, Coombelands, Addlestone, Surrey KT15 1HY.
Tel: 01932 855909. Fax: 01932 854750.
Subjects: Aviation, military, motoring, railways, road transport.

J.A.ALLEN & CO LTD
1 Lower Grosvenor Place,London SW1W 0EL.
Tel: 0171-834 0090. Fax: 0171-976 5836.
Subjects: Horses/equestrian.

AMBER BOOKS LTD/BROWN PACKAGING LTD (P)
Bradley's Close, 74-77 White Lion Street, London N1 9PF.
Tel: 0171-520 7600. Fax: 0171-520 7606.
Subjects: Aviation, crime, military, sport, reference, unexplained.

ANTIQUE COLLECTORS' CLUB LTD
5 Church Street, Woodbridge, Suffolk IP12 1DS.
Tel: 01394 385501. Fax: 01394 384434.
Contact: Diana Steel, Managing Director (by letter only).
Subjects: Antiques, architecture, art, gardening.

APPLE PRESS
The Old Brewery, 6 Blundell Street, London N7 9BH.
Tel: 0171-700 6700. Fax: 0171-700 4191.
Contact: Richard Dewing
Subjects: General,children's, cookery, crafts, decorative arts, gardening, health and fitness, leisure.

AQUARIAN – see HARPERCOLLINS PUBLISHERS

ARMS & ARMOUR – see CASSELL

ARNOLD – see HODDER HEADLINE PLC

AURUM PRESS LTD
25 Bedford Avenue, London WC1B 3AT.
Tel: 0171-637 3225. Fax: 0171-580 2469.
Subjects: General; art, design, film, travel.

BBC BOOKS
BBC Worldwide Publishing, Woodlands, 80 Wood Lane, London W12 0TT.
Tel: 0181-576 2000. Fax: 0181-749 8766.
Contact: David Cottingham, Picture Manager.
Subjects: General non-fiction, tie-ins to BBC TV and radio programmes; business, cookery, gardening, history, travel.

BANTAM PRESS
Transworld Publishers, 61-63 Uxbridge Road, London W5 5SA.
Tel: 0181-579 2652. Fax: 0181-579 5479.
Subjects: General; biography, cookery, health, history, music, new age, politics, science, travel.

BARRIE & JENKINS LTD
Random House, 20 Vauxhall Bridge Road, London SW1V 2SA.
Tel: 0171-973 9710. Fax: 0171-233 6057.
Subjects: Antiques, art, design, history, photography.

B. T. BATSFORD LTD
583 Fulham Road, London SW6 5BY.
Tel: 0171-491 1100. Fax: 0171-471 1101.
Contact: R H Reynolds, Senior Editor
Subjects: Architecture, bridge, chess, crafts, design, English heritage, entertainment, fashion, film, gardening, historic Scpotland, local history, management and personal investment.

BELITHA PRESS LTD
London House, Great Eastern Wharf, Parkgate Road, London SW11 4NQ.
Tel: 0171-978 6330. Fax: 0171-223 4936.
Subjects: Children's illustrated.

A & C BLACK (PUBLISHERS) LTD
35 Bedford Row, London WC1R 4JH.
Tel: 0171-242 0946. Fax: 0171-831 8478.
Imprints: Adlard Coles, Christopher Helm, Herbert Press.
Subjects: Arts and crafts, children's educational, children's music, nautical, ornithology, reference, sport, theatre, travel, ceramics.

BLACKWELL PUBLISHERS
108 Cowley Road, Oxford OX4 1JF.
Tel: 01865 791100. Fax: 01865 791347.
Subjects: Business, geography, history, politics, religion, sociology.

BLANDFORD – see CASSELL

BLOOMSBURY PUBLISHING PLC
38 Soho Square, London W1V 5DF.
Tel: 0171-494 2111. Fax: 0171-434 0151.
Subjects: General; biography, children's, current affairs, reference, travel.

BOXTREE
Macmillan Publishers, 25 Eccleston Place, Londonm SW1W 9NF.
Tel: 0171-881 8000. Fax: 0171-881 8280.
Subjects: General illustrated, cookery, gardening, history, popular music, sport.

BOUNTY – see REED CONSUMER BOOKS

BREEDON BOOKS PUBLISHING CO LTD
Breedon House, 44 Friar Gate, Derby DE1 1DA.
Tel: 01332 384235. Fax: 01332 292755.
Contact: Anton Rippon, Editorial Director.
Subjects: British heritage and local history.

BRESLICH & FOSS LTD (P)
20 Wells Mews, London W1P 3FJ.
Tel: 0171-580 8774. Fax: 0171-580 8784.
Subjects: Arts, children's, crafts, gardening, health.

CALMANN & KING LTD (P)
71 Great Russell Street, London WC1B 3BN.
Tel: 0171-831 6351. Fax: 0171-831 8356.
Contact: Susan Bolsom-Morris, Picture Manager.
Subjects: Arts and architecture, design.

CAMBRIDGE UNIVERSITY PRESS
The Edinburgh Building, Shaftesbury Road, Cambridge CB2 2RU.
Tel/fax: 01223 262811. Mobile: 0402 547411.
Contact: Callie Kendall, Picture Researcher.
Subjects: Archaeology, architecture, art, astronomy, biology, drama, geography, history, medicine, music, natural history, religion, science, sociology, travel.

CAMERON BOOKS (PRODUCTION) LTD (P)
P O Box 1, Moffat, Dumfriesshire DG10 9SU.
Tel: 01683 220808. Fax: 01683 220012.
Subjects: Architecture, fine and decorative arts, antiques and collecting, natural history, environment.

CASSELL PLC
Wellington House, 125 Strand, London WC2R 0BB.
Tel: 0171-420 5555. Fax: 0171-240 7261.
Imprints: Arms & Armour, Blandford, Gollancz, Ward Lock.
Subjects: General; art, crafts, cookery, equestrian, fishing, gardening, history, military, natural history, popular music, reference, religion, sport.

CENTURY
Random House, 20 Vauxhall Bridge Road, London SW1V 2SA.
Tel: 0171-973 9670. Fax: 0171-233 6127.
Subjects: Biography, current affairs.

CHAMBERS HARRAP PUBLISHERS LTD
7 Hopetoun Crescent, Edinburgh EH7 4AY.
Tel: 0131-557 4571. Fax: 0131-557 2936.
Contact: Ilona Bellos Morison, Pre-press Manager.
Subjects: General reference.

CHATTO & WINDUS LTD
20 Vauxhall Bridge Road, London SW1V 2SA.
Tel: 0171-973 9740. Fax: 0171-932 0077.
Subjects: General; biography and memoirs, current affairs, history, politics, travel.

CLARENDON PRESS – see OXFORD UNIVERSITY PRESS

RICHARD COHEN BOOKS
The Basement Offices, 7 Manchester Square, London W1M 5RE.
Tel: 0171-935 2099. Fax: 0171-935 2199.
Subjects: Arts, biography, current affairs, history, sport.

COLLINS – see HARPERCOLLINS PUBLISHERS

CONRAN OCTOPUS LTD
37 Shelton Street, London WC2H 9HN.
Tel: 0171-557 7700. Fax: 0171-836 9951.
Subjects: Antiques, cookery, crafts and hobbies, design, gardening, health and beauty, interior design.

CONSTABLE & CO LTD
3 The Lanchesters, 162 Fulham Palace Road, London W6 9ER.
Tel: 0181-741 3663. Fax: 0181-748 7562.
Subjects: General; biography, current affairs, UK guide books, history, military history, social sciences, UK travel, large-format photographic.

CREATIVE MONOCHROME
20 St Peters Road, Croydon CR0 1HD.
Tel: 0181-686 3282. Fax: 0181-681 0662.
Contact: Roger Maile, Managing Director.
Subjects: Monochrome photography – creative work and technique.

DAVID & CHARLES PUBLISHING LTD
Brunel House, Newton Abbot, Devon TQ12 4PU.
Tel: 01626 323200. Fax: 01626 323317.
Subjects: Arts and crafts, gardening, equestrian, natural history.

Are you working from the latest edition of The Freelance Photographer's Market Handbook? It's published on 1 October each year. Markets are constantly changing, so it pays to have the latest edition

---

EBURY PRESS
Random House, 20 Vauxhall Bridge Road, London SW1V 2SA.
Tel: 0171-840 8400. Fax: 0171-840 8406.
Imprints: Stanley Paul, Vermilion.
Subjects: Cookery, carfts, interiors, health and beauty.

FABER & FABER LTD
3 Queen Square, London WC1N 3AU.
Tel: 0171-465 0045. Fax: 0171-465 0034.
Subjects: Biography, film, music, politics, theatre, wine.

FARMING PRESS BOOKS
Wharfedale Road, Ipswich IP1 4LG.
Tel: 01473 241122. Fax: 01473 240501.
Contact: Claire Newberry, Senior Editor.
Subjects: Agriculture, countryside, gardening, wildlife.

G. T. FOULIS – see HAYNES PUBLISHING

W. FOULSHAM & CO LTD
The Publishing House, Bennetts Close, Cippenham, Berkshire SL1 5AP.
Tel: 01753 526769. Fax: 01753 535003.
Contact: Jane Hotson, Editorial Administrator.
Subjects: Crafts, collecting, cookery, DIY, gardening, health, hobbies, new age, sport, travel.

FOURTH ESTATE LTD
6 Salem Road, London W2 4BU.
Tel: 0171-727 8993. Fax: 0171-792 3176.
Subjects: Biography, current affairs, history, popular culture, popular science.

VICTOR GOLLANCZ
Wellington House, 125 Strand, London WC2R 0BB.
Tel: 0171-420 5555. Fax: 0171-240 7261.
Subjects: General; biography, current affairs, history, music, sociology, sport, travel.

GRUB STREET (P)
The Basement, 10 Chivalry Road, London SW11 1HT.
Tel: 0171-924 3966. Fax: 0171-738 1009.
Subjects: Aviation history, cookery, health.

GUINNESS PUBLISHING LTD
338 Euston Rd, London NW1 3BD.
Tel: 0171-891 4567. Fax: 0171-891 4501.
Subjects: General reference, sport and popular music.

ROBERT HALE LTD
Clerkenwell House, 45-47 Clerkenwell Green, London EC1R 0HT.
Tel: 0171-251 2661. Fax: 0171-490 4958.
Subjects: General; architecture, cookery, crafts, military, music, natural history, sports, travel.

HAMISH HAMILTON LTD
27 Wrights Lane, London W8 5TZ.
Tel: 0171-416 3100. Fax: 0171-416 3295.
Subjects: General; crime, current affairs, history, politics, travel.

HAMLYN – see REED CONSUMER BOOKS

HARPERCOLLINS PUBLISHERS
77-85 Fulham Palace Road, London W6 8JB.
Tel: 0181-741 7070. Fax: 0181-307 4440.
Imprints: Aquarian, Collins, Pandora, Thorsons.
Subjects: General.

HAYNES PUBLISHING
Sparkford, Yeovil, Somerset BA22 7JJ.
Tel: 01963 440635. Fax: 01963 440023.
Imprints: G.T.Foulis, Oxford Publishing Company, Patrick Stephens, Oxford Illustrated Press.
Contact: Alison Roelich, Editorial Department Manager.
Subjects: Biography, cars and motor racing, motorcycles, motoring.

HEADLINE BOOK PUBLISHING LTD
338 Euston Road, London NW1 3BH.
Tel: 0171-873 6000. Fax: 0171-873 6124.
Contact: Heather Holden-Brown, Publishing Director Non-Fiction.
Subjects: Biography, countryside, design, food and wine, gardening, music.

WILLIAM HEINEMANN LTD
Random House, 20 Vauxhall Bridge Road, London SW1V 2SA.
Tel: 0171-840 8400. Fax: 0171-233 6127.
Subjects: Popular non-fiction.

HELICON PUBLISHING LTD
42 Hythe Bridge Street, Oxford OX1 2EP.
Tel: 01865 204204. Fax: 01865 204205.
Subjects: Encyclopedias and reference.

CHRISTOPHER HELM PUBLISHERS LTD
35 Bedford Row, London WC1R 4JH.
Tel: 0171-242 0946. Fax: 0171-831 8478.
Subjects: Ornithology.

HERBERT PRESS – see A & C BLACK

HODDER HEADLINE PLC
338 Euston Road, London NW1 3BH.
Tel: 0171-873 6000. Fax: 0171-873 6024.
Imprints: Arnold, Headline, Hodder & Stoughton.
Subjects: General; academic, children's, cookery, history, music, religion, sport, travel.

HODDER & STOUGHTON – see HODDER HEADLINE

HUTCHINSON
Random House, 20 Vauxhall Bridge Road, London SW1V 2SA.
Tel: 0171-973 9670. Fax: 0171-233 7870.
Subjects: Biography, crime, current affairs, travel.

MICHAEL JOSEPH LTD
27 Wrights Lane, London W8 5TZ.
Tel: 0171-416 3000. Fax: 0171-416 3293.
Subjects: General.

THE KENILWORTH PRESS LTD
Addington, Buckingham MK18 2JR.
Tel: 01296 715101. Fax: 01296 715148.
Subjects: Equestrian.

KINGFISHER BOOKS – see LAROUSSE KINGFISHER

LAROUSSE KINGFISHER PLC
Elsley House, 24-30 Great Titchfield Street, London W1P 7AD.
Tel: 0171-631 0878. Fax: 0171-323 4694.
Imprint: Kingfisher Books.
Contact: Veneta Bullen.
Subjects: Children's non-fiction, natural history, reference.

FRANCES LINCOLN LTD (P)
4 Torriano Mews, Torriano Avenue, London NW5 2RZ.
Tel: 0171-284 4009. Fax: 0171-267 5249.
Subjects: General; cookery, gardening, health, interior design.

LITTLE, BROWN AND COMPANY (UK)
Brettenham House, Lancaster Place, London WC2E 7EN.
Tel: 0171-911 8000. Fax: 0171-911 8100.
Subjects: General.

THE LUTTERWORTH PRESS
P O Box 60, Cambridge CB1 2NT.
Tel: 01223 350865. Fax: 01223 366951.
Subjects: Arts, biography, children's non-fiction, crafts, educational, environment, history, leisure, reference, religion, science, sociology.

MACMILLAN GENERAL BOOKS
25 Eccleston Place, London SW1W 9NF.
Tel: 0171-881 8000. Fax: 0171-881 8001.
Imprints: Macmillan, Pan, Papermac, Sidgwick & Jackson.
Subjects: General; biography, cookery, crafts, current affairs, gardening, practical, travel.

MANCHESTER UNIVERSITY PRESS
Oxford Road, Manchester M13 9NR.
Tel: 0161-273 5539. Fax: 0161-274 3346.
Subjects: Architecture, design, art history, politics.

MARSHALL CAVENDISH BOOKS
119 Wardour Street, London W1V 3TD.
Tel: 0171-734 6710. Fax: 0171-439 1423.
Subjects: General; art, cookery, crafts, DIY, fashion, gardening, social history, sport, style, war and survival.

MARSHALL PUBLISHING/MARSHALL EDITIONS LTD (P)
170 Piccadilly, London W1V 9DD.
Tel: 0171-629 0079. Fax: 0171-834 0785.
Contact: Zilda Tandy, Picture Editor.
Subjects: General; crafts and hobbies, food and wine, gardening, natural history, photography, transport.

MILEPOST 92½
Newton Harcourt, Leicestershire LE8 9FH.
Tel: 0116 259 2068. Fax: 0116 259 3001.
Contacts: Colin Garratt, Director; Colin Nash, Picture Library Manager.
Subjects: Railways, light rail, transport in general.

MILLER'S – see REED CONSUMER BOOKS

MITCHELL BEAZLEY – see REED CONSUMER BOOKS

PRION
32-34 Gordon House Road, London NW5 1LP.
Tel: 0171-482 4248. Fax: 0171-482 4203.
Contact: Andrew Goodfellow.
Subjects: General; cookery, drink (beer, wine and spirits), natural history, new age, popular culture, travel.

JOHN MURRAY (PUBLISHERS) LTD
50 Albemarle Street, London W1X 4BD.
Tel: 0171-493 4361. Fax: 0171-499 1792.
Subjects: General; art and architecture, biography, crafts, geography, health, history, science, maths, travel.

NEW HOLLAND (PUBLISHERS) LTD
24 Nutford Place, London W1H 6DQ.
Tel: 0171-724 7773. Fax: 0171-258 1293.
Contact: Michaella Standen.
Subjects: Crafts, cookery, gardening, interior design, natural history, travel.

NEW LEAF BOOKS LTD (P)
BCM-New Leaf, London WC1N 3XX.
Tel: 0171-251 6242. Fax: 0171-251 6206.
Contact: Michael Wright.
Subjects: General; mainly practical and instructional.

NEXUS SPECIAL INTERESTS LTD
Nexus House, Boundary Way, Hemel Hempstead, Herts HP2 7ST.
Tel: 01442 66551. Fax: 01442 66998.
Subjects: Aviation, crafts, electronics, hobbies, maritime, military, model engineering and modelling, railways, woodworking.

OMNIBUS PRESS/BOOK SALES LTD
8/9 Frith Street, London W1V 5TZ.
Tel: 0171-434 0066. Fax: 0171-734 2246.
Contact: Chris Charlesworth, editor; Nikki Russell, picture researcher.
Subjects: Rock, pop and classical music.

OSPREY PUBLISHING LTD
Unit 6, Spring Garden, Tinworth Street, London SE11 5EH.
Tel: 0171-225 9857. Fax: 0171-225 9869.
Subjects: Aircraft, cars, military, motorcycles.

OXFORD ILLUSTRATED PRESS – see HAYNES PUBLISHING

OXFORD PAPERBACKS – see OXFORD UNIVERSITY PRESS

OXFORD PUBLISHING COMPANY – see HAYNES PUBLISHING

OXFORD UNIVERSITY PRESS
Great Clarendon Street, Oxford OX2 6DP.
Tel: 01865 556767. Fax: 01865 556646.
Imprints: Clarendon Press, Oxford Paperbacks.
Subjects: General; academic, educational, reference.

PAN – see MACMILLAN GENERAL BOOKS

PANDORA – see HARPERCOLLINS PUBLISHERS

PAPERMAC – see MACMILLAN GENERAL BOOKS

PARTRIDGE PRESS
Transworld Publishers, 61-63 Uxbridge Road, London W5 5SA.
Tel: 0181-579 2652. Fax: 0181-579 5479.
Subjects: Sports and leisure.

STANLEY PAUL – see EBURY PRESS

PAVILION BOOKS
26 Upper Ground, London SE1 9PD.
Tel: 0171-620 1666. Fax: 0171-620 1314.
Contact: Vicky Monk.
Subjects: Food and wine, gardening, interior design, music, sport, travel.

PENGUIN BOOKS LTD
27 Wrights Lane, London W8 5TZ.
Tel: 0171-416 3000. Fax: 0171-416 3294.
Imprints: Hamish Hamilton, Michael Joseph, Viking.
Contact: Lily Richards, Picture Research Manager.
Subjects: General.

PHAIDON PRESS LTD
18 Regents Wharf, All Saints Street, London N1 9PA.
Tel: 0171-843 1000. Fax: 0171-843 1010.
Subjects: Architecture, decorative and fine arts, design, photography.

GEORGE PHILIP LTD
2nd Floor, Unit 6, Citadel Place, Spring Gardens, Tinworth Street, London SE11 5EH.
Tel: 0171-225 9822. Fax: 0171-225 9841.
Subjects: Educational, guides, travel.

PIATKUS BOOKS
5 Windmill Street, London W1P 1HF.
Tel: 0171-631 0710. Fax: 0171-436 7137.
Subjects: Business, cookery, fashion, health, leisure, mind, body and spirit, women's interests.

PLAYNE BOOKS LTD (P)
Chapel House, Trefin, Haverfordwest, Pembrokeshire SA62 5AU.
Tel: 01348 837073. Fax: 01348 837063.
Contact: Gill Davies, Editorial Director.
Subjects: General illustrated books for adults and children.

PLEXUS PUBLISHING LTD
55a Clapham Common Southside, London SW4 9BX.
Tel: 0171-622 2440. Fax: 0171-622 2441.
Subjects: Biography, fashion, film, music, popular culture.

MATHEW PRICE LTD (P)
The Old Glove Factory, Bristol Road, Sherborne, Dorset DT9 4HP.
Tel: 01935 816010. Fax: 01935 816310.
Contact: Sue Davies.
Subjects: General children's books.

QUARTET BOOKS
27 Goodge Street, London W1P 2LD.
Tel: 0171-636 3992. Fax: 0171-637 1866.
Subjects: Biography, history, music and popular culture.

QUARTO PUBLISHING PLC (P)
The Old Brewery, 6 Blundell Street, London N7 9BH.
Tel: 0171-700 6700. Fax: 0171-700 4191.
Subjects: General; arts and crafts, cookery, home interest, reference, travel.

RANDOM HOUSE UK LTD
Random House, 20 Vauxhall Bridge Road, London SW1V 2SA.
Tel: 0171-973 9000.
Relevant imprints: Barrie & Jenkins, Century, Chatto & Windus, Ebury Press, William Heinemann, Hutchinson, Secker & Warburg.
Subjects: Various; see individual imprints.

THE READER'S DIGEST ASSOCIATION LTD
11 Westferry Circus, Canary Wharf, London E14 4HE.
Tel: 0171-715 8000. Fax: 0171-715 8181.
Subjects: General illustrated; cookery, crafts, DIY, encyclopaedias, folklore, gardening, guide books, history, natural history.

REED CONSUMER BOOKS
Michelin House, 81 Fulham Road, London SW3 6RB.
Tel: 0171-581 9393. Fax: 0171-225 9424.
Imprints: Bounty, Hamlyn, Miller's, Mitchell Beazley.
Subjects: Illustrated general reference and non-fiction.

ROBINSON PUBLISHING
7 Kensington Church Court, London W8 4SP.
Tel: 0171-938 3830. Fax: 0171-938 4214.
Subjects: Health, self-help, true crime, non-fiction anthologies.

ROUTLEDGE
11 New Fetter Lane, London EC4P 4EE.
Tel: 0171-842 2071. Fax: 0171-842 2298.
Contact: Suzanne Collins, Picture Researcher.
Subjects: Academic, professional and reference.

SALAMANDER BOOKS LTD
129/137 York Way, London N7 9LG.
Tel: 0171-267 4447. Fax: 0171-267 5112.
Subjects: Cookery, crafts, gardening, history, hobbies, military, music, natural history, pets, transport.

SAVITRI BOOKS LTD (P)
115j Cleveland Street, London W1P 5PN.
Tel: 0171-436 9932. Fax: 0171-580 6330.
Contact: M. S. Srivastava.
Subjects: General; crafts, ecology, natural history.

SECKER & WARBURG LTD
Random House, 20 Vauxhall Bridge Road, London SW1V 2SA.
Tel: 0171-840 8400. Fax: 0171-932 0761.
Subjects: Biography, history, jazz, politics, travel.

SHELDRAKE PRESS (P)
188 Cavendish Road, London SW12 0DA.
Tel: 0181-675 1767. Fax: 0181-675 7736.
Contact: Simon Rigge.
Subjects: General; architecture, cookery, design, history, music, travel.

SIDGWICK & JACKSON
25 Eccleston Place, London SW1W 9NF.
Tel: 0171-881 8000. Fax: 0171-881 8001.
Contact: Gordon Wise, Senior Editor.
Subjects: Biography, current affairs, history, music, sport.

SMITH GRYPHON LTD
12 Bridge Wharf, 156 Caledonian Road, London N1 9UU.
Tel: 0171-278 2444. Fax: 0171-833 5680.
Contact: Robert Smith.
Subjects: Celebrities, pop music, true crime, health, cookery, pets.

SOUVENIR PRESS LTD
43 Great Russell Street, London WC1B 3PA.
Tel: 0171-580 9307. Fax: 0171-580 5064.
Contact: Tessa Harrow, Editor.
Subjects: General; childcare, cookery, gardening, health, hobbies, practical, sociology.

SPELLMOUNT LTD
The Old Rectory, Staplehurst, Kent TN12 0AZ.
Tel: 01580 893730. Fax: 01580 893731.
Contact: Jamie Wilson, Managing Director.
Subjects: History and military history.

PATRICK STEPHENS LTD
Haynes Publishing, Sparkford, Nr Yeovil, Somerset BA22 7JJ.
Tel: 01963 440635. Fax: 01963 440023.
Contact: Alison Roelich, Editorial Department Manager.
Subjects: Aviation, cars and motorcycles, maritime, motor racing, railways, railway modelling.

SUNBURST BOOKS
Kiln House, 110 New Kings Road, London SW6 4NZ.
Tel: 0171-352 7936. Fax: 0171-351 0240.
Contact: J Messham.
Subjects: General illustrated; cookery, gardening, motoring, natural history, sport.

SUTTON PUBLISHING LTD
Phoenix Mill, Thrupp, Stroud, Gloucestershire GL5 2BU.
Tel: 01453 731114. Fax: 01453 884150.
Subjects: archaeology, aviation, biography, buildings, canals, history, military, motor transport, railways.

SWAN HILL PRESS – see AIRLIFE PUBLISHING

THE TEMPLAR COMPANY PLC (P)
Pippbrook Mill, London Road, Dorking, Surrey RH4 1JE.
Tel: 01306 876361. Fax: 01306 889097.
Subjects: Mainly children's reference; cities, geography, natural history, science.

THAMES AND HUDSON LTD
30-34 Bloomsbury Street, London WC1B 3QP.
Tel: 0171-636 5488. Fax: 0171-636 4799.
Contact: Jo Marsh, Head of Picture Research.
Subjects: Archaeology, anthropology, art and architecture, cinema, fashion, interior design, music, photography, practical guides, religion and mythology, theatre, travel.

THORSONS
77-85 Fulham Palace Road, Hammersmith, London W6 8JB.
Tel: 0181-307 4390. Fax: 0181-307 4278.
Contact: Amanda McKelvie.
Subjects: Complementary medicine, health, environmental issues, parenting and childcare.

TOUCAN BOOKS LTD (P)
Fourth Floor, 32-38 Saffon Hill, London EC1N 8BS.
Tel: 0171-404 8181. Fax: 0171-404 8282.
Subjects: General.

UNICORN BOOKS
16 Laxton Gardens, Paddock Wood, Tonbridge, Kent TN12 6BB.
Tel: 01892 833648. Fax: 01892 833577.
Contact: Ray Green, Managing Director.
Subjects: Railways.

USBORNE PUBLISHING
83-85 Saffron Hill, London EC1N 8RT.
Tel: 0171-430 2800. Fax: 0171-242 0974.
Contacts: Amanda Barlow, Steve Wright or Mary Cartwright.
Subjects: General children's; crafts, natural history, practical, reference.

VERMILION – see EBURY PRESS

VIKING – see PENGUIN BOOKS

VIRGIN PUBLISHING LTD
332 Ladbroke Grove, London W10 5AH.
Tel: 0181-968 7554. Fax: 0181-968 0929.
Contacts: Benn Dunn (sport); Ian Gittens (music); Carolyn Price (arts,m lifestyle, practical); Rebecca Levene (cult TV and film, erotica (male subjects only); Kerri Sharp (portraits, erotica, fetish fashion (all female subjects only)..
Subjects: As above.

WARD LOCK – see CASSELL

WARD LOCK EDUCATIONAL COMPANY LTD
1 Christopher Road, East Grinstead, West Sussex RH19 3BT.
Tel: 01342 318980. Fax: 01342 410980.
Contact: Rose Hill, Editor.
Subjects: General educational; geography, mathematics, music, science.

WEIDENFELD & NICOLSON LTD
Orion House, 5 Upper St Martin's Lane, London WC2H 9EA.
Tel: 0171-240 3444. Fax: 0171-240 4822.
Subjects: General; biography, cookery, history, travel.

PHILIP WILSON PUBLISHERS LTD
143-149 Great Portland Street, London W1N 5FB.
Tel: 0171-436 4490. Fax: 0171-436 4403.
Contact: Anne Jackson, Editorial Director.
Subjects: Applied and decorative arts, architecture.

YALE UNIVERSITY PRESS
23 Pond Street, London NW3 2PN.
Tel: 0171-431 4422. Fax: 0171-431 3755.
Subjects: Architecture, art, history, politics, sociology.

CARDS & CALENDARS

This section lists publishers of postcards, greetings cards and calendars, along with their requirements. Additionally, companies producing allied material, such as posters and prints, are also included, though there is considerable overlap with many of the companies listed here producing a range of products.

With the exception of traditional viewcard producers, who have always offered rather meagre rates for freelance material, fees in this area are generally good. However, only those who can produce precisely what is required as far as subject matter, quality and format are concerned, are likely to succeed.

Market requirements

Traditionally, these publishers have required larger format transparencies of the highest quality. While they still demand optimum quality, the requirement for the really large format has eased up in recent years and virtually all of the companies listed here will consider top quality 35mm. Nevertheless, if you want to make a real impact in this field, you should seriously consider working in the larger "landscape" formats, such as 6x7cm, 6x9cm or even 5x4in.

The need for material of the highest quality cannot be too strongly emphasised. The market is highly specialised with very specific requirements. If you aim to break into this field, you must be very sure of your photographic technique. You must be able to produce professional quality material that is pin sharp and perfectly exposed with excellent colour saturation.

You must also know and be able to supply *exactly* what the market requires. The listings will help you, but you should also carry out your own field study by examining the photographic products on general sale.

After a period in the doldrums the photographic greetings card has been making something of a comeback in recent years. Neverthless, the big mass-market card publishers still employ mostly art or graphics. Those that do use photography tend to be smaller, specialised companies, many of them publishing a full range of photographic products. These companies also use a lot of work from top photographers or picture libraries, which means that there is greater competition than ever to supply material for these products.

The calendar market is equally demanding, though fortunately there are still large numbers of calendars using photographs being produced every year. Many calendar producers obtain the material they need from picture agencies, but this is not to say that individual photographers cannot successfully break into this field. Once again, though, you must be sure of your photographic technique and be able to produce really top quality work.

Make a point of studying the cards, calendars or posters that you see on general sale or hanging up in places you visit. Don't rely solely on what *you* think would make a good card or calendar picture; familiarise yourself with the type of pictures actually being used by these publishers.

Rights and fees

Where given to us by the company concerned, fees have been quoted. Some companies prefer to negotiate fees individually, depending upon the type of material you offer. If you are new to this field, the best plan is to submit your transparencies (preferably after making an initial enquiry, outlining the material you have available), and let the company concerned make you an offer. Generally speaking, you should not accept less than about £75 for Greetings Card or Calendar Rights.

Remember, you are not selling your copyright in the transparency for this fee; you are free to submit the same transparency to any *non-competitive* market (for example, a magazine) at a later date. But you should not attempt to sell a transparency to another greetings card publisher once you have sold Greetings Card Rights to a competing firm.

BERKSWELL PUBLISHING CO LTD
PO Box 420, Warminster, Wiltshire BA12 9XB.
Tel/fax: 01985 840189.
Contact: John Stidolph, Managing Director.
Calendars, diaries, posters and books featuring Royalty. Good colour and B&W photographs of members of the Royal Family and Royal events always required.
Fees: By negotiation.

BRITANNIA PRODUCTS LTD
Dawson Lane, Dudley Hill, Bradford BD4 6HW.
Tel: 01274 688221. Fax: 01274 651218.
Contact: Gail Lanfranchi, Creative Manager.
Greetings cards. Will always consider images suitable for greetings card use: wedding subjects (no soft focus or '70s style still life), baby images, humour and nostalgia. 5"x4" transparencies required; will also consider high quality or hand-tinted B&W.
Fees: £190-£220 for World Greetings Card Rights for five years.

CANONBURY DESIGN (CAMDEN GRAPHICS)
46 Colebrooke Row, London N1 8AF.
Tel: 0171-226 2061. Fax: 0171-704 0616.
Contact: Monica Willett, Art Editor.
Greetings cards. Will consider original pictures of puppies/dogs, kittens/cats. Must look very sweet, cute or humorous. 35mm accepted but larger formats up to 5x4in always preferred.
Fees: £175 per image.

CARTEL INTERNATIONAL LTD
PO Box 918, Harlow, Essex CM20 2DU.
Tel: 01279 641125. Fax: 01279 635672.
Contacts: Trevor Jones, Licensing Director. Martin Carter, Product Manager.
Posters and greetings cards. All types of subjects considered, landscape, figurative, situation, fashion, humour, etc. Prefers 6x6cm or larger formats, but will consider 35mm if of the highest quality.
Fees: Greetings cards, around £200; posters on a royalties basis.

JOHN HINDE (UK) LTD
Dudnance Lane, Poole, Redruth, Cornwall TR15 3QR.
Tel: 01209 712617. Fax: 01209 612438.
Contact: Chris Spencer, Sales Manager.
Postcards and calendars. Local views of all UK areas, ranging from straightforward views to more "creative" images. Will also consider amusing animal pictures. 35mm acceptable.
Fees: £50–£75 dependent on rights purchased.

HOWITT PORTFOLIO PUBLISHING
Hope Rd, Bedminster, Bristol BS3 3NZ.
Tel: 0117 963 6161. Fax: 0117 966 4235.
Contact: Marion Wilson (Design & Art Manager).
Large format calendars for corporate customers. Requires very high quality colour images, 5x4in or medium format. 35mm only acceptable if very exceptional material and if justified by subject matter (i.e. wildlife). Top quality B&W also considered. Seeks wide range of subjects including British landscapes, European and Worldwide landscapes and scenes, waterscapes, natural wonders, wildlife, classic cars and glamour. Telephone in the first instance before submitting.
Fees: Variable depending on subject matter and usage. From £35–£200 for UK calendar rights for one year.

IMAGES & EDITIONS
Bourne Road, Essendine, Nr Stamford, Lincs PE9 4UW.
Tel: 01780 757118. Fax: 01780 754629.
Contact: Sandra Orme, Product Manager.
Greetings cards and stationery. Will consider British landscapes and wildlife, domestic pets (especially cats, dogs, horses), florals. Top quality 35mm acceptable but larger formats preferred.
Fees: By negotiation or on 5% royalty basis, for world rights for greetings cards for three years.

JARROLD PUBLISHING
Whitefriars, Norwich, Norfolk NR3 1TR.
Tel: 01603 227325. Fax: 01603 662748.
Contact: Ms Vivienne Buckingham, Photographic Librarian.
Calendars. Will consider picturesque scenes within the British Isles, flora, fauna, pets. Top quality 35mm and medium format transparencies only. Also publishes guide books (Britain only). Buying in period: all areas with the exception of Scotland 1 January - 31 March. Scotland: 1 August – 30 September.
Fees: £35–£50 outright purchase of full copyright, depending on format.

KARDORAMA
PO Box 85, Potters Bar, Herts EN6 5AD.
Tel/fax: 01707 652781.
Contact: Brian Elwood, managing partner.
Postcards. Always seeking new views of London – major tourist sights or subjects that tourists would consider typical such as red buses, phone boxes, policemen, taxis, etc. Should be good record shots but with "a hint of romance" and plenty of detail in the main subject. Also seek humorous images, any subject or location providing the image needs no explanation, but must be sharp and well exposed under good lighting conditions. 35mm transparencies (and even prints) are acceptable, but medium format is preferred.
Fees: Variable, depending on quality of work, subject matter and quantities.

THE MEDICI SOCIETY LTD
34-42 Pentonville Road, London N1 9HG.
Tel: 0171-837 7099. Fax: 0171-837 9152.
Contact: The Art Director.
Greetings cards and calendars. Limited requirement for transparencies of flowers, animals and birds in their natural surroundings, snow scenes, etc. 35mm transparencies can be accepted if of a high professional quality, but larger formats are preferred. Submissions should not consist of more than six transparencies. Please enclose a s.a.e.
Fees: From £170 approx.

THE ORIGINAL POSTER COMPANY LTD
Elephant House, Victoria Villas, Richmond, Surrey TW9 2JX.
Tel: 0181-332 0506. Fax: 0181-332 1286.
Contact: Samantha Gates, Production Assistant.
Greetings cards. Amusing or cute shots of animals in natural habitats (zoo pictures not normally acceptable unless captivity not apparent). Pictures must have the potential to be seen as amusing when a suitable caption is added. High quality 35mm acceptable.
Fees: £150–£200 for World Greetings Card Rights for five years.

PYRAMID
PO Box 219, Leicester LE2 7YX.
Tel: 0116 285 5080. Fax: 0116 285 4826.
Contact: Nic Wastell, General Manager.
Posters, prints and postcards. Will consider any subject suitable for high-quality poster or postcard

use – scenics, botanicals, animals (domestic and wild), etc. Always interested in humorous or "cute" material. Quality must be outstanding, both artistically and technically. Mainly colour but some B&W used. Top quality 35mm originals accepted but larger formats preferred. Always telephone before submitting.
Fees: £200–£400 for worldwide poster and/or postcard rights.

RIVERSIDE CARDS
Riverside Complex, Millfold Way, Rippondale, Halifax HX6 4JD.
Tel: 01422 824820. Fax: 01422 824830.
Contact: David Hardwick, Design Manager.
Greetings cards. Always interested in appealing photographs of pets/animals; black and white, hand-tinted or sepia images of children/couples, and other material suitable for greetings card publication. Portrait format preferred but landscape format will be considered.
Fees: By negotiation.

ROSE OF COLCHESTER
Clough Road, Severalls Industrial Park, Colchester CO4 4QT.
Tel: 01206 844500. Fax: 01206 845872.
Contact: E.R.Rose (Director).
Calendars, mainly for business promotion. Will consider top-quality, large format examples of traditional calendar subjects: British landscapes (landscape and upright formats), wildlife (British and worldwide), girls, classic cars, "nostalgia", cute children, domestic and farm animals, adventure sport. Must be top quality transparency material preferably in 10x8in or 5x4in formats. Minimum acceptable size 6x6cm. No 35mm. Submit December/January for annual selection process.
Fees: £120–£150 for UK calendar rights according to quality and quantity purchased.

SANTORO GRAPHICS
The Old Bank House, 342-344 London Road, Cricket Green, Mitcham, Surrey CR4 3ND.
Tel: 0181-640 9777. Fax: 0181-640 2888.
Contact: Meera Santoro, Projects Director.
Posters, postcards and greetings cards. Requires striking and attractive images appealing to the typical young poster/postcard buyer: nostalgic, contemporary, romantic, humorous. B&W a speciality, but colour images in contemporary styles are also sought.
Fees: By negotiation for worldwide rights.

SCANDECOR LTD
3 The Ermine Centre, Hurricane Close, Huntingdon, Cambridgeshire PE18 6XX.
Tel: 01480 456395. Fax: 01480 456269.
Contact: Mr Nigel Green, Sales Director.
Posters, prints, postcards and calendars. Will consider contributions mainly for poster/postcard use on a wide range of subjects: animals, cars, tasteful glamour, romance, humour, etc. Most interested in dramatic, powerful images or humorous shots likely to appeal to the youth market.
Fees: Depends on material, how it is used, and on whether international distribution rights may be required.

STATICS
41 Standard Road, London NW10 6HF.
Tel: 0181-965 3327. Fax: 0181-965 2317.
Contact: Natalie Barton, Art Editor.
Postcards, greetings cards, postercards and mini-calendars. Will consider cute or humorous shots of children or of "popular" animals (e.g. pigs, cats, dogs, orang-utans). Must be shot on location or in contextual settings, not in the studio. B&W and colour.
Fees: Postcards, £120; greetings cards, £160; postercards, £200; page in mini-calendar, £75.

AGENCIES

Picture libraries and agencies are in the business of selling pictures. They are not in the business of teaching photography or advising photographers how to produce saleable work – although they can sometimes prove remarkably helpful in the latter respect to those who show promise. Their purpose is strictly a business one: to meet the demand for stock pictures from such markets as magazine and book publishers, advertising agencies, travel operators, greetings card and calendar publishers, and many more. A typical agency has many thousands of pictures in its files, each one of which is carefully categorised and filed so that it can be easily located when an editor or picture buyer wants to see a selection of pictures of a particular subject.

Many photographers look upon an agency as a last resort; they have been unable to sell their photographs themselves, so they think they might as well try unloading them on an agency. This is the wrong attitude. No agency will succeed in placing pictures which are quite simply unmarketable. In any event, the photographer who has had at least some success in selling pictures is in a far better position to approach an agency.

Agency requirements

If you hope to interest an agency in your work, you must be able to produce pictures which the agency feels are likely to sell to one of their markets. Although the acceptance of your work by an agency is no guarantee that it will sell, an efficient agency certainly will not clutter up its files with pictures which do not stand a reasonably good chance of finding a market.

Agents handle pictures of every subject under the sun. Some specialise in particular subjects – sport, natural history, etc. – while others act as general agencies, covering the whole spectrum of subject matter. Any photograph that could be published in one form or another is a suitable picture for an agency.

Even if you eventually decide that you want to place all your potentially saleable material with an agency, you cannot expect to leave every aspect of the business to them. You must continue to study the market, watching for trends; you must continue to study published pictures. For example, if your speciality is travel material, you should use every opportunity to study the type of pictures published in current travel brochures and other markets using such material. Only by doing this – by being aware of the market – can you hope to continue to provide your agency with marketable pictures.

Commission and copyright

Agencies generally work on a commission basis, 50 per cent being the most usual rate – if they receive £100 for reproduction rights in a particular picture, the photographer will get £50 of this.

A 50 per cent commission rate may seem high, but it should be remembered that a picture agency, like any other business, has substantial overheads to account for. There can also be high costs involved in making prospective buyers aware of the pictures that are available – the larger agencies produce lavish colour catalogues featuring selections of their best pictures. Nevertheless, agencies are sometimes willing to negotiate a lower rate of commission with their more prized contributors.

Agents do not normally sell pictures outright; indeed, they should never do so without the permission of the photographer concerned, who would normally always retain copyright in all pictures placed with the agency. As would the individual photographer, they merely sell "reproduction rights", the transparency being loaned to the buyer for a specified period of time while printing plates are produced.

However a few agencies do sometimes offer to buy pictures outright from a photographer, instead of working on the normal commission basis. The price in these cases will be a matter for negotiation between photographer and agency, but it should be remembered that once a picture is sold outright, the photographer has effectively disposed of the copyright and has no further rights in the picture.

A long-term investment

When dealing with a photographer for the first time, most agencies require a minimum initial submission – which can consist of anything from 50–500 pictures. Most also stipulate that you must leave your material with them for a minimum period of anything from one to five years.

When an agency takes on the work of a new photographer, they are involved in a lot of work – categorising, filing, cross-indexing and, in most cases, re-mounting the transparencies in the agency's own standard mounts (or, at least, adding the agency's name to the existing mounts). The next step will often be to make it known to picture buyers that these new pictures are available, sometimes including reproductions of them in any new catalogues or publicity material currently being prepared. Having been involved in all this work and expense, it is not unreasonable for them to want to be given a fair chance to market the pictures. If the photographer were able to demand the return of the work after only a few months, the agency will have been involved in a lot of work and expense for nothing.

Dealing with an agency must therefore be considered a long-term investment. Having initially placed, say, a few hundred pictures with an agency, it could be at least several months before any are selected by a picture buyer, and even longer before any monies are seen by the photographer.

Normally, the photographer will also be expected to regularly submit new material to the library. Indeed, only when you have several hundred pictures lodged with the library can you hope for regular sales – and a reasonable return on your investment.

Making an approach

Many agencies prefer to meet new photographers personally to see and discuss their work. It is not a good idea, however, to turn up on their doorstep without an appointment. The best plan is to write to, or telephone, the agency of your choice, outlining the material you have available. It may also be worth mentioning details of any sales you have made yourself. If the agency is interested, they will suggest a mutually convenient appointment when you can bring your material along, or they may suggest that you initially post some samples to them.

But remember that there is little point in approaching an agency until you have a sizeable collection of potentially saleable material. Most agencies will not feel it worth their while dealing with a photographer who has only a dozen or so marketable pictures to offer – it just wouldn't be worth all the work and expense involved. And the chance of the photographer seeing a worthwhile return on just a dozen pictures placed with an agency are remote indeed; you'd be lucky to see more than one cheque in ten years!

In the listings that follow you'll find full information on over 80 agencies: the subjects they handle, the markets they supply, the formats they stock, their terms of business (including any minimum initial submission and retention period), and their standard commission charged on sales.

Prefacing the listings you'll find an Agency Subject Index; this is a guide to agencies which have a special interest in those subjects, though many other agencies may also cover the same subjects within their general stock.

Remember: simply placing material with an agency doesn't guarantee sales. And no agency can sell material for which there is no market. On the other hand, if you are able to produce good quality, marketable work, and can team up with the right agency, you could see a very worthwhile return from this association.

Subject Index

Aerial

Aerofilms Ltd
Geo Aerial Photography

Art & Architecture

Alvey & Towers
Ancient Art & Architecture Collection
The Bridgeman Art Library
Woodmansterne Picture Library

Botany/Horticulture

A-Z Botanical Collection Ltd
Garden Matters Photographic Library
Holt Studios
Houses & Interiors
NHPA
Natural Science Photos
Papilio Natural History Library
Planet Earth Pictures

Business & Industry

Ace Photo Agency
Alvey & Towers
Euroart Agency & Library
The Picture Book Ltd
Powerstock Photo Library
PictureBank Photo Library
The Telegraph Colour Library

Fashion & Beauty

Camera Press Ltd
The Picture Book Ltd
PictureBank Photo Library

Food & Drink

Bubbles Photo Library
Cephas Picture Library
The Anthony Blake Photo Library

General (all subjects)

Ace Photo Agency
Adams Picture Library
Alvey & Towers
Barnaby's Picture Library
J. Allan Cash Ltd
Cephas Picture Library
Colorific Photo Library Ltd
Eye Ubiquitous Picture Library
The Robert Harding Picture Library
The Hutchison Library
Photo Library International
Pictor International Ltd
Popperfoto
Spectrum Colour Library
Tony Stone Images
The Telegraph Colour Library
Topham Picturepoint
S&I Williams Power Pix

Woodmansterne Picture Library
ZEFA Pictures Ltd

Geography & World Environment

J. Allan Cash Ltd
Bruce Coleman Ltd
Ecoscene
Geo Aerial Photography
Holt Studios International
Link Picture Library
NHPA
Natural Science Photos
Oxford Scientific Films Ltd
Panos Pictures
Papilio Natural History Library
PictureBank Photo Library
Royal Geographical Society Picture Library
SCR Photo Library
Tropix Photographic Library
Windrush Photos

Glamour

Barnaby's Picture Library
PictureBank Photo Library
Rex Features Ltd
Spectrum Colour Library
S&I Williams Power Pix

Historical

Barnaby's Picture Library
The Bridgeman Art Library
Popperfoto

Landscapes

Oxford Scientific Films Ltd
Papilio Natural History Library
The Picture Book Ltd
PictureBank Photo Library
Planet Earth Pictures
Royal Geographical Society Picture Library

Music

Jazz Index Photo Library
Lebrecht Collection
Redferns
Retna Pictures Ltd

Natural History

Aquila Photographics
Bruce Coleman Ltd
Ecoscene
Frank Lane Picture Agency Ltd
NHPA
Natural Image
Natural Science Photos
Oxford Scientific Films Ltd
Papilio Natural History Library
Planet Earth Pictures
RSPCA Photolibrary
Windrush Photos

News & Current Affairs

Camera Press Ltd
Empics Ltd
Popperfoto
Rex Features Ltd

Personalities

Aquarius Literary Agency & Picture Library
Camera Press Ltd
Famous
Monitor Syndication
Popperfoto
Retna Pictures Ltd
Rex Features Ltd

Photojournalism

Camera Press Ltd
Popperfoto
Rex Features Ltd

Science & Technology

Powerstock Photo Library
Oxford Scientific Films Ltd
PictureBank Photo Library
Rex Features Ltd
Science Photo Library

Sport

Action Images Ltd
Alvey & Towers
Empics Ltd
PPL Ltd
Retna Pictures Ltd

Skishoot – Offshoot
Sporting Pictures

Transport

Ace Photo Agency
Alvey & Towers
The Bridgeman Art Library
Milepost 92½
Powerstock Photo Library
Quadrant Picture Library
Scotland in Focus
Telegraph Colour Library
Travel Ink

Travel/Tourist

Alvey & Towers
Cephas Picture Library
James Davis Travel Photography
Footprints Colour Picture Library
The Hutchinson Library
Jayawardene Travel Photo Library
Middle East Pictures Inc

Pictor International Ltd
PictureBank Photo Library
Royal Geographical Society Picture Library
Scotland in Focus
Skishoot – Offshoot
Spectrum Colour Library
The Still Moving Picture Company
Tony Stone Images
Topham Picturepoint
Travel Ink
The Travel Library
Travel Photo International
S&I Williams Power Pix
World Pictures

Underwater

Bruce Coleman Ltd
Footprints Colour Picture Library
Frank Lane Picture Agency Ltd
Natural Science Photos
Oxford Scientific Films Ltd
Planet Earth Pictures
Windrush Photos

*An asterisk against an agency name in the main listings indicates membership of the British Association of Picture Libraries & Agencies (BAPLA).

A-Z BOTANICAL COLLECTION LTD*
82/84 Clerkenwell Road, London EC1M 5RJ.
Tel: 0171-336 7942. Fax: 0171-336 7943.
Contacts: Johanna Lindsay-MacDougall (Director).
Specialist subjects/requirements: All aspects of plant life, not just flowers.
Markets supplied: Publishers and advertising agencies etc.
Stock: Colour only. 5x4in, medium format, 35mm.
Usual terms of business: No minimum submission, but contributors expected to continue supplying pictures on a regular basis. Minimum retention period: 3 years.
Commission: 50 per cent.
Additional information: Except for "scenic" shots, all plants should be captioned with Latin botanic name. Write in first before submitting. Wants lists supplied.

ACE PHOTO AGENCY*
Satellite House, 2 Salisbury Road, Wimbledon, London SW19 4EZ.
Tel: 0181-944 9944. Fax: 0181-944 9940.
Contact: John Panton (Chairman).
Specialist subjects/requirements: Abstracts, animals, beaches, business, celebrities, couples, families, glamour, industry, leisure, music & arts, natural history, people, skies/sunsets, sports, still-lifes, technology, transport, UK travel, world travel.
Markets supplied: Advertising; design; publishing.
Stock: Mainly colour. All formats acceptable, 35mm to 10x8in. Top quality, portfolio work only.
Usual terms of business: Minimum initial submission: 200 accepted images. Minimum retention period: 3 years.
Commission: 50 per cent.

ACTION IMAGES LTD*
Image House, Station Road, Tottenham, London N17 9LR.
Tel: 0181-885 3000. Fax: 0181-808 6167.
Contact: Tony Henshaw (Picture Editor).
Specialist subjects/requirements: High quality sports pictures, especially of any unusual or spectacular incident.
Markets supplied: Newspapers, magazines, books, etc.
Stock: Colour only. 35mm or medium formats.
Usual terms of business: No minimum initial submission, but please telephone first to discuss possible submissions.
Commission: 50 per cent.

ADAMS PICTURE LIBRARY*
156 New Cavendish Street, London W1M 7FJ.
Tel: 0171-636 1468. Fax: 0171-436 7131.
Contact: Carol Adams (Director).
Specialist subjects/requirements: All subjects except hot news.
Markets supplied: All markets including advertising, publishing, calendars and posters.
Stock: Colour only. All formats.
Usual terms of business: Minimum initial submission: 200 transparencies. Minimum retention period: 5 years; one year's notice required for withdrawal. required. Return postage must be included with all submissions.
Commission: 50 per cent.

AEROFILMS
Hunting Aerofilms Ltd, Gate Studios, Station Road, Borehamwood, Herts WD6 1EJ.
Tel: 0181-207 0666. Fax: 0181-207 5433.
Contact: P D O'Connell (Director).

Specialist subjects/requirements: Air-to-ground and air-to-air only. "We are prepared to consider for our library any aerial photography if not already included from our own photographers."
Stock: B&W and colour. Minimum 6x6cm colour transparencies.
Usual terms of business: Negotiable: "Our prime business is not that of an agency."
Commission: Negotiable.
Additional information: The exact location of every photograph must be specified. Will not look at 35mm transparencies nor any photographs that have been taken through the window of an aircraft.

ALVEY & TOWERS
9 Rosebank Road, Countesthorpe, Leicester LE8 5YA.
Tel/fax: 0116 277 9184.
Contact: Emma Rowen (Library Manager).
Specialist subjects/requirements: General; agriculture, architecture, commercial, industrial, leisure, people, sport, transport and travel. Specialist modern railway library incorporating all aspects of this particular industry.
Markets supplied: Advertising, books, magazines, corporate brochures, calendars, audio visual.
Stock: Colour transparency. 35mm, medium format and 5"x4".
Usual terms of business: On application.
Commission: 50 per cent.
Additional information: "It is essential that potential contributors contact us prior to making any submission so that we can discuss exactly the kind of images we are seeking. All images must be mounted, and numbered with captions on accompanying sheet of paper, not on transparency mounts."

ANCIENT ART & ARCHITECTURE COLLECTION
Suite 7, 401-420 Rayners Lane, Pinner, Middlesex HA5 5DY.
Tel: 0181-429 3131. Fax: 0181-429 4646.
Contact: The Librarian.
Specialist subjects/requirements: Historical art and artefacts mainly from pre-history up to the Middle Ages; everything which illustrates the civilisations of the ancient world, its cultures and technologies, religion, ideas, beliefs and development. Also warfare, weapons, fortifications and military historical movements. Statues, portraits and contemporary illustrations of historically important people – kings and other rulers.
Markets supplied: Mainly book publishers, but including magazines and TV.
Stock: B&W and colour. 6x6cm or larger formats preferred (though some 35mm accepted from remote overseas locations.)
Usual terms of business: 3 years minimum retention of material; 24 months notice of return.
Commission: 50 per cent.
Additional information: All submissions must be accompanied by return s.a.e. Only material of the highest quality can be considered.

AQUARIUS PICTURE LIBRARY*
PO Box 5, Hastings, East Sussex TN34 1HR.
Tel: 01424 721196. Fax: 01424 717704.
Contacts: Gilbert Gibson, David Corkill (Directors).
Specialist subjects/requirements: All aspects of showbusiness and the performing arts – vintage and current films, both stills and film star portraits; TV personalities and performers; pop stars; opera, stage and ballet artists.
Markets supplied: Television, newspapers, book publishers, magazines and advertising, etc.
Stock: B&W and colour. 35mm upwards for colour.
Usual terms of business: No minimum submission or retention period.
Commission: 50 per cent.
Additional information: "Most of our photographers operate in Hollywood, but we also have a constant demand for British material – old stock pictures as well as new. Lists of available subjects welcomed."

AQUILA PHOTOGRAPHICS*

PO Box 1, Studley, Warwickshire B80 7JG.
Tel: 01527 852357. Fax: 01527 857507.
Contact: Alan J. Richards.
Specialist subjects/requirements: All natural history. Birds a speciality.
Markets supplied: Books and magazine publishers, calendars, greetings cards, TV, video, etc.
Stock: Colour only. All formats.
Usual terms of business: Minimum initial submission of 200 transparencies.
Commission: 50 per cent.
Additional information: Phone or write for *modus operandi* before submission of material. All submissions must include return postage.

BARNABY'S PICTURE LIBRARY*

19 Rathbone Street, London W1P 1AF.
Tel: 0171-636 6128. Fax: 0171-637 4317.
Contacts: John and Mary Buckland (Directors).
Specialist subjects/requirements: All subjects, including large historic collection.
Markets supplied: Books, magazines, television, advertising, audio visual.
Stock: B&W and colour. All formats.
Usual terms of business: Minimum initial submission: 200 pictures. Minimum retention period: 4 years.
Commission: 50 per cent.

THE ANTHONY BLAKE PHOTO LIBRARY*

54 Hill Rise, Richmond, Surrey TW10 6UB.
Tel: 0181-940 7583. Fax: 0181-948 1224.
Contact: Clare Parker (Library Manager).
Specialist subjects/requirements: Food and wine related images. High quality, original material on all aspects from farming, fishing, country trades, markets and vineyards to raw ingredients, finished dishes, chefs, restaurants and kitchens. Also worldwide travel.
Markets supplied: Publishing, advertising, etc.
Stock: Colour only. All formats.
Usual terms of business: Minimum initial submission: usually 100+ images but depends on quality/subjects covered. Minimum retention period: 2 years.
Commission: 40 per cent to photographer in the first year, 50 per cent thereafter.
Additional information: "We are very selective about material submitted for the library. Always call before submitting." Do not commission but a regular "shooting list" is sent to contributors.

THE BRIDGEMAN ART LIBRARY*

17-19 Garway Road, London W2 4PH.
Tel: 0171-727 4065. Fax: 0171-792 8509.
Contact: Sarah Pooley (Marketing Manager).
Specialist subjects/requirements: American, European and Oriental paintings and prints, antiques, antiquities, arms and armour, botanical subjects, ethnography, general historical subjects and personalities, maps and manuscripts, natural history, topography, transport, etc.
Markets supplied: Publishing, advertising, television, greetings cards, calendars, etc.
Stock: Mainly colour but some B&W. Minimum 5x4in transparencies.
Usual terms of business: No minimum initial submission. Retention period negotiable.
Commission: 50 per cent.

BUBBLES PHOTO LIBRARY*

23a Benwell Road, London N7 7BL.
Tel: 0171-609 4547. Fax: 0171-607 1410.
Contacts: Sarah Robinson, Loisjoy Thurstun (Directors).

Specialist subjects/requirements: Babies, children, pregnancy, mothercare, child development, old age, family life, women's health and medical, still lives of food, vegetables, herbs, etc.
Markets supplied: Books, magazines and advertising.
Stock: Colour only. 35mm upwards.
Usual terms of business: Minimum submission: 100 transparencies. Regular contributions expected. Minimum retention period: 3 years.
Commission: 50 per cent.
Additional information: "Attractive women and children sell best. Photographers must pay close attention to selecting models that are healthy-looking and make sure that backgrounds are uncluttered. Best clothes to wear are light coloured and neutral fashion."

CAMERA PRESS LTD*
21 Queen Elizabeth Street, London SE1 2PD.
Tel: 0171-378 1300. Fax: 0171-278 5126.
Contact: Jacqui Ann Wald (Managing Editor).
Specialist subjects/requirements: Mainly photo reportage and portraits of newsworthy personalities. Also material suitable for women's magazines and general interest features, humour, science, pop, travel and stock.
Stock: B&W and colour. All formats.
Usual terms of business: "By mutual agreement."
Commission: 50 per cent.
Additional information: "Please submit only material that is excellent artistically, technically and, ideally, also journalistically."

J. ALLAN CASH LTD*
74 South Ealing Road, London W5 4QB.
Tel: 0181-840 4141. Fax: 0181-566 2568.
Contact: Alan Denny (Manager).
Specialist subjects/requirements: All subjects reflecting the world and its people.
Markets supplied: General and educational publishing, travel, advertising, design.
Stock: B&W and colour. 35mm transparencies accepted if of top quality; prefer larger formats.
Usual terms of business: Minimum initial submission: 100 pictures. Minimum retention period: 3 years; 12 months notice of withdrawal.
Commission: 50 per cent.
Additional information: "Please write for further details first."

CEPHAS PICTURE LIBRARY*
Hurst House, 157 Walton Road, East Molesey, Surrey KT8 0DX.
Tel: 0181-979 8647. Fax: 0181-224 8095.
Contact: Michael Rock (Proprietor).
Specialist subjects/requirements: All aspects of wine, vineyards, spirits, cider, beer and food. Top quality travel material – especially from wine producing countries – also required.
Markets supplied: Publishing, advertising etc.
Stock: Colour. Medium format preferred, but top quality 35mm accepted.
Usual terms of business: Minimum initial submission: 40 images "taken within past two years".
Commission: 50 per cent.
Additional information: "Write first with stamp for contributors' information sheet. A professional attitude is as important as top quality material. Library selling is long term – all things being equal the more pictures you have with us the greater your likelihood of sales."

BRUCE COLEMAN COLLECTION*
16 Chiltern Business Village, Arundel Road, Uxbridge, Middlesex UB8 2SN.
Tel: 01895 257094. Fax: 01895 272357.
Contact: Ian Thraves (Picture Editor).

Specialist subjects/requirements: Natural history, geographical, travel, scenics, archaeology, medical, science, anthropology, geological, horticulture, marine.
Markets supplied: Book publishers, magazines, advertising agencies, calendar publishers.
Stock: Colour only. 35mm, medium format and 5x4in.
Usual terms of business: Minimum submission: 250 transparencies. Minimum retention period: 5 years.
Commission: 50 per cent.
Additional information: Contributors are asked to write for library literature first.

COLLECTIONS*
13 Woodberry Crescent, London N10 1PJ.
Tel: 0181-883 0083. Fax: 0181-883 9215.
Contacts: Brian & Sal Shuel, Laura Boswell (Partners).
Specialist subjects: The British Isles and family life.
Markets supplied: All, particularly on the editorial side.
Stock: Colour in all formats, and B&W prints (which we frequently copy to transparencies).
Usual terms of business: By arrangement; "easy going and on the side of the contributor."
Commission: 50 per cent.
Additional information: "The Family Life section is not really open to new contributors at present. The British Isles side aims to stock pictures of as many places, things, happenings, on these islands as possible. You would be surprised what people ask for. England is pretty well covered, as is Wales. Ireland is coming along but we have little on Scotland and Devon. If you have any ideas we will be glad to hear from you."

COLORIFIC PHOTO LIBRARY LTD*
The Innovation Centre, 225 Marsh Wall, London E14 9FX.
Tel: 0171-515 3000. Fax: 0171-538 3555.
Contacts: Christopher Angeloglou (Editorial Director), David Leverton (Sales Manager).
Specialist subjects/requirements: General top quality photography: industry, agriculture, beaches, couples, generic, life style, travel, skies, high tech.
Markets supplied: Advertising, books, brochures, calendars and the whole editorial market.
Stock: Mainly colour. 35mm.
Usual terms of business: Minimum initial submission: 500 transparencies. Minimum retention period: 3 years.
Commission: 50 per cent.
Additional information: Material must be fully captioned and carry photographer's name. Introductory letters must include s.a.e.

JAMES DAVIS TRAVEL PHOTOGRAPHY*
65 Brighton Road, Shoreham, West Sussex BN43 6RE.
Tel: 01273 452252. Fax: 01273 440116.
Contact: James Davis (Proprietor).
Specialist subjects/requirements: Worldwide travel coverage – people, places, emotive and tourism.
Markets supplied: Travel brochures, publishing, designers and advertising agencies.
Stock: Colour. 6x6cm or larger preferred, on Fujichrome or Ektachrome, usually 50 or 100 ASA. 35mm only acceptable where it is impracticable or impossible to use larger format.
Usual terms of business: Minimum initial submission not less than 300 transparencies.
Commission: 50 per cent.

THE DEFENCE PICTURE LIBRARY (PHOTO PRESS DEFENCE)*
Sherwell House, 54 Staddiscombe Road, Plymouth, Devon PL9 9NB.
Tel: 01752 401800. Fax: 01752 402800.
Contact: David Reynolds (Director).

Specialist subjects/requirements: Military images covering all aspects of the armed forces worldwide, in training and on operations.
Markets supplied: Publishers, advertising agencies, UK MoD, national media.
Stock: Colour only. 35mm and medium format.
Usual terms of business: Minimum initial submission: 50 quality transparencies. Minimum retention period: 2 years.
Commission: 50 per cent.
Additional information: The library is the single biggest source of modern military photography in Britain. Pictures of general operations in Ulster, Bosnia and UK forces around the globe are always of interest.

ECOSCENE*
The Oasts, Headley Lane, Passfield, Liphook, Hampshire GU30 7RX.
Tel: 01428 751056. Fax: 01428 751057.
Contact: Sally Morgan (Proprietor).
Specialist subjects/requirements: Ecology and the environment, natural history with special emphasis on ecology and environmental issues worldwide.
Markets supplied: Books, magazines, organisations, etc.
Stock: Colour only. All formats.
Usual terms of business: Minimum initial submission: 50 quality transparencies. Minimum retention period: 2 years.
Commission: 55 per cent to photographer.
Additional information: Contributors' guidelines available on request – can also be found on the library's site on the World Wide Web along with details of specific current requirements.

EMPICS SPORTS PHOTO AGENCY*
26 Musters Road, West Bridgford, Nottingham NG2 7PL.
Tel: 0115 9455885. Fax: 0115 9455243.
Contact: Caroline Hoddinott (Sales & Marketing Director).
Specialist subjects/requirements: Sport; most interested in the unusual, not run-of-the-mill coverage. The agency has an electronic picture desk and wire service for extensive syndication.
Markets supplied: Newspapers, magazines, advertising agencies, governing bodies, etc.
Stock: Colour only. 35mm colour neg and transparency. Delivered in digital formats.
Usual terms of business: No minimum terms.
Commission: 50 per cent.
Additional information: "Always happy to consider unusual, exclusive and historical sports material."

EUROART AGENCY & LIBRARY
PO Box 533, London SE24 0QJ. 369 Shakespeare Road, London SE24 0QE.
Tel: 0171-733 7241. Fax: 0171-652 0251.
Contact: Mr P. M. Minyo (Principal).
Specialist subjects/requirements: Stock business images: depicting team work, decision making, meetings, training, work and stress, working with computers, using portable phones, business environments, business people at leisure and raising families, etc. Business concept photography: creative high quality business portrait and product photography on commission. Photographic postcards: creative images of London, new and unusual ways of looking at the city. Fine art photography suitable for offices.
Markets supplied: Business and commercial, company reports, brochures, business magazines, postcard publishers.
Stock: B&W and colour. B&W: minimum 10x8in, mostly require A4 size on glossy material. Colour: medium format and 5x4in, high quality 35mm (Kodachrome, Fujichrome) acceptable. Fine art photography: no minimum size of prints, 35mm transparencies.
Usual terms of business: No minimum submission. Minimum retention period: 3 years; 1 year notice of withdrawal.

Commission: 50 per cent.
Additional information: An innovative and professional approach with high quality images in all areas you are working in is essential. Use your own artistic style. Before supplying any material, write enclosing s.a.e. for more information about the particular subject area you are interested in submitting.

EYE UBIQUITOUS*
65 Brighton Road, Shoreham, West Sussex BN43 6RE.
Tel: 01273 440113. Fax: 01273 440116.
Contact: Paul Seheult (Proprietor).
Specialist subjects/requirements: General worldwide stock and social documentary material.
Markets supplied: Publishing markets, UK and European advertising agencies.
Stock: Colour only. All formats.
Usual terms of business: Suggested minimum submission 200 transparencies, but terms are open to discussion.
Commission: 50 per cent.

FAMOUS*
Studio 4, Limehouse Cut, 46 Morris Road, London E14 6NQ.
Tel: 0171-537 7055. Fax: 0171-537 7056.
Contact: Jenny Duval (Co-ordinator).
Specialist subjects/requirements: Celebrity photographs, especially personalities in the TV, movie, music, fashion and Royal fields. Taken in any situation: performance, studio, party, at home and paparazzi-style.
Markets supplied: General press and publishing.
Stock: Colour only. 35mm or medium format.
Usual terms of business: No minimum submission or retention period.
Commission: 50 per cent.
Additional information: Submissions can also be handled via digital transmission.

FOOTPRINTS COLOUR PICTURE LIBRARY*
Goldfin Cottage, Maidlands Farm, Broad Oak, Rye, East Sussex TN31 6BJ.
Tel: 01424 883078. Fax: 01424 883078.
Principal: Paula Leaver (Proprietor).
Specialist subjects/requirements: Worldwide travel and tropical beaches; underwater photography including scuba diving, snorkelling and marine life.
Markets supplied: Books, magazines, etc.
Stock: Colour only. 35mm.
Usual terms of business: No minimum initial submission. Minimum retention period: 2 years.
Commission: 50 per cent.
Additional information: All material must be up-to-date.

GARDEN MATTERS PHOTOGRAPHIC LIBRARY*
Marlham, Henley's Down, Battle, East Sussex TN33 9BN.
Tel: 01424 830566. Fax: 01424 830224.
Contact: John Feltwell (Principal).
Specialist subjects/requirements: Top quality close-up portraits of garden plants, garden portfolios from all parts of the world, garden design and embellishment, "how to" gardening material. Worldwide coverage.
Markets supplied: General.
Stock: Colour only. All formats, but mediums preferred.
Usual terms of business: Minimum initial submission: 200. Minimum retention period: 3 years.
Commission: 50 per cent.
Additional information: All submitted material must be fully and accurately captioned.

LESLIE GARLAND PICTURE LIBRARY
69 Fern Avenue, Jesmond, Newcastle-upon-Tyne NE2 2QU.
Tel: 0191-281 3442. Fax: 0191-281 3442.
Contact: Leslie Garland, ARPS, ABIPP (Proprietor).
Specialist subjects/requirements: General coverage of the North of England (North Yorkshire, Lancashire, Cleveland, Durham, Cumbria, Tyne & Wear, Northumberland, and Southern Scotland), especially places of interest, people and lifestyles, industry, engineering, science and technology. General coverage of Norway and Sweden.
Markets supplied: Advertising, books, brochures, exhibitions, magazines, etc.
Stock: Colour only. Medium format or larger transparencies preferred, exceptional 35mm considered depending on subject matter.
Usual terms of business: Minimum initial submission 50 accepted images. Minimum retention period: 3 years.
Commission: 50 per cent.
Additional information: All pictures must be of top quality professional standard with precise captions. Write enclosing s.a.e. for further details first.

GEO AERIAL PHOTOGRAPHY*
4 Christian Fields, London SW16 3JZ.
Tel/fax: 0181-764 6292 or 0115 981 9418.
Contact: John Douglas (Director), Kelly White (Consultant).
Specialist subjects/requirements: Worldwide oblique aerial photographs.
Markets supplied: Books, magazines, advertising, etc.
Stock: Colour only. 35mm or larger format.
Usual terms of business: Negotiable.
Commission: 50 per cent.
Additional information: Locations must be identified in detail. Do not send samples of work but contact by letter/telephone first.

ROBERT HARDING PICTURE LIBRARY LTD*
58-59 Great Marlborough Street, London W1V 1DD.
Tel: 0171-478 4146. Fax: 0171-631 1070.
Contact: Nelly Boyd (Picture Editor).
Specialist subjects/requirements: People, lifestyle.
Markets supplied: Publishers, advertising agencies, design groups, calendar publishers, etc.
Stock: Colour. All formats from 35mm up.
Usual terms of business: An initial sample of 200 transparencies "to enable us to judge quality and saleability." Minimum retention period: 3 years; 12 months notice of withdrawal.
Commission: 50 per cent.

HOLT STUDIOS INTERNATIONAL*
The Courtyard, 24 High Street, Hungerford, Berkshire RG17 0NF.
Tel: 01488 683523. Fax: 01488 683511.
Contact: Andy Morant (Commercial Director).
Specialist subjects/requirements: Pictorial and technical photographs of worldwide agriculture and horticulture, crop production and protection, livestock, pests, conservation, the environment and wildlife.
Markets supplied: Agricultural organisations, educational and technical publishers, advertising agencies, etc.
Stock: Colour only. 35mm and medium format.
Usual terms of business: To be negotiated.
Commission: Usually 50 per cent.
Additional information: "Our photographers combine specialist technical, scientific or agricultural knowledge with their photographic skills to produce outstanding photographs."

HOUSES & INTERIORS PHOTOGRAPHIC FEATURES AGENCY*
82-84 Clerkenwell Road, London EC1M 5RJ.
Tel: 0171-336 7942. Fax: 0171-336 7943.
Contact: Richard Wiles.
Specialist subjects/requirements: Stylish house interiors and exteriors covering all types of property, architectural and decorative details, home improvements, gardens, gardening techniques and cookery. Also complete illustrated feature packages on individual homes, step-by-step DIY and home improvements projects, etc.
Markets supplied: Magazines, books, partworks and advertising.
Stock: Colour, medium format preferred.
Usual terms of business: No minimum submission. Minimum retention period: 3 years.
Commission: 50 per cent for stock pictures; negotiable for speculative feature work. After first use feature pictures go into the stock library for further sales at the usual 50 per cent commission.

THE HUTCHISON LIBRARY*
118b Holland Park Avenue, London W11 4UA.
Tel: 0171-229 2743. Fax: 0171-792 0259.
Contact: Kate Pink (Library Manager).
Specialist subjects/requirements: Worldwide coverage of agriculture, industry, landscapes, festivals and ceremonies, decoration, religion, urban and village life, tourism, flora and fauna, medicine and education, architecture, art, craft, etc. etc.
Markets supplied: Publishing, company reports, calendars, advertising, audio visual.
Stock: Colour only. 35mm and medium format.
Usual terms of business: Minimum initial submission: 1,000 transparencies. No minimum retention period.
Commission: 50 per cent.
Additional information: "We only occasionally take on new photographers. Collections should either be in-depth documentary work (medical, environment, agriculture, supernatural, etc.) or be as varied as possible in geographical and subject coverage."

JAYAWARDENE TRAVEL PHOTO LIBRARY
7A Napier Road, Wembley, Middlesex HA0 4UA.
Tel: 0181-902 3588. Fax: 0181-902 7114.
Contact: Rohith Jayawardene (Proprietor).
Specialist subjects/requirements: Worldwide travel, covering cities, resorts, local life, market scenes, festivals, historic sites, landscapes, beaches/watersports, people on holiday, winter resorts and cruising.
Markets supplied: Travel industry, publishing, advertising.
Stock: Colour. 35mm and medium format only.
Commission: 50 per cent.
Usual terms of business: Minimum initial submission: 100 transparencies per country. Minimum retention period: 5 years.
Additional information: Transparencies must be supplied in card or plastic mounts and accurately captioned (preferably on a separate sheet). Telephone first to discuss submission.

JAZZ INDEX PHOTO LIBRARY
26 Fosse Way, London W13 0BZ.
Tel/Fax: 0181-998 1232.
Contact: Christian Him (Principal).
Specialist subjects/requirements: All forms of popular music, but especially jazz, blues and soul. Also pictures of musical instruments, clubs, crowds and atmospheric shots. Both contemporary and archive material of interest.
Markets supplied: Newspapers, book publishers, videos, television.
Stock: Colour, all formats; B&W: prints or negs.

Commission: 50 per cent.
Usual terms of business: No minimum submission.
Additional information: Contributors must phone first to enquire if material is suitable.

FRANK LANE PICTURE AGENCY LTD*

Pages Green House, Wetheringsett, Stowmarket, Suffolk IP14 5QA.
Tel: 01728 860789. Fax: 01728 860222.
Contacts: Jean Hosking, David Hosking (Directors).
Specialist subjects/requirements: Natural history and weather phenomena: birds, clouds, fish, fungi, insects, mammals, pollution, rainbows, reptiles, sea, snow, seasons, trees, underwater, hurricanes, earthquakes, lightning, volcanoes, dew, rain, fog, etc. Ecology and the environment. Horse, dog and cat breeds.
Markets supplied: Book publishers, advertising agencies, magazines.
Stock: B&W and colour. 35mm and medium format transparencies. Fujichrome preferred for 35mm.
Usual terms of business: Minimum initial submission: 250 transparencies. Minimum retention period: 3 years.
Commission: 50 per cent.
Additional information: "Competition in the natural history field is fierce, so only really sharp, well-composed pictures are needed. Sales are slow to start with, and a really keen photographer must be prepared to invest money in building up stock to the 1,000 mark."

LEBRECHT COLLECTION*

58b Carlton Hill, London NW8 0ES.
Tel: 0171-625 5341. Fax: 0171-625 5341.
Contacts: Elbie Lebrecht (Proprietor).
Specialist subjects/requirements: All aspects of classical music. Composers, musicians, singers, interiors and exteriors of concert halls and opera houses, instruments, tombs of famous composers in UK and abroad.
Markets supplied: Classical music press, national press, record companies, book publishers.
Stock: B&W and colour. All formats.
Usual terms of business: No minimum initial submission or retention period.
Commission: 50 per cent.
Additional information: Please submit top quality material only.

LINK PICTURE LIBRARY*

35 Greyhound Road, London W6 8NH.
Tel: 0171-381 2261. Fax: 0171-385 6244.
Contact: Orde Eliason (Proprietor).
Specialist subjects/requirements: General documentary coverage of countries worldwide, but particularly Africa – communications, culture, education, environment, health, industry, people and politics. Special interest in South Africa and South East Asia.
Markets supplied: General publishing.
Stock: Colour only. 35mm transparencies.
Usual terms of business: Minimum initial submission: 50 images. Minimum retention period: 3 years.
Commission: 50 per cent.

MILEPOST 92½*

Newton Harcourt, Leicestershire LE8 9FH.
Tel: 0116 259 2068. Fax: 0116 259 3001.
Contact: Colin Nash (Library Manager).
Specialist subjects/requirements: Railways – all aspects, national and international, contemporary and archive.
Markets supplied: Advertising, publishing, design, corporate railways.

Stock: Colour, 35mm or medium format. Archive B&W.
Usual terms of business: Minimum initial submission 25 pictures. No minimum retention period.
Commission: 50 per cent.
Additional information: All material must be of the highest quality. Transparencies must be mounted and captioned with brief, accurate details.

MONITOR SYNDICATION
17 Old Street, London EC1V 9HL.
Tel: 0171-253 7071. Fax: 0171-250 0966.
Contact: Stewart White, Grant Burton.
Specialist subjects/requirements: Portraits of personalities from sport, commerce, politics, show-business; Royals; well known buildings in London.
Markets supplied: National and international press, television, advertising, publishers, etc.
Stock: B&W and colour. 35mm and medium format.
Usual terms of business: No minimum submission.
Commission: 50 per cent, but may make outright purchase offer for suitable material.

NHPA (NATURAL HISTORY PHOTOGRAPHIC AGENCY)*
Little Tye, 57 High Street, Ardingly, Sussex RH17 6TB.
Tel: 01444 892514. Fax: 01444 892168.
Contact: Tim Harris (Manager).
Specialist subjects/requirements: Worldwide wildlife, domestic animals and pets, plants, landscapes, agriculture and environmental subjects. Endangered and appealing wildlife of particular interest.
Markets supplied: Books, magazines, advertising and design, cards and calendars, electronic publishing, exhibitions, etc (UK and overseas).
Stock: Colour only. 35mm, medium format and larger original transparencies. High quality large format dupes.
Usual terms of business: Minimum initial submission: 100 transparencies.
Commission: 50 per cent.
Additional information: Pictures should be strong, active and well-composed. Write before submitting material.

NATURAL IMAGE
Holly Cottage, 31 Shaftesbury Road, Poole, Dorset BH15 2LT.
Tel: 01202 675916. Fax: 01202 242944.
Contacts: Bob Gibbons (Proprietor).
Specialist subjects/requirements: Natural history, the countryside, gardens and gardening, worldwide travel with a wildlife or conservation bias.
Markets supplied: Books, magazines, etc.
Stock: Colour only. 35mm upwards.
Usual terms of business: Minimum initial submission: 50 slides. Minimum retention period: 1 year.
Commission: 50 per cent.
Additional information: Material must be accurately and informatively captioned, and be of very high quality.

NATURAL SCIENCE PHOTOS*
33 Woodland Drive, Watford, Hertfordshire WD1 3BY.
Tel: 01923 245265. Fax: 01923 246067.
Contacts: Peter Ward (Partner).
Specialist subjects/requirements: All types of living organisms including wildlife of every description, domestic animals and fowl, botany, ecology, geology, geography, climate and effects, astronomy, pollution and effects, primitive people and their ways of life, countryside topics and scen-

ics, latter mostly without artifacts. The building of an angling library, both sea and freshwater, is being undertaken.

Markets supplied: Books, magazines, newspapers, calendars, audio-visual, television and advertising, UK and overseas. Some inter-agency deals.

Stock: Colour only. Mainly 35mm, but larger formats accepted.

Usual terms of business: No minimum submission. Standard contract allows for 3 years retention and is non-exclusive.

Commission: 33 per cent.

Additional information: "All material to be clearly captioned and well documented – English and scientific names, locality and photographer; also any useful additional information."

CHRISTINE OSBORNE/MIDDLE EAST PICTURES.*

53A Crimsworth Road, London SW8 4RJ.

Tel/fax: 0171-720 6951.

Contact: Christine Osborne (Managing Director).

Specialist subjects/requirements: Islamic countries, especially Middle East and Arab Gulf states, Africa, Indian subcontinent, SE Asia – especially people interacting with their environment, family life, religious activities food production, tourism and backpacking.

Markets supplied: General publishing.

Stock: Mainly colour, 35mm.

Usual terms of business: Minimum initial submission: 40 to assess quality, following by 400 initial deposit. Minimum retention period: 2 years.

Commission: 50 per cent.

Additional information: Transparencies should be card-mounted, well captioned and of the highest quality.

OXFORD SCIENTIFIC FILMS LTD*

Lower Road, Long Hanborough, Oxfordshire OX8 8LL.

Tel: 01993 881881. Fax: 01993 882808.

Contacts: Dee Williams, Alex Harper, Suzanne Aitzemuller (Account Managers).

Specialist subjects/requirements: High quality wildlife photography, plus the environment, science, travel, pollution and conservation, landscapes, agriculture, high-speed photography, special effects, underwater, creative plant shots, indigenous people.

Markets supplied: Magazines, book publishers, advertising/design companies, merchandising etc.

Stock: Colour. All formats up to and including 5x4in.

Usual terms of business: Minimum initial submission 100 transparencies. Minimum retention period: 2 years.

Commission: 50 per cent on stock sales.

Additional information: All material must be of a very high technical standard – perfectly sharp and exposed, well composed, creative and visually stunning.

PPL LTD*

68 East Ham Road, Littlehampton, West Sussex BN17 7BE.

Tel: 01903 730614. Fax: 01903 730618.

Contact: Barry Pickthall, Eunice Bergin.

Specialist subjects/requirements: Sailing, marine sports and other maritime-related subjects. Plus British Steel industrial archive.

Markets supplied: Newspapers, magazines, advertising and publishing medias.

Stock: Colour only. 35mm and medium format.

Usual terms of business: No minimum initial submission, work accepted on a trial basis, but should be regular and continuous. 1 year notice of withdrawal.

Commission: 50 per cent.

Additional information: Always telephone before sending submission.

PANOS PICTURES*
1 Chapel Court, Borough High Street, London SE1 1HH.
Tel: 0171-234 0010. Fax: 0171-357 0094.
Contact: Adrian Evans (Director).
Specialist subjects/requirements: Documentary coverage of the Third World and Eastern Europe, focusing on social, economic and political issues and with special emphasis on environment and development. Also agriculture, education, energy, health, industry, landscape, people, religions.
Markets supplied: Newspapers and magazines, book publishers, development agencies.
Stock: B&W and colour. 35mm.
Usual terms of business: No minimum initial submission or retention period.
Commission: 50 per cent.
Additional information: All profits from the library are covenented to the Panos Institute, an international development studies group.

PAPILIO NATURAL HISTORY & TRAVEL LIBRARY*
44 Palestine Grove, Merton, London SW19 2QN.
Tel/fax: 0181-687 2202.
Contact: Justine Bowler (Library Director), Robert Pickett (Photographic Director).
Specialist subjects/requirements: All aspects of natural history worldwide: animals, plants, insects, birds, marine life and the environment generally, plus growing travel section covering people and places.
Markets supplied: Books, magazines, advertising, etc.
Stock: Colour only. 35mm and medium format.
Usual terms of business: Minimum initial submission 100 transparencies, though for certain images a smaller submission may be acceptable. Minimum retention period 3 years.
Commission: 50 per cent.

PHOTO LIBRARY INTERNATIONAL
PO Box 75, Leeds, West Yorkshire LS7 3NX.
Tel: 0113 2623005. Fax: 0113 2625366.
Contact: Kevin Horgan (Managing Director).
Specialist subjects/requirements: General, commercial, industrial and travel subjects.
Markets supplied: Advertising, travel brochures, greetings cards, publishers, etc.
Stock: Colour only. From 35mm up.
Usual terms of business: Minimum retention period: 3 years, with 12 months notice of withdrawal. Or pictures purchased outright.
Commission: 50 per cent – or outright purchase.
Additional information: List of current requirements sent on receipt of s.a.e.

PICTOR INTERNATIONAL LTD*
Lymehouse Studios, 30-31 Lyme Street, London NW1 0EE.
Tel: 0171-267 3717. Fax: 0171-267 5759.
Contact: Theresa Black (Senior Picture Editor).
Specialist subjects/requirements: General library handling all subjects.
Markets supplied: Advertising, calendars, posters, greetings cards, holiday brochures, books, encyclopedias, company reports, etc.
Stock: Colour, all formats. Black and white – will view prints but must be submitted as transparencies.
Usual terms of business: Minimum initial submission: 50–100 transparencies.
Commission: 50 per cent.

PICTUREBANK PHOTO LIBRARY LTD*
Parman House, 30–36 Fife Road, Kingston-upon-Thames, Surrey KT1 1SY.
Tel: 0181-547 2344. Fax: 0181-974 5652.

Contact: Martin Bagge (Managing Director).
Specialist subjects/requirements: Worldwide travel and tourism, UK cities and countryside, people (glamour, families, children, ethnic peoples), environment, animals (domestic and wild), business, industry and technology.
Markets supplied: Magazines, calendars, travel industry, advertising, etc.
Stock: Colour only. 35mm acceptable if subject matter is exceptional; larger formats preferred.
Usual terms of business: Minimum initial submission 100 transparencies. Minimum retention period 3 years.
Commission: Variable – maximum 50%.
Additional information: "We are keen to expand our files, but only with material of the highest quality."

THE PICTURE BOOK LTD
Units 161-167, Block F, Riverside Business Centre, Haldane Place, London SW18 4UQ.
Tel: 0181-877 9666. Fax: 0171-877 9643.
Contact: Christina Vaughan (Creative Director).
Specialist subjects/requirements: Solely involved in production of stock image catalogues for international distribution. Very high quality photography for the advertising and design industries. Exceptional images of lifestyle, beauty, business, industry, landscapes and travel.
Markets supplied: Advertising and design clients.
Stock: Colour and B&W, all formats.
Usual terms of business:N/A.
Commission: 50 per cent.
Additional information: We specialise in quality photography working closely with a small number of quality photographers. Initially we need to see a portfolio of the work you enjoy doing. People-related images should be very contemporary, styled and produced with the agency's client database in mind.

PLANET EARTH PICTURES*
The Innovation Centre, 225 Marsh Wall, London E14 9FX.
Tel: 0171-293 2999. Fax: 0171-293 2998.
Contact: Jennifer Jeffrey (Manager).
Specialist subjects/requirements: Natural history – marine and land, wildlife, landscapes, conservation, farming, fishing.
Markets supplied: Publishing, advertising and marketing.
Stock: Colour only. All formats.
Usual terms of business: No minimum submission, but "the more photographs that a photographer can leave in the library, the more chance he has of a reasonable return." Terms of business in more detail available on request.
Commission: 50 per cent.
Additional information: "We like to have a close working relationship with all our photographers." Photographers information booklet available on request.

POPPERFOTO*
Paul Popper Ltd, The Old Mill, Overstone Farm, Overstone, Northampton NN6 0AB.
Tel: 01604 670670. Fax: 01604 670635.
Contact: Ian Blackwell (Sales Manager).
Specialist subjects/requirements: General library of 13+ million images – historical/modern archive material and stock photography.
Markets supplied: All media worldwide including books, newspapers, magazines, TV and advertising.
Stock: B&W and colour. 35mm, medium format and 5x4in. B&W, 10x8in prints.
Usual terms of business: Retention period: 2 months.
Commission: Negotiable.

POWERSTOCK PHOTO LIBRARY (incorporating **ISE PHOTO LIBRARY**)*
9 Coborn Road, London E3 2DA.
Tel: 0181-983 4222. Fax: 0181-983 3846.
Contact: Ian Allenden (Creative Director).
Specialist subjects/requirements: World business centres: skylines and city views, people in business situations, technology, medicine, engineering, energy supply, transport, industry, agriculture, manufacturing. Also travel, sport, people, lifestyles, environment, nature.
Markets supplied: Advertising, publishing, audio visual, public relations, travel.
Stock: Colour only. All formats.
Usual terms of business: Minimum initial submission 50 transparencies.
Commission: 50 per cent.

QUADRANT PICTURE LIBRARY*
Quadrant House, The Quadrant, Sutton, Surrey SM2 5AS.
Tel: 0181-652 8888/3427. Fax: 0181-652 8933.
Contact: Kim Hearn (Head of Picture Library).
Specialist subjects/requirements: All aspects of transport and motorsport from the beginning of the century to the present day: classic cars, commercial vehicles, motorcycles, aircraft (including military), boats, ships, railways, roads, airports, etc. Also general travel material.
Markets supplied: Books, magazines, advertising, etc.
Stock: Mainly colour; B&W for archive material only. All formats, originals or dupes.
Usual terms of business: Minimum initial submission: 50 transparencies. Retention period: 5 years.
Commission: 50 per cent.

RSPCA PHOTOLIBRARY*
Causeway, Horsham, West Sussex RH12 1HG.
Tel: 01403 223150. Fax: 01403 241048.
Contact: Andrew Forsyth (Photolibrary Manager).
Specialist subjects/requirements: Wide range of natural history and animal welfare photographs. Mammals, amphibians, reptiles, British birds, pets, farm animals, environments and scenics. Unique and comprehensive photographic coverage of the work of the RSPCA.
Markets supplied: RSPCA publications and other publishers.
Stock: Colour only. 35mm and larger formats.
Usual terms of business: Minimum initial submission: 20–30 transparencies. Minimum retention period: 2 years.
Commission: 50 per cent.
Additional information: The library operates as a normal commercial library, but also supplies pictures for use in RSPCA publications and campaigning material. Prefer material submitted in plain plastic mounts, uncaptioned but numbered, accompanied by a corresponding sheet of detailed captions. Need to know what the subject is, where it was taken and if possible the date.

REDFERNS MUSIC PICTURE LIBRARY*
7 Bramley Road, London W10 6SZ.
Tel: 0171-792 9914. Fax: 0171-792 0921.
Contact: Dede Millar (Partner).
Specialist subjects/requirements: All forms of popular music from the 1920s onwards, but with special concentration on the past 40 years. Also related subjects such as musical instruments, dance, stage shows.
Markets supplied: Newspapers, magazines, books, record companies, advertising and design companies.
Stock: B&W and colour. 35mm and medium format.
Usual terms of business: Negotiable.
Commission: 50 per cent.

RETNA PICTURES LTD*
1 Fitzroy Mews, Cleveland Street, London W1P 5DQ.
Tel: 0171-209 0200. Fax: 0171-383 7151.
Contact: David Thompson.
Specialist subjects/requirements: Portraits and performance shots of rock and pop performers, actors and actresses, entertainers and other celebrities including politicians and business personalities. Expanding general stock library section covering lifestyle, travel, wildlife, people, sport and leisure.
Markets supplied: Newspapers, magazines, books, record companies, advertising.
Stock: B&W and colour, any format.
Usual terms of business: None specified.
Commission: 50 per cent.

REX FEATURES LTD*
18 Vine Hill, London EC1R 5DX.
Tel: 0171-278 7294. Fax: 0171-696 0974.
Contact: Mike Selby (Director).
Specialist subjects/requirements: Human interest and general features, current affairs, personalities, animals (singles and series), humour, travel, general library, stock material.
Markets supplied: UK national newspapers and magazines, book publishers, audio visual, television and international press. Daily worldwide syndication.
Stock: B&W and colour. All formats.
Usual terms of business: No minimum submission. Preferred minimum retention period: 2 years.
Commission: 50 per cent.

ROYAL GEOGRAPHICAL SOCIETY PICTURE LIBRARY/REMOTE SOURCE*
1 Kensington Gore, London SW7 2AR.
Tel: 0171-591 3060. Fax: 0171-591 3061.
Contact: Joanna Scadden (Manager).
Specialist subjects/requirements: Exploration and geographical coverage, both historic and current. Travel photography from remote destinations: indigenous peoples and daily life, landscapes, environmental and geographical phenomena, agriculture, crafts, human impact on the environment.
Markets supplied: Commercial publishing and academic research.
Stock: Colour, all formats. Historic B&W.
Usual terms of business: Minimum initial submission: 250 pictures. Minimum retention period: none specified, but like to hold material for at least 2 years.
Commission: 50 per cent.
Additional information: We like to have a close working relationship with our photographers.

SCR PHOTO LIBRARY
Society for Co-operation in Russian and Soviet Studies, 320 Brixton Road, London SW9 6AB.
Tel: 0171-274 2282. Fax: 0171-274 3230.
Contact: Andrew Lord (Research Administrator).
Specialist subjects/requirements: Pictures from Russia and all Republics of the former Soviet Union. General/everyday scenes, landscapes, architecture, towns and cities, politics, arts, industry, agriculture, science, etc.
Markets supplied: General.
Stock: All formats.
Usual terms of business: No minimum initial submission. Minimum retention period: 2 years.
Commission: 50 per cent.

SOA*
87 York Street, London W1H 1DU.
Tel: 0171-258 0202. Fax: 0171-258 0188.
Contact: Sabine Oppenländer.

Specialist subjects/requirements: Very high-quality, modern, creative, avant-garde images of varied subject matter.
Markets supplied: Mainly advertising and design via catalogue distribution and worldwide network of other small agencies.
Stock: Colour and B&W. All formats.
Usual terms of business: No minimum submission required. Individual arrangements for catalogue inclusion.
Commission: 50 per cent.
Additional information: We provide photographers with a personalised service with regular sales reports and prompt payment.

SCIENCE PHOTO LIBRARY*
112 Westbourne Grove, London W2 5RU.
Tel: 0171-727 4712. Fax: 0171-727 6041.
Contact: Rosemary Taylor (Director).
Specialist subjects/requirements: All types of scientific, industrial and medical imagery, from micrography to astronomical photography. Also includes photographs of equipment, laboratories, factories and relevant personalities.
Markets supplied: Books, magazines, advertising, design, corporate, audio visual.
Stock: Mainly colour. 35mm accepted, but prefer medium format.
Usual terms of business: No minimum submission. Minimum retention period: usually 4 years.
Commission: 50 per cent.
Additional information: All photographs must be accompanied by full caption information, but preferably in non-technical language.

SCOTLAND IN FOCUS and THE SCOTTISH WILDLIFE LIBRARY
22 Fleming Place, Fountainhall, Galashiels, Selkirkshire TD1 2TA.
Tel: 01578 760324. Fax: 01578 760256.
Contact: Bob Lawson (Proprietor).
Specialist subjects/requirements: All areas of Scotland and aspects of Scottish life, particularly town and city life, transport, industry, communications, environment and wildlife.
Markets supplied: Books, brochures and magazines, design and advertising, cards and calendars.
Stock: Colour. 35mm transparencies welcome; medium and larger formats preferred.
Usual terms of business: Minimum initial submission 100 transparencies.
Commission: 50 per cent.
Additional information: "Only interested in sharp, well-composed images suitable for reproduction. We would rather see quality than quantity. For selection purposes we prefer transparencies in slide wallets or black mask sleeves, each transparency captioned and numbered including a separate list for identification."

SKISHOOT – OFFSHOOT*
Hall Place, Upper Woodcott, Whitchurch, Hants RG28 7PY.
Tel: 01635 255527. Fax: 01635 255528.
Contact: Fiona Foote, Jane Blount.
Specialist subjects/requirements: Skishoot: skiing and snowboarding, ski resorts in Europe, Australasia, Japan and North America. Offshoot: major cities and tourist areas in France. Special interest in offbeat shots of people and local colour.
Markets supplied: Travel industry and general publishing.
Stock: Colour only. 35mm and medium format.
Usual terms of business: Minimum initial submission: 10 transparencies. No minimum retention period.
Commission: 50 per.cent.

SPECTRUM COLOUR LIBRARY*
41/42 Berners Street, London W1P 3AA.
Tel: 0171-637 1587. Fax: 0171-637 3681.
Leeds Office: Unit 13, Holly Park Mills, Calverley, Pudsey, West Yorkshire LS28 5QS.
Tel: 01132 394020. Fax: 01132 361506.
Contacts: Keith Jones, Ann Jones (Directors). Leeds Office: Peter Dransfield (Manager).
Specialist subjects/requirements: Travel, natural history, people, general.
Markets supplied: Advertising, publishing, travel brochures, etc.
Stock: Colour only. 35mm transparencies if exceptional, but prefers larger formats.
Usual terms of business: Minimum initial submission: 500. Minimum retention period: 5 years.
Commission: 50 per cent.

SPORTING PICTURES (UK) LTD*
7a Lambs Conduit Passage, London WC1 4RG.
Tel: 0171-405 4500. Fax: 0171-831 7991.
Contact: Justin Downing, Stuart Cranston.
Specialist subjects/requirements: Leisure activities and extreme sports (primarily for advertising), model-released if possible.
Markets supplied: Magazines, books, advertising etc.
Stock: Colour 35mm.
Usual terms of business: No minimum initial submission.
Commission: 50 per cent.

THE STILL MOVING PICTURE COMPANY*
67A Logie Green Road, Edinburgh EH7 4HF.
Tel: 0131-557 9697. Fax: 0131-557 9699.
Contacts: John Hutchinson, Sue Hall (Directors).
Specialist subjects/requirements: All Scottish subjects; scenics, travel, commerce, industry, wildlife, sport and culture. Also worldwide travel material.
Markets supplied: Publishing, advertising, tourism, etc.
Stock: Colour only. All formats.
Usual terms of business: No minimum initial submission. Retention period variable, but usually at least 1 year.
Commission: 50 per cent.
Additional information: A full "wants" list can be supplied on request.

TONY STONE IMAGES*
Worldwide House, 101 Bayham Street, London NW1 0AG.
Tel: 0171-267 8988. Fax: 0171-722 9305.
Contact: Andy Saunders (Creative Director).
Specialist subjects/requirements: All subjects, as commonly used in advertising, design, publishing and the travel industry.
Markets supplied: Advertising agencies; travel industry worldwide.
Stock: B&W and colour. All formats.
Usual terms of business: On application. Send ten outstanding pictures in first instance.
Commission: 50 per cent.
Additional information: "Our commitment to creative and technical quality has made us one of the top five agencies worldwide. We are always enthusiastic about marketing outstanding photography."

THE TELEGRAPH COLOUR LIBRARY*
The Innovation Centre, 225 Marsh Wall, London E14 9FX.
Tel: 0171-987 1212. Fax: 0171-538 3309.
Contact: Colin James (Director).
Specialist subjects/requirements: General: animals, commerce, ecology, education, entertain-

ment, health, industry, landscape, occupations, people, personalities, technology, transport, space exploration, sport, etc.
Markets supplied: Advertising and publishing.
Stock: B&W and colour. All formats.
Usual terms of business: Minimum initial submission: 100 to start contract, to be followed up with regular additional submissions. Minimum retention period: 5 years.
Commission: 50 per cent.
Additional information: "We're always seeking new top quality material on a variety of subjects, particularly action, animals and sports, natural and man-made disasters, bad weather (including electrical storms), people (especially crowds, children and families), industry and technology."

TOPHAM PICTUREPOINT*
PO Box 33, Edenbridge, Kent TN8 5PB.
Tel: 01342 850313. Fax: 01342 850244.
Contact: Bernice Fairchild (Stock Manager).
Specialist subjects/requirements: World coverage; sports, pastimes, industry, agriculture, travel.
Markets supplied: Books, travel industry, advertising, etc.
Stock: Colour only. 6x6cm or larger preferred (but top quality 35mm acceptable on subjects demanding this size).
Usual terms of business: Minimum initial submission must produce at least 100 retained transparencies. Minimum retention period: 5 years.
Commission: 50 per cent.

TRAVEL INK*
The Old Coach House, 14 High Street, Goring-on-Thames, Berkshire RG8 9AR.
Tel: 01491 873011. Fax: 01491 875558.
Contact: Briony Phillips, Lisa Hiller.
Specialist subjects/requirements: All aspects of travel and tourism, from destinations to forms of transport, food, things to buy, famous sights, hotel shots to native lifestyles. All countries including the UK. Interested in looking at all excellent stock.
Markets supplied: Travel industry, magazines, books, newspapers, advertising etc.
Stock: Colour, all formats.
Usual terms of business: Minumum submission: 200. Minimum retention period 3 years.
Commission: 50 per cent.

THE TRAVEL LIBRARY*
Unit 7, The Kiln Workshops, Pilcot Road, Crookham Village, Fleet, Hants GU13 0SL.
Tel: 01252 627233. Fax: 01252 812399.
Contacts: Philip Enticknap (Proprietor), Val Crisp (Administrator).
Specialist subjects/requirements: Top quality tourist travel material covering destinations worldwide.
Markets supplied: UK tour operators and travel industry publishers.
Stock: Colour only. Medium or larger formats.
Usual terms of business: Minimum initial submission: 100 transparencies. Minimum retention period 3 years.
Commission: 50 per cent.

TRAVEL PHOTO INTERNATIONAL
8 Delph Common Road, Aughton, Ormskirk, Lancashire L39 5DW.
Tel/fax: 01695 423720.
Contact: Vivienne Crimes (Director).
Specialist subjects/requirements: World travel and tourist material.
Markets supplied: Travel brochures, books, general advertising.
Stock: Colour only. 35mm accepted but larger formats preferred.

Usual terms of business: Minimum initial submission: 100 pictures. Minimum retention period: 3 years.
Commission: 50 per cent.
Additional information: "Pictures must be taken in clear sunlight, have excellent colour saturation, be critically sharp and accurately exposed."

TROPIX PHOTOGRAPHIC LIBRARY*
156 Meols Parade, Wirral, Merseyside L47 6AN.
Tel: 0151-632 1698. Fax: 0151-632 1698.
Contact: Veronica Birley (Librarian).
Specialist subjects/requirements: The developing world and environmental issues.
Markets supplied: Book and magazine publishers internationally, national press, etc.
Stock: Colour only. Normally 35mm.
Usual terms of business: Subject to negotiation.
Commission: 50 per cent.
Additional information: At the time of going to press, this library was not taking on new photographers. Photographers with suitable material may, however, telephone to enquire whether the situation has changed.

S&I WILLIAMS POWER PIX
Castle Lodge, Wenvoe, Cardiff CF5 6AD.
Tel: 01222 595163. Fax: 01222 593905.
Contact: Steven Williams (Director).
Specialist subjects/requirements: Girl pix of all kinds, natural history, travel, people, children, families, sub-aqua, industry, mood, abstracts and still life.
Markets supplied: Publishers, advertising, record companies, calendar and greetings card publishers, travel brochures, encyclopedias. Worldwide coverage – agents in Spain, Germany, Japan, Australia and USA.
Stock: Colour only. 35mm acceptable but medium format preferred where practical.
Usual terms of business: Minimum submission 50 transparencies, but contributors must be in a position to submit regularly to build up their stock. Minimum retention period: 5 years.
Commission: 50 per cent.
Additional information: Contributors should write with s.a.e. for free "Photographer's Information" before submitting.

WINDRUSH PHOTOS*
99 Noahs Ark, Kemsing, Sevenoaks, Kent TN15 6PD.
Tel: 01732 763486. Fax: 01732 763285.
Contact: David Tipling.
Specialist subjects/requirements: High quality bird photography. We specialise in birds and birdwatching and act as ornithological consultants.
Markets supplied: Magazines, book publishers, etc.
Stock: Colour only. 35mm upwards.
Usual terms of business: No minimum initial submission. Minimum retention period 3 years.
Commission: 50 per cent.
Additional information: Do not submit on spec – always telephone first to discuss requirements.

WOODMANSTERNE PICTURE LIBRARY*
1 The Boulevard, Blackmoor Lane, Watford, Herts WD1 8YW.
Tel: 01923 228236. Fax: 01923 245788.
Contact: Johanna Woodmansterne.
Specialist subjects/requirements: Archaeology, architecture, arms and armour, ballet and opera, birds, castles, cathedrals, churches, costume, countryside, decorative arts, furniture, historic houses, interior design, natural history, painting and sculpture, parks and gardens, religious subjects, sea-

sonal scenes, state occasions, travel, etc.
Markets supplied: Publishing, souvenir/novelties, tourism, travel trade.
Stock: Colour only. All formats.
Usual terms of business: Subject to negotiation.
Commission: 50 per cent.
Additional information: "Only top quality pictures per subject, ranging from the record shot to the unusual."

WORLD PICTURES*
85a Great Portland Street, London W1N 5RA.
Tel: 0171-437 2121 and 0171-436 0440. Fax: 0171-439 1307.
Contacts: Joan Brenes, David Brenes (Directors).
Specialist subjects/requirements: Travel material: cities, resorts, hotels worldwide plus girls, couples and families on holiday suitable for travel brochure, magazine and newspaper use.
Markets supplied: Tour operators, airlines, design houses, advertising agencies.
Stock: Colour only. 6x7cm, 6x9cm and 5x4in. No 35mm.
Usual terms of business: No minimum submission but usually likes the chance of placing material for minimum period of 2 years.
Commission: 50 per cent.

ZEFA PICTURES LTD*
PO Box 210, 20 Conduit Place, London W2 1HZ.
Tel: 0171-262 0101. Fax: 0171-724 2274.
Contact: Harold Harris (Director).
Specialist subjects/requirements: General library handling most subjects.
Markets supplied: Advertising, publishing, etc.
Stock: Colour, and historic B&W. 35mm and medium format transparencies.
Usual terms of business: Minimum initial submission: 200–500. Minimum retention period: 3–5 years.
Commission: 50 per cent.

SERVICES

This section lists companies providing products and services of use to the photographer. A number of those listed offer discounts to BFP members. To obtain the discounts indicated, members should simply produce their current membership card. In the case of mail order transactions, enclose your membership card with your order, requesting that this be returned with the completed order or as soon as membership has been verified. But in all cases, ensure that your membership card is valid: the discount will not be available to those who present an expired card.

Accessories & Specialised Equipment

CAMERA BELLOWS
Units 3-5, St Pauls Road, Balsall Heath, Birmingham B12 8NG.
Tel: 0121-440 1695. Fax: 0121-440 0972.
Bellows for all photographic purposes in leather and other materials. Replacements for modern and antique cameras.
Discount to BFP members: 2%.

COURTENAY PHOTOGRAPHIC LIGHTING
Paterson Group International Ltd, Vaughan Trading Estate, Tipton, West Midlands DY4 7UJ.
Tel: 0121-5222120. Fax: 0121-5222573.
Courtenay electronic flash systems.

THE FLASH CENTRE
54 Brunswick Centre, London WC1N 1AE.
Tel: 0171-837 6163. Flashline Information: 0171-833 3466. Fax: 0171-833 4737.
Specialist suppliers of studio flash systems and photographic lighting equipment.

FOTOLYNX LTD
CCS Centre, Vale Lane, Bedminster, Bristol BS3 5RU.
Tel: 0117 9635263. Fax: 0117 9636362.
Distributors of Camera Care Systems, Kaiser Fototechnik, Fotospeed Chemistry, Hermafix.

JESSOP'S PHOTO CENTRES
Head Office: Jessop House, 98 Scudamore Road, Leicester LE3 1TZ.
Tel: 0116 2320033. Fax: 0116 2320060.
Specialist suppliers of all photographic and digital imaging equipment including Portaflash portable studio flash, a full range of darkroom equipment and accessories.

KJP
Promandis House, Bradbourne Drive, Tilbrook, Milton Keynes MK7 8AJ.
Tel: 01908 366344. Fax: 01908 366322.
Branches: London, Aberdeen, Belfast, Birmingham, Bristol, Croydon, Edinburgh, Glasgow, Leeds, Liverpool, Manchester and Nottingham.
Distributors of Bowens, Cambo, Colourshade, Fidelity, Manfrotto, Norman, Savage, Wein, Zone VI, etc.

S. W. KENYON
PO Box 71, Cranbrook, Kent TN18 5ZR.
Tel/fax: 01580 850770.
K-Line dulling sprays.

OCEAN OPTICS
13 Northumberland Avenue, London WC2N 5AQ.
Tel: 0171-930 8408. Fax: 0171-839 6148.
Specialist suppliers of underwater photography equipment.

THE PROCESS CONTROL COMPANY
Griffin Lane, Aylesbury, Buckinghamshire HP19 3BP.
Tel: 01296 484877. Fax: 01296 393122.
Makers of processing equipment: sinks and anti-static equipment. Water service equipment. Makers of densitometers. Importers of electronic darkroom doors.

JAMIE WOOD PRODUCTS LTD
Cross Street, Polegate, Sussex BN26 6BN.
Tel: 01323 483813. Fax: 01323 483813.
Makers of photographic hides. Suppliers of photo electronic equipment.
Discount to BFP members: 5%.

Art Services

COLOUR PROCESSING LABORATORIES LTD
Head Office: Fircroft Way, Edenbridge, Kent TN8 6ET.
Tel: 01732 862555. Fax: 01732 866560.
Branches in London, Birmingham, Bristol, Eastleigh, Nottingham, Brentwood, Reading and Portsmouth.
Exhibition design facility, retouching, etc.

LONDON LABELS LTD
20 Oval Road, London NW1 7DJ.
Tel: 0171-267 7105. Fax: 0171-267 1165.
Self-adhesive labels for 35mm slides, printed with name, address or logo. Also plain labels.

MALLARD IMAGING
Graphic House, Noel Street, Kimberley, Nottingham NG16 2NE.
Tel: 0115 9382670. Fax: 0115 9458047.
Full service colour laboratory. Exhibition printing, typesetting and graphic arts department.

OBSCURA LTD
8 Chaple Place, Vere Street, London W1M 9HN.
Tel: 0171-499 3030. Fax: 0171-499 2060.
Electronic retouching, conventional photocomposition and retouching, etc.

M. A. POPE PRINTERS
'Gomer', Maynard Green, Heathfield, East Sussex TN21 0DG.
Tel: 01435 812738.
Flush-fitting printed labels for 35mm slides, including name, address and copyright symbol.

QUICK IMAGING CENTRE
23 Sherwood Road, Bromsgrove, Worcestershire B60 3DR.
Tel: 01527 871648. Fax: 01527 575763.
Full range of professional laboratory services plus Photoleaflets, Photolabels.
Discount to BFP members: 10% against c.w.o.

STEEPLEPRINT LTD
5 Mallard Close, Earls Barton, Northampton NN6 0LS.
Tel: 01604 810781. Fax: 01604 811251.
ABLE-LABELS – printed self-adhesive labels.

STONELEIGH PHOTO GRAPHIC IMAGING
Queensway, Leamington Spa, Warwickshire CV31 3JT.
Tel: 01926 427030. Fax: 01926 833539.
Comprehensive laboratory service. Graphic artwork and design, vinyl cutting service, Dicomed imaging centre, bureau services, pre-press services.
Discount to BFP members: Quantity discounts.

NATHALIE TIERCE
28-29 Eastman Road, London W3 7YG.
Tel/fax: 0181-740 8044.
Freelance scenic artist producing backgrounds for photo stills/advertising.

TREADAWAY PRINTING
Unit 7, Princes Works, Princes Road, Teddington, Middlesex TW11 0RW.
Tel: 0181-943 4188. Fax: 0181-943 2600.
Design, artwork and litho printing. Publicity cards, folders, posters and brochures etc.
Discount to BFP members: 10%.

WALKER PRINT LTD
Classic House, 4th Floor, 174–180 Old Street, London EC1V 9BP.
Tel: 0171-253 1200. Fax: 0171-253 0890.
Design and publicity printers. Photographers' index cards, posters, catalogues, etc.
Discount to BFP members: 10%.

Computer Software

IRIS AUDIO VISUAL
Unit M, Forest Industrial Park, Forest Road, Hainault, Essex IG6 3HL.
Tel: 0181-500 2846. Fax: 0181-559 8780.
Cradoc Captionwriter and Cradoc Photomanagement programs for labelling and library management of transparencies, prints, etc. Versions available for Mac, IBM DOS, Windows, Windows 95 and Windows NT.

TYPECAST
4 Geldof Road, New Lane, Huntington, York YO3 9JT.
Tel/fax: 01904 416684.
Photo File stock management software for Microsoft Windows, including caption label printing. Also supply blank or printed (to order) labels for transparencies/prints and Viewpack filing systems.
Discount to BFP members: 10% off RRP of software packages.

Equipment Hire

ANGLIA CAMERAS
15-15a St Matthew's Street, Ipswich IP1 3EL.
Tel/fax: 01473 258185.
AV equipment, overhead projectors, screens, etc.

EDRIC AUDIO VISUAL LTD
Oak End Way, Gerrards Cross, Bucks SL9 8BR.
Tel: 01753 884646. Fax: 01753 887163.
Also at: Manchester, Tel: 0161-773 7711 and Bristol, Tel: 01454 201313.
Hire and sale of AV equipment, film production and video production equipment.

GEORGE ELLIOTT PLC
London Road, Westerham, Kent TN16 1DR.
Tel: 01959 562198. Fax: 01959 564709.
Large format camera, Schneider Lenses, studio and darkroom equipment. B&W filters.

KJP
Promandis House, Bradbourne Drive, Tilbrook, Milton Keynes MK7 8AJ.
Tel: 01908 366344. Fax: 01908 366322.
Branches: London, Aberdeen, Belfast, Birmingham, Bristol, Croydon, Edinburgh, Glasgow, Leeds, Liverpool, Manchester and Nottingham.
Comprehensive equipment hire service featuring cameras, lenses, lighting, tripods, backgrounds, digital & AV equipment & accessories.

LEOPOLD CAMERAS LTD
17 Hunter Street, London WC1N 1BN.
Tel: 0171-837 6501. Fax: 0171-916 1217.
Comprehensive equipment hire service.

Equipment Repair

BOURNEMOUTH PHOTOGRAPHIC REPAIR SERVICES
251 Holdenhurst Road, Bournemouth, Dorset BH8 8DA.
Tel: 01202 301273. Fax: 01202 301273
Professional repairs to all makes of equipment. Full test facilities including modern electronic diagnostic test equipment.
Discount to BFP members: 10% off labour charges.

CAM SERV
56 Yeoman Street, Stoke-on-Trent, Staffs ST4 4AP.
Tel/fax: 01782 412938.
Repairs to all makes of cameras, camcorders, flash units, etc.
Discount to BFP members: 20%.

CAMTEC PHOTOGRAPHIC REPAIRS
40C Devonshire Road, Hastings, East Sussex TN34 1NF.
Tel: 01424 718314. Fax: 01424 718313.
Repairs to all makes of photographic equipment, binoculars and telescopes.
Discount to BFP members: 10%.

CENTRAL CAMERAS
29 Salters Road, Walsall Wood, West Midlands WS9 9JD.
Tel: 01543 370263. Fax: 01543 454144.
General photographic repairs (not AV). Specialist in 35mm cameras, lenses and medium format equipment.
Discount to BFP members: 10% of labour costs.

COUSINS & WRIGHT
5 The Halve, Trowbridge, Wiltshire BA14 8SB.
Tel: 01225 754242.
Camera, camcorder and photographic equipment servicing and repair.

THE FLASH CENTRE
54 Brunswick Centre, Bernard Street, London WC1N 1AE.
Tel: 0171-837 6163. Flashline Information: 0171-833 3466. Fax: 0171-833 4737.
Specialists in studio flash repair.

LESLIE H. FRANKHAM, FRPS
166 Westcotes Drive, Leicester LE3 0SP.
Tel: 0116 2550825.
Equipment repairs and testing services. Optical instrumentation testing. Representing the original Zeiss Foundation. Special rapid delivery for BFP members where possible.

H. A. GARRETT & CO LTD
300 High Street, Sutton, Surrey SM1 1PQ.
Tel: 0181-643 5376. Fax: 0181-643 8914.
Camera and equipment repair.
Discount to BFP members: 5% off labour charges.

INSTRUMENT SERVICES CO LTD
208 Maybank Road, London E18 1EU.
Tel: 0181-504 8885. Fax: 0181-505 8005.
Sole accredited service centre for Weston Master exposure meters. Repairs to Gossen and other quality instruments.

A. J. JOHNSTONE & CO LTD
395 Central Chambers, 93 Hope Street, Glasgow G2 6LD.
Tel: 0141-221 2106. Fax: 0141-221 9166.
All equipment repairs, including AV equipment. Authorised service centre for Canon, Olympus, Nikon, Bronica and Jobo processing equipment. Canon warranty repairs.
Discount to BFP members: 10%.

KJP
Promandis House, Bradbourne Drive, Tilbrook, Milton Keynes MK7 8AJ.
Tel: 01908 366344. Fax: 01908 366322.
Branches: London, Aberdeen, Belfast, Birmingham, Bristol, Croydon, Edinburgh, Glasgow, Leeds, Liverpool, Manchester and Nottingham.
Full equipment repair and rental loan service whilst equipment is in for repair.

LENCOL
62 Forest Drive, Chelmsford, Essex CM1 2TS.
Tel: 01245 256845.
General repair service. Also photographic sales, accessories and D/P.

SENDEAN LTD
105-109 Oxford Street, London W1R 1TF.
Tel: 0171-439 8418. Fax: 0171-734 4046.
General repair service. Estimates free.
Discount to BFP members: 10%.

VANGUARD PHOTOGRAPHIC SERVICES
156 Boston Road, Hanwell, London W7 2HJ.
Tel: 0181-840 2177. Fax: 0181-566 3361.
All photographic equipment repairs.

Framing & Finishing

AVONCOLOUR LTD
131 Duckmoor Road, Ashton Gate, Bristol BS3 2BH.
Tel: 01179 633456. Fax: 01179 635186.
Mounting and laminating and display systems.
Discount to BFP members: Up to 20%; Tel: Ron Munn.

KAY MOUNTING SERVICE LTD
351 Caledonian Road, London N1 1DW.
Tel: 0171-607 7241. Fax: 0171-700 2208.
Mounting, canvas-bonding and heat-sealing. Bonding of prints and transparencies to Perspex.

KIMBERS
94 Westbourne Street, Hove BN3 5FA.
Tel: 01273 326907. Fax: 01273 820663.
Mail order wholesale and retail of frames, mounts and wedding albums.
Discount to BFP members: 2.5% on orders over £120.

POLYBOARD LTD
Unit 10, Wealden Industrial Estate, Farningham Road, Jarvis Brook, Crowborough, East Sussex
TN6 2JR.
Tel: 01892 667608. Fax: 01892 667548.
Sole agents for Polyboard and Polyframe.
Discount to BFP members: 5% cash with order.

JAMES RUSSELL OF WIMBLEDON
17 Elm Grove, Wimbledon, London SE19 4HE.
Tel: 0181-947 6171. Fax: 0181-944 2064.
D&F Maxima etc. Albums and accessories. Frames to size wood/metal, many colours.
Discount to BFP members: 5% on orders over £150.

DENIS WRIGHT LTD
2 Barnsbury Street, London N1 1PN.
Tel: 0171-226 2628. Fax: 0171-226 6890.
Manufacturers of albums, mounts and frames.

Insurance

AUA INSURANCE
Peek House, 20 Eastcheap, London EC3M 1LQ.
Tel: 0171-283 3311. Fax: 0171-283 0968.
"All Risks" insurance for professional and semi-professional photographers, minilabs and photo-processors. Comprehensive package including professional negligence.
Discount to BFP members: 71/2****%.

ALLIANCE MULTIMEDIA INSURANCE
Alliance House, 66 St George's Place, Cheltenham, Gloucestershire GL52 3PN.
Tel: 01242 584001. Fax: 01242 226710.
Full range of specialist insurance for photographers, including insurance for photographic and video equipment, photographic negatives, computers, Public Liability and Professional Indemnity. Also household insurance that includes a 10% discount to BFP members working from home.
Full range of cover available to BFP members at special rates: details available from the above address.

CAMERASURE INSURANCE CONSULTANTS LTD
Funtley Court, Funtley Hill, Fareham, Hampshire PO16 7UY.
Tel: 01329 826260. Fax: 01329 825625.
A complete insurance service for the professional photographer including a comprehensive policy covering equipment, studios, work in progress and legal liabilities (Public, Products and Employers).
Discount to BFP members: 5%.

ENTERTAINMENT & LEISURE INSURANCE SERVICES LTD
PO Box 100, Ouseburn, York YO5 9SZ.
Tel: 01423 330711. Fax: 01423 331008.
Specialist photographic insurance scheme covering private, domestic or commercial photo equipment.

GOLDEN VALLEY INSURANCE
The Olde Shoppe, Ewyas Harold, Herefordshire HR2 0ES.
Tel: 01981 240536. Fax: 01981 240451.
Comprehensive insurance cover for all photographic, video and sound recording equipment, binoculars and telescopes, computers, home office/studio etc.
Discount to BFP members: 10%.

HINTON AND WILD (INSURANCE) LTD
Bank House, 2 Ditton Road, Surbiton, Surrey KT6 6QZ.
Tel: 0181-390 4666. Fax: 0181-390 4660.
Specialist photographic insurance scheme.

MICHAEL PAVEY INSURANCE BROKERS
Berywn House, 70-72 Abbey Road, Torquay TQ2 5NH.
Tel: 01803 211236. Fax: 01803 211307.
"Home Office" insurance for the person working from home.

PRIVILEGE INSURANCE
Tel: 0113 243 2211; Quoteline: 0113 292 5555. Fax: 0113 280 1259.
Direct-line motor insurance offering competitive rates for those in so called "high-risk" professions such as photographers.

A SAUNDERS & CO
70 Watling Street, Radlett, Herts WD7 7NP.
Tel: 01923 858339/858359. Fax: 01923 859895.
Flexible All-Risks insurance package for photographers, including Public and Products Liability cover.

Material Suppliers

COLORAMA PHOTODISPLAY LTD
Ace Business Park, Mackadown Lane, Kitts Green, Birmingham B33 0LD.
Tel: 0121-783 9931. Fax: 0121-783 1674.
Suppliers of photographic background products including Colorama Background Paper, Colorcrepe, Rainbow, Colormatt, Colorgloss, Colormaster canvases and fabrics. Special effects backgrounds, support systems and Colorcove and Cove-lock coving systems.

KJP
Promandis House, Bradbourne Drive, Tilbrook, Milton Keynes MK7 8AJ.
Tel: 01908 366344. Fax: 01908 366322.
Branches: London, Aberdeen, Belfast, Birmingham, Bristol, Croydon, Edinburgh, Glasgow, Leeds, Liverpool, Manchester and Nottingham.
Complete range of standard and specialist films, papers and chemicals.

KENTMERE LTD
Staveley, Kendal, Cumbria LA8 9PB.
Tel: 01539 821365. Fax: 01539 821399.
Manufacturers of the Kentmere range of black and white photographic papers, including variable contrast and graded materials, and Kentint coloured base papers. Also offers a comprehensive range of photobase ink jet media including K. Tapestry, an art surface media and specific media for the Iris system.

LEEDS PHOTOVISUAL LTD
20-26 Brunswick Centre, London WC1N 1AE.
Tel: 0171-833 1661/1641. Fax: 0171-833 1560.
Other branches in Leeds, Newport, Manchester, Birmingham and Glasgow.
Professional photographic wholesalers – photographic, a/v, video and electronic imaging equipment.
Discount to BFP members: 10% on materials; for equipment prices please phone.

MID COUNTIES PHOTOGRAPHIC SUPPLIES
617 Jubilee Road, Letchworth, Hertfordshire SG6 1NE.
Tel: 01462 679388. Fax: 01462 675860.
Comprehensive wholesale supplies of film, paper, chemicals, albums, mounts, etc.

SILVERPRINT LTD
12 Valentine Place, London SE1 8QH.
Tel: 0171-620 0844. Fax: 0171-620 0129.
Specialist suppliers of B&W materials. Importers of Oriental Seagull and Forte Fibrebased and wide range of other papers, toners, liquid emulsions, tinting and retouching materials. Products for archival mounting, and archival storage boxes and folio cases. Mail order service.

Are you working from the latest edition of The Freelance Photographer's Market Handbook?
It's published on 1 October each year. Details are subject to change,
so it pays to have the latest edition

Model Agencies

CHARMERS INDEX
29 Alexandra Way, Norwich, Norfolk NR17 1YW.
Tel/fax: 01603 613834.
General model agency.
Discount to BFP members: 10%.

DEREK'S HANDS AGENCY
153 Battersea Rise, London SW11 1HP.
Tel: 0171-924 2484. Mobile: 0831 679165. Fax: 071-924 2334.
Model agency specialising in hands.
Discount to BFP members: 10% agency fee waived.

G. H. MANAGEMENT
Heathbarn Farm, Midhurst, Sussex GU29 9RL.
Tel: 01730 814679. Fax: 01730 814679.
Model Agency. Individual photographic tuition in portrait and glamour work.

CLIVE GRAHAM MODELS INTERNATIONAL
Pembury Lodge, 56 Castle Hill Avenue, Folkestone, Kent CT20 2QR.
Tel: 01303 255781. Fax: 01303 221192.
Top models available for photographic, fashion, television, video and films.
Discount to BFP members: 10%.

MANCHESTER MODEL AGENCY
14 Albert Square, Manchester M2 5PF.
Tel: 0161-236 1335. Fax: 0161-832 2502.
Photographic models – female, male and children for fashion and advertising.

MODELS PLUS MODEL AGENCY
Royal Arcade, Christchurch Road, Boscombe, Bournemouth, Dorset BH1 4BH.
Tel: 01202 393193. Fax: 01202 301156.
Agency specialising in fashion, glamour, photographic and promotional models.
Discount to BFP members: 10%.

NUMBER ONE MODEL MANAGEMENT
The Mezzanine Suite, 30 St Paul's Square, Birmingham B3 1QZ.
Tel: 0121-233 2433. Fax: 0121-233 2454.
Also at: 50 Westminster Buildings, Theatre Square, Upper Parliament Street, Nottingham NG1 6LG.
Tel: 01159 240055. Fax: 01159 240033.
Model agency specialising in commercial advertising. Suppliers of fashion, photographic and promotional assistants.

Postcard Printers

ABACUS (COLOUR PRINTERS) LTD
Lowick, Near Ulverston, Cumbria LA12 8DX.
Tel: 01229 885361/885381. Fax: 01229 885348.
Quality printers specialising in colour postcards & greetings cards. Minimum quantity postcards: 1,000. Price £132 + VAT. Minimum quantity greetings cards: 1,000. Price £170 + VAT.

DENNIS PRINT & PUBLISHING
Melrose Street, Scarborough, North Yorkshire YO12 7SJ.
Tel: 01723 500555. Fax: 01723 501488.
Quality sheet fed printers. Postcards a speciality. Minimum quantity: 3,000 for £180; 5000 for £215.00; 10,000 for £320. Special rates for composite cards. All prices exclude VAT.
Discount to BFP members: 5%.

GRAHAM & SONS (PRINTERS) LTD
51 Gortin Road, Omagh, Co. Tyrone, BT79 7HZ.
Tel: 01662 249222. Fax: 01662 249222.
Minimum quantity: 500. Price £58 + VAT.

JUDGES POSTCARDS LTD
176 Bexhill Road, St Leonards on Sea, East Sussex TN38 8BN.
Tel: 01424 420919. Fax: 01424 438538.
Minimum quantity postcards: 1,000 and greeting cards: 1,500.
Discount to BFP members: 10%.

LEACH LITHOPRINT LTD
Church Lane, Brighouse, West Yorkshire HD6 1DJ.
Tel: 01484 406021. Fax: 01484 406002.
Minimum quantity: 2,000. Price: £150 + VAT; 5,000. Price: £225 + VAT.
Discount to BFP members: Variable depending on number of subjects ordered.

THE SHERWOOD PRESS
Hadden Court, Glaisdale Parkway, Glaisdale Drive West, Nottingham NG8 4GP.
Tel: 0115 928 7766. Fax: 0115 928 0271.
Quality printers specialising in the production of greetings cards, fine art prints, postcards and calendars, etc.

THE THOUGHT FACTORY
Group House, 40 Waterside Road, Hamilton Industrial Park, Leicester LE5 1TL.
Tel: 0116 276 5302. Fax: 0116 246 0506.
Minimum quantity: 250. Price: £54 + VAT.

Processing & Printing

ACT
4 East Street Industrial Estate, Rhayader, Powys LD6 5ER.
Tel: 01597 810003. Fax: 01597 811265.
Specialist transparency duplicating services using state-of-the-art equipment for optimum quality results.
Discount to BFP members: 5% on orders over £150.

ATLAS IMAGE FACTORY
Unit 33, Sutton Business Park, Earley, Reading RG6 1AZ.
Tel: 0118 926 0494. Fax: 0118 966 9086.
Comprehensive professional colour and black and white printing and processing service.
Discount to BFP members: 20%.

AVONCOLOUR LTD
131 Duckmoor Road, Ashton Gate, Bristol BS3 2BH.
Tel: 01179 633456. Fax: 01179 635186.
Comprehensive colour processing services, including duping and copying, mounting and laminating, hand printing and duratrans up to 8x4ft. Presentation Direct catologue available containing over 3,000 products to help the presenter show and sell more effectively.
Discount to BFP members: Up to 20%; Tel: Ron Munn.

C.C. IMAGING
39 Belle Vue Road, Leeds LS3 1ES.
Tel: 0113 233 0024. Fax: 0113 233 0016.
Comprehensive colour and black and white processing services. Specialist reversal print service. Full mounting and finishing services. Colour laser copying. Digital imaging, retouching and printing.
Discount to BFP members: 15%.

CHANDOS PHOTOGRAPHIC SERVICES LTD
5 Torrens Street, London EC1V 1NQ.
Tel: 0171-837 1822/7632. Fax: 0171-837 2705.
Comprehensive colour and black and white processing services. Full range of duplicate transparencies.

CITY COLOR LTD
426-432 Essex Road, London N1 3PJ.
Tel: 0171-359 0033. Fax: 0171-226 0435.
Comprehensive professional colour and black and white processing services. digital imaging, bleach etching, mounting and framing.
Discount to BFP members: 10%.

COLAB LTD
Herald Way, Binley, Coventry CV3 1BB.
Tel: 01203 440404. Fax: 01203 444219.
Comprehensive colour processing and digital imaging services.

COLCHESTER COLOUR PROCESSORS
7 Brunel Court, Severalls Park, Colchester, Essex CO4 4XW.
Tel: 01206 751241. Fax: 01206 855134.
Colour and black and white processing, electronic imaging.
Discount to BFP members: 5%.

COLORLABS INTERNATIONAL
The Maltings, Fordham Road, Newmarket, Suffolk CB8 7AG.
Tel: 01638 664444. Fax: 01638 666360.
Comprehensive colour and black and white processing services.

COLOUR CENTRE (LONDON) LIMITED
41a North End Road, Kensington, London W14 8SZ.
Tel: 0171-602 0167. Fax: 0171-371 2464.
1½ hour E6 processing. Also C41, contacts, R-Types & C-Types. All hand made. Trade counter for films.

COLOUR PROCESSING LABORATORIES LTD
Head Office: Fircroft Way, Edenbridge, Kent TN8 6ET.
Tel: 01732 862555. Fax: 01732 866560.
Branches: London, Birmingham, Bristol, Southampton, Nottingham, Brentwood, Reading, Portsmouth.
E6 and C41 processing. All forms of photographic printing including giant photo-murals, leaflets, etc. Cibachrome and Duratrans.

COALVILLE PROCESSING LABORATORY
45 Park Road, Coalville, Leics LE67 3AE.
Tel: 01530 833785.
Colour D&P and reprints to 20x16in. Kodak Ektamax. B&W prints from 120/35mm colour/B&W negs up to 12x8in. Postal service available.

DKG PHOTOGRAPHIC SERVICES
PO Box 80, Manchester M16 8PZ.
Tel/fax: 0161-232 0242.
Black and white hand processing and printing.
Discount to BFP members: 15%.

LYNN DRISCOLL
Basement Unit 2, Enterprise House, 59-65 Upper Ground, London SE1 9PQ.
Tel: 0171-401 3825. Fax: 0171-207 0557.
E6 processing, from 8.30am Monday to 8.30pm Friday. Cheap overnight rates for library and stock photographers.
Discount to BFP members: 10% over £100.

DUNNS PROFESSIONAL IMAGING LTD
Unit 16, Summerhill Industrial Park, Goodman Street, Ladywood, Birmingham B1 2SS.
Tel: 0121-200 3226. Fax: 0121-236 9009.
Comprehensive colour and black and white processing, professional Photo CD and electronic retouching services.

G. GROVE PHOTOGRAPHIC SERVICES
61 Mareham Lane, Sleaford, Lincs NG34 7LA.
Tel: 01529 303867.
Specialist B&W hand printing and hand colouring services.
Discount to BFP members: 10%.

HAWORTH PHOTOGRAPHIC LTD
The Old Forge, Rossendale Works, Chase Side, Southgate, London N14 5PJ.
Tel: 0181-886 6008. Fax: 0181-886 3524.
Comprehensive colour and black and white processing services.

HOME COUNTIES COLOUR SERVICES LTD
12-14 Leagrave Road, Luton, Bedfordshire LU4 8HZ.
Tel: 01582 731899. Fax: 01582 402410.
Photographic processing services for photographers and industry.

THE IMAGING LAB
23-25 Great Sutton Street, London EC1V 0DN.
Tel: 0171-250 1471.
Duplicate and enlarged transparencies to 11x4in. Transprints to 20x16in. C-type prints to 20x16in. Black & white prints to 16x12in.

P. & P. F. JAMES LTD
496 Great West Road, Hounslow, Middlesex TW5 0TS.
Tel: 0181-570 3974/8951. Fax: 0181-569 4397.
Full range of colour and black and white services from 35mm dupes to 30x40in display panels plus R-types, duratrans, mounting and framing.

JOE'S BASEMENT
113 Wardour Street, London W1V 3TD.
Tel: 0171-434 3210. Fax: 0171-287 5867.
Also: 82-84 Clerkenwell Road, London EC1M 5RJ. Tel: 0171-253 3210. Fax: 0171-336 0489.
And: 111 Hammersmith Road, London W14 0QH. Tel: 0171-371 3210. Fax: 0171-602 4161.
Full service lab. 24-hour/7-day E6 processing/C41 Dev & Print, Pictostat and laser copy print service/trade counter. Colour and B&W hand printing, exhibiition printing, duping, computer graphics, complete film processing including exclusive Agfa Scala processing, dry mounting and framing. Full range digital imaging service.

MALLARD IMAGING
Graphic House, Noel Street, Kimberley, Nottingham NG16 2NE.
Tel: 0115 9382670. Fax: 0115 9458047.
Comprehensive colour and black and white processing services, exhibition printing.

GRAHAM NASH LTD
12 Stephen Mews, London W1A 4WP.
Tel: 0171-580 4152. Fax: 0171-580 9361.
Comprehensive colour and B&W processing and printing services. System 70 transparency duplicating service for low-cost reproduction-quality dupes.

NESS VISUAL TECHNOLOGY
Kershaw Street, Widnes, Cheshire WA8 7JH.
Tel: 0151-424 0514. Fax: 0151-424 1792.
Comprehensive professional colour processing services. Schools package printing.

PHOTO SPORTS LTD
52 Harvest Bank Road, West Wickham, Kent BR4 9DJ.
Tel: 0181-462 4885.
Specialists in E6 processing.

PHOTOMATIC LTD
Dellsome Lane, North Mymms, Hatfield, Herts AL9 7DX.
Tel: 01707 262506. Fax: 01707 276553.
Black and white printing services. Runs of postcards etc., from customers' own originals.

PICTURECRAFT PHOTOGRAPHY
16 Park View, Cleethorpes, NE Lincs DN35 7TG.
Tel: 01472 340491.
Specialist black & white hand process and printing service, contact prints, hand enlargements – phone or write for price list.
Discount to BFP members: 10%.

PORTFOLIO PHOTOGRAPHY
2 Woodfield Road, Chorley, Lancs PR7 1QT.
Tel: 01257 265914.
Black and white hand and machine printing from processed negs, negs 35mm to 5x4in.
Discount to BFP members: 10%.

PROFOLAB
Unit 4, Surrey Close, Granby Industrial Estate, Weymouth, Dorset DT4 9TY.
Tel: 01305 774098. Fax: 01305 778746.
E6, C41 processing and printing up to 30x40in; specialist reproduction-quality slide duplicating service.

PROPIX LTD
Rockingham House, Broad Lane, Sheffield S1 3PP.
Tel: 0114 2737778. Fax: 0114 2768808.
Comprehensive professional colour and black and white processing services.
Discount to BFP members: 10% on lab services.

JAMES RUSSELL OF WIMBLEDON
17 Elm Grove, Wimbledon, London SE19 4HE.
Tel: 0181-947 6172. Fax: 0181-944 2064.
Comprehensive colour processing services; 2-hour E6 processing, C41, dupes, copy trans, copy negs, machine and hand line printing, exhibition printing and mounting service. Also complete B&W service.
Discount to BFP members: 5%.

SCL
16 Bull Lane, Edmonton, London N18 1SX.
Tel: 0181-807 0725. Fax: 0181-807 2539.
Comprehensive colour and black and white processing services.

STONELEIGH PHOTO GRAPHIC IMAGING
Queensway, Leamington Spa, Warwickshire CV31 3JT.
Tel: 01926 427030. Fax: 01926 833539
Comprehensive laboratory services. Exhibition and mural printing. Silk screen printing. Point of purchase volume printing. Electronic and digital printing. Dry mounting and encapsulating. Slide and OHP production. Vinyl cutting service.
Discount to BFP members: Quantity discounts.

SUPERDUPES
1-4 Pope Street, Off Tower Bridge Road, London SE1 3PH.
Tel: 0171-403 3295. Fax: 0171-407 6687.
Specialist transparency duplicating service – 24-hour turnaround.

RAYMOND THATCHER STUDIOS
18 Queen Street, Maidenhead, Berkshire SL6 1HZ.
Tel: 01628 25381. Fax: 01628 778921.
Comprehensive colour and B&W processing.
Discount to BFP members: 10%.

TRANSCOLOUR LTD
Unit 1, Tyers Gate, London Bridge, London SE1 3HX.
Tel: 0171-403 0048. Fax: 0171-403 1944.
Image manipulations, 1½ hour E6 processing (8am–8pm; 24-hours by arrangement), dupes, retouching, R-Types & C-Types.

WEYCOLOUR LTD
Moss Lane, Godalming, Surrey GU7 1EF.
Tel: 01483 417670. Fax: 01483 427267.
Comprehensive colour processing service.

MICHAEL WHITE
PO Box 105, Newbury, Berkshire RG14 7YL.
Tel/fax: 01635 49879.
Superior black and white processing by a professional photographer.

WRIGHT COLOR LTD
29 Millers Road, Warwick, Warwickshire CV34 5AN.
Tel: 01926 494345. Fax: 01926 410932.
Comprehensive colour and black and white processing services.
Discount to BFP members: 5%.

Storage & Presentation

AIRFLOW
17 Lumen Road, GEC East Lane Estate, Wembley, Middlesex HA9 7RE.
Tel: 0181-385 0385. Fax: 0181-385 0450.
Archival transparency storage systems for all needs for film and photos, wallets, pockets, folders, binders, all types of masks – plastic and card, specials made to order, high frequency plastic welders. Plus overprinting.
Discount to BFP members: 5%, rising to the value of order.

AUDIO VISUAL MATERIAL LTD
AVM House, Hawley Lane, Farnborough, Hants GU14 8EH.
Tel: 01252 510363. Fax: 01252 549214.
Optia storage systems; lightboxes, Draper projection screens.
Discount to BFP members: 10%.

BRAYTHORN LTD
Phillips Street, Aston, Birmingham B6 4PT.
Tel: 0121-359 8800. Fax: 0121-359 8412.
Suppliers of cardboard tubes and envelopes. Minimum quantities: 250 envelopes, 50 tubes.

CHALLONER MARKETING LTD
Raans Road, Amersham, Buckinghamshire HP6 6LL.
Tel: 01494 721270. Fax: 01494 725732.
Suppliers of Fly-Weight envelope stiffener. Minimum quantity: 100.
Discount to BFP members: 5% on orders over 5,000.

DW VIEWPACKS LTD
Unit 7/8 Peverel Drive, Granby, Milton Keynes MK1 1NL.
Tel: 01908 642323. Fax: 01908 640164.
Filing and presentation systems, masks, mounts, wallets, storage cabinets, lightboxes, slide sorting and viewing equipment.
Discount to BFP members: 10%.

FLASH FOTO LTD
4 Parkmead, Flower Lane, London NW7 2JW.
Tel: 0181-959 4513. Fax: 0181-959 1388.
Slide presentation and storage systems, including "Trippelmask" black card mask system, Arrowfile archivally-safe photo pockets, lightboxes, negative/slide location systems, suspension files.
Discount to BFP members: Telephone for latest improved discounts and catalogue.

NICHOLAS HUNTER LTD
Unit 8, Oxford Business Centre, Osney Lane, Oxford OX1 1TB.
Tel: 01865 727292. Fax: 01865 200051.
Plastic wallets for presentation of prints, slides and negatives.
Discount to BFP members: 5% if c.w.o.; 10% on orders over £100.

IRIS AUDIO VISUAL
Unit M, Forest Industrial Park, Forest Road, Hainault, Essex IG6 3HL.
Tel: 0181-500 2846. Fax: 0181-559 8780.
Photographic and audio visual accessories including slide and negative care and storage systems, slide mounts, computer labels for slides and prints. Supplier of Cradoc Captionwriter and Cradoc Photomanagement programs for labelling and library management of transparencies, prints, etc. Versions available for Mac, IBM DOS, Windows, Windows 95 and Windows NT.

KJP
Promandis House, Bradbourne Drive, Tilbrook, Milton Keynes MK7 8AJ.
Tel: 01908 366344. Fax: 01908 366322.
Branches: London, Aberdeen, Belfast, Birmingham, Bristol, Croydon, Edinburgh, Glasgow, Leeds, Liverpool, Manchester and Nottingham.
Complete stockists of a full range of storage & presentation equipment and materials, including lightboxes, mounts, frames, storage bags and albums.

KENRO LTD
Greenbridge Road, Swindon, Wilts SN3 3LH.
Tel: 01793 615836. Fax: 01793 513561.
Black card transparency masks, slide storage systems, library systems and other presentation products.

S. W. KENYON
PO Box 71, Cranbrook, Kent TN18 5ZR.
Tel/fax: 01580 850770.
Slide storage systems.

KRYSTAL TRADING LTD
Unit 2, Wessex Industrial Estate, Avenue 3, Station Lane, Witney, Oxfordshire OX8 6BP.
Tel: 01993 773401. Fax: 01993 778668.
High quality plastic wallets and folders for the storage and presentation of slides, prints and negatives. Wedding preview pages to fit most albums. Plastic stationery. Custom design and printing service available.
Discount to BFP members: 5%.

MID COUNTIES PHOTOGRAPHIC SUPPLIES
617 Jubilee Road, Letchworth, Hertfordshire SG6 1NE.
Tel: 01462 679388. Fax: 01462 675860.
Wholesalers of albums, mounts, film, frames, papers, chemicals, etc.

SLIDEPACKS
16 Temple Mead Close, Stanmore, Middlesex HA7 3RG.
Tel: 0181-954 7048. Fax: 0181-954 1110.
Binders, folders. mounts and wallets for transparency presentation, storage and filing. Custom-made service also available. Also supply labels, lightboxes, lupes and other accessories.

WILTON OF LONDON LTD
Stanhope House, 4-8 Highgate High Street, London N6 5JL.
Tel: 0181-341 7070. Fax: 0181-341 1176.
Manufacturers of re-cycled, hand-finished cardboard envelopes.

As a member of the Bureau of Freelance Photographers, you'll be kept up-to-date with markets through the BFP Market Newsletter, published monthly. For details of membership, turn to page 9

Studio & Darkroom Hire

BEEHIVE CENTRE OF PHOTOGRAPHY
37 Camden High Street, London NW1 7JL.
Tel: 0171-388 6261.
Three large studios with electronic flash, plus three darkrooms.
Discount to BFP members: 50% off first annual subscription to centre.

CEDAR WAY STUDIOS
5 Cedar Way, Camley Street, London NW1 0PD.
Tel: 0171-387 2637. Fax: 0171-387 5824.
Well-equipped studio with comprehensive equipment hire.

FILM PLUS STUDIO
216 Kensington Park Road, London W11 1NR.
Tel: 0171-727 2570. Fax: 0171-727 3433.
Small hire studio with comprehensive Godard flash equipment. Also hire and sales of Godard equipment. Technical advice and processing also available. Trade counter and camera hire.
Discount to BFP members: 10%.

HOLBORN STUDIOS LTD
49/50 Eagle Wharf Road, London N1 7ED.
Tel: 0171-490 4099. Fax: 0171-253 8120.
12 studios to hire, plus very comprehensive equipment hire.
Discount to BFP members: 10% on full week bookings.

MANCHESTER MODEL AGENCY
14 Albert Square, Manchester M2 5PF.
Tel: 0161-236 1335. Fax: 0161-832 2502.
Fashion studio available for hire.

NOMAD STUDIO HIRE
School Buildings, Great Leigh Street, Ancoats, Manchester M4 5WD.
Tel: 0161-236 2008. Fax: 0161-236 9621.
Three well-appointed studios for hire. Wide range of flash equipment. In-house design and construction service for sets and props.

SHOOT PHOTOGRAPHIC
Larchwood, Chiddingfold Road, Dunsfold, Surrey GU8 4PB.
Tel: 01483 200079.
Large studio, 2 acre garden and house for hire.

Studio Services

ALLISTER BOWTELL MODEL MAKER AND EFFECTS DESIGNER
59 Rotherwood Road, London SW15.
Tel: 0181-788 0114. Fax: 0181-785 4012.
Design and construction of models and all kinds of special effects for film and stills.

Services

THE DISPLAY STAND COMPANY
5 Rickett Street, London SW6 1RU.
Tel/fax: 0171-381 0255.
Specialists in design and manufacture of clear and coloured acrylic display props. Also supply large acrylic covers for displaying prints for exhibitions, both wall-mounted, free-standing and hanging.
Discount to BFP members: 5% minimum.

CHARLES H. FOX LTD
22 Tavistock Street, London WC2E 7PY.
Tel: 0171-240 3111. Fax: 0171-379 3410.
Suppliers of theatrical and photographic make-up and books on make-up technique.

LAUREL HERMAN
18a Lambolle Place, London NW3 4PG.
Tel: 071-586 7925. Fax: 071-586 7926.
Ladies' modern designer day/evening clothes and accessories: hire and discounted sales outlet.

LEWIS & KAYE (HIRE) LTD
3b Brassie Avenue, London W3 7DE.
Tel: 0181-749 2121. Fax: 0181-749 9455.
Large collection of silver, glass, china and *objets d'art* for hire as studio props.
Discount to BFP members: 10% where hire charge is £500 or over.

USEFUL ADDRESSES

ASSOCIATION OF MODEL AGENTS
122 Brompton Road, London SW3 1JE.
Tel: 0171-584 6466.

ASSOCIATION OF PHOTOGRAPHERS
9/10 Domingo Street, London EC1Y 0TA.
Tel: 0171-608 1441. Fax: 0171-253 3007.

BRITISH ASSOCIATION OF PICTURE LIBRARIES AND AGENCIES
18 Vine Hill, London EC1R 5DX.
Tel: 0171-713 1780. Fax: 0171-713 1211.

BRITISH INSTITUTE OF PROFESSIONAL PHOTOGRAPHY
Amwell End, Ware, Hertfordshire SG12 9HN.
Tel: 01920 464011. Fax: 01920 487056.

BRITISH PHOTOGRAPHIC IMPORTERS' ASSOCIATION
Ambassador House, Brigstock Road, Thornton Heath, Surrey CR7 7JG.
Tel: 0181-665 6181. Fax: 0181-665 6447.

BRITISH SOCIETY OF UNDERWATER PHOTOGRAPHERS
12 Coningsby Road, South Croydon, Surrey. CR2 6QP.
Tel/fax: 0181-668 8168.

BUREAU OF FREELANCE PHOTOGRAPHERS
Focus House, 497 Green Lanes, London N13 4BP.
Tel: 0181-882 3315. Fax: 0181-886 5174.

CHARTERED INSTITUTE OF JOURNALISTS
2, Dock Offices, Surrey Quays Road, London SE16 2XU.
Tel: 0171-252 1187. Fax: 0171-232 2302.

DESIGN & ARTISTS COPYRIGHT SOCIETY
Parchment House, 13 Northburgh Street, London EC1V 0AH.
Tel: 0171-336 8811. Fax: 0171-336 8822.

GUILD OF WEDDING PHOTOGRAPHERS UK
13 Market Street, Altrincham, Cheshire WA14 1QS.
Tel: 0161-926 9367. Fax: 0161-929 1786.

MASTER PHOTOGRAPHERS ASSOCIATION
Hallmark House, 2 Beaumont Street, Darlington, Co Durham DL1 5SZ.
Tel: 01325 356555. Fax: 01325 357813.

NATIONAL ASSOCIATION OF PRESS AGENCIES
41 Lansdowne Crescent, Leamington Spa, Warwickshire CV32 4PR.
Tel: 01926 424181. Fax: 01926 424760.

NATIONAL COUNCIL FOR THE TRAINING OF JOURNALISTS
Latton Bush Centre, Southern Way, Harlow, Essex CM18 7BL.
Tel: 01279 430009. Fax: 01279 438008.

NATIONAL UNION OF JOURNALISTS
Acorn House, 314 Gray's Inn Road, London WC1X 8DP.
Tel: 0171-278 7916. Fax: 0171-278 1812.

PA NEWS (PRESS ASSOCIATION)
292 Vauxhall Bridge Road, London SW1V 1AE.
Tel: 0171-963 7000. Fax: 0171-963 7191.

PHOTO MARKETING ASSOCIATION INTERNATIONAL (UK) LTD
Peel Place, 50 Carver Street, Hockley, Birmingham B1 3AS.
Tel: 0121-212 0299. Fax: 0121-212 0298.

PROFESSIONAL PHOTOGRAPHIC LABORATORIES ASSOCIATION
35 Chine Walk, Ferndown, Dorset BH22 8PR.
Tel: 01202 590604. Fax: 01202 590605.

ROYAL PHOTOGRAPHIC SOCIETY
Octagon Galleries, Milsom Street, Bath BA1 1DN.
Tel: 01225 462841. Fax: 01225 448688.

THE PICTURE RESEARCH ASSOCIATION
455 Finchley Road, London NW3 6HN.
Tel: 0171-431 9886. Fax: 0171-431 9887.

SOCIETY OF WEDDING AND PORTRAIT PHOTOGRAPHERS
5 Liverpool Road, Ashton Cross, Wigan WN4 0YT.
Tel: 01942 711763. Fax: 01942 725448.

INDEX

A

AA Publishing   179
ACT   233
AUA Insurance   230
A-Z Botanical Collection Ltd   203
Abacus (Colour Printers) Ltd   232
Academy Editions   179
Accountancy Age   50
Ace Photo Agency   203
Action Images Ltd   203
Active   83
Active Life   79
Adams Picture Library   203
Addison Wesley Longman   179
Adlard Coles   179
Aerofilms Ltd   203
Aeroplane Monthly   37
Africa Economic Digest   50
Air Gunner   134
Air International   37
Air Pictorial   38
Airflow   238
Airforces Monthly   38
Airlife Publishing Ltd   179
Airports International   38
Albion Press Ltd   179
All About Cats   29
All About Dogs   30
Allan, Ian, Publishing   179
Allen, J A, & Co Ltd   179
Alliance Multimedia Insurance   230
Alvey & Towers   204
Amateur Gardening   76
Amateur Photographer   121
Amber Books Ltd   179

American, The   79
Ancient Art & Architecture Collection   204
Angler's Mail   27
Anglia Cameras   227
Angling Times   27
Animal Action   30
Animal Life   30
Antique Collector's Club Ltd   179
Apparel International   94
Apple Press, The   180
Aquarian   180
Aquarist & Pondkeeper   85
Aquarius Picture Library   204
Aquila Photographics   205
Architecture Today   46
Arena   103
Arms & Armour   180
Arnold   180
Art of Bonsai, The   85
Asian Hotel & Caterer   74
Association of Model Agents   242
Association of Photographers   242
Athletics Weekly   134
Atlas Image Factory   233
Attitude   103
Audio Visual   121
Audio Visual Material Ltd   238
Aurum Press Ltd   180
Auto Express   107
Autocar   107
Automobile, The   107
Automotive Management   107
Aviation News   37
Avoncolour Ltd   229, 234

B

BBC Books 180
BBC Gardeners' World Magazine 76
BT Today 95
Babycare & Pregnancy 119
Back Street Heroes 63
Badminton 134
Bantam Press 180
Barclays News 50
Barnaby's Picture Library 205
Barrie & Jenkins Ltd 180
Bathrooms and Kitchens: The Magazine 46
B T Batsford Ltd 180
Beehive Centre of Photography 240
Belitha Press Ltd 180
Bella 158
Berkswell Publishing Co Ltd 194
Best 158
Best of British 80
Big! 56
Bike 64
Bird Keeper 85
Bird Life 30
Bird Watching 31
Birds 31
Birdwatch 31
Bizarre 80
Black, A & C, Publishers Ltd 180
Blackwell Publishers 181
Blake, Anthony, Photo Library 205
Blandford 181
Bloomsbury Publishing Ltd 181
Blues & Soul 113
Boards 40
Boat Angler 27
Boat International 41
Boating Business 41
Bookseller, The 148
Bounty 181
Bournemouth Photographic Repair Services 227
Bowtell, Allister, Model Maker 240
Boxing Monthly 134
Boxtree Ltd 181
Braythorn plc 238
Breedon Books Publishing Co Ltd 181
Breslich & Foss 181
Bridgeman Art Library, The 205
Britannia Products 194
British Airways News 38
British Association of Picture Libraries
    & Agencies 242

British Baker 148
British Institute of Professional Photography 242
British Journal of Photography 121
British Photographic Importers Association 242
British Railway Modelling 85
British Society of Underwater Photographers 242
Broadcast Hardware International 34
Brown Packaging Ltd 179
Brownie 56
Bubbles Photo Library 205
Buckinghamshire Countryside 57
Build It 46
Builders Merchants Journal 46
Building Services 47
Bureau of Freelance Photographers 9–10, 242
Business Life 155
Business Opportunity World 51
Business Traveller 156
Buying Cameras 122

C

CA Magazine 51
CC Imaging 234
Cabinet Maker 148
Cage & Aviary Birds 86
Calmann & King Ltd 181
Cam Serv 227
Cambridge University Press 181
Camcorder User 122
Camden Graphics 194
Camera Bellows Ltd 224
Camera Press Ltd 206
Camerasure Insurance Consultants Ltd 230
Cameron Books (Production) Ltd 181
Camping & Caravanning 54
Camping Magazine 54
Camtec Photographic Repairs 228
Canal & Riverboat 41
Canon User Magazine 118
Canonbury Design 194
Car & Accessory Trader 108
Caravan Industry 55
Caravan Life 55
Cars & Car Conversions 108
Cartel International 194
Cash, J Allen, Ltd 206
Cassell plc 181
Cat World 31
Caterer & Hotelkeeper 148

Catholic Gazette 130
Catholic Herald 131
Catholic Times 131
Cats 31
Cedar Way Studios 240
Central Cameras 228
Century 182
Cephas Picture Library 206
Challoner Marketing Ltd 238
Chambers Harrap Ltd 182
Chandos Photographic Services 234
Charmers Index 232
Chartered Institute of Journalists 242
Chat 158
Chatto & Windus Ltd 182
Chemist & Druggist 149
Chemistry & Industry 132
Choice 80
Church Times 131
Cipher 113
Citizen's Band 68
City Color Ltd 234
Clarendon Press 182
Classic American 108
Classic Bike 64
Classic Boat 41
Classic CD 114
Classic Motorcycle, The 64
Classic & Sportscar 108
Classical Music 114
Classics 109
Clean Air & Environmental Protection 132
Climber 135
Clocks 86
Club International 103
Club Mirror 35
Coach & Bus Week 154
Coalville Processing Laboratory 235
Coarse Angling 27
Coarse Fisherman 28
Cohen, Richard, Books 182
Colab Ltd 234
Colchester Colour Processors 234
Coleman, Bruce, Collection 206
Collect It! 86
Collections 207
Collins 182
Colorama Photodisplay Ltd 231
Colorific Photo Library Ltd 207
Colorlabs International 234
Colour Centre (London) Ltd 234
Colour Processing Laboratories Ltd 225, 234
Commerce Magazine 51
Commercial Motor 154

Commuter World 39
Company 159
Company Car 109
Computer Weekly 68
Conde Nast Traveller 156
Conran Octopus 182
Constable & Co Ltd 182
Containerisation International 154
Convenience Store 149
Cosmopolitan 159
Cotswold Life 58
Country 58
Country Homes & Interiors 91
Country Life 58
Country Origins 58
Country Walking 59
Countryman, The 59
Courtenay Photographic Lighting 224
Cousins & Wright 228
Crafts Beautiful 86
Creative Monochrome 182
Cricket World Monthly 129
Cricketer International, The 135
Crops 72
Cumbria & Lake District Magazine 59
Cycle Sport 64
Cycling Plus 65
Cycling & Mountain Biking Today 65
Cycling Weekly 65

D

DKG Photographic Services 235
DW Viewpacks Ltd 238
Daily Mail 168
Daily Mirror 168
Daily Record 168
Daily Sport 168
Daily Star 168
Daily Telegraph, The 168
Dairy Farmer 72
Dalesman, The 59
Dance & Dancers 35
Darkroom User 122
Darts World 135
David & Charles Publishing Ltd 182
Davis, James, Travel Photography 207
Defence Helicopter 39
Defence Picture Library Ltd 207
Dennis Print & Publishing 233

Derek's Model Agency 232
Design & Artists Copyright Society
242
Design Engineering 47
Desire Direct 81
Director 51
Display Stand Company, The 241
Dogs Today 32
Dorset 60
Dorset Life 60
Drapers Record 149
Driscoll, Lynn 235
Driving Magazine 109
Dunns Professional Imaging Ltd 235

E

ETI 68
Ebury Press 183
Echoes 114
Economist, The 126
Ecoscene 208
Edric Audio Visual Ltd 227
Education In Chemistry 133
Electrical Times 95
Electronics World & Wireless World
69
Elle 159
Elle Decoration 92
Elliott, George, plc 227
Empics Sports Photo Agency 208
Energy In Buildings & Industry 47
Engineer, The 47
Engineering 48
Engineering In Miniature 87
English Garden, The 77
Entertainment & Leisure Insurance Services
230
Entrepreneur 52
EOS Magazine 123
Equestrian Trade News 70
Escort 103
Esquire 103
Essentially America 156
Essentials 159
Essex Countryside 60
Eternity 114
Euroart Agency & Library
208
Eurofruit Magazine 149
European, The 126
European Rubber Journal 95

Eva 159
Executive Travel 156
Export Times 52
Express 168
Express on Sunday Magazine
168
Eye Ubiquitous 209

F

FC 135
FHM 104
FW 150
FX 150
F1 News 136
Faber & Faber Ltd 183
Famous 209
Farmers Weekly 73
Farming Press Books 183
Fashion Extras 150
Field, The 60
Fiesta 104
Fighters – The Martial Arts Magazine
136
Film Plus Studio 240
Financial Pulse 84
Financial Times 168
Fire Prevention 99
Fire & Rescue 99
First Down 136
Fishing Monthly 150
Flash Centre 224, 228
Flash Foto Ltd 238
Fleet News 109
Flight International 39
Florist Trade Magazine 151
Fly-Fishing & Fly-Tying 28
Flyer 39
Focus 133
Folk Roots 115
Food Industry News 95
Football Europe 136
Football Monthly 137
Footprints Colour Picture Library
209
Fore! 137
Forecourt Trader 151
Forum 81
Fotolynx Ltd 224
Foulis, G T, 183
Foulsham, W, & Co Ltd 183
FourFourTwo 137
Fourth Estate Ltd 183
Fox, Charles H, Ltd 241

France 157
Frankham, Leslie H, FRPS 228
Fun For Kids 119
Furniture & Cabinetmaking 87
Future Music 115

G

GH Management 232
GPMU Journal 126
GQ 104
Gallop! 70
Garden, The 77
Garden Answers 77
Garden Matters Photographic Library 209
Garden News 78
Garden Trade News 78
Gardens Illustrated 78
Garland, Leslie, Picture Library 210
Garrett, H A, & Co Ltd 228
General Practitioner 83
Geo Aerial Photography 210
Geographical Magazine, The 133
Gibbons Stamp Monthly 87
Glass Age & Window Construction 96
Goal 137
Golden Valley Insurance 230
Golf Monthly 137
Golf World 138
Gollancz, Victor 183
Good Housekeeping 160
Good Woodworking 87
Graham, Clive, Models International 232
Graham & Sons (Printers) Ltd 233
Great Outdoors, The 60
Grove, G, Photographic Services 235
Grub Street 183
Guardian, The 169
Guiding 56
Guild of Wedding Photographers UK 242
Guinness Publishing Ltd 183

H

H&V News 48
Hale, Robert, Ltd 183
Hamilton, Hamish, Ltd 183
Hamlyn 184
Harding, Robert, Picture Library 210
Hardware & Garden Review 151
Harpercollins Publishers 184

Harpers & Queen 160
Harpers Sport & Leisure 138
Haworth Photographic Ltd 235
Haynes Publishing 184
Headline Book Publishing Ltd 184
Health & Efficiency 84
Health & Fitness 84
Heavy Duty 65
Heinemann, William, Ltd 184
Helicon Publishing Ltd 184
Helicopter World 40
Hello! 160
Helm, Christopher, Publishers Ltd 184
Herald, The 169
Herbert Press 184
Here's Health 84
Heritage 81
Herman, Laurel 241
Hertfordshire Countryside 61
Highbury House Communications 81
Hinde, John, (UK) Ltd 194
Hinton & Wild Insurance Ltd 230
Hockey Sport 138
Hodder Headline plc 184
Hodder & Stoughton 184
Holborn Studios Ltd 240
Holt Studios International 210
Home 92
Home Counties Colour Services Ltd 235
Home & Country 160
Homes & Gardens 92
Homes & Ideas 93
HomeStyle 92
Horse Magazine 71
Horse & Pony 71
Horse & Rider 71
Horticulture Week 78
Hotel & Restaurant Magazine 74
House Beautiful 93
House Builder 48
House & Garden 93
Houses & Interiors Photographic Features Agency 211
Howitt Portfolio Publishing 194
Hunter, Nicholas, Ltd 238
Hutchinson 184
Hutchison Library, The 211

I

Images & Editions 195
Imaging Lab, The 235
Improve Your Coarse Fishing 28

Independent , The 169
Independent Caterer 75
Independent Magazine 169
Independent on Sunday, The 169
Independent Retail News 151
Industrial Diamond Review 96
Industrial Fire Journal 96
Infomatics Digest 69
Ink & Print 96
Inside Rugby 138
Inspirations 93
Instrument Services Co Ltd 228
International Boat Industry 42
International Broadcasting 35
International Milling Flour & Feed 73
International Off-Roader 110
International Railway Journal 128
Iris Audio Visual 226, 239

J

J17 56
James, P & P F 235
Jane's Defence Weekly 126
Jarrold Publishing 195
Jayawardene Travel Photo Library 211
Jazz Index Photo Library 211
Jessop Photo Centres 225
Jet Skier & Personal Watercraft 42
Jewish Chronicle 12
Joe's Basement 236
Johnstone, A J, & Co Ltd 228
Joseph, Michael, Ltd 184
Journal, The 52
Judges Postcards Ltd 233
Junior Education 100
Just Parrots 88

K

KJP 225, 227, 228, 231, 239
Kardorama 195
Kay Mounting Service Ltd 229
Kenilworth Press Ltd, The 185
Kennel Gazette 32
Kenro Ltd 234, 239
Kentmere Ltd 231
Kenyon, S W 225, 239
Kerrang 115
Keyboard Player 115
Kimbers 229
Kingfisher Books 185

Knave 105
Koi Carp 88
Krystal Trading Ltd 239

L

Lady, The 161
Lancashire Life 61
Land Rover Owner 110
Landworker, The 73
Lane, Frank, Picture Agency Ltd 212
Larousse Kingfisher plc 185
Leach Lithoprint Co Ltd 233
Lebrecht Collection 212
Leeds Photovisual Ltd 231
Legal Action 100
Legion 82
Leisure Week 35
Lencol 229
Leopold Cameras Ltd 227
Lewis & Kaye (Hire) Ltd 241
Liberal Democrat News 127
Lincoln, Frances, Ltd 185
Lincolnshire Life 61
Link Picture Library 212
Little, Brown & Co UK Ltd 185
Loaded 105
Local Government News 100
London Labels 225
London 2000 157
Looks 161
Lutterworth Press, The 185

M

MEED 53
Macmillan General Books 185
Mail on Sunday, The 170
Mallard Imaging 225, 236
Management Accounting 53
Manchester Model Agency 232, 240
Manchester University Press 185
Manufacturing Chemist 97
Marie Claire 161
Marine Engineers' Review 48
Marketing 53
Marshall Cavendish Books 185
Marshall Editions Ltd 185
Marshall Publishing 185
Martial Arts Illustrated 139
Master Photographers Association 243
Match 139

Maxim 105
Mayfair 105
Meat & Poultry News 152
Meat Trader 152
Medici Society Ltd, The 195
Melody Maker 116
Men Only 106
Men's Health 106
Menswear 152
Metal Hammer 116
Mid Counties Photographic Supplies 231, 239
Middle East, The 127
Middle East Pictures Inc 214
Milap Weekly 127
Milepost 92½ 186, 212
Miller's 186
Mitchell Beazley 186
Minx 161
Mizz 57
Model Boats 88
Model Engineer 89
Models Plus Model Agency 232
Mojo 116
Monitor Syndication 213
More! 162
Mother & Baby 119
Motor Boat & Yachting 42
Motor Boats Monthly 42
Motor Cycle News 656
Motor Trader 110
Motorcycle Classics 66
Motorcycle International 66
Motorhome Monthly 55
Motoring & Leisure 110
Mountain Biker International 67
Mountain Biking UK 67
Ms London Weekly 162
Municipal Journal 101
Murray, John, (Publishers) Ltd 186
Muzik 116

N

NHPA 213
Nash, Graham, Ltd 236
National Association of Press Agencies 243
National Council for the Training of Journalists 243
National Union of Journalists 243
Natural Image 213
Natural Science Photos 213
Natural World 32
Navin Weekly 127

Ness Visual Technology 236
New Christian Herald 131
New Civil Engineer 49
New Holland Publishers 186
New Leaf Books Ltd 186
New Musical Express 117
New Scientist 133
New Statesman 128
News of the World 170
Nexus Special Interests Ltd 186
Night & Day 170
911 & Porsche World 111
19 162
Nomad Studio Hire 240
North East Times County Magazine 61
Northern Picture Library
Now 162
Number One Model Management 232
Nursery World 119
Nurseryman & Garden Centre 79

O

Obscura Ltd 226
Observer, The 170
Observer Life 170
Ocean Optics Ltd 225
Off Road and Four Wheel Drive 111
OK! Weekly 82
Old Glory 154
Omnibus Press/Book Sales Ltd 186
On the Ball 139
Options 163
Original Poster Company Ltd 195
Osborne, Christine 214
Osprey Publishing Ltd 186
Our Baby 120
Oxford Illustrated Press 186
Oxford Paperbacks 187
Oxford Publishing Co 187
Oxford Scientific Films Ltd 214
Oxford University Press 187

P

P A News 238
PPL Ltd 214
PTC Journal 127
Paddles 139
Pan 187
Pandora 187
Panos Pictures 215

Papermac 187
Papilio Natural History & Travel Library 215
Parents 120
Parentwise 131
Partridge Press 187
Paul, Stanley 187
Pavey, Michael, Insurance Broker 230
Pavilion Books 187
Penguin Books Ltd 187
Penthouse 106
People, The 170
People Management 53
People & the Planet 128
Perfect Home 93
Performance Ford 111
Period Living & Traditional Homes 94
Personal Magazine 170
Perspectives On Architecture 49
Peter Purves' Mad About Dogs 33
Phaidon Press Ltd 187
Philip, George, Ltd 187
Photo Answers 123
Photo Library International 215
Photo Marketing Association International Ltd 243
Photo Sports Ltd 236
Photo Technique 123
Photographer, The 124
Photomatic Ltd 236
Photon 124
Piatkus Books 187
Pictor International Ltd 215
Picture Book Ltd, The 216
Picture Research Association, The 243
Picturebank Photo Library Ltd 215
Picturecraft Photography 236
Pig Farming 73
Pilot 40
Planet Earth Pictures 216
Planning 101
Playne Books 187
Plexus Publishing Ltd 188
Police Review 101
Polyboard Ltd 229
Pony 71
Pope, M A, Printers 226
Popperfoto 216
Popular Crafts 89
Popular Flying 40
Portfolio Photography 236
Post Magazine 54
Pot Black Magazine 140
Poultry World 74
Powerstock Photo Library 217

Practical Boat Owner 43
Practical Caravan 55
Practical Craft 89
Practical Fishkeeping 89
Practical Householder 94
Practical Photography 124
Practical Wireless 69
Press Association, The 243
Prestige Interiors 152
Price, Matthew, Ltd 188
Prima 163
Prion 186
Puffin 183
Privilege Insurance 230
Pro Sound News 69
Process Control Company 225
Professional Engineering 49
Professional Landscaper and Groundsman 49
Professional Photographer 124
Professional Photographic Laboratories
   Association 243
Profolab 236
Promotions & Incentives 54
Propix Ltd 237
Pub Food 75
Publican Newspaper, The 75
Pulse 84
Pyramid 195

Q

Q 117
Quadrant Picture Library 217
Quartet Books 188
Quarto Publishing plc 188
Quick Imaging Centre 226

R

RIBA Journal 50
RSPCA Photolibrary 217
RYA News 43
Racing Pigeon Pictorial 140
Radio Times 36
Rail 129
Rail Express 129
Railnews 129
Rally Sport 111
Rambling Today 62
Random House UK Ltd 188
Rangers News 140

Reader's Digest 82
Reader's Digest Association Ltd 188
Real Business
Redferns Music Picture Library 217
Reed Consumer Books 188
Regatta 43
Retna Pictures Ltd 218
Revs 111
Rex Features Ltd 218
Rhythm 117
Ride 67
Rider 184
Riding 72
Right Start 120
Riverside Cards 196
Roadway 155
Robinson Publishing 188
Rose of Colchester Ltd 196
Roustabout Magazine 97
Routledge 188
Royal Geographical Society Picture Library 218
Royal Photographic Society 243
Rugby Leaguer 140
Rugby News 141
Rugby World 141
Runner's World 141
Russell, James, of Wimbledon 229, 237

S

SCL 237
SCR Photo Library 218
SOA 218
Safety Education 101
Saga Magazine 82
Sailing Today 43
Salamander Books Ltd 189
Salmon, Trout & Sea Trout 28
Santoro Graphics 196
Saturday 168
Saunders, A, & Co 231
Savitri Books Ltd 189
Scale Models International 89
Scandecor Ltd 196
Science Photo Library 219
Scootering 67
Scotland in Focus 219
Scotland on Sunday 170
Scots Magazine, The 62
Scotsman, The 169
Scottish Field 62
Scottish Licensed Trade News 76

Scottish Sporting Gazette 141
Scottish Wildlife Library, The 219
Scouting 57
Scuba World 142
Sea Angler 28
Secker & Warburg 189
Select 117
Sendean Ltd 229
She 163
Sheldrake Press 189
Sherwood Press, The 233
Shoe & Leather News 153
Shoot! 142
Shoot Photographic 228, 240
Shooting Gazette, The 142
Shooting Times & Country Magazine 142
Show Jumping 72
Sidgwick & Jackson Ltd 189
Sign World 97
Silverprint Ltd 231
Sinclair-Stevenson Ltd 184
Ski & Snowboard 143
Skier and Snowboarder Magazine, The 143
Skishoot – Offshoot 219
Sky Magazine 82
Slidepacks 239
Smash Hits 117
Smith Gryphon Ltd 189
Snooker Scene 143
Snowboard UK 143
Society of Wedding & Portrait Photographers 243
Somerset Magazine, The 62
Souvenir Press Ltd 189
Sovereign 112
Special Beat 102
Spectrum Colour Library 220
Spellmount Ltd 189
Sporting Pictures (UK) Ltd 220
Sports Boat & Waterski International 44
Sports In The Sky 144
Sports Trader 144
Stage, The 36
Statics 196
Steam Classic 129
Steam Railway 130
Steam Railway News 130
Steel Times 97
Steepleprint Ltd 226
Stephens, Patrick, Ltd 189
Steve Grayston's Martial Arts 144
Still Moving Picture Company 220
Stillwater Trout Angler 29
Stone, Tony, Images 220

Stoneleigh Photo Graphic Imaging
    226, 237
Street Machine 112
Subpostmaster, The 153
Sugar 57
Sun, The 169
Sunburst Books 190
Sunday Magazine 170
Sunday Mail, The 170
Sunday Mirror 170
Sunday Post 171
Sunday Sport 171
Sunday Telegraph, The 171
Sunday Telegraph Magazine, The 171
Sunday Times, The 171
Sunday Times Magazine, The 171
Superbike 68
Superdupes 237
Surf Magazine 44
Sussex Life 63
Sutton Publishing Ltd 190
Swan Hill Press 190
Swimming Times 144

T

TV Times 36
Target Gun 145
Tax-Free Trader 153
Teacher, The 102
Team Talk Magazine 145
Teddy Bear Scene 90
Telegraph Colour Library, The 220
Telegraph Magazine 168
Templar Co plc 190
Tennis World 145
Thames & Hudson Ltd 190
Thatcher, Raymond, Studios 237
That's Life! 163
Theatre 36
This England 63
Thorsons 190
Thought Factory, The 233
Tierce, Nathalie 226
Timber Grower 98
Times, The 169
Times Magazine, The 169
Tin International 98
Today's Golfer 145
Today's Runner 146
Top Gear Magazine 112
Top of the Pops 118
Topham Picturepoint 221

Total Football 146
Total Guitar 118
Total Sport 146
Toucan Books Ltd 190
Touring Car World 146
Toymaking 90
Trace 118
Traction 130
Tractor and Farm Machinery Trader 74
Trail 63
Transcolour Ltd 237
Travel Ink 221
Travel Library, The 221
Travel Photo International 221
Traveller 157
Treadaway Printing 226
Treasure Hunting 90
Triumph World 113
Tropix Photo Library 222
Trout Fisherman 29
Trout & Salmon 29
Truck 155
Truck & Driver 155
Typecast 227

U

Unicorn Books 190
Urethanes Technology 98
Usborne Publishing 190
Utility Week 98

V

VW Motoring 113
Vanguard Photographic Services 229
Vermilion 190
Veterinary Practice 33
Viking 190
Virgin Publishing Ltd 191
Vox 118

W

Walker Print Ltd 226
Wanderlust 157
Ward Lock 191
Ward Lock Educational Company Ltd 191
Water Craft 44
Waterways World 44

Weekend Guardian   169
Weidenfeld & Nicolson Ltd   191
Weycolour Ltd   237
What Digital Camera   125
What Hi-Fi?   70
What Satellite TV   36
What Video & TV   125
White, Michael   237
Widescreen International   125
Wild Cat   33
Wildfowl & Wetlands   33
Wildlife Photographer, The   125
Williams, S&I, Power Pix   222
Wilson, Philip, Publishers Ltd   191
Wilton of London Ltd   239
Windrush Photos   222
Windsurf Magazine   45
Wine & Spirit International   76
Wisden Cricket Monthly   147
Woman   164
Woman Alive   132
Woman & Home   164
Woman's Journal   164
Woman's Own   164
Woman's Realm   164
Woman's Weekly   165
Wood, Jamie, Products Ltd   225
Woodcarving   90
Woodmansterne Picture Library Ltd   222
Woodturning   91
Woodworker   91
Works Management   99
World Fishing   153
World of Interiors, The   94

World Pictures   223
World Tobacco   99
Wright Colour Ltd   238
Wright, Dennis, Ltd   229

X

XL   147
Xtreme   147

Y

Yachting Monthly   45
Yachting World   45
Yachts & Yachting   45
Yale University Press   191
Yes Magazine!   170
You Magazine   170
You & Your Baby   120
Young Dancer Magazine, The   37
Young People Now   102
Your Cat   34
Your Dog   34
Your Garden   79
Yours   83

Z

Zefa Pictures Ltd   223

Join the BFP today and get next year's Handbook hot from the press!

As a member of the Bureau of Freelance Photographers, you'll be kept right up to date with market requirements. Every month, you'll receive the BFP *Market Newsletter*, a unique publication telling what picture buyers are looking for now. It will keep you informed of new markets - including new magazines - as they appear and the type of pictures they're looking for. It also serves to keep The Freelance Photographer's Market Handbook up to date between editions, since it reporst important changes as they occur.

And as part of membership, you receive the Handbook automatically each year as it is published. For details of some of the other services available to members please see page 9.

Membership currently costs just £40 a year. To join, complete the form below and post with your remittance to the BFP. You'll receive your first Newsletter and membership pack within about 14 days.

Please enrol me as a member of the Bureau of Freelance Photographers for 12 months. I understand that if, once I receive my initial membership pack, I decide that membership is not for me, I may return it within 21 days for a full refund.

☐ I enclose cheque/po value £40

☐ Debit my Access/Visa card no_____

Expiry Date_____Series No (Switch only)_____in the sum of £40.

NAME _____ BLOCK
CAPS
ADDRESS _____ PLEASE

_____

_____ Postcode_____

Post to:
Bureau of Freelance Photographers,
Focus House, 497 Green Lanes, London N13 4BP.